London Voices
London Lives

London Voices
London Lives

Tales from a working capital

Peter Hall

with photographs by
Bill Knight

First published in Great Britain in 2007 by
The Policy Press
Fourth Floor, Beacon House
Queen's Road
Bristol BS8 1QU
UK

Tel no   +44 (0)117 331 4054
Fax no   +44 (0)117 331 4093
Email   tpp-info@bristol.ac.uk
www.policypress.org.uk

ISBN 978 1 86134 983 5 paperback
ISBN 978 1 86134 984 2 hardcover

British Library Cataloguing in Publication Data
A catalogue record of this book is available from the British Library.

Library of Congress Cataloging in Publication Data
A catalog record for this book has been requested.

Typeset in Aldine and Humanist by PNR Design, Didcot, Oxfordshire.
Front cover: photograph kindly supplied by Bill Knight
(www.knightsight.co.uk/index.html).
Cover design by Qube Associates, Bristol.
Printed and bound in Great Britain by Hobbs the Printers Ltd, Southampton.

THIS BOOK IS DEDICATED TO COLLEAGUES
FROM THE WORKING CAPITAL RESEARCH TEAM

Especially to Belinda Brown for her assistance on the first draft
and also to
Nick Buck
Ian Gordon
Michael Harloe
Mark Kleinman
Karen O'Reilly
Gareth Potts
Laura Smethurst
Jo Sparkes

But now behold,
In the quick forge and working-house of thought,
How London doth pour out her citizens.
SHAKESPEARE, Henry V

Contents

Preface

As Chapter 1 explains, this is a book linked by an umbilical cord to another, published five years ago: *Working Capital: Life and Labour in Contemporary London* by Nick Buck, Ian Gordon, Peter Hall, Michael Harloe and Mark Kleinman (London: Routledge, 2002). But which book is the child of which is a little difficult to say.

Working Capital was the first to get published, and was intended from the start as an academic tome. But it was based in large part on over one hundred interviews with ordinary Londoners – in their homes and at work. The research team were able to use only a minute part of these interviews in their book. So they decided that they should be mined more deeply, to give some of the rich flavour of all these London voices telling of their London lives. This book, dedicated to the team, is the result.

The acknowledgements include all those who helped in different ways on the original study. But particular thanks are due here to one team member, Michael Harloe, and to Paul Barker, our 'writer in residence', who read a first draft of this manuscript and made invaluable comments which have immeasurably improved it. For remaining deficiencies, needless to say, the author alone remains responsible.

The gestation and publication of this book were made possible by two charitable foundations. The Institute of Community Studies (now the Young Foundation) supported its writing when the author was concluding his three-year term as Director in the summer of 2004. And a grant from the Balzan Foundation, forming part of the 2005 Balzan International Prize awarded to the author, has assisted in its publication.

Peter Hall
London
April 2007

Acknowledgements

As the preface has explained, this book is uniquely linked to another: *Working Capital: Life and Labour in Contemporary London* by Nick Buck, Ian Gordon, Peter Hall, Michael Harloe and Mark Kleinman (London: Routledge, 2002). *Working Capital* was the primary product, and always the intended final product, of a 3-year research project, made possible by a substantial grant (L130 25 1027) from the ESRC *Cities: Competitiveness and Cohesion* programme, as one of four 'integrative city studies' whose brief was to examine how a wide range of processes affecting these concerns interacted in particular places. This grant supported a strong interdisciplinary team of researchers who worked together with the five principal investigators and authors, researching and writing and meeting, monthly and sometimes more frequently, for 3 years. Within this team Karen O'Reilly was responsible in the first year for much of the quantitative sociological work, particularly on issues of social capital, before moving on to a lectureship at the other end of the country. The other four members of the research team – Belinda Brown, Gareth Potts, Laura Smethurst, and Jo Sparkes – were responsible for the area-based fieldwork which was the focus of later phases of the project, and which provides the raw material for this book. Each was responsible for scoping studies, on which large parts of Chapters 2 and 10 of that book were based, and then for interviews in a particular pair of areas, while each of them also took the lead in generating information on one sub-set of themes, designing relevant parts of the semi-structured interview programme, and feeding through information for writing up the main findings in relation to these: Belinda took primary responsibility for issues of community and crime; Gareth for business and employment issues; Laura for services, social exclusion and social capital; and Jo for education and governance. Supplementary interviews were carried out by Henrietta Owusu Ansah in Southwark and by Tad Heuer in the City.

But it was always clear that most of the material from the hundreds of interviews could never be used in *Working Capital*. So, during its writing, the team agreed that this rich treasury of survey material should be deposited into the care of the Institute of Community Studies (now the Young Foundation), where Peter Hall as Director would work with the assistance of Belinda Brown as Fellow to prepare richer extracts for a more discursive book on London and its people. *London Voices London Lives* is the result.

Because of the linkage between the two books, it is appropriate here to repeat some of the earlier acknowledgements to those members of London's research community. I want particularly to acknowledge our debt to those who participated in the ESRC-sponsored 'London' research seminar which we convened through the 4-year period preceding this study, including Irene Bruegel, Les Budd, Tim Butler, John Davis, Michael Edwards, Dan Graham, John Hall, Chris Hamnett, Michael Hebbert, Michael Keith, Michal Lyons, Ann Page, Judith Ryser, and Andy Thornley; to colleagues from Llewelyn Davies Planning who worked with us on the ALG-sponsored London study, *A Socio-Economic Assessment of London*, which was published in 1997; and to counterparts on other projects within the ESRC *Cities: Competitiveness and Cohesion* programme, particularly the other 'integrative city studies' – Martin Boddy in Bristol, Alan Harding in Liverpool-Manchester and Ivan Turok in Glasgow – and also with researchers from 'thematic' projects working on aspects of development in the region, including Sophie Bowlby, Tim Butler, Jo Foord, Norman Ginsburg, Geoff Meen and James Simmie. The Programme Director, Michael Parkinson, actively supported the work with stimuli of various kinds, and some indulgence regarding deadlines.

I also recognise the contributions made by discussions with collaborators on related projects – Nick Banks, Paul Cheshire, Martin Crookston, Christian Lefevre, Ray Pahl, Tony Travers and Christine Whitehead – and with members of the Global Cities Working Group – John Mollenkopf, Pierre Beckouche, Toshio Kamo, Takashi Machimura, Edmond Preteceille, Masayuki Sasaki and Barney Warf.

On a number of occasions we also benefited substantially from the presence and contributions of Paul Barker as 'our journalist in (intermittent) residence' and from Susan Fainstein as our one-person 'international (occasionally visiting) advisory committee'. Paul, as Honorary Research Fellow at the Institute of Community Studies, has continued to play a very full role in reading the manuscript of this book and making invaluable suggestions about its readability. One of the authors of *Working Capital*, Michael Harloe, took time out from his day job as Vice-Chancellor of the University of Salford to play an equally invaluable role as reader.

The arduous and detailed work of re-editing sections of the transcripts, with new name identifiers, was undertaken with great speed and efficiency by Jill McComish at the Institute of Community Studies. Bill Knight toured London to provide brilliantly appropriate illustrations in very short order, while Richard Burton of PNR Design produced elegant and accurate camera-ready copy. And the original manuscript of *Working Capital*, as of this companion volume, both benefited hugely from the close personal attention and detailed commentary given to it by Ann Rudkin as editor. Both books owe a great deal to her devoted work.

This book, like so many predecessors, would never have come into being at all without the devoted logistical support of Magda, domestic manager without peer, who fuelled the machinery of authorship with endless culinary innovation and much more besides.

As explained in the Preface, publication of the book was made possible by a grant from the Balzan Foundation as part of the 2005 Balzan International Prize awarded to the author.

Most of all I am very grateful to the several hundred Londoners who gave their time for extended interviews, providing us with rich insights into the circumstances, often difficult, in which Londoners in different parts of their vast city-region live and work.

Finally, I want to acknowledge the stimulus that came from our *Working Capital* colleagues as we researched and wrote, above all in our enormously rewarding monthly all-day meetings at the LSE, when we shared ideas and criticised each others' contributions. None of us, we suppose, will ever fail to look back on those days without a sense of pleasure and delight. In recollection of that experience, I dedicate this further product of our labours to them: a small token, but one deeply felt.

Peter Hall
London
March 2007

St Paul's and the Millenium Bridge

© Bill Knight

Part One

London Places,
London People

In this introductory chapter, we find that London remains the unique city, as the Danish writer Steen Eiler Rasmussen described it in the 1930s. It is unique not only because – as he pointed out – it spreads at relatively low densities; it has also achieved a new uniqueness, in being the sole major British city that is again growing. And this is because, again uniquely, it forms one of the world's greatest magnets to migrants from other parts of the world: one of the very few global cities. These are making it a multi-ethnic, multicultural city that remains unique in Britain, and only comparable with other global cities like New York and Los Angeles.

St John's Hill, Battersea   © Bill Knight

Chapter One

Voices from the London Streets

You hear London voices everywhere: on the streets, in the tube, in restaurants and pubs; more often than not, nowadays, on mobile telephones. Often, they are exotic voices: people overheard in London seem to speak a hundred different languages, some recognisable as European, many not. And, of those that are speaking English, many are doing so in accents that show they were not born or raised in this city. But evidently, when you overhear their conversations – nowadays, thanks to those omnipresent mobile phones, you can hardly avoid doing so – most of their owners are Londoners, not tourists.

There is another funny thing about these voices, especially for an older Londoner. Often you will overhear a typical London voice, and when you see its owner you will find that he or she is what the 2001 Census calls Black and Minority Ethnic (BME), who now number nearly 30 per cent of all Londoners. It was not like that forty years ago, and it is still not like that for some of the parents of these Londoners; certainly not for their grandparents. They spoke, and speak, other varieties of English, which they learned to speak in their own childhoods in far-distant parts of the British Empire or the new nations into which that empire dissolved. They gave, still to some extent give, a huge and attractive variety to all those voices on the London streets. But, in the second or third generation, they are all melding into a single accent, forged in the world of the London schools: a flat sub-cockney accent some call Estuary English, but strangely shot through with cadences derived from other accents and other languages, so that it ceases to be a surprise to find a variety of Jamaican patois spoken by a crew-cut young white male with an earring.

All these voices appear to be heavily involved in business, evidently urgent and needing their immediate attention. Any traveller across London would soon conclude that its economy rests on a vast and infinitely complex network of communication, in which every step needs talk, talk, talk. And that of course would be true: at the start of the new century most Londoners do not make things, they provide services for other Londoners and the world, and that demands that they are in almost constant contact with each other and with the rest of that world.

This book puts on record an infinitesimal part of all those overheard London voices: specifically, just over a hundred of them, interviewed and recorded in a research project on life and labour in London in the year 2000. The researchers did much more than interview them: they sought them out, and talked to them at length about their lives and their reactions to life in London in that auspicious year. Their reflections make up a unique record of what a cross-section of Londoners felt about their lives and the lives of those around them. We felt that they were telling us significant stories, worth recording for posterity. Hence this book.

The Global City

As our researchers conducted and transcribed their interviews, we reflected on the extraordinary character of the city which they revealed. Truly, in European if not in global terms, London is unique. As all these voices show, something very special has been happening and is happening here. London has become the archetype of a term that is in danger of becoming a cliché but deserves a better fate: it is one of the great *global cities* of the world.

Academics and other scribblers have been debating the meaning of that word for nearly a century, since the pioneer Scots planner Patrick Geddes coined a closely related title, the World Cities, in 1915 (Geddes, 1915). But what they essentially mean by it is a city at some kind of pinnacle of a hierarchy of all other cities, a city defined by its connectivity to networks of people and information that flow out to other cities. It is no accident that Heathrow is the busiest international airport in the world, or that London sits at the centre of one of the world's largest and most complex telecommunications networks. It is no coincidence either that London remains, together with New York and (perhaps) Tokyo, one of the three (or two) leading financial centres of the world, or that it is the headquarters of some of the world's largest companies providing financial and business services across the globe, or that the BBC is one of the greatest global media corporations, or that London is one of the world's great destinations for worldwide tourism.

There are multiple reasons for this, some going back centuries, some much more recent in origin. But they are cumulative, and their combined effect has been to put London on a lonely pinnacle among cities, equalled by very few others in the world.

London: The Unique City

So London is the unique city. But that is not exactly new. It was the title of a book published in 1937 by Steen Eiler Rasmussen, a distinguished Danish architect-planner: an English version of a book he had written in his native language three years earlier. *London: The Unique City* (Rasmussen, 1937) remains perhaps the best book on London ever written. It argued that London was different from all other European cities because, unconstrained by the city walls that had been necessary to defend those other places from enemy invaders, it had been free for centuries to spread out at relatively low densities; thus, it was a city of suburbs, and creating successful suburbs was what London was all about.

Rasmussen concluded that Londoners, especially Londoners in power, should heed his plea and defend their city from another form of invasion: from the siren voices of continental European architects, who urged high-density solutions that would turn their city into an imitation of Paris or Berlin or Barcelona. He was only partially successful: in the great rebuilding of London after World War Two, new skyscraper offices and apartment towers changed the London skyline for ever. Yet, for all these changes, London remained – and remains – remarkably un-dense by continental European standards: a city of suburbs, as Rasmussen immortally described it.

That was partly because London went on thinning out – even more than the planners had intended. Londoners showed a quite unnatural enthusiasm for quitting their city: they moved out in their hundreds of thousands not only to the planned new towns – eleven of them, by 1970 – but also to suburbs all over the Home Counties and beyond, in rings of growth that rippled ever farther from London each decade. The government became so alarmed that, at the end of the 1970s, it made an historic policy shift: money that had gone into planned decentralisation would henceforth be diverted to urban regeneration. Despite the seismic shift in British politics represented by Thatcher's victory in 1979, she continued that policy by new means: the huge Docklands reconstruction is her memorial.

And from 1983 – as the London Docklands Development Corporation got into its stride – a remarkable reversal occurred: London's population, after a steady forty-year decline since the wartime blitz years, began to increase again. From a low point of 6.7 million, nearly two million below the 1939 peak of 8.6 million, by 2001 London's population had crept back to 7.2 million and was projected to climb almost back to its 1939 level by 2016. The economy, wracked by de-industrialisation and dock closures in the 1970s and early 1980s, expanded through new jobs in financial and business services, representing London's climb to the summit of the new global economy. The new reality, as revealed in the Mayor's *London Plan* of 2004, was a city in the throes of dynamic growth.

So London proved itself again to be the Unique City. But unique, this time, no longer in comparison merely with its European rivals, but also with other British cities. For, as the 2001 Census demonstrated to much grinding of civic teeth, these other cities still face demographic and economic decline. They too are generating new service jobs in both public and private sectors, but they are not compensating for the loss of traditional manufacturing and goods-handling jobs. They too are attracting new inhabitants to live in new apartments and conversions around their attractive and dynamic city centres, but these places are surrounded by tracts of urban wasteland, because other people – especially people with children – are leaving for homes in the greenfield counties outside. In the 1990s, Manchester's population dropped by 10 per cent, Liverpool's by 8 per cent, Newcastle's by 6 per cent and Birmingham's by 3 per cent. London in contrast grew by nearly 5 per cent (Anon, 2003, 23).

Urban analysts argue that such global cities are steadily becoming disconnected from their national economies, to become members of a global Premier League. That may well be an exaggeration. Our research for *Working Capital*, a book that was based on close examination of London's economy and society at the millennium, suggests that though its economy has a global core, overall it is less globalised than commonly imagined (Buck *et al*., 2002, Chapter 3). But what is clear is that it is much more successful overall than the economies of what have come to be called the core cities – Britain's major provincial cities.

And, viewed more closely, London's demography proves if anything to be even more special than its economy. The *London Plan* decomposes the trends: it turns out that Londoners are still leaving the capital in as large numbers as ever before, but now their places are being taken by immigrants from abroad. These immigrants come in all shapes and sizes: they include international bankers from New York and Tokyo and Frankfurt, Australasian backpackers working their way around the world with odd jobs in fast food outlets and office temping, people from Commonwealth countries coming to join their families or to marry resident citizens born in London, asylum seekers from the latest world hotspots, and – almost certainly, though difficult to count – large numbers who arrive for various purposes but somehow lose their return tickets. Between 1991 and 2000, while London lost about 51,000 people a year to the rest of the UK, in-migration from abroad averaged 62,000 a year, a net gain of 11,000 per annum; according to Migration Watch, a lobby group, two-thirds of immigrants into Britain since the mid-1990s have come to London. And some of these migrants – especially those who mislay their tickets – have high birth rates, both because they are young and because they belong to cultures where having large families is still the norm. Natural increase – the excess of births over deaths – averaged 40,000 a year during the 1990s. Overall, then, London gained an average of 51,000 people a year during the 1990s (Mayor of London, 2002, 17–18; Anon, 2003, 23).

So Rasmussen was more right than he could ever have known: London remained unique because it remained, relatively speaking, the city without walls. In consequence, London has a demographic profile quite unlike any other part of the country; it is almost like a different country. In 2001 1.57 million, 21.8 per cent of the population, were born outside the EU, against 6.6 per cent in England and Wales; London's non-EU-born constituted 45.8 per cent of the national total. According to the same Census 2.07 million Londoners, 28.8 per cent of the total, were non-white, against 8.7 per cent nationally; London non-whites represented no less than 45.4 per cent of the England and Wales total: 6.1 per cent were Indian; 5.3 per cent Black African; 4.8 per cent Black Caribbean. Muslims made up 8.5 per cent of Londoners, against 3.0 per cent in England and Wales as a whole. And for Inner London the distinction is even starker: here over a quarter, 26.8 per cent, were born outside the EU, while over a third, 34.3 per cent, were non-white. Individual boroughs were even more distinct. In Brent 140,756 people, 38.2 per cent of the total, were born outside the EU. In Newham 147,761 people, 60.5 per cent, were non-white. In Tower Hamlets 71,389 people, 36.4 per cent, were Muslim.

Clearly, there is some kind of connection between London's special kind of economy and its special attraction to all these very varied groups of people. Indeed, a 2003 survey, reported in *The Economist*, suggests that London is now the number one magnet city for international migrants in the world, outpacing even New York and Los Angeles. No less than 67 per cent of new immigrants to Britain come from high-income countries, according to *The Economist*, against a mere 30 per cent of entrants into Germany and 24 per cent of those into France.

'The foreigners' arrival has changed London visibly', *The Economist* reported:

New ethnic villages have sprung up all over the place. The Arabs have long been in Bayswater, the West Indians in Brixton, the Punjabis in Southall and the Bangladeshis in Tower Hamlets. Now the Poles are in Lambeth and Southwark, the Algerians and Moroccans are in Finsbury Park, the Kosovans and Albanians are in Enfield and Newham, the Iraqis in Barnet and the Congolese in Croydon.

The Europeans and Americans are all over central London. Foreign accents have long been as common as local ones in Mayfair; now that is true in large parts of Kensington, Chelsea, Holland Park and Notting Hill. Indigenous professionals, who would have lived in those areas in the 1970s and 1980s, have been forced to colonise dodgier boroughs such as Hackney and Lambeth (Anon, 2003, 24).

There is of course a downside to the process, very evident in the stories many people tell in this book. In Inner London, only 38 per cent of children get five or more good GCSEs, against 48 per cent in England as a whole. Housing costs make it hard to recruit teachers: 12 per cent are unqualified or temporary, against 6 per cent in England as a whole. Those with money send their children to expensive private schools: 16 per cent of London secondary school children go to independent schools, against 8 per cent nationally.

And so there is a circular connection between the inflow and the outflow. As the costs of living – above all the costs of housing – in London rise ever higher, and as public services are seen (rightly or wrongly) as deteriorating still further, more Londoners cash in the value of their homes, and leave for the rural counties beyond the green belt. But not just beyond – because here, housing pressures and housing prices are as fierce a deterrent as in London itself. The 'sunbelt', as urban analysts call it – the zone of maximum growth that stretches across southern England from Dorset through Wiltshire, Oxfordshire and Northamptonshire to Cambridgeshire and Suffolk – is moving steadily ever outward, especially northward: in 2000–2001, according to Health Authority statistics, the biggest migration gains were recorded by Lincolnshire, closely followed by Norfolk.

This then is the new reality of London at the start of the twenty-first century: a city that is itself large and hugely dynamic, but is only the core of an even larger, even more dynamic polycentric city region, a hundred or more miles across: a mega-city region, as I have described it (Hall, 2003). It is almost too much for academic analysis – though, precisely as we were writing this book, there was published a study that analyses the phenomenon across North West Europe (Hall and Pain, 2006). In this book, for the sake of manageability, I limit the analysis geographically to a more modestly-circumscribed region: the so-called London Metropolitan Area, a concept much used in the 1960s but recently fallen into disuse, covering an area about 40 miles (70 km) in radius and thus extending to Reading in the west, to Stevenage in the north, to Southend and Medway in the east and beyond Crawley in the south.

This is deliberate, because we need to convey as fully as possible something of the everyday lives of people in this vast city, and that means trespassing outside the strict limits of Greater London and its 32 London boroughs, to look at life in at least one or two places beyond the M25. For our central thesis is that London is so intrinsically dynamic that all its parts, and almost all its people, are drawn into a process of constant, almost frenetic change – and this change is felt just as deeply in these areas beyond the London boundary, as in London itself. It is the same area used in the companion book, with which this is indissolubly associated: *Working Capital* (Buck *et al.*, 2002). As already explained in the Preface, that book had a different purpose from this one: it was to investigate the relationships between economic competitiveness and social cohesion, a key theme central to the entire research programme of which it formed a part.[1] It did so through a combination of statistical analysis and evidence from over one hundred interviews of Londoners in their different roles – as employers, as professionals, and above all as citizens in the course of their everyday lives in their own neighbourhoods.

These in particular formed a vast mine of information: the transcripts, thousands of pages of them, give an extraordinarily vivid picture of London in the millennial year, in which people quite openly and often movingly tell of their own lives, their fortunes and misfortunes, their hopes and frustrations, their own views of the city in which they live and work. As the research team extracted the briefest of quotations from this rich collection, it became more and more evident to them that they must find a way of using it more fully, through a companion volume that could give longer and richer extracts, conveying something of the flavour of the original conversations. Hence this book – which, paradoxically, is a sort of by-product of the other, while at the same time it represents the raw material out of which the other was written.

Specifically, this material represents interviews in some ten residential areas and in associated centres of employment (Figure 1.1). With the exception of three sample areas outside Greater London – one in the inner Newtown district of Reading, one in the suburb of Earley in the neighbouring Wokingham District to the west of London,[2] and one in Greenhithe, a village becoming a suburb within the Thames Gateway Dartford district to the east – all these interviews were conducted in London itself, in six areas running in a belt across London from west to east. Three are in inner London as the Office of National Statistics defines it[3] – Battersea (in north Wandsworth); Bermondsey and Peckham (in north Southwark); and Upton Park (in Newham) – and three in outer London – Heston (in Hounslow); Gants Hill (in Redbridge); and Eltham (in Greenwich). In each case, a socially distinct residential area – or, in Greater Reading and Southwark, two contrasting areas – and a local employment centre were selected, and defined in terms of one or two Census wards. In this book, we have drawn almost exclusively on the residential interviews, though at the very end, discussing policies in Chapter 15, we also draw on some of the other material.

We chose these areas by looking at statistics and using our own knowledge of London and its constituent parts. We were looking for places with distinct economic and social characteristics, resulting from different historical trajectories over the second half of the twentieth century. And we were not disappointed; rather, we were quite startled to find just how distinctive some of these places proved to be. Each had a very different and special character, such that a special theme or themes emerged insistently

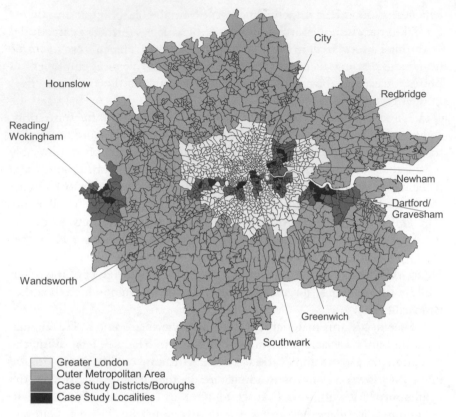

Figure 1.1. The interview neighbourhoods.

in each place. But one point emerged tellingly as we interviewed in each area, and as we then discussed our results in the regular monthly meetings of the *Working Capital* team: there were a number of dominant cross-cutting themes that occurred and recurred, in different degrees, across all our study areas.

And that logically suggested, even dictated, the form of this companion volume. First, in Part Two, we visit in turn each of the neighbourhoods,[4] describing its distinct feel and character, outlining its evolution and giving a quick statistical sketch of its key social and economic features. And we let the inhabitants speak for themselves; these are truly *London Voices*, and in each area they have a distinctively different tale to tell. Then, in Part Three, we turn the emphasis around: we attempt a more complex, less direct exercise in comparison and contrast, a contrapuntal exercise combining different voices. Here we seek to understand the common themes, and also some of the differences, in the experiences of different Londoners across this vast city. These are *London Lives*. Then, in a concluding chapter which introduces Part 4, we try to extract from the interviews the views of Londoners on the policy and political issues that shape their lives: the major problems London faces as a city and some of the possible answers. Finally, we try to bring together the main findings and their possible relevance for all who care about the future of their city. These are *London Futures*.

'We' is a collective term, deliberately ambiguous: it means you, the reader, and I, the author; but it also means we, the team of five professors and five researchers who together did the work from which this book is the product. The book is individually authored but in a deep sense is a collective product of all those to whom, in a spirit of remembered comradeship, it is dedicated.

Notes

1 The ESRC (Economic and Social Research Council) *Cities: Competitiveness and Cohesion* research programme

2 For reasons of space, we omit the Reading interviews from this part of the book. But we draw on them when we discuss cross-cutting issues in Part Three.

3 The ONS (Office of National Statistics) definition is different from the one earlier used, and still popularly used, which was equivalent to the former Inner London Education Authority and the even older London County Council: it also included the London Borough of Greenwich, but excluded the Boroughs of Haringey and Newham.

4 Except Reading; see note 2, above.

Pub conversation

© Bill Knight

Part Two

London Voices

In Part Two, we visit each of the neighbourhoods, describing its distinct feel and character, outlining its evolution and giving a quick statistical sketch of its key social and economic features. And we let the inhabitants speak for themselves; these are truly London Voices, and in each area they have a distinctively different tale to tell.

Battersea high rise

© Bill Knight

Chapter Two

New Melting Pot

Battersea

'South Chelsea': during the 1990s, Battersea became celebrated, even slightly notorious, as the latest piece of London to undergo frenetic yuppification. Or gentrification; the favoured term varied from one decade to another, but the process was always the same: an inner-city neighbourhood, once predominantly working class, where artisan terraces were snapped up by the young middle class who flocked here from the fashionable area next door. And, symbol of a vanishing past, public housing in the form of high-rise tower blocks and medium-rise maisonettes, is now itself part-privatised. The townscape of Battersea is replicated, with minuscule local differences, across inner London: in Camden Town and Islington, in Stockwell and Peckham, in Hackney and Tower Hamlets.

It is the outward manifestation of deeper changes – demographic, ethnic, social – that have visited these areas, in a series of waves, over the last 50 years. They have been described in broad London-wide terms in Chapter One, but of course their precise impacts vary from neighbourhood to neighbourhood, mediated by local conditions that may have roots far back in history. In Battersea they include a long-established working-class population which came to occupy the less attractive lower-lying land intersected by railway viaducts; a history of intervention to improve housing conditions, first by nineteenth-century philanthropic landlords and then by an activist local borough council and the London County Council; the arrival in the 1950s and 1960s of new immigrants, especially from the Caribbean; the 1965 reorganisation of London local government, with a new borough council that soon became a flagship Conservative administration; and the spread of gentrification from neighbouring Chelsea, immediately opposite Battersea on the other, north, side of the Thames.

As a result of these fast-succeeding changes, Battersea is the archetype of the inner London neighbourhood, mixed in every way: the tower block rising next to the street of two-storey artisan terraces, the young living next door to the old, the new rich to the old less-rich, black next to white.

Some History

Situated on the south bank of the Thames in the inner west London borough of Wandsworth, Battersea is the area that tens of thousands of Londoners see daily from their train windows as they travel into and out of Waterloo: a landscape of typical yellow stock-brick terraces, interspersed with scores of distinctive tower blocks that the historian would immediately identify as the proud product of the London County Council Architect's department in its 1950s and early 1960s heyday. And this landscape demonstrates a complex socio-economic geography, reflecting both Battersea's location and its history. Cheap riverside land, on what had traditionally been the 'wrong' side of the river, facilitated extensive nineteenth-century suburban housing development, some of very good quality, providing an obvious target for gentrification a century and more later. But a basic division – between a physically more elevated, higher-class south Battersea and a lower-lying riverside, working-class north Battersea – was massively underlined by nineteenth-century railway building and riverside industrialisation. A little later, from about 1900 through to the 1960s, came large-scale public housing schemes in the lower northern areas, many of which still survive. Then, during the 1980s and 1990s, the demographic and housing structure was transformed through the efforts of a radical Conservative borough council, greatly accelerating the gentrification process.

South Battersea, on the higher and healthier ground away from the river, developed as a salubrious rural suburb; in the nineteenth century, first Clapham and then Stockwell became select residential areas for commuters to the city. But, except for the perimeter of Battersea Park, these did not extend down to the lower ground of North Battersea: the railways, which brought the working classes in, blighted the land and kept the middle classes out. In fact, until the second half of the nineteenth century lower Battersea remained predominantly agricultural, although a wide range of industries grew up on the riverside – some using the Thames for transport or its tributary, the Wandle, for power, others simply because the land was cheap upstream of the port. With the coming of the railways, which by the late 1860s had brought a great 'tangle' of interconnecting tracks to Battersea, more substantial industries followed, employing working-class people displaced from the centre of London by railway building that took away their homes, and by rising rents.

Only with the arrival in the 1900s of the LCC's electric trams, with their substantially cheaper workmen's fares, did much working-class housing follow. This was provided by a mixture of speculators, philanthropic trusts, and – from 1901 – Battersea Borough Council, which under Labour control prioritised house building, together with an ambitious range of social services. While its estates attracted the skilled artisan and upper-working-class families, poorer people went into inferior developments with growing multi-occupancy, on damp, low-lying, polluted land. Slums developed; then, from the 1920s, the LCC started to replace them with walk-up flats, increasing the concentration of public housing in North Battersea. Heavy bomb damage during World War Two added to housing needs, which were met by LCC/GLC and borough council construction of tower blocks. Built at lower densities, these meant the export of population from Battersea; and, by cutting across established community areas and destroying traditional settings for social life, they served to weaken neighbourhood life. This process was accentuated when the borough was swallowed up by Wandsworth in the London government reorganisation of 1965.

After 1965, at first under Labour control, Wandsworth responded to continuing housing need with a mixture of municipalising repairable rented properties, improving the existing stock, and supporting owner-occupation rather than further redevelopment. But the area steadily became more attractive to middle-class residents because it offered improved air quality, plus nearness to central London and its rapidly-multiplying professional and managerial jobs; increasingly, properties from the private rental sector were bought up by a new wave of gentrifiers, for conversion back to larger family homes. By 1974 it was reported that in North Battersea:

An increasing number of young professional people have moved into the area. A whole range of shops and services have sprung up to serve them, like wine bars, specialist and antique shops, which also have the effect of squeezing out those that previously met the needs of the existing population. (Beresford and Beresford, 1978, 24–25)

With Conservative control of the Council from 1978, followed from 1979 by the Thatcher government's promotion of council house sales, both to sitting tenants and on the open market, gentrification got more active public support. The Council targeted improvement grants at pre-1919 houses needing substantial repairs, with the consequence that by late 1983 80 per cent of grants were going to owner-occupiers, rather than for rented properties. Council house sales were advanced by ploughing back proceeds into improvement of council estates, making it attractive to buy flats (at substantial discounts), and thus populating areas of the borough dominated by council housing, such as Battersea, with potential Conservative voters. The process was further accelerated through sales of whole blocks to developers, with the effect that owner-occupation in the borough rose to 54 per cent in 1991, the highest level in inner London, while the proportion of local authority renters fell to 21 per cent (from 35 per cent in 1981). These processes were operated in a way which led to a much less even spread of local authority housing across areas of Battersea. In some wards it has virtually disappeared, while remaining estates in North Battersea seem to have been increasingly left with the role of taking 'problem' tenants from other areas, as older-established tenants were provoked to leave.

Battersea Today

As we took our interviewers' recorders through the Battersea streets, further changes were under way: luxury apartment conversions were appearing in former industrial areas on the riverside, and – after a gap of more than half a century – signs were everywhere advertising property TO LET. These are taking a stage further the transformation of Battersea from the working-class community of 1950 (and even 1975) into a haven for young middle-class couples and singles wanting easy access to City work and ample local restaurants and bars in which to relax. This is reflected in house prices, which though much lower than in Hammersmith or Chelsea across the river, are well above the London average (a borough average of £364,000 for all properties in early 2006). But in North Battersea these affluent incomers are still juxtaposed with a rump of disadvantaged tower block residents who have no real choice over their location.

Across Wandsworth as a whole, there are now very few jobs in manufacturing (about 5 per cent); the bulk of employment is spread across a wide range of service activities. Almost all of these, apart from finance, are more heavily represented here than in the national employment profile, but the degree of specialisation is generally low, albeit strongest in business services and in health. Wandsworth has one of the lowest proportion of jobs, just one-fifth, in manual work among all our case study districts – though uniquely, this proportion actually grew during the 1990s, thanks to expansion in both transport and wholesale distribution (including the relocated New Covent Garden food markets), while growth in business services generally was offset by public sector job losses in education and health services. Professional and managerial jobs were less well represented than junior or (especially) intermediate level non-manual jobs, suggesting that the borough as a whole occupies a niche somewhere below the core areas of gentrification, presumably because of the mix of properties on offer, notably those transferred from the council sector. This, and the age structure – with an above-average proportion between 20 and 35 – are also presumably related to the tenure mix, which is distinguished by a higher proportion in private rented property, especially furnished lets.

Wandsworth also records an above-average share of single-parent families and one-person households. The lone parents (9 per cent of households in 2001, drastically down from 23 per cent in 1991) tend to be educationally disadvantaged. They might have benefited from gentrification had the newcomers sent their children to the local schools and pushed for higher standards, but the gentrifiers did not do so. One consequence was that in 2000, despite strong but ineffectual local protest, two primary schools in North Battersea were being closed, following a negative Ofsted report on one and falling rolls in both.

Ethnically the borough population is quite mixed: 22 per cent came from non-white origins in 2001, of whom just under 5 per cent were Black Caribbean and just under 4 per cent Black African. By 1999 there was a majority (53 per cent) from non-white ethnic origins within local maintained schools, though the proportion with English as a second language (30 per cent) was significantly lower than in most Inner London boroughs. All ethnic groups have shown a shift from private and council tenancies into owner-occupation – 52 per cent of households in 2001 – if rather more among whites than Afro-Caribbeans. But in the process, ethnic minorities have become more and more concentrated in particular wards, reversing the trend of the 1970s. The process is not simply one of segregation, however; some significant ethnic pockets (with 30 to 40 per cent minority population in a ward) seem to have all but disappeared during the 1980s as these areas became solidly owner-occupied. It appears that while white gentrifiers were buying up Victorian cottages, ethnic minorities were more commonly purchasing flats on council estates.

The area as a whole is steadily becoming more middle class: every year, thousands of affluent young private tenants or owner-occupiers move in, while a roughly equivalent number – including, it is thought, less-affluent pensioners – move out. So there are increasing divisions between long-term residents, restricted to the council estates, and highly-mobile newcomers who can afford to buy.

Wandsworth seems to be easily the most affluent of our case study boroughs – though its affluence appears unevenly distributed, since its local unemployment rate was higher than in most of them. It stands near the middle of national deprivation rankings – except in housing, where a majority of wards register in the worst 10 per cent nationally and all in the worst 20 per cent. This reflects typical London housing pressures; in 2001, the borough ranked as the 16th worst in England and Wales for overcrowding. But there are also wards which come in or near the worst 10 per cent for income and employment deprivation – with, in particular, a concentration of child poverty in four wards with a large proportion of social housing, three in north Battersea, reflecting the incidence of lone parenthood. The numbers of children and young people on the child protection register, and the rate of secondary school pupil exclusion, are among the highest in London. Crime rates are high by national standards, but very close to the London average.

The three Battersea wards where we interviewed rather neatly represent the three different Batterseas that had come into existence in the last quarter of the twentieth century. Logically enough, they also represent altitude above sea level; following an old London rule, even small differences in height can represent big differences in perceived salubriousness and so in social cachet.

Starting at the top, then: Shaftesbury Ward, the highest and most southerly, itself divides into two. One, the southern half, is essentially West Clapham: the ward boundary follows the north side of the common, and north of it are solid streets of two- and three- and four-storey late Victorian houses, the largest divided into flats, the majority in single-family owner-occupation. This was early gentrification territory – part of it, indeed, gentrified from the first development of the area. The other, north of Lavender Hill, where the shops interestingly show sharp contrasts between a gentrified west and a very traditional working-class east end, is another world: on the steep slope down to the river and on the flat floodplain below, the large Shaftesbury Estate of the 1870s, a pioneering exercise in high-quality housing for the deserving poor, now a conservation area where the occasional house for sale – most still belong to the trust – is eagerly sought.

Latchmere Ward comes next, to the north, on the flat floodplain north of the main line from Waterloo to Clapham Junction but itself divided by a tangle of tracks leading to the West London Line. Its eastern half is a huge council housing estate, mixed borough and LCC in origin, with the usual high-rise low-rise mixture of the postwar years, plus a Shaftesbury-style estate next to the railway. The western half is much more of a mixture: more council housing, gentrified two-storey late Victorian terraces with a mixture of white and black gentrifiers, huge luxury blocks along the river. Latchmere contains some of the borough's most deprived public housing, and regularly returns three of the few Labour councillors in the borough.

Finally St Mary's Park, the ward that breaks the rule: two-storey late Victorian bow-windowed artisan housing, built originally adjacent to the many factories and workshops that lined the river and the railway tracks, now gone; wholesale signs of gentrification everywhere, with the wine-bar culture heavily in evidence in Battersea Square and Battersea Bridge Road; here, too, converted warehouses and new riverside luxury apartment blocks; behind, old LCC interwar walkups and postwar high-rise, some evidently converted and sold as luxury housing; plus grand nineteenth-century apartment blocks lining Battersea Park. This eastern end of the ward always had social status; what is new is the wholesale gentrification of what, not so long ago, was less-than-desirable working-class housing hemmed in by railway tracks and workshops.

Taken together, they contain a mix of tenures, although with a proportion of residents in social housing which is well above average.

Average property prices here in summer 2001 were around £295,000, reflecting a location advertised as 'only minutes from the Kings Road'. The population mix is preponderantly white, but with a significant black minority (especially in St Mary's Park where in 2001 it represented 23 per cent of the population, the vast majority British-born). Socially, the most distinctive feature is a relatively high proportion of lone parents (12.5 per cent of all households in Latchmere).

Tiffany

Tiffany, a Jamaican-born Black Caribbean divorced mother and council tenant in her thirties, employed part-time as a dinner lady in the local school, has tried hard to work her way up through the system. At one point she took out a loan through the Prince's Youth Business Trust but in the long run the business didn't work out and she paid the loan back. More recently she has thought about studying for a qualification, but finds it impossible to do so because of Catch 22s in the benefits system. As she explained:

… you're on benefit yeah? And … now you go into full time education, they're telling you that they're going to take your benefit away from you because you're in full time education, and if you're gonna be in full time education you can go and work full time. Now that is stupid, innit? But that's how they work… They give you in one hand but they take it out the other so there ain't nothing, you go back, you actually go back to where you start from.

Most of her energy is spent on the trials and tribulations of bringing up two teenage boys:

The teenage hormones. I keep telling them I'm tired. 'Tell your friends don't bother my 'phone before 12 O'clock in the morning, don't buzz my buzzer before 12 O'clock, don't come to my door cos I'm gonna be nasty.' And I'm telling them to tell so that I don't be nasty to them you see, but then I tell them anything, about, last night I was lying there, about six times the 'phone ring, I don't answer it no more cos 'e ain't mine.

And trying to get money to support the youngest son:

And when we first split up it was, you know what I mean, hard, but no, my friends used to say I'm wicked cos I used to 'phone him up and I used to go, 'Shane needs the money, where's Shane's money? I can't work because I've gotta look after him'. You know what I mean? And especially he's got his difficulties and whatever, I need the money, so I make sure I get money from him every week.

Tiffany has been living on the Doddington and Rollo Estate since she came to England in 1978 as a child from Jamaica. She missed home terribly at first:

I cried, I cried, I cried for about a year... All my friends, all the thing, I missed the freedom mainly ... the freedom to go and come, you know, it was different over here cos you couldn't get up and go. Like back home you'd get up in the morning and just disappear and go, everybody's neighbours are there, you know, you know everybody.

It was just like much safer?

Yeah. And over here it's just, everybody's just closed in.

But since then, she has become very attached to the place where she lives:

I like it here, like it right where I am ... I'm used to it. I can go out the area and I still come back to Battersea, I feel safe... Yeah, I feel, yeah cos I've been here for so long so... To me this is home and I know most of the people around here anyway, so this is my area... Yeah, this is my safe zone, safe zone.

She feels safe because she knows many people here:

I know a lot of them... I think that's why I feel safe, cos I know most, even the boys are like supposed to be bad, whatever, whatever, I know them, they ... 'Hello, Tiffany, hi'. ... I will tell them, 'These are my children, if anybody, any one of you touch them you lot are dead'.

But this is gradually changing, as increasingly new owner-occupiers move into the estate:

... when they come and live in the area do they mix in with the other people? Are they part of the community...?

Not much, not really, just keep themselves to themselves.

This is part of the overall process of gentrification which is happening everywhere:

Yeah ... because they're tryin'a, they changed over to New Chelsea but nobody calls it New Chelsea, do they?

Who's trying to call it New Chelsea?

... some ... Government ... people ... they're tryin'a make it rich. I mean a lot of businesses closed down and it's all this restaurants, posh restaurants and all that business, you walk down to Latchmere, all them rich people's business coming in, I mean we couldn't buy any of those things, you know, I mean it's all very high class coming in.

And this is parallelled, she believes, by another social divide on the estate, between black and white. Perhaps this is a matter of lifestyle and, underlying that, disposable income. But perhaps, also, it is a matter of fear – or at least nervousness:

Yeah, cos there's things going on in the park tomorrow and you'll see all the black people going over there...

Really, and not the white people? What do the white people do?

I don't know, they go out, they go away, they go camping, go somewhere... Yeah, they stay more to themselves... I think maybe black, white people's a bit threatened... Yeah, I think they feel threatened by so much black people together. Which is quite silly.

Sandra

Sandra is a single Afro-Caribbean mother in her forties, who works in a care home for the elderly. She is a council tenant in a tower block very close to the estate where Tiffany lives, and has been here for 12 years. She lives on her own but has two grown-up daughters who also live in South London. Before that she was:

... in York Road. And I stayed there for about 5, 6 years and then I was going to buy another one, then my mother died. Then I had to go home for the funeral, I took my, I've got two daughters, I took them with me for the funeral. When I came back I just, I didn't have enough, cos I spent the money on the funeral, so I didn't bother to buy a house, so I went to the Council, I told them I was homeless I didn't have ... so they said they couldn't house me because I had made myself intentionally homeless, and so I said, 'I haven't got anywhere to stay'. So anyway, they helped me out and they gave me this flat and I've been here now about 12 years in December.

Like many other residents, she feels that the area has become safer in recent years:

I think it's got better, cos when I first moved in here, I've got a garage now for my car, but when I first moved in there was always muggings and car breaking in and ... people's houses being burgled, but ... they've made it, I think the Council's done a good job, it's more secure now anyway. It's, you know, it's not so frightening going out any more. Although it still happens, but it's, yeah, it's better round here now. I think so anyway. I've never had any ... touch wood, problems that way.

She thinks that improvements in the facilities for young people have helped here, by allowing them to spend their time more productively:

they've opened more places for the kids to go, cos when they haven't got anything to do really, they just do what comes naturally, you know, if they've got places to go and relax and do something, cos there's the down the bottom, they can go there in the day time, do things, you know, so they occupy theirselves during the day time if they're not working.

Like Tiffany, she finds this a friendly area, one that has generous resources of what the sociologists call social capital:

Everybody's very friendly around here, I must say... If anything happens to anyone everyone's interested to know why, who, and ... you know, and what happened.

Is that just in this block or do you mean in the area in general?

The area in general, cos you're walking up the road and somebody'll just say, 'Hello, good morning, good afternoon'. People don't usually do that, you know, people just walk straight past you if you drop down in the road, nobody bothers they jump over you to go over to what they're doing, but here people are...

But in this regard, she may be unusual. She had taken the initiative to start a local tenants' association and had worked doggedly to get improvements made. She is a mover and a shaker:

You know what I'm saying. And I thought 'What the ... going on?' and I used to be phoning up, phoning up, phoning up, and there's people in, there's old people in the block and there's people in the block with kids and babies, and some of them lives on this floor, some of them live on the top floor, you know, higher level, and I thought, no, that's not right, man, so I thought they have to get, and I used to go every single day I used to go to the Council, every single day... Soon as I walk in they said, 'Oh, here comes trouble'.

Excellent. Oh, so it's good to know that you can change, you can change the world around if you put your mind to it.

I said, once you are determined to do something and you say right, and you don't sit on it, you will get it done. You will get it done, yeah.

Consequently she has been able to win major improvements from the Council, starting with her own flat:

It was in a shitty state. So I went round to the Council and I said … 'Excuse me, have you seen the flat you've offered me?'. 'No', he said, 'Why?' I said, 'Have you got a dog?' He said, 'No'. I said 'Well, if you had a dog you wouldn't put it in the flat you offered me'. I said, 'It's not because you said that I made myself intentionally homeless that you have to give me …', so he said 'Oh, is it that bad?' I said, 'Yes'. I said, 'Haven't you seen it?' He said, 'No'. So he and the other lady, manager came to look at the place and she said 'Yes, it's in a bad way'. So they told me to come back and have a look at it and write down everything I want done. There was no electric meter, there was no gas meter, there was no handles on the doors, there was … on the wall everywhere, and the bath … the bath and the sink was like this aluminium, it was so dirty, the bath was like … unit top. So I wrote everything down. I said, 'I want new handles, I want new doors, I want new bath, I want new toilet, I want a new sink bowl'. I wanted this and I wrote it all down and I took it to them, they said okay, so I gave them the list and within a week they wrote me back again and they said, 'We've done all what you wanted, would you…'.

She looked back on those early weeks, and at how she worked herself to turn the place into a home:

… now I've been 12 years now, and I moved in about, like one week before Christmas, and I really worked in this flat and the man from the Council that gave me the flat, he came to see me just before Christmas, I said, 'Would you come over for a drink'. He came and he said, 'Flippin' hell, it looks like you been here a long time and you've only been here a week'. He said, 'You've really done it up, you've really worked nice'. And I thought, well, that's it, it's my home now. And it's nice because you don't get rooms that big any more.

And as a tenant she has nothing but praise for the level of service the Council gives her – a sentiment repeated by many other Wandsworth residents we interviewed, whether council tenants or owner-occupiers:

Mm, I mustn't complain, I have, cos I haven't had any complaint, if ever anything's wrong or anything needs doing they do it. I just go to the office and say 'My window's broken' or 'Blah blah blah', whatever, and within the week I get it done. And now they're doing…

Although she has been living here since she was a child she has never had an experience of racial discrimination:

I've never ever had that… Never. Never. Never. Never. Never.

She does not at all regret her move to work in the old people's home:

I've worked in the office for about 8 years, and I've done that and I've done this, so I've worked in a solicitors, I've been a legal executive for about 2 years and so I thought I'll just have a go at working with the elderly and mentally handicapped and I just got into that and it's different, you know, so I can always go back to whatever I wanted but the older you get the harder it gets for you to get a job in the office, if you see what I'm saying, so this is alright, I thought I'd give that a go, and it's okay, I'm enjoying it… It's really, it's good, I do, I really appreciate my job.

So she has a job as well as a council flat. But life is still a struggle. Yet she is philosophical about it:

There are lots of things I go without, love. *(Laughs)* If I haven't got it I just don't bother, do you know what I'm saying? I just make sure my rent is paid, my bills are paid and what you don't have you don't miss anyway. So you have to make sacrifices.

She maintains close contact with her family:

I haven't really got friends, cos friends always let you down … I've got acquaintances. I've got a friend who I can trust and depend on and … which is a friend, but I've got a lot of acquaintances, but my family, we're very close. Very very close.

They live quite locally you said…?

Yeah. Not too far away. Not too far away. And they sort of, if I come in they phone me, my kids phone every night and say 'Are you home?', cos they know what time I get in…They phone and say 'Are you home? Are you there?' or there's a message on the answering machine 'Mum, can you phone me when you get in please'. So I phone them and they say 'Where've you been, where did you go?' *(Laughter)* 'Why are you so late?' *(Laughter)* So it's, it's nice. No, they really, they really care about you, it's really nice. It makes me feel good.

Daniel

Daniel is a British-born Afro-Caribbean in his early twenties, and a father whose relationship has broken up. He is employed and has two children who live with his former partner; they come over to stay with him and his family at the weekends. He lives on a council estate in Battersea with his parents, and gives us a frank assessment of it. It does not have too good a reputation locally, but he thinks it is fine:

It's mixed, yeah. It's mixed. You've got a lot, you've got certain people who's unemployed, you've got people who's working, you've got people from Guyana and there's Jamaicans and … there's a Spanish family from Spain, and you've got … some Italians, so it's a different mixture of people. Different ethnic minorities. It's kind of cool though.

In fact this area was once home to the notorious 'So Solid Crew'. But, listening to the positive things Daniel has to say, it is hard to believe that they come from the same place. Like Sandra, he stresses the strong sense of neighbourliness, the feeling that this is a safe and secure place to live:

Erm … it's cool living on this estate, it's really nice.

So what are the things that make it a nice place to live?

Erm … well, they got a lot of playgrounds for the children … they've knocked down the old playgrounds and brought in new playgrounds and made 'em bigger, okay. And they made the estate safer, you know, there's a lot of police who patrol the estate and there's hardly, there's, they've got a anti-burglary scheme, and they've got cleaners on the estate and that's important. If you notice, you don't hardly see any graffiti, in most estates you see a lot of graffiti and a lot of mess.

What about crime, is there much crime?

Not around here. Not, not, not on this estate. But obviously there's crime everywhere, isn't there … the good thing about this estate is that everyone knows each other so there's a sense of unity and that's important…You know, and like I could, I could leave my door open, yeah, and just go to the shop, and you know the granny, she could look after my door … like we've got a community centre and basically everybody looks out for everybody in the community centre. And one of the ways I could say they help people, sometimes the postman delivers letters to different addresses so someone might come up to you and go, 'This is your letter and it's addressed to my house'. You know, they might do that. And looking after children.

I think one more important thing, that I told you earlier was that we all look out for each other… Like … if a stranger, obviously if there was a stranger around and he's tampering with your house then they'd either call the police or they'd inform you about it, and if you're not in, obviously they'd call the police and they would tell you this such and such person came around your house and they looked like this, and you would know if you recognised them or you didn't know them by the description what they're telling you.

But there was no doubt, he felt, that if you lived here you automatically acquired a bad reputation in the wider London beyond the immediate boundaries. And this extended even to the attitude of emergency services like police and ambulance, who were reluctant to answer calls:

We do have neighbourhood watch, yeah. But I think that the people on the estate prefer to do things by themselves. Because the police has, on a number of occasions they have let us down. There've been a lot of incidents… Cos what happened, there's been a number of occasions where people's houses got burgled on this estate and there's been fights and domestic violence and the police have taken long to come here. And we had a guy who fell down the stairs, erm, the fifth floor of the stairs and the police was contacted and the ambulance took about half an hour to come. Cos the ambulance was thinking, 'Oh, it's an estate, there's trouble, blah, blah, blah'. And the guy was in agony, the guy was literally in agony. And there was this guy who came along and he called an ambulance from his mobile phone and the ambulance came. But when they use the house phone the ambulance wouldn't come. So the police has let the estate down on a number of occasions. You know, but other than that, everyone works together and it's a really good estate.

On top of that, the estate is not very well placed in terms of access to facilities:

The thing I don't like about this area, another thing is the roads, there's quite a lot of roads, you know, and there's hardly any safety for the children. And, what else? It's a distance, it's a distance to go to the shops... It's a walking distance and if you haven't got a car, you know, then it could be a bother. But with me, with me and my two children I've found it could be difficult because I haven't got a car at the moment, so I have to walk with them and take buses … to the nearest sports centre. It's … it's okay. I suppose, I suppose the best one is in Brixton.

Carol

Carol is a white divorced mother, in her fifties, with four children, two of whom are already grown up. She is currently unemployed and rents from a housing association in a street where all the other properties are owner-occupied. So she feels anomalous: a poor person, struggling to make ends meet, living in an up and coming area where everyone else is not merely getting by, but getting on. So, strange to say, she seems to feel a sense of exclusion, which never seemed to exist among the people who lived on the council estates.

She came here from Putney; but she never chose to live here, and sees it as rather threatening:

I felt, Battersea to me seemed more threatening somehow. I didn't feel so safe walking on the streets, whereas in Putney, I lived there for about 2 years and … was very friendly and it's beside the river which was nice. I … it's a nicer environment, it seems more leafy. Battersea's very dense, it's … area and it's got lots of dense, high-rise blocks, it's altogether much more claustrophobic, but I didn't have any choice, so I had to take what was offered.

In fact, rather remarkably, she has now lived here for 21 years. Yet she feels no more at home than when she first arrived; rather the reverse.

She sees the area as dangerous, and thinks her gentrifying neighbours are deliberately failing to see the problem:

The over-riding fear of crime, it's, it's always there and if I walk along the street, it's an ever present thing. And if I didn't have a car I wouldn't go out after dark, it's also the feeling that… You would never let your children go to school on their own. In five minutes going to school, they could be bullied or lots of things. When you read the local paper it's very depressing, when I read the *Guardian* it's just horrid, and when I do go away from Battersea, and come back … it's, yuppies would hate you to say it because they want everything rosy in the garden, I think it's a real, a real problem here, and I wouldn't live here if I could move elsewhere. But I don't have … cos I don't own this house. So … I can't sell up and go somewhere else. But I think it's horrible.

She also finds the house and area quite claustrophobic, and has clashed with her neighbours:

… he's complained about the children, they have nowhere to play except that tiny little patch there. I can't stress how horrid, and I only know how horrid… I really do despise it. And if I had the money and this was my own house I would sell.

You see we're just like a load of rats, we were all on top of each other and if you get a load of anything on top of each other then you get on each other's nerves, and that's just what happens at… If you're driving along, if you stop literally for one second to see where you were going, it's toot, toot, toot, toot, drivers are so aggressive and people … I've noticed so much more friendly when I go out…

She recognises that there have been improvements, but perceives that many of them have in effect been negative for her own quality of life:

… it's better in that the, there are some nice shops, some nice shops and some nice wine bars, and this triangle feels quite safe. I think it's got worse in that it's much more dense, traffic is terrible…

Yes. I mean it has changed, in that it's become gentrified, it's, there are pockets of affluence, especially round Battersea, Wandsworth Common. There are a lot of … independent prep schools which have started up to meet that need of the affluent people who've moved in. There are lots of middle class services, such as wine bars and bookstores and restaurants, which weren't here … when I first moved here. And the Northcote Road has changed dramatically. My son's at *** School, which is just near the Northcote Road and years ago that was just stalls, vegetable stalls, not, selling horrible things mouldy old veg and everything, *(laughs)* but they, that's what it used to be, now it's all gift shops and restaurants and wine bars.

On the one hand, gentrification has produced social tensions:

So there has been a dramatic change in Battersea, yes, but there are still pockets of poverty and these co-exist side by side, and I think that creates a lot of tension because there's a lot of burglaries around here, I've been burgled, my son had a brand new, well, four months old ... bike we put it in the garden and he still had the guarantee and receipt and the trellis was all broken down, somebody came over the back garden. They'd seen it from the window, I suspect it was a neighbour, in actual fact another neighbour knew it was because she saw him, but she wouldn't testify in court and the new bike was dragged over the backs and she actually saw this.

But her neighbours, she finds, are reluctant to acknowledge that crime exists in their upmarket arcadia:

... you can't have people who own their own houses saying 'Well, it's crime ridden, we have to put all the mortice locks on and lock up the door and put our window grills up'. You can't say that kind of thing because you're not going to sell your house, and the estate agent can't say that either, because he's not going to sell the house. The idea is that you market the area as desirable, you can't talk about undesirable things, it's a slant. What goes on below the surface is quite different. It ... I think it's the fact that ... actually it's ... it's become, what happened about 20 years ago ... people who couldn't move to Chelsea, which is the sort of people who live round here are the sort of people who'd really much prefer to live in Chelsea, but they can't actually afford it, because you get a mini little house like this for maybe two hundred and fifty thousand, in Chelsea you'd get ... thousand, so they have to come here, and then they drive over the bridge to Chelsea or they take the bus.

But, beyond this feeling of constant physical insecurity, there is also social insecurity. She feels that her neighbours look down on her:

No, no. They're the sort of people around here who look down their nose at you if your child doesn't go to prep school. I mean, Prem goes out in his old jogging bottoms and sweatshirts and trainers... And I get into my scruffy old 2CV and... Single parent, urgh, you know, tatty old... You can feel it, it's, it's almost a tangible thing, mm. Yes. I mean, it's quite nice to know that you don't ... feel threatened by the people, by violence but that's... You know, it's the innate snobbiness... Because in actual fact I think they're rather sad because they don't want to live here, once they have children they don't, do not want to live in these poky little houses without the gardens, they want to move up by the Common but they can't, so it's all about a hierarchy, I mean, people who live around by the common in their eight hundred to one million pound houses look down on people... 'Fancy living in north Battersea. Urgh, tatty old part of Battersea.' ... but it's all a hierarchy, but that's what, that's what society is, it is hierarchical, and Wandsworth's no different. So I get looked down on, but likewise people here would be looked down on as well. I think it's quite funny really.

In fact, she believed they had no idea that she was a housing association tenant, which would merely add to the social tension between them:

... if they knew I didn't own this house you can imagine what, the fuel that would add to the fire... You know, the lowest of the low. I can imagine that. I can really imagine that. Yeah, horrible. Because it's all about status round here, having your V registration car and your nice curtains... And being seen to be going somewhere up the ladder, and it's not about just being a housing trust tenant, divorced with four children, who's going nowhere... during the boom, which I can't remember, was it the eighties?... The for sale boards were going up and down like yo-yos, they were buying houses cos it's property speculation, bought the house, rejuvenate it, renovated it then sell it for a huge profit ... there aren't so many boards going up now. Just lofts going up actually. A couple of years ago the first loft went up and now everybody's got a loft. They're actually, they're actually a bit sad I think. They're like a load of sheep round here. One puts a loft up, everyone will do it.

David

David is in his thirties, self-employed, Jewish, an owner-occupier living with his partner in a street of terraced housing. Previously he worked for a large business consultancy, but recently he decided to go it alone, running a company from home. Unlike the other residents of his neighbourhood, he is a newcomer to London. Battersea for him was simply a consumer choice, not a decision based on a real attachment to the area:

... neither of us had lived in London before and we both had to move to London because of our jobs. So we just did a, we did a drive on one day from Docklands all the way out through, to er, Putney, Barnes, Richmond, and out the other side ... we picked a few areas which we liked on the way sort of, there were bits of Docklands which are nice and then Battersea, Clapham was a bit too expensive and bits of Putney ... and then we started looking more closely in these areas and then this just came up.

The area also has good facilities, which is fortunate because, as he later explains, he is keen to avoid central London:

... in terms of facilities I think it's very well provisioned, we've got a leisure centre, two leisure centres erm, here, and we've got the park, which is only five minutes walk away, Battersea Park. And there's a lot of sports going on there. And in terms of restaurants and things you've got er, Battersea Park Road, which is, got some really nice restaurants on it, for sort of quick meals and things and if you want to get out a bit more you've got Lavender Hill which is only ten minutes walk at the most.
It has good parking. It's good for parking. (Laughs) So, you know, a lot of the

people don't work very far away, I don't think, or er, they don't have cars so, you don't have to sort of, overcrowding you have in places like Clapham.

And, the key consideration in his economic rationale, it is affordable in comparison with Clapham:

Oh yeah, for the same, for a two double bedroom flat, when we were looking, you wouldn't get anything below sort of, a hundred and fifty, at least and that was normally one double bedroom and a sort of, small box room or a kiddy's room. Whereas here you could get a two proper double bedroomed flat for around the hundred and fifty mark at the time so...

He recognises that this is also a mixed area, and this can have its disadvantages. To him, coming into London as a provincial from outside, this close social mixture is quite exotic and quite unusual, something he has never previously experienced and with which he is trying to come to terms:

It's quite, it's quite mixed I think. Er, these are, used to be council owned properties and some of them still are, so you've got a mixture of council tenants and er, sort of, working couples and families, over in that side, cos that side's houses and this side flats. So those are two bedroomed houses I think, then if you look at the buildings they're narrower, er and these are purpose built flats.

Are there any problems with crime in the area?

My bike got nicked from right outside the house. *(Laughs)* Within about a week of bringing it up to London. Er, generally I don't think, this is not a, a bad neighbourhood. Er, I, I, I just was amazed when I first came to London, the sort of, mix of properties and if you walk that way you're into some really horrible council, you know, these old seventies concrete blocks which can't be a pleasant place to live at all. Er, and yet if you go sort of, that way there's some ludicrously expensive you know, cottage, maisonettes and things like that. It's just a very strange mix round here.

But, he felt, this is probably quite a good area for children:

... in the school holidays, yes. Er, and that, I would say if you're gonna bring up kids in central London this is as good a area as any. This estate there's not so much traffic, er, people go haring up and down that road there but I suppose you'd keep your kids away from there. You've got a little park there with some swings and stuff. Er, there's good school facilities, I think, there's two nurseries, there's one just opposite the leisure centre and there's one behind it. Er, I don't know where the nearest school is but generally the facilities are quite good and then, you know, you've got the park and things. You've got access to central London so it's all right.

Despite this, he only came to London because his work brought him here. And, he makes clear, he is not all keen to stay:

... are you thinking of moving somewhere else?

In the short term. I mean, I probably would like to be out of London in 3 years, but...

... why do you think that eventually you'd want to get out of London?

Quality of life really. Er it's not that pleasant being here, er, I enjoy outdoor pursuits and one of my hobbies is para-gliding, and there's, er, it's er, just to get out of London it takes an hour, and then you know, it's just getting around. Whereas if you were somewhere like, living on the South Coast, Portsmouth, Southampton they're still, you know, they're still thriving towns but you've got much more, sort of, in the way of outdoor facilities.

Unlike the people on the council estates, David does not really have contact with the local community:

... my lifestyle isn't really a community one, I don't tend, this is very much a place, or used to be very much a place where I would just, you know, leave in the morning and come home to at night. Whereas if you can get hold of the chap downstairs you probably get a very different response from him. And he's been here a very long time, he knows a lot of people in the area, er, and he's sort of, a pillar of the community, effectively.

So ... there is some kind of community but you're not really that much part of, that much of it.

No I don't. I just don't have time really. Well, I used to get home sort of, half past seven, eight at night, but you've missed all the, any sort of, residents' meetings and things. And we're not here a lot of the weekends cos we go para-gliding...

Amir

Amir is a single father, in his forties, from Morocco, and has lived in England for twenty years. He earns a good income, helping to run a chain of coffee shops and restaurants. He is currently living in council accommodation but is saving up to buy his own home. He would like to move outside London because he hopes to have a family with his current (Polish) girlfriend and does not think that London is a suitable place to bring children up.

Amir has managed very well by using the loopholes in the system; he even got his permanent residency through roundabout means. He was studying for a diploma in France but suddenly realised that his rights to be there legally would shortly run out and he would have to return to Morocco:

… we were friendly with some English and Irish girls, that were staying in university, doing same course, very good friends. And we were sitting in a cafe on a Friday, I said … one of them, she said, 'I'll do you this favour, why don't you marry me and you can go to England if you want' … I said, 'Well'. We decided on Friday afternoon, we get married on the Monday, she went to New York up to now and I came here… Yeah, so on Friday, yeah, it was so easy. On Tuesday I went to the British Embassy in France … then … I came here. I'd never ever thought about going to England or anything like that.

He obtained his first council accommodation in a similarly opportunistic fashion. He had many friends in Italy whom he used to visit. One asked if he could keep an eye on her brother who was dying of Aids. Some sense of duty prompted him to do as his friend requested, but he did not have a particularly altruistic or charitable approach towards his work:

No, I didn't live there, no, I didn't live with him, no… No, God forbid, no. I used to come like every fortnight, bring him bag of shopping and… At the time, people, I mean, I myself, I didn't know a lot about Aids and all that, you know, I was worried to drink a cup of tea in his house. So always, listen I'm in a rush … this is the stuff … and walk out.

But he was well rewarded for his pains:

And he came to a stage when he was really deteriorating, you know, really bad and he had, I don't know what they call it, anyhow a woman used to come. Yeah, well, she, she said, 'Oh, it's very nice of you, you know, people like you don't …', she kind of liked what I did for that guy. And … she told me this … Mario, his name, she said, 'He's not gonna make it, so why don't you take over this place', and she arranged it somehow, she arranged it, put my name on the rent book… But when he passed away, that woman, she … that's where, I think there was some back-hander … yeah, I gave her about £500. And she gave me the flat.

Then, he had good luck with housing a second time:

Normally, I'm on my own, normally I shouldn't get moved, probably I should be lucky, people like tell me I'm lucky to get a one bedroomed to start with, you know.

This, he explained, was because at the time he had had his sister living with him:

Yeah, I managed to get this area because I've been there, it's one bedroomed flat for a long time, I had my sister living me, she's got two kids.

She was in France?

And, but no, just with kids and all that.

Yet even this proved to be untrue:

But if you were with your sister and she had children?

Well, I used that, she moved back ages ago.

He evidently understands only too well how to operate the system:

There's a lot of backhanding things going on … if you know people you get moved to where you want.

That incident, it should be emphasised, did not occur with Wandsworth Council. But his story strongly suggests that he is well qualified to comment on what really happens in at least one London borough housing office.

Amir's urban street skills did not end with housing, though. He also used alternative mechanisms to get work:

… for foreigners they don't, foreigners they don't trust Job Centres that much…You don't get, you don't get much jobs through Job Centres… You find like they go to private places like mostly Italians, you go to restaurants with the Italians, yeah, cos everything down there is dodgy. You go there … I'll give you, when you're, I'll give you in your hand like two hundred and fifty, three hundred … and I give you a payslip of £120, yeah. I'm happy, because you take more money, yeah. I know for a fact that if I say I want a counter-hand…

He currently had a management position, running twelve outlets which altogether employed 74 staff. In that job Amir found that these alternative mechanisms were the ones that worked:

For a very good counter-hand you are very fast and good one, I know he's not gonna be happy, I need to give him at least £300 a week. And if I … if I deal with Job Centres, I can't tell them I'm offering £300 a week, you understand, because I can get an English one, I can get someone, you know, stick to the rules … and they will think that you have £300, they want £300 … payslip and that. Yeah, it's a lot of hassle, so the best way for me is, find me the counter-hand, I'll get one of the ones… 'Do you know anyone that works somebody else who's very good', so … around without, without going through the Job Centre. There are, there are a couple of agencies, yeah, which they are fully aware of what's going on. If I tell them this and I'll spend, I will, if I say, 'I work 2 years for David Visconti', yeah, I'm hot cake. Yeah, but if you stayed 2 years in … you're good, you must be damn good… High pressure, it's a very busy place in the middle of West End, you get twenty people coming out of the tube at once and they all want a cappuccino, blah, blah, blah. You serve them all within five, six minutes, bit faster than that, so it can go round like… It's another world *(laughs)*.

He had also learnt that his company could do much better if it avoided employing English people altogether. They were too conscious of their working rights:

An Englishman to come and work for us, yeah, they send me an Englishman, yeah. They are, they know too much. It isn't that they, like I want my break, I want my break, which is one hour and a half and I don't care if that, within that hour suddenly you've got forty people that just walked into that shop, yeah, and you try to make a compromise, 'Listen, I know this is your break time, but because I've just got forty people come in here and your colleagues are in a mess, so you know, give and take. I mean, you get up, you stay there a little bit longer and after that', 'No, this is my break'. You know, you can't, it's his right, all right, but then again, you don't show that, you know what I mean?… And I can't, like I start 8 O'clock, I come at, I get here at half past seven here, I can make my egg and bacon sandwich and all that, and there is something wrong, someone left the fridges off the night before and there is water everywhere, 'I ain't gonna be bothered, I start at 8 O'clock … I don't care' you know, this is their attitude.

Amir regards this area as rather rough to live in: he sees high levels of unemployment, and like other interviewees he is aware of drug dealing in the area. On the positive side he values the signs of gentrification which are evident everywhere:

I'm very happy with the high street … trendy now… Yeah. So it's somewhere that, I can spend all day there really.

But oddly, because it seems to contradict that last observation, he also notices that a subtle process of racial segregation seems gradually to be taking place. He notices this in the schools, and he ascribes it to out-movement of the white middle class:

And what kind of people are living in this area?

Well, there is very few English people … I would say one in four … I don't know, but I know … when I go and pick up my sister's kids from school, yeah, it's, they were only white kids in the whole school… Not that it bothers me, I mean … think of it as good thing. Because it's … things like … kinds of things. Like, just when you see like forty kids and there is only one, it is a bit, you know, odd.

… Do you think it's cos the white people are sending their children to school in a different area?

No, the white people are moving into different areas, the white people are … they don't, white people don't like, they move out of the area, because they don't like to mix up with black people… And black people, they like to stay with each other, yeah. And I remember, meeting someone was in hospital in Kingston and … and … she's a black lady, she's got a very good job, she works in a bank and all that … she said, 'I would never live in Kingston'. I said, 'Why?', she says, 'There's no brothers round there', it's all white people … and she moved back because… Well, this, this, they tend to like to be with, to mix up with each other whereas the other ones, they like to move away from them and that's what happened… They don't want, put it this way, white people don't, don't like to live in the same area with a lot of black people. They move out and black people like to stay with each other, so they move in, yeah. That happened…

At a more personal level Amir also shows how issues of race and discrimination play themselves out. He explains how, when he goes to visit the large companies for which his company caters, he is always accompanied by his employer's wife. As a white English woman, she conveys the right image for the company. But, when it comes to discussing the finer business details – what they are going to charge, what they are going to do – he does all the talking. If having the right image were not so important, he could easily manage on his own.

He also describes how, in terms of day to day socialising, relationships tend to be more likely to develop along ethnic lines. People live together, they respect each other, but they socialise separately:

… to be honest, over the last 20 years I think, I think the foreign communities somehow gave up on the, on that … that we can be mixed up together and be all right. Now we are here, we, we abide by the rules here, we, we work and make sure, this is, this is the rules, make sure you never need them…If I'm stuck for money, yeah, I know Paul for … I know Paul for 15 years, I took him with me to Morocco, yeah, he come and have brilliant holidays and all that.

Paul's your boss?

No, he's a friend of mine. And … if I'm stuck for fifty quid, I will go and ask Abdullah or Mohammed that I met a week ago, but I wouldn't ask Paul… Because, I don't know, because it's, it's always, it seems to me that it's in their way of thinking that, 'We're all spongers and we're all … come here and we all go and sign on and we all go and', you know. You know, if I buy a nice car or something, that's ... how much did you sell that, Moroccan hash or something like that. It's things like that, all stereotypes, it puts ... in their mind, yeah. The only way I impose myself on them is that I have to be better than all of them, you understand? Wear better clothes, buy a better car, spend more money when we go there, you know, I have to do that extra effort, you know. You do that, you need that extra effort to, to come up to the level, yeah.

The race does play a part of it, like if, if I go down the West End and I'm having a drink and I met like an English bloke yeah, and we start ... two or three hours, yeah and like we enjoy each other's company so probably say, 'All right, take care, goodbye', and that's it, 'See you sometime', but if it was like Moroccan and the exactly same thing happened again, you, you're dead sure you get his number and say, and you're dead sure he's going to ring you up two or three days later. And you know, that extra ... like give it that extra push.

Amy

Amy is a white woman in her thirties, employed, who lives with her husband and baby in an owner-occupied house in one of the more up-market streets in Latchmere Ward. From the interior décor it was clear that they are very much part of the new affluent gentrifying class. She had forgotten about the interview and was still in her dressing gown with her very little baby.

They had chosen the area because it provided relatively easy access to Hammersmith where they both work – she in marketing for a big American media company. They have been living here less than a year and like David they are not originally from London:

Well, we lived in Pimlico before because, and we were living, well we were living in North Yorkshire and my sister lives in Pimlico so we naturally moved to Pimlico just as an area to, you know, begin, and then the reason we came here is, one, money, what we could afford cos we wanted, cos we were in a flat before, a basement flat, so ideally we wanted our own place which was a bit bigger with a bit, with a bit of garden and, and this is one of the areas we could have afforded a house, but not too far from London, and commutable cos we go to Hammersmith, both of us work in Hammersmith. So it's not too bad.

Although not originally from the area, or even from London, she has many friends who live locally:

Right, and have you got, like your networks of friends, do they tend to be in this area or are they spread out all over London?

Umm. Ironically a lot of them are in this area, umm, near Brixton, Brixton, Balham, there's one in ... Southfields, so all this kind of area, Fulham.

And, perhaps because she is now at home all day with her baby, she is aware of the existence of a local community:

I have, I have a great, no, definitely I, I think it's a very good community actually. Already there's, I know an awful lot of neighbours here. So yeah, no, it is good, and there's shopkeepers and what have you. Yeah, it is.

Moving to London was part of a very obvious next step in a very mobile lifestyle; after she and her husband finished university, they moved to places where they could find work:

… in 10 years I've, I've had something like six jobs actually I suppose… I think the maximum I've stayed in a job is the one I'm in now, which is 3 years … you see Mike and I have lived all over the country … so we've not been bothered about moving because when we came out of college it was a really bad time, so you had to move, and, and the first job we had we were made redundant, so we had to move. *(Baby noises)* So … we know that if we want to get on … you always say that if that's where you want to be in 3 years or 2 years then you've gotta go, and also, you know, the money factor … you have to be prepared to move.

This area, she found, is also a good one in terms of local facilities:

Umm, I love it, I love, because I mean you've got Clapham just down the road, which is great for the shopping, you've got Battersea which is great for the park and for the kids … a lot of kids' things going on, which is really good, and, umm.

But, like David, she has no sense of long-tem commitment to the area: they plan to move out of London altogether as their child grows:

Yes. I don't know about when he starts to walk and what have you because the traffic is very bad so he couldn't really run around on his bike or whatever.

… do you intend to sort of live in the area for a long time and…?

I reckon, the plan at the moment is, by the time he's three and if we have another child we may have to move on because he'll be running around the place, and then what we'll probably do is go back to the country… Or Bath, we. We'd like to move to Bath…

Megan

Megan is a young white woman of sixteen, unemployed, and in bureaucratic terms a single mother. In fact, she lives with the father of her child and his family in a council flat. When her baby was even younger she was separated for a while from the father and lived in the same area as her mother in Margate. She is now back with the father and lives with him, his mother and a lodger in a small flat on the same estate as Daniel. But, because she is officially a single mother, she is eligible for Income Support and is looking forward to being moved to bed and breakfast accommodation in the near future. There are many reasons why she would rather live in London than near her mother in Margate; one is that London offers her an unusual degree of privacy:

It's just everybody just gets on with their own business, and nobody's…

What, you found that, like there, those people weren't minding their own business, or…?

… Yeah, not really. They're just very watchy watchy. But I was living in ⸱⸱⸱ before, but we lived in Chatham, and then we moved to Colchester. And then we split up, and I went to Margate, to live near to my mum, and then we got back together, and that's how we ended up here.

Another important consideration is that London offers work opportunities:

… it was better really, a lot easier, I could find a job of work, you see. There's people who can look after me… I love it. I really prefer it.

Although she does receive Income Support, she would very much like to work. And she is perhaps in a better position to do so than most single parents, since she lives with her partner and his mother:

(Laughs) I think it's definitely a bit of a pinch! I think that … because I get Income Support as a lone parent at the moment, because I was living by myself, and when he goes back to university, I still will. I only get £67.20 a week, so I'm going to be much much much better off, going and getting a job.

At the moment she has a very relaxed approach to the kinds of jobs she does:

Yes. Yes. Mmm. You see, when I don't feel happy with my job, then I just leave and get something else. I know that's very irresponsible… At the end of the day, I'm so young, and I, like, I didn't have any responsibility, so why am I going to be, like, 16 years old, sitting in a stupid job that I hate, when I can just as easily go and get another job, and enjoy it for three months or … if I get … well …

She does however have some longer term ambitions about what she would like to do:

I want to be a social worker, so I'm going to college in September, to do Health and Social Care... They've accepted me, but I need to go in and do an exam before I can go there, because I haven't got any GCSEs to get on to the course, and because it's quite a hard course, I need to do the exams to see if I'll be able to follow with it...

There are other lines of work which seem to get her more fired up, though she seems to find it difficult to decide exactly what:

Do you know what sorts of jobs are available?

It's ... sales, cleaning. There's everything ... executives, police officers, Sainsbury's, you know ... everything ... building. There is everything. Even down to, like, phone sex lines and things ...

That must be a very very funny job to do.

I would love to ... really, I would love to do it! I would just have so much fun at work! You would really enjoy it, wouldn't you! You have to be 21, though.

So when you need to earn a bit of cash on the side for your university studies, you could go and ...

I would do that, because it's not dirty, is it, really, at all ... I don't think. I'm sure there's much worse. And it's probably really well paid, really. But it's acting, isn't it... It's acting. That's what I said to my friends... It is acting, because I'm sure that, in every job, you have to act, you have to role play. I said, 'The same as strippers. When they're dancing', I said, 'It's a job. They're acting, they're dancing'. I said, 'It doesn't matter that they're taking their clothes off. Just forget that. But they probably, if you saw them in the street, you wouldn't know that they were a stripper', because it's kind of... I wouldn't do it myself, but ... like the phone, one's acting, and they can't see you. You can be ... you know, they can't get to you or touch you, or hurt you, or anything, because it's so...

In the meantime she has more modest but perhaps more realistic plans:

Yeah, well, I start a cleaning job on Monday, but it's only, like, two hours a day, five days a week... But it's rubbish money. But it's a bit of extra money.

Can I ask you what sort of money it is? Because I know cleaners that make £7 an hour.

I don't think it's £7 an hour. Maybe it's £5 an hour, or something like that. I think it's £5 an hour.

Is that, like, would that be, like, an early morning job?

Yeah, 5.30 until ... 7.30.

She finds problems in doubling up with her partner's family:

There isn't the space, it's just cluttered. We've got one bedroom and, you know…

… It's not one bedroom for all three of you?

Yeah.

Not ideal.

But it's only a three-bedroom flat anyway, so it's not very big, and a lodger has his dining room, and…

Although she lives on the same estate as Daniel, she doesn't see it in nearly such a favourable light:

… this estate's bad… It's just a lot of rough people live on this estate. I mean, I don't think it's as bad as it used to be, but it's associated as a rough … you know. Like if you put in you live at *** Court, on a job interview, and they know where *** Court is, you probably won't get the job!

Seriously?

I think so. That's what somebody told me.

But, like Amir, she feels the area is improving and sees this in a very positive light:

You can see … not that I really know, but from what I hear, there used to be only really … there used to be a very black populated area before. Not to say that that's a bad thing! Obviously, I wouldn't say that! But, you know, the estate wasn't like this. So it was associated. There was a lot of crime and … and now, there's a lot of, like, more well-to-do people, really, if they're black or white, or Asian, or whatever … moving in. So there's more wine bars opening up, and restaurants, and it's getting very trendy.

… Would you like that?

Yes, I like … I think a lot of people round here have a problem with that, actually… Oh, I'd love to be a yuppie! *(Laughs)* I would! Really! No, I don't have a problem with that at all, because it means that there's nice places to go out for a change, and … you know, lots of nice places to eat. But I suppose it's getting expensive as well, really, so maybe that's why people are complaining. And lots of … because the council properties are being bought out now.

Ronnie

Like Tiffany, Ronnie is a long-term resident on his council estate; he has lived here for 16 years. Afro-Caribbean, a father in his fifties, living with his partner, he is a homeowner. He previously worked as a maintenance officer for the Council and therefore has good insight into the workings of the Council and local issues. He now does maintenance for a private company. He has always been active in various kinds of groups, including the Labour Party, and appears to be very well integrated into the local community; he seems to know 80 per cent of the people on what to the outside visitor appears an extremely large estate. This knowledge may give him a greater awareness than most of the area's problems and their causes.

He described how the government's 'care in the community' policies had had a negative impact on the local area:

But it's not, I think that the only thing …was this so-called care in the community. The block next to me is called *** … and what was happening is because Wandsworth prison is in Wandsworth, if you get somebody coming out of prison, like one of these drug addicts or whatever, they support people… I don't know if you know special needs?… So because *** is a one bedroom flat, a lot of them you know in *** , you know and sometimes, you know you've got needles down there. You've got needles on the landing if the lift is not working and you go down the stairs. You know, so that can be quite stressful, you know so, you know.

Perhaps related to the use of drugs, there also appeared to be high levels of burglary and theft:

What about crime, is crime a problem on the estate in particular?

No more than anywhere else. I think at one time, going back to what we was talking about is, there was another block called *** Court, we had the same problem. *** Court was for, well no-one under fifty really gets into *** Court. It was specially reserved for the elderly or senior citizen yeah… And it was specially, it was really a good block. But then you had the same problem it was a one bedroom, so when, right an older person moved out or something like that, they was putting young people in there and they was breaking into people's flat … there was one guy, you know and he, Oh he came out of Wandsworth prison and was living in *** Court, he probably done nearly all the flats.

There were also other more everyday forms of anti-social behaviour:

And that is the, that is one of the problems. The other problem we've got on the estate, after all the money that had been spent, is the dogs. You know sometime people, their, what is happening, they don't allow, they don't exercise their dog enough. They leave it till the last minute and sometimes the dogs don't even make the lift or the stairs and you know it can be quite, you know and that causes friction between you and your neighbours.

And those who insisted on playing their music too loud:

What happened is like when the sun is shining and during the summer it can get quite noisy on the estate, you know different music, if you come like on a Sunday here, one body is playing Jim Reeves, the other one is playing ... and you know there's no peace, you know. It really does get noisy like, you know what I mean?

And what happens when you say, turn the radio down, do they?

They open the window and put the speaker in the window ledge.

These problems, he thought, arose in part because many people who had bought their flats were forced to rent them out in order to be able to pay their mortgage. And this brought a new kind of tenant into the area, one who was here for a short time and had no particular commitment or concern for the area in which they lived:

And what was happening is that a lot of people, they, a lot of the mortgage companies, they just had so much money, they just wanted to, they would lend anybody money. So a lot of people just like what I'm saying to you, I mean a hundred and seventy a week, that's what you have to find. It's not easy, so a lot of people was renting them out as a profit but they had no choice, otherwise they would have got repossessed or whatever, you know. The most problem it create is like noise and music, they have parties cos they're mostly youngsters from Spain and France and things like that, you know and they have these parties and that's the only problem, mostly the noise.

And while the incomers into the area praise access to local facilities, the opening of the new large supermarkets has meant that many of the local shops on the estate have had to close down:

What happened as you are aware, all the local shops has closed down because they can't take on this, the big supermarkets, like Tescos and Kwik Save and all of them. But all these people is in certain area and if you look at Asda is Clapham Junction and then next door to Asda and Sainsburys and Arndale Centre, they all got one thing, a car park. So you need your car to even do simple shopping, yeah.

These shop closures can perhaps also be attributed to the high levels of unemployment on the estate:

And you see as people become bored, I mean half of the girls on the estate was on Valium, you know that is really serious and because as they become bored, they turn to drugs, you know. So all this about, unemployment, the level haven't dropped, not around here. I mean you had people on the estate who is thirty-four and thirty-five,

I was forty and still working and they just give them a book, like a pension book, a Social Security book, do you know?

This may be partly because many Wandsworth jobs are being filled by people outside the area. Ronnie says this may be because local people simply don't have the skills:

…we done research the other day, we had a meeting and 90 per cent of people that work in there, doesn't live in Wandsworth. They come in from places like Leytonstone and whatever. They don't even live in Wandsworth and that is throughout the whole borough. I mean if you look at the town hall, half of them doesn't come from round, doesn't live in Wandsworth.

Why is that?

Somehow probably the lack of skills in the area and the people that apply for the job doesn't met, meet the criteria, it's not, you know, you know.

Part of the reason for this lack of skills, he thinks, is probably the poor quality of the local schools:

Some of the kids don't even go to school there, you can find them hanging about in the landing, in the, some of them you find around Clapham Junction in the arcade and things like that, all around, you know and they beat up the teacher and all them kind of things. It's not a very good school. Not a very good school. You won't find a good school within, I would say 5 miles of this area.

But, despite this rather bleak picture, there are some positive things too. Like others, he refers to the big improvements which have taken place on the estate in recent years:

But probably if you'd go back about 8 to 10 years ago, everybody wanted to get out. It was really bad. We had bridges linking the buildings together. I don't, I should have keep a picture for you … so if they break into one flat, they can easily get away, you know and this was the main problem, you know. So everybody wanted to get out, going back 10 years and then it was revamped with trees, one time, I mean these trees, some of these trees is no more than 8 years old if that.

He also has many of his family living in the area, and this provides him with support:

I would say 90 per cent of my family is in the area, niece, great niece, nephews, sister, you know and I suppose that helps, cos you've got, I've got support.

And, he felt:

> … there's still a good community spirit because then most of the people that's on the estate at the moment was here for over 30 years. You know, over in that block, 30 years, 30 years, some of them have been here from day one.

Right, so how many people would you reckon you'd know to say hello to, sort of as many people as fifty?

> Oh no I would say about 80 per cent… Eighty per cent of the estate. Even the new people, well I've been lucky because the new people that at one time Wandsworth was just selling off the flats, like the top … penthouse, where a lot of them was involved in, like local community groups and things like that. So you get a chance to meet them, so about 80 per cent. Plus as I said to you my sister and all her friends and all them, moved here from 1979, 1980, around that era when it was first built. So what's happened is that their sons and daughters and grand-daughters, you get a chance to know them, yeah.

And to continue the story Ronnie told earlier, strong community cohesion meant they had effective if perhaps unconventional means for dealing with crime:

> So it didn't take them long to find out who was doing it because he was trying to sell some of the stuff. So when he come to me and says well I lost a video, I says what does it look like, what make is it and it didn't take long to really pin him down… So some of the lads on the estate had a quiet word with him and then I think there was a fight outside the paper shop, they grabbed him out there one day. He had to run and leave his shoes, he hasn't come back since, you know, when he was threatened, you know. But the police wouldn't do nothing about it… No the police says they have to catch him and they didn't even take fingerprints, nothing like that…

So the local community, there's actually a strong enough community that they resolved the problem themselves?

> Yeah. Yeah they dealt with it, you know.

Perhaps because the estate is so noisy, if he got the chance he would like to move out:

> No again there's a place in Streatham Common in Streatham area that, you know that I was after but it was too much, I couldn't afford it but if I got the opportunity… I would like to live somewhere near the seaside or somewhere where I can get a little bit more peace and quiet.

Angie

Angie is a white single mother in her twenties, unemployed, who has been living with her children in a council flat for 3 years. She chose to live here because she had family living locally and Wandsworth gave her a flat in the locality she had requested. Her partner (he is a black Jamaican) was also present at the interview, and it appeared that he lived in the flat with her. As a single mother Angie struggled on Income Support:

(Laughter) Do you know anyone on the Social who's got adequate income? No, I must say it's a struggle but it has to be done.

Her partner, however, did work and appeared to have a flexible approach towards employment – as his replies show:

He: I've done security, labouring, site labouring ... assistant, worked in a circus for a couple of weeks and I've like I've done a few things.

Do you find it easy, is it quite easy to find work ?

He: It is if you really sit down and think about it. If you just say to yourself 'Well I want to do this', you can go and do it. If you decide that you don't want to do it, then don't do it. If you're willing to try and say 'Oh I'll try that out', then you're OK.

And when you find work, when you're finding those jobs is that through people you know or Job Centre or advertisements or ...?

He: Basically newspapers and walking into, basically walking into places and just ... and saying 'Have you got a job here? Is there anything going on? Oh can I have an application form blah, blah, blah' and bumph. Basically I talk myself into some jobs.

When you look for work do you look for work locally or you go...?

He: I look for, basically I look as far as my moped can take me, as far as I'm, within an hour distance from where I am. If I can get there within an hour I'm fine, if I can't get there within an hour I don't really want to do it cos it's like taken most of the day to get there and basically get home again.

Angie also found it difficult living in such cramped accommodation. But, since moving to the flat, she has had another child and is therefore eligible for another move, as her partner explains:

He: Rooms and doors going on, you think Oh, great lots of space here, when you work it out these buildings are not built for families, these buildings are built for people who have as they call it the average two point two kids, you know. And hopefully both of them have, both of those children happen to be either all boys or all girls because if you get a girl and then you get another you end up with a load of boys then you're in real trouble cos you can't say to them well you can stick a load of boys together, when you get girls you can't. So it's like at the moment that's why, one of the reasons why they have to move us out of here cos she's getting too old to stay in a room with her brothers. It doesn't help that she's got to completely constantly be tidying up and then you've got these two destroying everything.

But, despite these cramped living conditions they feel, like Ronnie, that the area is improving:

He: Well they've cleaned it up a bit compared to how it was a few years back. Battersea's basically, as they call it, one of the brighter boroughs. Well if you go back to about 19, 1970 ... it was, this area was one grey, dull, dismal area but lately it's been getting brighter and better. Which makes it easier for her a lot of the times because walking around here, especially on this estate, a few years you couldn't walk around this estate, no young lady could walk around this estate especially after nine because it was just that gloomy... It frightened the life out of you when you walked on it ... the buildings actually interconnected so basically you could start at one block and without even touching the ground you could end up at the last block... They knocked them all down because of all the trouble that was going on... Not the blocks, they just knocked down the walkways, about eleven ... of walkways, so there was no way for anybody, basically this was a really bad crime scene round here cos you could basically get to this estate and you disappeared. It's not easy to catch somebody round here. But then they started saying 'Right block this area off, put bollards up'. And now it's like the estate seems to have quietened down a heck of a lot compared to how it used to be like.

These improvements appear to have considerably reduced the amount of crime:

He: Only in, only where the shops are. I mean they were thinking about doing it around this area but it got so, it basically just went from one very noisy bad estate to one very quiet and no-one's ever heard anything on this estate any more. I mean the trouble's moved from here, it's gone all the way to *** area... Burglaries, robberies, rape, we've had a murder down the end here, well a couple of murders on this estate to tell you the truth... It just disappeared, it's basically calmed down. Seriously cos I mean I've actually not seen, it used to be you could walk down the road and you was guaranteed to see somebody get robbed.

There also appear to be good facilities in the area in terms of bringing up children:

He: When I was young it was like it was fun because you got a humungous park,

Battersea Park...Then you've got Clapham Common further down if you really wanted to go somewhere, but they usually have festivals and stuff like that going on. I mean ... *Ronnie stop that please*. What else? You've got lots of leisure centres around, I mean in Battersea you've got what, you've got Battersea Leisure Centre down the bottom. Across the bridge you've got the Chelsea one which is not that far away from here, you can go over and use that one too. Schools, apart from them shutting down a lot of them which is like how they're supposed to be trying to tell us, the government is trying to tell us that they're supposed to ... keep these schools open and try and get primary kids school places. It's like that's not what I see, and I'm seeing is they're having problems getting kids into school.

The area also seems to have quite a strong community feel about it, she feels, associated with the presence of mothers and their children:

... At three thirty, at three thirty you always get them, by the time 3 O'clock comes the mothers are actually sitting up, lined up outside, there about half an hour ahead of the school OK, they're all sitting there, they're all talking about what's going on for the rest of the day. Oh the people done this and Oh got this party going on and Oh yeah we'll organise that. I'm walking along I'm going 'I'm leaving them alone'. They have their meetings but everyone, I mean they're sociable around here, once the mothers and fathers are out they're all really sociable. I mean I've never actually even heard anybody arguing really.

Race relations, they think, also appear to have considerably improved in this area. As a mixed race couple coming from mixed race families, they may be particularly sensitive to these issues:

You mentioned the National Front, did this used to be quite a racist area?

He: Oh yeah we had a march, we had one time, this was, and it must have been about the middle of the seventies as I say there was a march went through the middle of this estate. And it didn't, it got as far as three steps into the estate before the police, and I'm not talking about a few police I'm talking about several van loads of police, jumped into this crowd and told them to go back the other way cos they were walking into the biggest crap they could ever imagine. We were all, there was a load of guys waiting for these people to walk around one corner and they would have been jumped. And that's how it used to be, basically you could walk down the road and it would be, you'd be run down by two skinheads but then it would be the same thing would happen, those two skinheads would go round the corner and they'd be mugged by ... and it would turn round and be all back the other way. That's how it used to be. Now it just seems to have just gone.

So do you think they've just moved out of the area and that it's just generally less racist?

He: No, I think people have just slightly got smartened up. What's the use of arguing over people who come in here and live with you all their lives yeah? They are, as far as I'm concerned they are West Indian, African... OK so why get prejudice from people... As far as I'm concerned most of the friends I've ever had have all been white. I mean I've got, my cousins are all black and I've got one, two, I can say I've got about three black friends. Most of the rest of them are white.

Like everyone else, they are also highly conscious of the social changes that are happening around them, as new people move in. But they are far from happy about it:

Have you noticed much of people moving into the area, like yuppies?

He: Oh yeah.

She: Well, they don't like kids screaming and ... and they don't like the look of two people together, walking down the road.

He: Or if you're not dressed in a particular way, they kind of stare at you, as if to say, 'You're supposed to have designer clothes on'.

The ideal for them would be to move out of London, but they sense that this is unlikely to happen – and in any case, they do not seem to have a very clear idea of what life would be like beyond the M25:

What makes you want to move out of London?

I dunno just it'd be quieter. There's not as much going on and the air's supposed to be fresher. I can't see it somehow but...

Lisa

Lisa is a widow, still only in her thirties, with two sons – one a teenager and one in secondary school. White, employed, she is a housing association tenant. She previously lived on an estate by Clapham Junction, where her husband was caretaker. But when her husband died the housing association moved her to this house:

I moved, I was widowed a couple of years ago so Peabody gave me this house. Because I had to move because my husband was a caretaker for them, so the property came as, came as part of the parcel so they gave us this house, and I just ... so much difference. I didn't feel as safe and as comfortable there, and besides my husband died, but I just didn't feel as safe, ... I felt really ... kinda protected, all the neighbours and everything and there is lots of children around here too and lots of children around my younger sons age ... and Paul's age as well, but Paul doesn't socialise much.

She has had experience of social housing since she lived in council accommodation in Brixton before she got married:

Love it. We all love this area. Most of our life we have lived in Brixton, I lived in Durham for a little while in the north-east, umm but most of it down here and I absolutely love it here.

What do you really love about being in this area?

Umm, main thing. The train station for getting around, there is plenty of transport round here. Umm I am happy with the schools around here and so are the children… Craig goes to *** on *** Road, Paul went to the ADT College in Putney, he now travels to Epsom to Nescott, he just transferred to college. Umm he went to quite a local school. I am really really happy with the house, considering it is worth a fortune and considering that it belongs to Peabody, I am really happy with the house… What else do I like about the area? I like the Latchmere Centre I have got all the facilities down at Latchmere as well. Everything is handy, our doctors are down … everything seems to be on hand … I feel it is. I work in Crystal Palace and I am going against the traffic, so I actually drive to work … I feel as though most things around here I am happy with. I feel safe, I feel quite safe here, although there are a couple of back streets and I do drive a lot. I do feel … well maybe it's because, well I have lived in rougher areas, I have lived in an estate and everything so being on a street I do feel a lot safer.

A key factor is that this is a safe area for her younger child to play in. Compared with where she used to live:

… there is another difference, I wouldn't have been happy with Craig playing out, I mean he is nine now and he was six or seven when we lived on the estate. I wouldn't have been as happy with him playing out, although I allow him to play on the street although the road is quite a fast road, although it shouldn't be, I don't mind him playing out because of lots of other children and I know everyone has got their door open … and he doesn't go off this road and at least I feel as though it is as safe as you can be and there are lots of adults about.

So safety is the main thing. As to whether there is a strong sense of community here, she doesn't have a clear sense:

And what about the community, do you feel there is a strong community here?

There probably is, but to be really honest I don't involve myself so much because I work full time anyway so I don't see as many people. But I do feel it, and I do remember when I first moved in here everyone said to me, you don't need an alarm… I mean I was very security conscious because it was the first time I had been on my own, umm but all the neighbours were saying, you know you will be OK, we will all look after you, you know so there is some kind of community spirit although I am not involved so much.

She also compares her home with Brixton, where she used to live:

That's nice. How do you find living here compared to Brixton?

Totally different ... I find ... I am not happy to go back into Brixton I'll stay with my sister, personal safety I just don't feel as happy going into Brixton, and I travel there in my car most of the time. I wouldn't be happy walking around the streets or anything. I don't know, it could be me losing my confidence, because I am on my own losing my confidence more. Community spirit definitely, the community spirit.

There wasn't one?

No.

Did you live in a street or on an estate?

I lived in a block of flats and I had a couple of friends who were in the flats at the time. I think it is quite a hostile place to live. Wherever I live, I like people I smile at everyone in the street and I want the same response and the same reaction, the same hello good morning. Old fashioned whatever, but that's what I like and I don't expect to be treated. In Brixton, I feel that even now you are ... and know that white people are a minority and not part of there so ... it is difficult, really difficult.

Do you think amongst themselves, the black community is more...

Oh it is a lot stronger, but I just think it is unbalanced, it's the minority of people, I am sure that is what it is. There's no way that I am racist, I love working in a multicultural school, but it feels quite hostile I feel, being here is totally, totally different.

Perhaps the strongest indication that she is comfortable with the area is that she would like to live there permanently:

I don't ever intend to move anywhere, I feel as though I will be here for life, I would want to be here for a long time, unless anything drastically changed, I am happy with the house and the area.

A Place Called Home

Like many Batterseans, Lisa has found a place she can call home. This we found is Battersea's chief characteristic: it is a place in which people feel comfortable and with which they can identify.

Perhaps because so many people here are young and have grown up in a multicultural environment, most respondents feel their quality of everyday social life is good. People know their neighbours and feel on good terms with them. Many have children, and make friends through them. Others have friends they made at university, through work or through a rich social life, quite often in the same locality. They have middle-class jobs, and reasonably high incomes; lifestyles are affluent, Sunday magazine style. That can make them vulnerable to crime, and some certainly feel it.

Unsurprisingly, easy access to facilities and services was seen as a big advantage; transport links were good too, despite lack of a Tube. Above all, here and elsewhere, people most frequently wanted some local 'convenience' stores and chemists, doctors, dentists and post offices as well as easy access to one of the supermarket chains that suited their budgets and requirements. And local government services were judged to be outstandingly good, by many council tenants as well as others. Above all, people felt their area was improving and that the Council was a strong contributory factor.

Of course, not all residents shared in this lifestyle. A few found themselves shut off from social interaction with their neighbours, and their overall evaluation of the neighbourhood was coloured accordingly. Less extreme, but still notable, was the sense that their relative poverty meant they were being relentlessly excluded from the good things that the neighbourhood offered. Many working-class residents, decanted from their council estates to make way for newcomers, felt resentful that they and their children had been deprived of the chance to stay in their area. Yet the council estates also showed rich social interaction: families have close ties and a close support system, reinforced by proximity. Because they are less mobile than the yuppifiers, their patterns of friendships and family links were far more concentrated in and around their neighbourhoods. But, despite such differences, generally people in Battersea seem on good terms with their neighbours; although Battersea is divided by class, this does not seem to lead to trench warfare in its neighbourhoods.

True, there are exceptions. For some, especially the elderly, the new multi-ethnic neighbourhood was perceived negatively, as a sign of decline, socially and in terms of local facilities. Some suggested that both blacks and whites segregate themselves, in pubs or in parks, and identify with one community or the other. But others argued that the real discrimination was by class, and that nowadays class was determined by lifestyle, and therefore by income.

And, true, this feel-good quality dissipates on some of the area's problem estates. Some feel in all kinds of subtle ways that they do not quite belong here. But even here, vigorous policies seem to have brought a big improvement. The most striking feature of Battersea, in which it probably resembles many other London neighbourhoods, is how all sorts and conditions of people – old-time residents, newcomers, young, old, gentrifiers and welfare-dependent – live in relative tranquillity together. It is this quality that makes life in so many parts of London not merely bearable, but positively liveable.

On security, responses were again mixed. Some felt that crime was rife, partly because pockets of poverty persisted among the affluence, partly because of drugs. They talked about needles on stairwells, of drug-dealing on the estates. The arrival of new tenants on housing estates could trigger anything from noisy parties to a local crime wave, ruining the quality of people's lives overnight. But others felt perfectly safe for themselves and their children, probably because they knew the area and its people well; other neighbourhoods, they suggested, were far worse. In a few places, we found an informal and old-fashioned system of crime control, independent of the police: if someone caused trouble, 'the lads on the estate had a quiet word with him'.

So generally, people liked it here. Yet many, both tenants and gentrifiers, expressed a desire to leave London, generally for the country, sometimes for the coast. They wanted space, they wanted peace and quiet, for themselves and their families. The city by its very nature could not offer this. Perhaps it was simply a matter of age and lifecycle, the factors that have always sucked so many young people into London and cities like London, but have equally caused them to leave again later on.

Flight path above Battersea

Bermondsey street scene © Bill Knight

Chapter Three

Pressured Proletarian Island

Bermondsey

On a superficial first glance, walking the streets east of London Bridge station and past London's new riverside City Hall, Bermondsey might appear as a variant of Battersea: an old-established white working-class community, living in a stable housing area with strong family and neighbourhood networks, now undergoing gentrification. But, down in these streets and talking to these people, Bermondsey emerges as a very different kind of place from Battersea – even, perhaps, its diametric opposite. Here too, people have experienced multi-dimensional change: the loss of traditional jobs in docks or factories, the arrival of newcomers to the public housing estates, the gentrification of working-class streets, and the loss of a tight sense of community. But the impacts on them have been drastic and often quite negative. That makes it all the more important to try to understand how such a situation could have developed – which involves delving back into history.

Some History

Southwark, the borough in which Bermondsey lies, presents an intriguing comparison with Wandsworth borough and its Battersea neighbourhood. Four miles farther north-east along the south bank of the river, its early development was in many ways similar, although it has always been closer to the economic heart of the city. Its recent political evolution has shown distinctive twists and turns, as control shifted from Old Labour in the 1960s to militant Labour in the 1970s and 1980s; then to very New Labour in the 1990s, actively encouraging gentrification like the radical Conservatives in Wandsworth; and finally to no overall control in the early twenty-first century. But three in five of its residents still live in social housing, much of it substandard, and the borough continues to suffer the full range of 'inner-city' problems. In particular, while new jobs are arriving, many locals lack the qualifications needed to fill them.

These problems have deep roots. For centuries, at least since Shakespeare's day, Southwark has always been the poor neighbour of the City of London across the river. Developing first along the Borough High Street that led south from London Bridge – the only river crossing, down to the mid-eighteenth century – it became a place of intense traffic of goods and people. It was a place of markets, including the still-surviving Borough Market, while along the wharves which lined the 'Pool of London', for a mile or more below the bridge, was concentrated all of London's port activity until enclosed docks were built on clear land further east in the nineteenth century.

By then, packed into the intervening space was a mixture of industry, including noxious activities such as leather tanning, and one of the worst slum districts in London: Jacob's Island, immortalised in Dickens's *Oliver Twist*. Above the bridge, Bankside was traditionally London's red light district, a place of theatres, bear pits, taverns and brothels. The High Street was also a centre for coaching inns until London's first rail terminus was built nearby at London Bridge. Two major commuter railways, serving the City of London across the river, then produced a huge complex of east–west railway tracks on high arches, effectively severing the area in two. Below the tracks lay a tangled mass of slum housing, warehousing and industry, and trades ancillary to the City, such as printing and food processing, as well as heavier industry – including a gasworks on Bankside, replaced in the 1950s by London's last power station, itself transmogrified into the Tate Modern gallery shortly before we interviewed.

Slowly, from the mid-nineteenth century, charitable trusts and then municipal endeavour began to replace the worst of the slums, squeezing new housing into the limited spaces between the viaducts. This process accelerated in the twentieth century, as Southwark and Bermondsey Councils built as much public housing as their powers and finances would allow them. And after 1934 they were joined by the London County Council, as Herbert Morrison's Labour administration switched emphasis from peripheral out-county estates to denser inner-London renewal schemes. Then as later, one effect of reconstruction was to lower residential densities; even as early as the 1890s, with the arrival of LCC tram termini and then of Tube services, out-movement of population began, initially to new LCC cottage homes. It continued through most of the twentieth century, hugely accelerated by the Blitz, taking the combined population of the (pre-1965) Southwark and Bermondsey boroughs from a peak of 337,000 in 1901 to just 158,000 by 1951. Then, in the 1950s, a comprehensive renewal strategy brought huge new public estates on either side of a relocated Jamaica Road, but again housing and area improvements entailed reduced densities and substantial population overspill from these areas.

But for a time the riverside area of wharves and warehouses remained more or less untouched, until quite suddenly – between 1967 and 1981 – competition from more entrepreneurial east coast container ports led to the sudden and unexpected contraction and then closure of the Port of London, leaving a vast stretch of derelict land along 8 miles of riverfront. During the 1970s there were successive redevelopment schemes, involving much paper and much talk but very little action. To remedy this situation, in 1981 the Thatcher government removed both initiative and veto powers from the local authorities, and imposed a London Docklands Development Corporation with a single-minded remit to secure redevelopment of the entire dockland area, including the Southwark waterfront. It was fought all the way up to the High Court, delaying the LDDC's inauguration for a year. Even after this, Southwark Council – whose traditional working-class trade-union leadership had been displaced by a group of left-wing activists – pursued a bitter guerrilla war against the government, producing a rival development plan which had to be struck down in the High Court, and rejecting any collaboration with the LDDC.

Beyond simple issues of power, there was a fundamental conflict about the kind of area that this should be. The Council's priorities were to preserve traditional land uses and activities employing the existing working-class population; the LDDC saw the future in terms of an informational economy, and was determined to attract jobs in the service sectors and to build homes for the predominantly middle-class people who would work in them.

The LDDC's main impact was logically in the area it took over: the enclosed docks, both on the north bank and further east in the Surrey Docks. But its territory also included the line of riverside warehouses stretching up to London Bridge, most of which were converted into shops, restaurants, bars and luxury apartments, through two major developments in the 1980s: Hay's Galleria near London Bridge and Butler's Wharf just below Tower Bridge. The early 1990s collapse of the property market delayed a third major scheme, London Bridge City, beyond the LDDC's winding-up in 1998. By then, however, the Southwark riverside (like that opposite in Tower Hamlets) displayed two starkly dissimilar landscapes: one of public-sector rebuilding, 1934 to 1981, and another of commercial redevelopment under public-private partnership, 1982 to 1998, separated by a kind of invisible Berlin Wall.

When the LDDC was wound up in 1998 its initiatives passed back to the local authority. But by then, ironically, the Council had transformed itself into a model of Blairite New Labour. Southwark eagerly accepted the revolution that the LDDC had wrought, and sought to push it towards its logical conclusion, pursuing both private investment and a more affluent population. It extended the area of extensive development and regeneration from the waterfront base to encompass a wide area across the northern half of the borough, especially in five areas: the riverine areas of Bankside and London Bridge (home to the new Greater London Authority); North Peckham; the Aylesbury Estate; and the Elephant and Castle. The entrepreneurial strategy – promoted by Southwark's then director of development, Fred Manson, in conjunction with a Cross-River Partnership – involved linking Southwark as a whole into the City and Westminster economies, with Bankside as the crucial bridgehead, all boosted by completion of the Jubilee Line extension in 1999.

Since the 1970s, during periodic boom spells this area has attracted overspill business service development from the City. But the key to its recent transformation is its incorporation into an extended cultural quarter, with the rebuilt Globe Theatre (1996), Tate Modern (2000) and associated development (including Vinopolis and smaller galleries) linking along the riverside westward to the postwar South Bank arts complex and eastward to the yuppified Hay's Galleria and beyond. This in turn has brought gentrification, as evidenced by house prices which have risen faster than in most other parts of London since the mid-1990s, with average prices for all properties in Southwark reaching £273,000 in early 2006, putting it in sixteenth place, midway among London boroughs.

Bermondsey Today

There have been vast changes in Southwark's economy since 1970: the docks have gone, and most manufacturing industry has either shut down or moved away. Between 1991 and 1998 a further 4,000 manufacturing jobs were lost. What survives is mostly printing, which retains its traditional advantages of proximity to CBD customers, and now operates alongside newspaper publishing, television and video production.

But, as in other parts of east and south-east London, employment in Southwark now means office employment. There are two major categories: public services – public administration, railway transport, post, telecommunications – which have been affected by reorganisation or privatisation, but overall seem to have remained stable in employment through the 1990s; and financial and business services, which have grown at no more than average rates but account for a third of all employment. More recently, regeneration policies on Bankside have brought new jobs in the creative, cultural and tourist industries. Even before the arrival of the Globe Theatre and the Tate Modern, there was an important local cluster of creative industries, and the area can now boast some sixteen art galleries and many advertising and design companies, as well as media operations. During the 1990s, borough employment in recreational and cultural services more than doubled, though they still only employed 6,000 people in 1999. A similar number work in catering and hotel services, where there has also been substantial growth, though this sector remains under-represented in the borough as a whole, and growth probably owes as much to expanding local demand as to that from tourists.

Overall, employment grew in Southwark during the 1990s – by about 8 per cent between 1991 and 1998. Even manual sector jobs contracted only a little, about 3 per cent, while non-manual work grew healthily. It seems that, after a low point in the 1970s and early 1980s, the borough economy has turned. But, of course, it has done so only by transforming itself from goods handling to knowledge production.

And this shows starkly in the social structure of the resident population. Its most striking feature – at least in comparison to areas farther west – is the high proportion of people who are economically inactive: just over 40 per cent in 2001, including 6.2 per cent unemployed, 8.0 per cent retired, and 5.3 per cent permanently sick or disabled. Significantly, though nearly 35 per cent have a degree level or higher, over 24 per cent have no qualification at all. In 2005, the largest single group of workers were managers and senior officials, closely followed by associate professional and technical and by administrative and secretarial and professional occupations, but next after those came elementary occupations – the clearest possible index of the economic and social polarisation that now characterises Southwark.

In 2001 only 31 per cent of households owned their homes, and no less than 58 per cent of Southwark households remained in social housing. But in household composition Southwark is close to the London norm: almost 50 per cent of the population fall in the single never married category, 37 per cent of households have only one person and only 20 per cent are married couples, while 14 per cent are lone parent households – 10 per cent with dependent children.

Southwark is typical of inner London in another way: it has an exceptionally high proportion, 37 per cent, of non-white people. The largest ethnic minority is one that has arrived quite recently, the Black African with 16 per cent, followed by Black Caribbean with 8 per cent. Significantly, though, negligible numbers recorded themselves as other than Christian, no religion or religion not stated. In 1981 the ethnic minority population of the borough had been only 18 per cent; growth since then – including relatively large numbers of refugees and asylum seekers, estimated at around 4 per cent of the resident population by 1997 – has reversed a long-term pattern of population decline. The change is highlighted within the school population, where by 1999 55 per cent were from ethnic minorities (including 15 per cent Afro-Caribbean and 26 per cent African) and 36 per cent had English as a second language.

Unsurprisingly, Southwark appears among the four London boroughs with the greatest concentrations of deprivation; in 2004 it was seventeenth among all English local authority areas on the government's indices of deprivation. Average incomes of taxpayers in the borough are actually on a par with those in most of our other case study districts, but the large numbers of economically inactive people mean that the average conceals huge disparities: rich and poor are living side by side. As elsewhere in London, the level of housing deprivation is particularly severe: the 2001 Census showed an overcrowding rate of 25 per cent, eighth worst both in London and nationally. Other indicators of deprivation include a quarter of the primary school population with special education needs, and relatively high rates of child protection registration. Crime rates for almost all types of offence are the highest among the case study districts, most notably for drug offences, where they are more than twice the London average.

Our interviews took place in two distinct neighbourhoods: Bermondsey, along the river east of Tower Bridge, and the North Peckham estate, about a mile inland.

Bermondsey, like many other neighbourhoods where we interviewed, is not a single homogenous place at all, but at least two – or maybe, three. There is the vast area of public housing south of the dual-carriageway Jamaica Road passing the new Bermondsey Jubilee Line Tube station – which was itself a postwar creation, diverted during the course of the great rebuild of the 1950s and 1960s. This, the 'four squares' area, is the almost standard mixture of the 1950s and 1960s: a mixed area of four-storey maisonettes and seven-storey slab blocks, quite well planned and maintained, and generally peaceful. In the heart of it is Lockwood Square, a series of rather massive seven-storey slab blocks with deck access, arrayed around a nicely landscaped square, in a quiet area with some good character. Here also is the rather isolated and anomalous Casby House: a massive twenty-storey tower block on the south side of Jamaica Road, close to the Tube station, and rather unusual for this area, which is generally not more than seven storeys. Farther east, on Tooley Street on the other side of Tower Bridge Road, are Devon Mansions: tall Victorian blocks which you can see from the railway line into London Bridge.

North of Jamaica Road is a rather different landscape resulting from the great rebuild of the 1960s: the Dickens Estate and Pynfolds next door towards the Rotherhithe Tunnel, quite pleasant, with four-storey maisonettes, well landscaped, but with some traffic noise for the blocks directly facing onto Jamaica Road, and with some two-storey houses immediately behind. This, even more than the area south of Jamaica Road, is an oasis of peace: a reminder of just how good the postwar planners were at their best, especially now the vegetation has grown around their creations.

Finally there is the third Bermondsey: on the rear side of Hay's Galleria, an itsy-bitsy mixture of old warehousing and new infill construction. Here is an 'urban village' street: a mixture of warehouse conversions and new infill apartments, including a large LSE hall of residence, in an area full of trendy wine bars and restaurants, just behind Butlers Wharf near the Design Museum.

This physical distinction of course results from history. The first two areas are closely identified with the area's former port functions and remain essentially a white working-class community, with local internal divisions stemming from the physical division by Jamaica Road and by the wide rail viaduct a few blocks to the south, and also from the family linkage policies of local housing associations, typified by the father-son tenancies of the Peabody Estate. These can produce quite inward-looking and also backward-looking feelings: communities increasingly feel squeezed out of their own borough, because they find it hard to access the office jobs that have replaced dock jobs as the area's mainstay, and also because their traditional amenities have been replaced by offices or tourist facilities. They also see rents rising beyond their means. On top of that, there is a shortage of local secondary school places, so that many of their children have to travel long distances to school while others stay at home. So – as in their futile campaign against the development of London Bridge City, an office development around the new City Hall – they tend to dig in and oppose further change.

North Peckham is very different: it is an area of huge 1960s and 1970s council estates, consisting of massive blocks with deck access, which became problematic during the late 1970s and 1980s, causing them to be rebuilt under the aegis of the Peckham Partnership with mixed tenures and lower densities, and with an upgraded town centre including an award-winning public library. For many older residents, this provided a welcome opportunity to leave a claustrophobic and crime-ridden estate, while those who remained have benefited both from housing standards higher than in many private developments and falling crime rates. But there have been teething problems, with delayed construction of social facilities, and bureaucratic problems in resettling families, while schools have been hit by steeply declining registers. The most vulnerable were the hardest hit; elderly residents, in particular, sometimes did not survive the move. Most recently the area achieved notoriety for gang activity, with the much-publicised manslaughter of the ten-year-old Nigerian child, Damilola Taylor. Property prices here remain low, averaging just £211,000 in early 2006.

Serena

Some Bermondsey residents appear to exist almost miraculously in islands of communal cohesion, while almost everything in the world around them has dissolved and changed. One of these is Serena, a divorced mother of two in her twenties, white, unemployed and a council tenant. She came from a large local family and has no less than eleven brothers and sisters.

She describes the feeling of community on her local estate in words that are almost lyrical, making it sound like something out of an almost forgotten age of social harmony, an almost rustic village quality where everyone knew everyone and where social controls were effortlessly maintained, informally and almost unconsciously:

They've got the ... one of the best estates in London. Everybody on this estate knows everyone else ... everyone on here just makes you feel welcome. We all sort of go out on day trips together on coaches. And ... I think it's a brilliant area. I think everyone keeps their eye on everyone else's children round here. As soon as one of the kids goes off the estate, you know about it.

How do you know?

One of the others will come and knock on the door and say. They'll say to you ... or even if one of them's talking to someone they shouldn't be speaking to, one of the older ones will come round and say, 'Oh, so and so's talking to ... a stranger'. But most of them know not to talk to strangers. Oh yeah. I mean, the teenagers on here, they're unbelievable. They really are unbelievable, the teenagers.

In what sorts of ways?

Um ... I don't know. If I needed my garden done. I could say to the boys, 'Oh, I'm doing my garden, I've got to cut the grass. Can you take all the rubbish down to the chute for me?' And they'd all do it. That's just the way that they've been brought up round here, though. And in terms of people who live in the area, would you know ... I mean, how many people do you think you'd know, just generally, in the area? I would say about 40 ... you walk down the street and you know more or less everyone. I could go down ... Southwark Park Road, and I'd know more or less everyone that I walk past.

Really? Like a village? How many people would you reckon that you knew? If you'd just, like, to say hello to? I mean, if you had to put a figure on it?

To say hello to? Just in Bermondsey? About 150. Yeah. It's like ... I can be walking along with my friend Donna, and she'll stop and talk to somebody that she knows, and then next time I'm walking down the street, that person will say hello to me, and I'll say hello to them. And that's how it goes.

She thought that this contributed to a minimal, almost non-existent level of crime on the estate:

And if the teenagers have been making too much noise on the estate, then somebody has a word with them. But, basically, no, it's a very very good estate. I think we've had one burglary in 3 years, because everyone knows everyone on here, and they know who shouldn't be on here at certain times, so…

In her view, the estate was so hospitable because of its small size and intelligently-planned layout:

I don't know. I think it's because it's so small, and all the blocks face each other, and they've got, like, a communal area, obviously, in the middle. And it's got such a different age range.

She contrasted this to the design of other local estates which have a bad local reputation:

But it's just areas that they look at, that they don't have a community any more, like the *** Estate. I can't see them having a community ... the tall blocks, because you don't know who lives two floors down from you. Whereas probably everyone in that block could tell you who lives on the ground floor and ... and who lives opposite them as well.

But, she had no doubt, the local facilities contributed to the quality of life on the estate as well:

The shops are, literally, right in front of my front door... Yeah. The Tube station's right next door, that's in Jamaica Road. And the school's across the road. The bus stops are right in front of me as well... Yeah. And there's a park about 50 yards away. And there's swings in the back garden! So you don't really need to go anywhere else.

It was the same with the local tenants' association, which was extraordinarily lively and active:

... when I first moved on here, because I didn't really know anyone ... and the Tenants' Association, the first thing they do is come round and introduce theirselves to everyone that moves in... And they ask for a pound a month off each household, and then all the children get a card at Christmas, with £5 in it, and they also go on a day trip in the summer, which is where we're going next Sunday, actually ... to Broadstairs. So we've got a 72-seater coach. But everyone gets the choice of going or not. And we're just going to go and have a day out in Broadstairs.

All these factors meant that – unlike some other parts of Bermondsey – this estate had a low turnover; no one wanted to leave:

No, a lot of people don't tend to give their flats up on this estate. It's very, very hard to get a flat on here, and it's very rarely you actually see one going, unless it's for a specific reason, like if it's an old person that's got stairs in their flat. But I think that they ... they'd actually rather move into one of the ground floor ones, rather than move off of the estate.

Liz

Liz echoed many of Serena's sentiments. Like Serena she had grown up in a nearby area, in her case the East End on the other side of the river, and had fifteen brothers and sisters. In her thirties, a council tenant, she was also white, divorced and had three children.

Although Liz lived on a much larger estate than Serena, she found it surprisingly congenial:

Yeah, yeah, I've got, there's a few good friends, yeah. Yeah, there is. No I can honestly say it's a nice, it's a nice area to live, I wouldn't live nowhere else, I wouldn't go back over the East End … even though my family live over there, I don't think I could … go and live back over in that area. Even though, I mean I go over there quite a lot, but I don't think I'd like to live where they live, I really like it here. The people, they are, they're all quite nice really … they're quite friendly and you get the odd one, but then … you get that anywhere don't you?

And this made her feel safe:

I feel very safe, I mean, I can honestly, cos like, I do know, sort of, everyone to say hello to, so I would feel safe, yeah, walking round here, I wouldn't have no qualms about…

Any time of the night?

Yeah, I wouldn't have really no, that is because I know everyone and…

And this feeling of safety comes from her familiarity with the area:

Yeah, yeah… But as for crime, I think everyone gets a little bit of crime, but I can honestly say, like I say, I'd feel safe walking round this area, this particular part, you know what I mean. I don't know about down the Blue, down that way late at night, I wouldn't, you know, I'm not saying that cos I don't really know it down there so.

She also appreciated the convenient local facilities, especially the shops, and the easy access by public transport:

Well I can't, we're on top of everything really here aren't we? We've got Surrey Quays, you only have to get a bus at the top here, it takes you right into the Quays. We got the Bermondsey Station, that takes me right to my sister's, takes you right through to Stratford Shopping Centre, up the West End. So I've really got no complaints about the transport. You know, I mean, where I can go sort of anywhere from here, you know, it is so easy. I mean, I'm in walking distance to London Bridge, Tower Bridge, couldn't be better really.

But there were a few concerns in her mind too. One, almost inevitably, was the progressive 'yuppification' of the area and its effect in breaking down the old close social relationships:

I don't really know, you don't really know who lives over there to be honest. Do you know what I mean, you might see 'em at the window, but … I can't honestly … say that … you don't really know who lives there.

And this was associated with a certain feeling, amounting to mild paranoia, that the Council was encouraging the process while allowing traditional local services to run down:

No, there's no improvements, it's just… I mean, I don't know if you've seen the chute just there, you know, when you come in… I can't understand it, because like the dustmen'll come, and they … take the rubbish, but leave half of it on the floor just seems, they've got no time, it's all being built up round here, it seems it's like for, you know, them that can afford their houses and that. That's what it seems to me.

At an everyday level, she felt that the Council could cater better for local needs – for instance, of mothers looking after small children during the day:

I think they could do with like a nice little play park or, or anything, you know, a little park on there. I don't mean for the big uns, I mean for the little children, cos obviously you can't let 'em out, so wouldn't it be nice if they could just come down and their parents could watch 'em from the window, you know, and play along. They're lovely the flats, they're beautiful, they're very nice but don't forget us, do something for us.

But, as her own children were now all of secondary school age, her main concern is with the trials and tribulations of the local school system, typical of a borough like Southwark but compounded by the sheer shortage of school places:

The schools are terrible, the trouble I've had with the three of mine, my boy is 17, he never went to school, because he couldn't get in a school, and he was on the waiting list at ***, and you know they didn't even know he was off school until he was 13. And then I got a letter to say I had to go … to go up there, but by the time he was 13 they sent him ***, and he couldn't get on because he hadn't been to school, and then he went to a centre. I had the same trouble with my two girls, one was off for a year, the other one, to be honest, I've, be truthful, I went to the Catholic Church because I wasn't Catholic, and I went all through the things for two years to get 'em into the school, one of 'em got in, one of 'em never. Now … she, the one that was at ***, she's gone *** now because she couldn't get on round there.

Del and Kenny

Del and Kenny are two brothers in their thirties, one single, one a divorced father, one unemployed, the other employed, living in council housing in a tower block on the Jamaica Road in Bermondsey. Both grew up in the area and went to school there. Like Liz, Del and Kenny are starting to feel the consequences of gentrification and had strong views about the process:

You've got wharves and all that over there that have been converted for, like, people coming into the area. It's all progress, I know. But they're splashing, like, we're getting windows put in now, right? It ain't like… They're having a spruce up… *Oh, let me finish, mate, please? Right.* The reason we've put, like they're putting the windows in now, it's not because all of a sudden we all need windows now, it's because all of a sudden, this looks like an eyesore. I'm telling you, that door's been hanging off for, like, 3 years, no one's wanted to know… Basically, yeah. 'Let's make Jamaica Road a little bit picture perfect', that's all it's about. And everywhere you go round here, you'll see the same thing. It's exactly the same thing.

Del has mixed feelings about this. He concludes:

The more the merrier. If it improves the gaff, I'm all for it. But, like, I don't like the hypocrisy of why we're getting things done, and then expecting us to thank them and vote for them. We ain't that stupid. I resent the fact that they're insulting my intelligence, by like, 'Well, we put your windows in, mate', they should have put them in years ago. We needed them, seriously.

As two typical young 'Bermondsey boys', Del and Kenny didn't exist in quite the same universe as Liz and Serena. Their formative experiences ranged more widely and their impression of their neighbourhood was far less benign:

I'll be honest with you, love, right, this area alone, right, people I've grown up with, we go to work for a living. He ain't no hard man, he's just … we're just normal people, we like a laugh more than … like all our … not egotistical that way, don't believe in violence or nothing like that, but I swear to you, if you walked out that … you know, if you wanted to go in any pub round here, you'd find the equivalent, because that was then and this is now, and now, I'm afraid, you've got bits of kids 17 and 18, who are tooled up in pubs, meant to be having a social drink. And I don't understand that. I don't understand it. And a lot of people I've known have either been killed or shot, or whatever. I've known a few deaths in my time, and I'm nothing special, I don't know everybody. But there's a lot of spiteful people round here, and there's a lot of capable people round here, and it don't really take too much to set them off.

Consequently there were few local people Del felt he could trust:

…when it really boils down to it, I mean, living, coming from round here, I know what friends mean, but I wouldn't know how to define it. I would not know how to, like, you know, if I was talking to you about a friend … I mean, my mate in the Army, I trust him, simple as that. But round here, well, I wouldn't know where to begin, because there is very few people that, like, I'm likely to, like, leave my money on the table in front of. Or talk about things that … that somebody could … tuck you up over, or … you know, anything. I mean, you don't put your wealth on offer, and you don't let on too much. You know, you play, what is the saying? You play your cards close to your chest

Del had explanations for the causes:

Political correctness has ruined, like, it's ruined, it's ruined so many things for so many people, because at the end of the day, they've tried to teach people a new (way) of seeing right from wrong, and dealing with it. And basically, it's something you know, everybody knows the difference between right and wrong. And, like, the thing with it is, with this political correctness, right, say you saw a guy who was looking really sultry like, look like how you'd imagine a paedophile, and he's got a kid by the hand, and he's dragging the kid, and the kid's crying, right? Ten years ago, longer, you'd have walked over and gone, 'What's the matter with that child, mate?' And you'd have been justified in doing it. You can't say nothing like that nowadays. You can't say nothing to nobody. You've just gotta bury your head in the sand. And when things go off…

And he had decided ideas about solutions too:

Be honest with you… I'll be honest with you. I honestly believe, and I don't believe … if this is possible, without sounding like an hypocrite, I don't believe in violence, right? But, at the same time, right, how do you … like, where discipline's concerned, right, a lot of people … there's a lot of people, right, in this world, who would be better people if someone had either kicked them up the arse, or slapped them round the head, put them in their place. And that goes right through the board. Don't matter where you're born, who you are, your preferences, nothing. At the end of the day, there's people running round in this world, thinking they can do what they like, because the punishments, I mean, let's face it, they're almost like fucking treats!

Perhaps part of Del's cynicism towards life stemmed from the difficulties he had experienced over the years in earning a living:

I was in a mortuary up until last Christmas, at St. Thomas's, I think I was on the minimum wage.

You were in a mortuary?

Yeah, I was playing with all the dead bodies and that, like that was my job, and wheeling people in and out who were virtually not far off of dead. And that was the minimum wage… I tell you what I was clearing, and this is a bit embarrassing, really, for a grown man, right, bearing in mind that, yeah, I've got commitments that I can't get out of all the time, moneywise. And basically, I was clearing, after tax, after I'd paid me fares as well, I was clearing 23 quid a day. And that's eight to five.

Del felt that he was actually very capable:

And to be truthfully honest, there's no … like, I mean, I can do quite a few things. I'm no expert, but I can turn my hand to most things. And the thing of it is, I won't go and work for £2.50 an hour, and be spoke to like a moron, right.

But his lack of a CV meant it was difficult for him to find a job:

But the thing is, I mean, nowadays, you go for a job, and you've gotta have a CV. I mean, what is a CV? It's a French car, isn't it? I mean, like, what can I put on it? Like … at the end of the day… I mean, my CV reads … I'm the first man to swim the Channel without getting wet, or I was an astronaut, I was this or that. If you put the truth, at the end of the day, somebody will look at it, and go, 'phoah' You know what I mean? That ain't gonna get you a job, that's gonna get you hung!

Despite all his difficulties, Del had carried on working. But his brother Kenny had not been able to overcome similar problems:

So, anyway, this geezer signs me up. I went, he went, 'Have you got steel toe-cap boots?' I went, 'No', he went, 'Oh, we'll supply you with them, then'. He didn't tell me I had to pay for them, you know what I mean? My first wage packet…

Oh, they took it out your wage packet?

Yeah. Right, soon as I started … it was a Bank Holiday, I started on the Tuesday or something, so I done four days, right, in these new boots, right, going down roads, somewhere where I've never been before, with a fucking broom, you know what I mean, sweeping up leaves in the winter. You can imagine it in Putney, it's all full of trees. So the boots are killing me, I can hardly walk, I get me wage packet, I've got fucking about two quid in it, because he took the score out for the boots straightaway, you know what I mean!

As well as earning very little money, Kenny suddenly found himself in the notorious poverty trap: because he was no longer on benefit, he had to start paying bills that he had never before had to face:

You're in debt, like, as soon as you go to work, cos… Because you had to pay rent, and then you get banged Council Tax, bang, bang, bang. They don't give you no grace, do you know what I mean? You've gotta start paying from when you start work. I was getting up at half past four in the morning. I was writing to the Council, 'What am I now paying, like a rent, right?' Didn't get a reply off them at all, like, after four letters. So I was getting up half four in the morning, by the time I get home, they're shut anyway, and it's pointless trying to phone them, because they're useless down the phone. So anyway, I ended up in court over that, because of non-payment of rent, and all that shit. Do you know what I mean?… I was going to work, and coming back and just crashing out. Getting up and going to work, crashing out. It was just… And then I was taken to court and in debt over it.

His conclusion was one that many others in a similar position had reached:

Well, I'm better off not working, because I can't find a thing that'll pay the actual … a living fucking wage, you know.

As Del explained, there was a very basic psychological aspect to this: by coming off benefits, you gave up the whole cocoon of Social Security that had protected you, leaving you on your own in a harsh world with virtually no protection:

Cos … it's, see, you get on the dole, I've been on the dole before, and there's this paranoia of … it's like, it's like leaving the nest. You sign off, right, and then you're out in the big wide world, 'Where am I going to get my money from?' This, that and the other, you know. And it's a psychological thing, I think, because that's how I felt when I come off the dole.

Gary and Dawn

Gary and Dawn are a married white couple in their forties, with five young children, and live in housing association accommodation. Gary had worked as a taxi driver, but ill health had caused him to give up that job and become a radio controller:

I work in, as a controller in an office three nights a week because I was chauffeuring up till last week but me back went and they told me I couldn't do that sort of work any more, like sitting behind a wheel. So all I do is Sunday, Monday and Tuesday night, 8 hours a night, just sitting on the phones, answering the phones. But apart from that I can't really do anything…

Faced with a debilitating injury, he found that his benefits ran out and he had to find some kind of work:

I don't know what the hell it was, they didn't know... I could stay on the sort of sick for so long, you know what I mean, but they wasn't going to put me down and, and I'm not disabled, you know. They wasn't going to put me down for that so I had to go back to work but I obviously couldn't do the sort of work that I've been doing all me life, you know, like sort of driving and lifting luggage and that. I just couldn't do it, I don't know, I don't know what happened. I suppose it's a bit of old age as well but...

Jobs like his previous one, or the one he was now doing, were never advertised: you heard about them by word of mouth, by being connected into an informal network:

I mean no-one kind of like advertises a job, someone always knows someone who knows someone who's looking for someone who's doing this, you know what I mean, and I don't think, well that chauffeur firm it was only that someone I knew, he started there and I see him and I said 'Oh I'll have some of that' and I had it for about 2 years but this time last year I was like a cripple when I did me back... But, so, so the job I'm working for, you know, it was never advertised, you know what I mean, someone I knew I was talking to in the park, phoned up ... phoned me up. And that's how it is...

Like Serena and Liz, Gary is part of the traditional Bermondsey community:

I suppose ... well for years we all stayed in the area, family stayed in the area, and everyone, I mean if I walk down the street I always see someone I know, whether it's, you know, if it's not someone's ... I know, I know their mum, their dad, their brother, their sister, their uncle, their aunt, their cousins, everyone knows everyone. But...

But Dawn, who had grown up in Welwyn, was not. And, even after years in the area, she still felt it:

I mean even with me, I could be with his friends and I feel OK but there's always that little bit that tells you you're not one of them. It's strange, it's a strange feeling... Yeah. Cos they always tend to make you feel as if you're an outsider, they say they don't but they do... Yeah. They can be friendly, they're nice and friendly to you but deep down you just get that, you know when you get a feedback, you feel... They don't like adapting, they're like little, they like, all I can explain like a little village...

And, like Del and Kenny, both Gary and Dawn were pretty cynical about the way the area was changing:

She: We're more worried about the children really and the crime and everything and what they can get into, this is the problem.

He: You wouldn't dream about it, but now things have changed. They've got a, they've got to get money for drugs. They'll break into a car, you know, and nick a £400 radio ... to sell it for £20, you know, just to get something to shove up their nose.

She: No, they don't work, I don't think they work. That is their living, going out nicking, and they nick to, nick and then go and sell... Yeah, they go into places, there's a business centre, they go round there, there's units, and people when they've got their pay day and they'll go round there and they'll be selling stuff.

They blamed these problems on new arrivals in the area – not this time the yuppies, but incomers of a different sort, brought in by what they saw as a social engineering operation on the part of the borough:

She: No, I think there's an African over the back, an African on the corner ... Irish, there was an Irish lady lived there. Other than that ... but most of these, we were the only ones who come from Bermondsey, the rest of them were all brought in from, you know when they pulled the five estates down in Peckham, they all come from there.

He: We're the only ones that are not. That causes problems because they're not like us, not being snobbish or, but it does cause a lot of...

She: No, they do say, they do say hello but ... I shouldn't really say this but it does bring it down a bit, you know. It's a terrible thing to say.

He: ... in the last years it's changed because the Council, they've done it as a purpose, they've decided that they'll make like 50 per cent of the borough, well not of the borough, 50 per cent of any new properties will be an ethnic thing, like which can be Irish, so, African, whatever, you know. So a lot of the people that lived here, they're getting the hump because they see places like this being built, we was lucky, you know, and they...

At the same time, they believed that the Council was encouraging colonisation by yuppies at the expense of old-established working-class residents like them:

Have you found, do you know in Bermondsey generally do you notice gradually like, are there more like yuppies moving in?

He: Well I think since the Tube's opened they're buying up more and more places and that's going down as a selling point.

She: This is another thing the Council are trying to do, they're trying to sell off all the housing stock and actually bring in people like that and really try and move all us away.

Because of all these changes, despite Gary's attachment to the area, Dawn no longer wanted to stay. And she felt that her husband was beginning to feel the same:

She: At one time I would have said no because he was born here and he said he wanted to go out in a box here, you know, but I think he's changing his mind because it is changing a lot.

Janice

Janice is a British-born half-white, half-Afro-Caribbean woman in her thirties, unemployed, living as a single mother with three children in a council flat. She is an 'immigrant' to the area: she previously lived in Walworth Road, south of the Elephant and Castle, only a couple of miles away, which nevertheless she seemed almost to regard as a different world. She moved into this area when her previous flat became too small for the children:

Well, what it was was, they said to me, because I was in a bit of arrears, so they wouldn't move me on that ground. Then … my son's the eldest of them all, then I had a girl, and then I went back to them, and I said, 'Well, look, I've got a daughter'. And they said, 'Oh, not till when she was 5'. And when she got to 5 years old, they measured up the flat, and told me … because I had a kitchen and a dining room, they told me I could make my dining room into a bedroom, which was totally stupid! And after that, I had two more. And it was only until … when my other daughter, my last one was born, when they decided that I was…

As a mixed-race woman coming from outside the area, she experienced the disadvantages of trying to settle into a close-knit community:

I've got a couple of people I say hello to, but I more keep myself to myself. When I first moved in the area, I had a lot of racialists.

What sort of form did that take?

… when the kids were outside playing underneath, because I didn't want them to go too far, he would come in drunk and he would start swearing at them and everything, and telling them to go over there and play. So I went out and I shouted back at him, and the man just started spitting at us all, and calling us names. So I said, well, I wasn't having that.

She lived on an estate just slightly farther out from the Jamaica Road, which meant that she didn't have access to quite the same facilities as some of the other people:

… they haven't really got, like, much for the children to do round here. All they've got is that grass. And they used to have two slides and a swing. They knocked that all out and put in a baby slide. So the big kids ain't got nothing, and they're not supposed to play ball games, so there's nothing for them to do. And you can't really let them wander off somewhere, because it's too dangerous.

What about in terms of, like, shopping, leisure facilities, and that kind of thing, is it…?

Quite hard, because I don't drive. So I have to go all the way to either Surrey Quays, Deptford, Peckham, or … for instance, I've got quite a long journey to keep going backwards and forwards to get what I need. One, there isn't no decent shops around here, so it's very hard for me, with the three kids, to get around and get what I need. Two, buses are not direct enough. I mean, to get to certain places, I have quite a walk a certain distance, then take a bus, or I have to just walk all the way. Three, not really a lot of schools round here, like in secondaries. Well, I'm just trying to keep … once they give me the forms for her, because I should get them this year, then I can work out from them what to do.

As a single parent, not currently working, she was also plagued by the difficulties of trying to make ends meet. And for her this was not cushioned, as it was for Serena and Liz, by having a loose network of sibling support:

Clothes, because I can only afford to give them a certain amount of clothes once a year, so most of the time they go without. I mean, right now, my daughter's in need of trainers, and I've just said she's got to wait until I can actually afford to get it for her. And certain foods, because I suffer from a B_{12} deficiency, Oh, I can't even say that word! I've got problems with my B_{12}, my body's not storing what it's supposed to. So the hospital wanted to get in touch with the Social, for them to give me a little bit extra, for me to buy the certain food that I need.

So she was looking to move out of Bermondsey, although still in the borough. In fact, she wanted to move back to the southern part from where she had come, and where she clearly felt at home. The Old Kent Road, that great south-east London boundary, obviously resonated in her consciousness.

Do you want to stay in Southwark, or are you looking to move out of Southwark?

I actually want to stay in Southwark … because all my family, well, part of my family is still in Southwark. I don't want to go too far.

Which part of Southwark would you like to live in?

I'd like to go back to Walworth Road, but on the outskirt of it, not actually on the Aylesbury Estate itself. A certain part of Peckham, more like the Dun Cow end. And they're my main two options. And Old Kent Road. I quite like Old Kent Road.

Is that just because you know it really well, after living in Walworth Road?

My nan used to live in Old Kent Road, so, as a little one, I've just grown up … and I've always been in Old Kent Road.

And always, presumably, would be.

Mark

All the council tenants interviewed, except Dawn, had grown up within 2 or 3 miles of the area. That made sense, of course, in terms of council allocation policies and also the limited mobility of most of the tenants. In contrast, Mark, a single employed white man in his thirties living as a private tenant in a new build housing development, had come in from outside London, from a country town:

I was living in Horsham, in West Sussex, before this, and the other guy that lives here, he was just moving down from Glasgow, he was part of a promotion in his job. So I wanted to move up here to move to a job in the City, so I just decided to move nearer the area. And just sort of looking through … *Loot*, actually, and found it.

Coming originally from Scotland, he had moved to London mainly to take advantage of work opportunities:

Would that be the main reason you moved to London?

… partly it was professional career, because I believe that, in London, there's a lot of people who get places without trying very hard, and from my experience, when I moved to London at first, I was a restaurant manager, and I found it was … it's hard to get young people to work. I find there's a sort of bad ethic, or a different work ethic. And provided you apply yourself down here, you can get promoted, or you can do well, reasonably well.

Although someone like Mark would be seen as a yuppie, he too, like the others, is having to scrimp and save, especially at the start:

For a long long time, there are lots of things that I had to go without, until I actually started to earn any money at all. I had to, for a time, from the moment I get paid, until the end of the month, I'd have to budget myself on £3 a day, which would cover food and … and would also incorporate bills, so if I could, that would bring it down to £2 a day. So I had to really scrimp and save all the time, I couldn't afford nights out, but eventually, that started to build up. It's just so expensive to … to … I don't know why. I mean, it's not a terribly expensive place to rent here, compared to the rest of London, but…

But some compensation, as he anxiously scanned his living costs, seemed to come from the community spirit he found in the private development where he lived:

Oh, it's one of the big points that I like about the area, is that there is actually a definite community spirit, just the fact that they've got a Residents' Association, everyone's been here a while, so they all want to know who their neighbours are, and we have, like, clean up days, where everyone does their gardens, and everyone just wants tools and things round about, and then we have the Annual Barbecue, where that whole parking bit there is closed off, and we have a big barbecue and outdoor music, and we just have a big sort of street party, till about midnight. There's all ages of people there. It's just, it's just nice to … I think it's refreshing to actually get to know who your next door neighbours are.

But, while he sees his immediate area as being very friendly, if he ventures into local pubs he is immediately made aware of the tensions – also mentioned by Dawn and Janice – experienced by anyone coming in from the outside:

When you go in there sometimes, it's not because I'm Scottish, but sometimes, it's almost intimidating to go in the pub there. You have to go in a few times. It's almost like being a lone wolf trying to get into a pack of wolves, because it just takes a bit of … seeing your face, to accept you, because everybody knows each other, even if they're sitting outside, and somebody's driving by in a car, they know who that is. A very close community. I don't mean to say that's making any reference to the … at all, but they're very … that's what they are, they're just like sort of … not racist, but…

It seemed not so much a matter of hostility, as the fact that the locals were so closely bonded together in a common culture, constituting almost a private club:

They're all sort of predominantly male 40-something Millwall fans, or West Ham fans, so … you start talking about football, and you're accepted. But if you sit there, or if you're going in with a couple of friends, which I've done, and just sit there, and everyone else in there knows each other, if you're not talking to anybody else, then you are aware of people looking at you out the corner of their eye.

Henrietta

Henrietta is a resident in Butler's Wharf, close to the river, and therefore lives on the 'right' side of Jamaica Road: the north side, scene of big warehouse conversions and new blocks next door to older council estates.

Single, in her twenties, employed, white, a private tenant, well educated and in a well-paid job, she occupies an entirely different universe from the other women to whom we spoke. Her parents lived in Essex; in moving to Bermondsey, she thus reversed the traditional outward movement. Where other residents are very rooted in their local area, Henrietta had only lived there a year when we spoke to her. And she travels a great deal:

I spend 50 per cent of my time in Surbiton, 50 per cent out on the road. So far this year I have been in Zürich for two weeks, Amsterdam for nearly three months and two weeks in Utrecht in Holland and the rest of the time I have been in Surbiton.

She was also planning to move permanently to Sydney in a few months' time.

While the other women are not working, Henrietta is an asset management software consultant whose job means a lot to her:

Probably it's the challenge. The challenge of what they are going to ask me to do. If it is too easy I won't want to do it, if its too hard I won't want to do it but it also has to be money. I've gone beyond living in shitty student digs. I won't do that anymore. I did that then and now I am not doing that. I lived for two and a half years without central heating and I'm not doing it again. So money plays a big part but not a huge part otherwise I'd have a job earning more money. The experience of what I'm doing – not so much. Who I'm doing it with – not so much. The challenge, the adventure being able to do it. Power to a certain extent as well. Not power that's not the right word. Kudos? I don't know how to say it. Every job has to be better than the last one. Has to be perceived by my peers to be better than the last one. Tragic isn't it.

Although she lived very close to the other residents we interviewed, the world she occupied could have been a million miles away:

I *love* it here. I love getting up and going down for a coffee at the shop and getting the freshly baked bread 'cause there is a bakery here and I love … the All Bar One has made a big difference. You can go round there for a drink, it's a proper bar erm I love being near the water. I love coming into all the lovely restaurants, the Chop House or you know the … I haven't actually been to the Pont de la Tour restaurant erm but I have been to all the others, Cantina… Pizza in here and the little shops for gifts if you've got to buy something and there is always taxis round here, there is always taxis round here so…

She has a low opinion of the world on the other side of Jamaica Road, which she sees as proletarian, unpleasant and alien:

… the prices have already gone up quite considerably. They charge 182 grand for the nasty flat I was in just 'cause it's on Tower Bridge Road even though its about 2 miles down Tower Bridge Road, it's a bit much and its too near the nasty Old Kent Road.

And although she knows the council estates exist, she simply sees them as an unpleasant fact of life:

There are really expensive flats round here and then so many you know, really nasty council estates just across the road; it is really quite a strange place.

But they do not impinge upon her consciousness.

You mean you are not really aware of the estates in the area?

Not at all.

Whereas other residents had complained about local health facilities, her ability to pay meant that she could keep these at a distance:

Doctors are a total pain in the arse. They are only open from nine to five and they are only open for ... you have got to be actually dying, emergencies, for one hour on a Saturday morning. So even though the doctor is reasonably close to where I live ... its actually in one of the council estates up the road, but its hardly open. It means that I would have to take half a day off work to go to a doctor that is open from nine to five. It's ridiculous I have no choice so what I sometimes do and it's a bit cheeky and I shouldn't really do it but what I sometimes do is go to the medical centre at Waterloo...

Why do you think it's cheeky?

Cause you shouldn't really waste your money going to a private doctors should you?

But it sounds as if there is not actually much choice in the matter, if you think of it in terms of the hours you have to take off work to go to a doctor...

Absolutely. If I'm getting the train to Waterloo then the Medicentre, I can get an appointment at 6 O'clock and any prescription I get is private I have to pay for it but I don't have to take any time off work to do that, so if I have to go that's what I usually do...

And the public transport, which other residents praised, played no part in her world:

Where we are here, we are right in the middle of Bermondsey and London Bridge Tubes. I hate the Tube anyway ... I always get, I hate being underground, I like to watch the world go by … I always get a taxi. I'm a devil for taxis I can't stop myself … if I walk out of here I can always get a taxi and 20 minutes later at the absolute maximum I'm at Waterloo station and I'm not stressed I'm not, I haven't had to stand in a smelly bus and I get to where I'm going that much more relaxed. So its worth it, but its expensive its about six or seven pounds each way. I only get in one way I get the bus home but even still…

Interestingly, in complete contrast to other residents, she does not find her immediate area quite so friendly:

I say hello to anyone I meet in the lift cause that's just being polite. But they are quite reasonably friendly. A little bit stand-offish. I mean you would say hello but you wouldn't necessarily talk to them.

And, unlike many of the other residents of the area, she did not feel safe:

The crime and the fear and the scariness of London is getting worse. And I don't necessarily… I'm a reasonably nervous person about walking alone at night anyway but my best friend is half Swiss white and half Jamaican black and she feels London is becoming very racist and she's very scared and she wants to leave.

The more we talked to her, the more we sensed that though she liked certain features of her local life, she wasn't really a natural city dweller at all.

Hard Lives and High Hopes in the Proletarian Island

Her sentiment, unfortunately, was shared by others. There were undoubtedly those in Bermondsey, whether old-time Bermondseyans or new-time yuppifiers, who felt that this was not an area in which they felt physically safe or emotionally comfortable. Some were finding it hard enough to struggle for a living or keep their heads above water. Others were doing well materially but still felt threatened. They saw problems in their neighbourhoods and in their children's schools. Some were battling valiantly to try to change their circumstances; for others, flight was the obvious option.

Doubtless, some of these problems were those of any area in any city undergoing rapid demographic and social transition; doubtless, eventually the area would reach some kind of stability. And it must also be said that there were many, perhaps the majority, who cared deeply about the area, who had a deep attachment to it, and were actively working to make it a better place to live. What we found most remarkable in Bermondsey was that ordinary people, without any special qualifications for the task, found their own feet and their own voice, assuming not merely active roles but even the leadership of local civic or tenants' organisations. And these included especially the children of the old Bermondsey working class, who were seeking to recreate the sense of solidarity, of community, that they remembered from their childhood.

True, some people – the newly-arrived gentrifying minority – were living comfortably enough in the middle-class niches they had colonised, especially in Bankside, as abundantly marked by the presence of shopping, culture and entertainment that caters for their interests and their lifestyles. Here, we found places and people reminiscent of Battersea: people who rate the quality of their neighbourhood highly, because here they find the facilities they value and the access to others close by. But for the working-class majority, it could not be more of a contrast. Their reactions to change have been very different: they desperately try to defend their turf against newcomers, whether decanted black and white tenants from neighbouring council estates in Peckham, or asylum-seekers, or gentrifiers. They are doubly frustrated and very angry: they see 'their' housing disappearing to the gentrifiers on the one hand, and to 'outsiders', especially non-white ones, on the other. And it is the older members, who have the strongest memories of a sense of community now lost, who are the angriest of all.

They see rising crime and insecurity everywhere, affecting them and their children, and they seek to contest it, often by informal means ('The lads will have a word with you'). Frequently there is a racial divide: whites report problems with noise and mayhem, blacks report abuse and harassment. A poor physical environment adds to this: lack of space directly affects quality of life, causing people to feel claustrophobic, trapped, or cramped. High density and limited space amplifies the noisiness of a neighbours' music or their playing children, increases the possibility of a football going through a window, the likelihood of bored children being naughty, the offence caused by uncollected rubbish and dog mess, and even the problems presented by badly-parked cars. Unsurprisingly, all but the gentrifiers seem to want to move out.

The sense of stress can become almost intolerable on some problematic estates, where different groups are brought suddenly together in layouts which provide little protection against crime or mayhem. These, we found, are among the unhappiest neighbourhoods in contemporary London: places where perceptions of the quality of neighbourhood life, especially by contrast to how it once was, are of the lowest. Mercifully, such neighbourhoods seem to be very uncommon in London.

Bollywood comes to Upton Park

© Bill Knight

Chapter Four

Transit Centre

Upton Park

There is yet another kind of place that is emblematic of London in the millennium years. It is neither a comfortable melting pot like Battersea, nor a slightly paranoid place like Bermondsey, where the ingredients are curdling rather than blending. Unlike either, it is a place in a state of constant toing and froing: a place full of new arrivals, who might take up sticks and move on, or might just lay down roots there. It is in this kind of place, perhaps, that we may most truly discover what is happening in contemporary London and where the city might go in the future.

Stratford Broadway and its neighbouring area of Upton Park are as precise an archetype of this kind of place as you could hope to find. They lie in the east London borough of Newham, 16 minutes from Bermondsey on the Jubilee Line. This is the newest piece of the London underground, and on the way it passes under Docklands, the largest piece of urban regeneration in Europe. As the train emerges from the tunnel at Canning Town, the passenger can see Canary Wharf on one side, and the huge new ExCel exhibition centre on the other. But from then on, the scene is less prepossessing as the line runs up the Lower Lea Valley, the most intensive of the surviving industrial areas in London: a chaotic sequence of tin sheds, sewerage outfalls, and old mills. For centuries this was one of London's main dumping grounds, particularly so after the formation in 1888 of the London County Council, when West Ham (of which Stratford forms the north-western corner) became home to a range of noxious activities, exiled from the LCC area.

So it is an area with a clouded past, but a bright future. Already Stratford is the second best-served location in London in terms of public transport, with two Tube lines, main line suburban services, the Docklands Light Railway and buses; in 2007, a new station on the Channel Tunnel Rail Link will further enhance it; and Crossrail, a new west–east express transit line, may eventually complete the process. Already, a commercial consortium has drawn up a masterplan for a huge development around the new station, incorporating a huge shopping centre, offices and high-density residential areas. And, next door, is the site of the stadium that will be the centrepiece of London's successful bid to host the 2012 Olympic Games. That summer, part of Stratford City's residential area will form the Olympic Village, housing athletes from across the world. Later, these apartments will be released on to the market, triggering a transformation of this part of London – perhaps into a new Canary Wharf, perhaps something more dramatic still.

Some History

But that is still for the future, and meanwhile Stratford is one of London's more seriously deprived areas. It started life as a small market town at a bridgehead on the river Lea, at the junction of main roads out to Cambridge and Colchester. It was already an industrial area before the nineteenth century, with mills, gunpowder manufacture, distilling, oil and timber milling, calico and silk weaving, and a pottery. Coming in 1839–1840, the railway likewise forked here, making Stratford a railway town complete with locomotive works, a vast complex of railway yards, and a new town built to house the workers.

Then, extending in 1874 from its original Bishopsgate terminus to Liverpool Street, the Great Eastern Railway was required to offer cheap early-morning workers' trains. The result, during the last thirty years of the nineteenth century, was the rapid spread of cheap working-class housing along the lines north and east of Stratford, producing a mass of uniform terraced streets across the neighbouring areas of Leyton, Leytonstone, Maryland, Forest Gate, and Manor Park. In parallel, 2 miles to the south, the London Tilbury and Southend Railway had opened in 1858 and soon produced a very similar manifestation around its stations at West Ham, Plaistow, Upton Park and East Ham. Built quickly and cheaply by speculative builders as standard by-law minimal housing, without much charm or character, and situated downwind of the Lea Valley's noxious industries, these eastern suburbs of London never had the social cachet of their western counterparts; they housed impecunious junior City clerks and those whom the City solicitor Charles Pearson described as 'the superior order of the mechanical poor' (Kellett, 1969, 367). Immediately to the south, the terrace streets of Canning Town were built to house casual workers from the Port of London's new Royal Docks.

In 1965, when this area was incorporated in the new Greater London Council, East Ham and West Ham were combined into the London borough of Newham. They had always been working-class districts and even areas of poverty and deprivation, but very soon their situation took a turn for the worse, with dock closures and attendant deindustrialisation. And, almost simultaneously, the area became a destination for immigration.

The dock closures came later here than in Tower Hamlets, because these were the latest and largest docks in the system, the so-called Royal Docks, built to accommodate seagoing vessels; but they too were all derelict by 1981. And, from the 1970s, large and small industrial undertakings alike were buffeted by huge structural forces: overseas competition, technical changes (such as the replacement of coal gas by North Sea gas, which brought the closure of huge gasworks at Bow and Beckton), and the struggle for greater efficiency which led to mass redundancies. Between 1960 and 2000, industrial employment in the borough contracted by two-thirds. Large areas in the south of the borough, comprising the Royal Docks, were included in the London Docklands Development Corporation (LDDC) area, but logically the Corporation made regeneration of the closer-in inner docks its first priority; then development plans stalled in the recession of the late 1980s, and many have been completed only after the demise of the Corporation in 1998. Dwelling prices are among the lowest in London, with Newham prices for all property averaging just £210,000 in early 2006, though prices were beginning to rise around Stratford as the gentrifiers began to come in from neighbouring Hackney, attracted by the excellent train services and the promise of an Olympics effect.

Newham today

In the aftermath of deindustrialisation, Newham's economy is dominated by small service firms. Typically for east London, this reflects not small business vitality but a failure to replace those large establishments which were once central to the economy. Ethnic minority businesses are common in distribution and catering, but tend to have a small turnover. Manufacturing continues to employ a higher proportion of workers than in most parts of London (7.3 per cent per cent in 2006, against a London average of 5.5 per cent), especially in chemicals, food (in Forest Gate) and clothing. But – again typical for east London – the biggest employers are in public services, especially public administration and education, as well as in transport and storage, the ExCel exhibition centre, and an insurance company's headquarters office in Forest Gate.

Unusually for London, manual work (production, wholesaling and transport) has continued to lose jobs: between 1991 and 1998 5,000 jobs went, a loss of 23 per cent. So gains in non-manual sectors, especially business services, merely counterbalanced these losses – and overall employment declined very slightly in the 1990s. Newham thus remains strongly working-class – more so than any other area we surveyed. It has by far the lowest proportion of professional and managerial heads of households (9 per cent in 2001), the highest proportion of manual workers (31 per cent) and one of the highest proportion of economically inactive people (nearly 50 per cent); no less than 17 per cent describe themselves as having a limiting long-term illness, 10 per cent describe their health as 'not good'. It has one of the lowest proportions in the entire country of owner-occupiers, 43.6 per cent in 2001. Lone parent households with dependent children, 11.9 per cent of all households, represent the highest proportion of any English local authority – while married couple households, at only 26.0 per cent, are among the lowest.

Newham is also very diverse ethnically. Over 35 per cent of its people were born outside the EU, according to the 2001 Census – the second highest proportion in the country. And over 60 per cent are non-white, the highest proportion of any English local authority, and a huge leap from 31 per cent in 1981. The largest groups are Black Africans (13 per cent), Indians (12 per cent), and Bangladeshis (nearly 9 per cent). And 24 per cent are Muslim. Most of the non-white population have come here through migration from the areas of original settlement, as a second generation sought affordable owner-occupation: Pakistanis and Bangladeshis have moved from Whitechapel to the Upton Park area of East Ham, and Black Africans and Afro-Caribbeans from Dalston and Hackney to Stratford. But there has also been a huge recent wave of refugees and asylum-seekers: in 2006 Newham had the largest population of refugee children in the country, numbering no less than 7,128. Mainly from Asia and Africa, they also include Poles, Vietnamese, Russians and Somalis. The borough schools have more than 400 refugee children on their rolls.

In 1999, 70 per cent of Newham school children were non-white, the majority were bilingual, and 42 per cent needed help with English. It is all too easy to link these characteristics with poor educational outcomes: 80 per cent of primary schools fail to achieve national average performance levels, with worse results still in maths and science. But there is no clear relation between school results and ethnic mix; low performance more directly seems to reflect family poverty. The Education Action Zone established to deal with serious schooling problems covers Canning Town, an ex-dockland area with a majority white British intake.

Newham is without doubt the most deprived of our study areas: its 6.7 per cent unemployment includes over 2 per cent long-term unemployed, and average incomes among taxpayers in 1999 were significantly lower even than Southwark, reflecting much more limited gentrification. On the IMD2004 index of area deprivation Newham stands eleventh among the 355 English districts; 70 per cent of its population live in the most deprived small areas (Super Output Areas or SOAs) in the entire country.

Upton Park, the neighbourhood which we chose for our household interviews, lies east and south-east of Stratford Broadway, comprising

Victorian/Edwardian terraced housing, some quite substantial, together with a couple of council estates, parts of which (including one high-rise block) were being refurbished by a council/housing association partnership, and some infill areas of small new terrace houses. To the north, around Forest Gate station, are truly grand mid-Victorian villas worthy of Canonbury or Barnsbury (or perhaps, since some even have Australian-style verandas, redolent of Woolloomooloo or Carleton). And the gentrifiers are clearly at work here – though evidently, the majority of them are Indian professional and business people, who seem to have discovered the area before anyone else.

Further south, on the other side of the busy Ilford High Road, the great Indian emporium of Green Street runs for a mile down to Upton Park station, packed with every imaginable variety of business: greengrocers selling fruit at wholesale prices, Indian restaurants and takeaways offering exotic meals at minimal cost, women's clothing stores selling Indian styles, cut-price air travel shops, immigration lawyers, jewellers, and banks with exotic names. On either side run long streets of late Victorian terraced housing, every house impeccably renovated and lovingly maintained: a vast exercise in urban regeneration South Asian style, all aided and abetted by Newham Council's provision of new street trees and traffic calming. And the work evidently still goes on. Upton Park, it seems, is the place to which Bangladeshi Whitechapel migrates in search of the middle-class good life. But, back on Green Street, there are frequent appearances of a rather special kind of estate agency, which offer lettings: evidently, many of these houses are for income as well as residence. And, viewed more closely, Green Street's undoubted exotic quality – Dhaka or Sylhet transhipped to London E13 – tends to obscure the fact that, like so many other neighbourhoods, this is actually very mixed: white working-class mothers and their children, whose red or ginger hair may suggest Irish roots long ago, mix with older Afro-Caribbeans. This is the heart of melting-pot London.

Most housing here is either owner-occupied or privately rented; many of the bigger houses are subdivided into very small flats, or one-room lets with shared facilities. Conditions vary, but in some parts both overcrowding and poor/unsafe housing conditions have led to council prosecution of private landlords and/or compulsory purchase. Housing is generally cheap by London standards, with average prices in early 2006 around £186,000, similar to Peckham. But, as in Newham generally, price increases have accelerated since 2000, reflecting the area's position within Newham's 'Arc of Opportunity', the recently improved rail access to Canary Wharf and Central London via the West Ham station on the Jubilee Line, and the opening in 2007 of the Channel Tunnel Rail Link station.

Nonetheless the local population is poor, with an unemployment rate in the ward of 16 per cent in winter 1999 and 20 per cent receiving income support: the area appears within the most deprived small areas in the country on the IMD 2004 index. There is a large and diverse ethnic minority population, including many of Pakistani origin, the remains of a local Sikh population (others having prospered and moved further out in the 1990s), a growing Bangladeshi population (including outward movers from Tower Hamlets), some Africans and newer waves of migrants from areas such as Somalia, Eastern Europe, Kosovo and Afghanistan. The last group tend to live in particularly poor and overcrowded housing, with a significant element of unregistered refugees in the worst position.

As well as local shops, the area has the Green Street market, supported by a very active Green Street Partnership, undertaking education, environmental and health related projects as well as promoting local business; in 2006 it successfully fought a proposal by a leading supermarket chain to redevelop the market. Community support is also provided by a very wide range of religious establishments, including mosques, temples, a synagogue and various types of church (from both English and minority traditions) – whose activities extend into education and (in some cases) even business advice – together with an array of voluntary and statutory organisations.

Our interviews covered a wide sweep – wider than in any other area surveyed – of races, religions, cultures, ages, social circumstances and personal histories. Logically we will begin with longer-established residents and end with the most recent arrivals.

Linda

Linda is as archetypical a member of the older-established residents as you could hope to find: a white married mother in her mid to late forties, in part-time employment and living in an owner-occupied modern semi-detached house. She has lived in this area all her life, and moved to this house because they needed more space for the children:

All my life, yeah, yeah ... I was born in Osborne Road, that's just by Forest Gate Station... Seven years, yeah about 7 years I've lived in this house... Before that I lived with me parents and then we bought a house in Osborne Road, it's only a two-bedroomed house, we sold that and we bought this because the boys was getting, I've got two sons, the children was getting older and we bought this 'cause this is three ... this is three bedrooms, yeah.

She has deep roots in this area, and her close family members are all around her:

No, no, I've got all my family round me, I've always, you know, I'm so used to Forest

Gate... Living here all me life, I've got quite a few friends, I went to primary school up the road, I went to secondary school up the road, so you know... When it was still Stratford Grammar School, yeah ... a few years ago, and yeah, I've got quite a few friends round here. My sister only lives at Stratford, my mother only lives at Manor Park, we're all 10 minutes away and my mother-in-law lives at Stratford, so you know, they're all like in the vicinity, a car away or a bus ride away, you know so...

Some of her friends still live locally, but others have joined the great exodus out to Essex. Yet she still manages to keep contact:

Yeah, yeah, I've got a few friends at Basildon and that, but quite a few that I went to school with, I still see 'em on a regular basis. I work with one of them that I went to secondary school with. She's a welfare officer, so...

She feels very comfortable in her neighbourhood, which seems to have almost the feeling of life in an extended family:

Been here 7 years, we all roughly moved in the same week, you know, and there's been children born and they're very nice people, I've never ever had any problems, never any problems at all.

And do they do things for you or do you do things for them or...?

Well if I could help 'em I would, yeah, yes, definitely, they're all very, they're just all sort of like family people, you know, what I mean, they're very nice people.

Yet, even so, it is evident that the area does not feel completely safe:

Does it feel safe around here at night?

Yeah, mind you, saying that, I have got an alarm... (*goes to switch it off*). Yeah, but as soon as we moved here I had the alarm – yeah, and I've got like sensors in the rooms and that and I feel quite safe and I've got a panic button upstairs and things like that, but round here we've had quite a few burglaries in 7 years, yeah – that poor love up there at number nine's been burgled three times.

And she thinks the area has changed: it has hugely developed since she was a child:

Well personally ... it's got more houses, everywhere you look is houses. When I was a kid, I'd come out of Godwin Road School and we'd go on Wanstead Flats for an hour but now it's houses everywhere and shops, you know, when I used to live in Osborne Road, it used to be all tree-lined, now it's all gone, you know, I find ... I know it's all in the name of progress but ... I think I preferred it the way it was.

Nostalgically, she recalls an idyllic world, remembered from childhood, now gone. And this was within the brief span of 30 years:

… the kids that used to play on the green, you know, there used to be loads of kids and then the Council put a swing and a slide and that on it, wonderful, Oh my God I'm going back 30 years but … like you know, now it's all houses, they've built all housing and a nursery on the green and that.

She also recalls a lost world of small shops and personal service:

Well, before like it used to be Finefare and I can remember my Mum going over and saying to me, 'Get me a quarter of ham and don't take the bit off the…', they always used to put a little bit on the top – 'Don't take the bit off the top'. And Oh yes, you know, 'Get me a piece of cheese about 10 shillings and if they slice it, don't take the end bit, like…', you know, I always used to nick the bit on the top and that, but now everything is self-service, you go round and there's no sort of like delicatessen where you can get your ham sliced and their bacon and everything is sort of like pre-packed and that now … you don't know nobody when you go in the shops, it's all sort of like checkouts and bleeps and you know, like, sad really.

She finds no fault with the local authority services. And she has special needs, for her youngest son has educational problems:

And the school encourages him and everything?

Oh really, really, I can't fault the school, they've really, you know, and even with my son that's on, my little un's on special needs, excellent, everyday for 15 minutes they sit down and read with him, help him with his letters, really I can't fault them…

And what's the Social Services like in Newham, are they quite good?

Well again I can't fault them because every time I've had to call Social Services in or call police or anything, I've got no complaints whatsoever, and they listen and then they act. That's what I've found anyway, they're very good backup support, very good.

They used to struggle somewhat:

Ten years ago when I had two little 'uns, I was on a basic housekeeping money, I used to think 'Oh I won't get that this week, I'll save a bit this week and get it next week', but now we're both working, you know, that makes a hell of a difference.

But now, they are in comfortable circumstances:

Yeah – my husband's a marine engineer and he's got a pretty good job … they've got loads of work, my husband works every Saturday, he works 6 days a week, so they've got loads of work and some Sundays he goes in if there's rush jobs and that, but he also sometimes, he goes away quite a lot, like this weekend he wasn't far, but he was called to Southend, one of the schooners had broke down or something so he'd gone out and fixed it and all this lark, so…

So he's often away?

He worked for 3 months in Miami and all this lark. What was it, about 3 years ago was the last time he done Miami, he can do it every year but he doesn't, you know, he's refused … there's plenty of work abroad, the Caribbean and everything.

With two incomes, they have no money worries. But she also values her financial independence:

… that is why I work, mind you I never pay a bill or the mortgage or nothing, he pays for all the bills, the mortgage, everything, but saying that I do like my own independence, having me own money, not having to say to him 'Can I have some money, I want…'.

You can spend it on what you like…

That's right, that's right, my wages is mine, end of story – that sounds rotten, but it's true, it is the truth…

Roland

Roland is one of the older immigrants, who came in the first wave to settle here. Afro-Caribbean, a father in his sixties, he is recently retired, and homeowner of a terraced house; he is married to a Filipino Catholic. Originally from Jamaica, he went to Birmingham in 1961 and then moved down to London in 1973. He seems to have no regrets about his move to England:

Since I've been in this country em touch wood I never have a racist remark passed against me. You know, I try to be nice to people and people be nice to me.

In fact, he has lost contact with Jamaica and his family:

I have one sister, one brother, but we don't really get on so well. No, no, we em don't, don't care about…

Like many Afro-Caribbeans in Britain, he started by doing a succession of relatively unskilled jobs but worked his way up the hierarchy through his diligence and reliability:

No, no, em my first job in this country was British Rail, and I work on British Rail 1962 up until em 1972, I came to London 1972. I start to work into a laundry in Golders Green, and then em 1975 they make us redundant and the manager said to me, she would, because being I was a good worker and, you, you know, really skilful and dutiful to my job, she said to me: 'Oh Roland, I would like to, em, you know, find a job give to you'. So she said to me: 'Would you like to go and work into a hotel?' And I said: 'Well, you know, I never worked in a hotel before, but I said all right, I'll give it a try' yeah and er she get me the job and I start working Intercontinental on 29 December 1975, and I finish up on the, the last of May 1999... I first started work as a machine operator in the laundry, then I move up move up my way to er supervisor.

Now he is retired, enjoying relaxation after a life of hard work:

I just em relax and do some housework, you know, bit of cleaning, go to the launderette, you know, go to the park, little bit of shopping, you know, keep myself busy.

Did you find it difficult when you first retired?

No, no ... so I was working when I was 14 years old I goes to work and goes to school. You know, em I wake up at 5 O'clock in the morning yeah and I do some work, then I go to school, then I come back and work again, and I go back to school.

So it was quite nice to stop?

Yeah, so retiring now, it's not really so early because some of my mates them say: 'Oh, you're gonna get fed-up, what are you gonna do?' But I don't get fed-up because I used to drink and I stop through a medical reason, yeah, so you know, and I've got everything inside my house. I've got my television, my music, my kids em you know, I can go for your walk if I wanna go anywhere I've got a free bus pass, and you know.

He budgets carefully, and feels financially comfortable:

I'm not really worried, you know, and I've got my pension, you know, and got a pension from the hotel, I finished pay for my house, so...

And did that make a difference to your financial situation?

I try and you know, keep my budget to a certain amount, a level. You know, I don't wanna put myself into too much debt and say when I finish work Oh my wife have to pay this, my wife have to pay that.

... and is it quite a good pension?

Er, well they give you a lump sum yeah, plus they er they give you £94, £96 a month.

Asked if there was anything in life he would want, he replies:

Well, I'm trying to win the Lottery.

Yes, aren't we all?

And that would change my lifestyle completely.

Completely, yes.

Yes, but otherwise than that I'm doing fine, you know, em cos well, I wouldn't say financially I'm well-off, but it's enough to…

To manage.

Uhmm, uhmm.

But he is not in good health and is very unhappy about the National Health Service:

Like, for instance, now em I've got roughly this appointment now what they send me last week and is the fourth one yeah?… They will send the one this month and then they cancel it yeah?… And then em, next month they will say: 'Oh, Mr Richards, em we have got a bed for you', yeah, for such-and-such a date, then they will send the next appointment again. So this one is the fourth one.

Why do you think that is, do you think they just don't have the staff, or the beds or…?

Well, I, I don't know … probably claim to say that they haven't got the resources, they haven't got the bed, they haven't got the amount of doctors to do, do the kind of job what you know, the physician to do the work what you're supposed to come in for. You know, they, they make lots of excuses, but what can you do? You know, it's either you go private, or you wait on their time, you know, and to be honest, I don't really fancy going private, as I've been in this country half my life and I've been working, so… So it's only fair for me to get something back.

He came to Newham in 1983, from South Hampstead. He seems to have arrived in Newham almost by accident, and clearly at some level he regrets it. Shopping and transport are convenient, he finds. But he has a definite lack of enthusiasm for the area, and clearly finds it less than friendly:

Well, it's all right, you know, most of the neighbours them are Indians, you know, my next door neighbour, she's English, and my next door neighbour is em Indian, so you know, everybody kind a keep themself to themself…

So you don't see the neighbours very much then?

Well, no, I don't have to see them, or hear the noise they're making, because they are, em they're refurbishing the house ... they make a lot of noise, so I don't have to see them, I can tell they are in.

The area is quite peaceful and crime-free, basically because it is not easy to break into the houses:

... not much crime really goes on in the street, but sometime you know when you buy the Newham paper you hear there's a lot of crime commit in some other, you know, East Ham and all those places, but in this area it's, it's pretty quiet, because you know, the police, they patrol round here sometime, plus they have a Neighbourhood Watch and ... these houses here now it's like, em it's very difficult for people to really break into your house.

He says that the character of the place has changed hugely in the years he has lived here:

You did see a mosque, yeah em if you come at 2 O'clock it's very difficult for you to pass on the pavement, because they pray six times for the day and when they finish they all stand up outside but they can't really do about that. You know, I mean every shops in our row it's Indians and it's all right, it just er bothers me, you know ... when I come over here and live, most of these houses used to be white people living there... But em now 90 per cent of this people live on this street are Muslim.

He obviously feels the area is no longer diverse, and this makes him uncomfortable:

One bloke offered to buy my house... He meet me in the launderette and he said to me: 'If you're selling your house, sell it to me'...he said to me: 'I don't even wanna come and have a look at it, I just buy it'... Cos it's near to the, his brother is the owner for the laundry, so he want to live near to his brother.

But he felt he was being cheated:

... he offered me £75,000 ... and you know, have you seen the prices of houses, a one-bedroomed flat a hundred and odd thousand. So I just say: 'OK, when I'm ready I will tell you'.

And you won't?

No, I just give him that to keep him off of my back.

He feels the houses are becoming overcrowded and the neighbourhood is going downhill:

Yeah, when, when people get to be knowing, you know, then you have too much crowd. You know, like if I'm living here and a few friends will know I live here and then in time you realise you have here 9, 10 people in your house, you know.

Kamal

Kamal is an Indian male in his fifties, unemployed and living in a private rented house; his 18-year-old son also participates in the interview. Born in Madras and a Tamil speaker, he worked from 1950 to 1971 for the British navy in Singapore. When they handed over to the Singapore government, he returned to India but came here in 1973. With his first wife he had seven children; when she died he remarried in India, and had four more. The children of the first marriage are now themselves all married and living with their own families in East Ham:

Son: We're not in touch with them as much as we are with the other. We go: 'Are you all right?' 'All right'. 'Come cup of tea, come cup of tea', that's all.

Right, so you see them for a cup of tea and everything – not very close.

No, because … because everybody, everybody got their own problem … we don't want to, you know, going to help me … no.

They lived in the Manor Park area of East Ham. Then disaster struck them:

I have big operation here … that's where … I move … 6 month coma in hospital. Everything, he knows my problem, but can't help me – I don't know why – in disable, everything… Hernia operation. Before it was bad blood remove … something happen, 6 months go to coma … coma stayed 6 months in hospital.

Son: They messed the operation up, or something.

You were in a coma for 6 months. And it was after that that you decided you were going back to India for a few years?

Yeah, yeah, I take all the children to India, sell house … I let them get the house only £15,000.

Evidently, he decided that it would be better to return to India. But that proved to be a disastrous decision:

Unfortunately, unfortunately in ninety-one I made a mistake because those children, small boys - I sold my house, I take all children to India – mother language want to study … children with my family more. That's why I sold my house, that's the main problem.

But then he was forced to return:

Now India is … you can't live now without permission. Now they give you only 5 years visa – after 5 years you can't live in India… Because the children born this country – all British passport holder.

Now he is completely dependent on his dialysis:

I can't get this facility anywhere, because transport they send it to me – he pick up me, I bring the hospital, he put the machine, 4 hours every time, and they give 2 O'clock a cup of tea and two biscuit, and at 4 O'clock, or 4 to 4.30, sandwich, fruit, tea, and finish 7 O'clock, we're waiting for the transport.

And they take you home as well?

Yeah, and bring back here, sometime 8.30, sometime 7.30, which time I always have transport.

And you're going in every other day, is that right?

Yeah, every day – Tuesday, Thursday and Saturday.

And have they said how long you're going to have to keep doing dialysis for – forever?

Until life, until life…

His finances are tortuous. A former Ford employee, he gets a state pension of £352 a month plus a Ford pension of £60 a month as well as Income Support of £92.50 a week.

I borrow … you know, until now I borrow money in the bank, more than £6,000, I have a balance standing on … what can I do, this? The children want to … they didn't pay any children money, you know, Income Support, because he is over 18, two children.

His rent is £160 a month of which the Council pays £125, requiring him to find the other £35. His landlord is trying to evict him for arrears of rent:

Because he didn't get the … money, £160 I agree with them, but like the Council pay only £125. I can't afford £35 from my budget every week.

He tries to explain:

I can't afford it because I am Income Support, I've got four children and wife, and those four children full-time education… So especially I am disabled, I am disabled people under dialysis, kidney failure, I've been weekly three times – now I'm waiting for the transport will come collect me half-past eleven. I am going to hospital and come back 8.30/9 O'clock… I send to everybody letter, my problem, but I didn't get any reply until now… I get copy of letter which I am sending, so I prove everything… I have medical letter, hospital letter, my sickness, everything, but no reply at all. So I been solicitor, I take the solicitor … you know, this is the problem, all this round this … I made complaint, you know, I am disabled people, I have to stay here, I am living with four children, with the wife - but he didn't, don't bother about me … landlord… 'You move this house'.

Has he – he can't evict you though unless he goes through the courts, can he?

Yeah, that's why I take now my solicitor … solicitor say: 'You're going to the possession order in court'. Then after I'm homeless – where I am go – that's what I'll ask them.

That's what you're worried about.

Yeah, I'm worried – four children going to college and the school – where I am go. Last time same problem with me 145 Telegraph Road … I am living 3 years … the housing … the landlord want the house back, you know… I apply, I didn't get any council house, so he draw up with me, I'm going to homeless place of person.

He talks about his experience with the housing department after that eviction:

Yeah, everything, you know, before I do that … yeah, before I explain everything and letter, everything, and then one day, you know, 24th, move the house, you come there early morning, 9 O'clock there. OK, hand over key…

Son: This is on the day we vacated the house, 9 O'clock in the morning we had to go.

All things I put in my son house.

And you went…

I went to there … went to there, me and my son. All day I wait there … so many people… And the evening, 6 O'clock only the officer call me: … 'we've got a hotel arranged'. So I said: 'Where – hotel', I say, 'is it somewhere here – we want to live here', you know. (*Makes groaning noise*) 'Southend'. Hotel, Southend, far away from Southend. 'You go there, that hotel, you can stay there'. So I say … I explain my dialysis say: 'I'm going weekly three days dialysis St Bartholomew Hospital – how can I come – without dialysis be dead'. 'I don't know – you want take this or not?' I come back home.

What's the consequences of not taking the accommodation?

Son: If you don't take it you have to see for arrangements yourself.

Right, so they only make one offer to you?

Son: Yeah, 10 days till school was to open in September.

Ten days before school started?

Yeah, because I decide leave the children there, you know, things all right, put it somewhere then on the storage, TV, everything I put there. So what can I do...

Thus they ended up here, in Forest Gate. He has had an application for public housing on the file since 1991:

And do you know where you are on the list?

No, no, nothing, I didn't get anything reply, because I move here to other – East Ham to Manor Park – Manor Park to Forest Gate – so many application I make. There's a copy of letter.

His children go to school in East Ham, and he has to pay his son for transport to take them:

Because we can't find a house in East Ham, we have to come all the way over here, and it's not really good changing schools for the kids all the time, so I have to go there every morning and drop them off and pick them up in the evening.

On top of this they were burgled and lost everything:

We just had this flat and he was out of breath or something and we had to take him to hospital. When we got there and come back, someone ... there's a basement here as well, someone else lives there ... comes in this house, robbing everything – all my wife's jewellery, video camera, video, everything ... unfortunately I didn't take any insurance, because I move, this new house, because also I get the, you know, insurance, housing insurance.

His circumstances are extraordinary. He does not know any of his neighbours at all:

And do you know your neighbours here?

Son: Not really.

No, I get nothing ... next door was mixing people, English and Jamaican.

Son: Next door's like a flat or something, people renting out rooms.

And this side is Bangladesh, but I don't speak to them ... I... nobody knows them, even name also so I don't know what...

Their only source of support appears to be his son in East Ham, whom they regard as living a long way away, though it is only just over a mile distant:

Son: Well my brother's like really the one that helps us out, because when he goes to hospital he's the one that has to come over from East Ham every now and then check on him. And since we moved into here because it's far away not many people come – when we were in East Ham there used to be a lot of people around and everything, but since we moved here there's not much people really.

... We are living far away from them.

Yeah. And you go over to your brother's, what, once a week...

Son: No, we go to his house quite often ... because every time – children go to the same school – *** School, East Ham... So I drop his kids off at school as well ... when I go to East Ham.

He is reluctant to take them out of the school:

That's why I don't want to change, you know ... the children, the children got some friends, school mates ... they don't want to break with them. That's where my expensive ... the car, every day I send them, because of the children education.

They seem completely bewildered by life in Forest Gate, as if they are in a different country:

Son: Forest Gate – we're not usually that sure about the high street – we have to go East Ham all the time because we are usual ... we know the places there ...we don't really know the streets over here.

School was all right, the son said. Though they had experienced some racism from other children when they first returned from India, now there was not much of a problem. He was now taking biotechnology at university:

Son: (*Hesitation*) I don't ... for me, I don't really think that I'm losing out as much cos Dad usually provides everything for me. Basically it's just this thing I'm worried about, the university loan and stuff like that ... and probably there's other expenses like trips and all that, I have to do investigations and all that sort of thing. So I was thinking of getting a part-time job or something to probably help out a bit.

And do you think it would be difficult or easy to get a part-time job?

Son: Yeah, it will be difficult to get a job, but even if I do it's going to be hard to go through college and work… And then I have to drop my brothers and everyone off at East Ham as well…

He was undecided about his future career:

Son: I'm not really sure – when I do biotechnology I've got options, I can either go into the science bit of it, or I can have a go at marketing. I'll probably be more interested in marketing. I'll just see how that goes over 3 years and see what I want.

In the longer term, we asked the son, did he think things were going to get better or worse for the family? He was cautiously optimistic:

Son: Yeah, I think if … when my brother finishes his education I think it would be a bit easier. What we were thinking is probably like once we've finished we will probably get a house and then move into a house rather than keep waiting for a council house… He's got another 2 years… And then when I finish we'll probably buy a house together … it will be better, he's got more money coming in.

His father was not looking so far ahead:

Life better – I get the council house, I'm quite happy until I'm dead – that's all I say… Anywhere – I don't bother – Stratford, Plaistow, anywhere … if we've got the council house I can settle one place… Which is our own house … look after children … I'm quite happy until I'm die – that's all I want. But nobody help me.

His son drew a different conclusion: that his father had made a basic mistake and that nowadays people knew better:

Son: Yeah, at the moment many people know not to do what my dad did, like sell their houses when it'll be hard to get another house.

Sanjula

Sanjula is an older-established immigrant on her way out: a Hindu Indian, married, in her thirties, with two children, employed as a teacher but taking a year off; she lives with in-laws in an owner-occupied terraced house. She has lived at this address for 11 years, but in Newham for over 20 years. She evidently is a person whose life is centred around her family – both her husband and children, and her own parents and in-laws. So she has a good local support system. But they are moving out to Redbridge.

Asked what she likes about this area, she says, with hesitation:

The park's wonderful, down the road (*amusement*)...Yeah. I think it's, in terms of convenience, you know, its shops and other facilities, it's quite good, I mean and especially this location, sort of 5 minute drive to the Asian shops – Green Street – and we've got a few large, two large supermarkets in Stratford, and in terms of, yeah, convenience I think...

But she finds health care here in Newham appallingly overloaded and unable to cope:

I don't know the details of the area we're going to be moving into. I don't know sort of the health service there and things like that – the GP we're with, GP clinic, I should say, the surgery, is just appalling really... It is, it's awful ... you know, you can't, you can't get an appointment for maybe 10 days or 2 weeks there. If your child's ill ...then you really have to kick up a fuss before they say: 'OK, bring them in' ... I mean we book appointments, go there and we probably don't get seen until, you know, an hour and a half later. So when your child's ill and they're whingeing, you'd much rather be at home and then go just in time for your appointment, but it doesn't happen like that. And for adults you might as well forget it, you'd be better...

The neighbourhood, she said, is friendly:

... they're all very friendly here – we haven't really got anyone who's a nuisance. No, it's nice ... it's nice to be living where you know you've got friendly neighbours.

But crime was an issue:

It's getting worse – this particular road was very quiet, very safe when I came here not so long ago, just 11 years, and there've been a few burglaries on this road in the last year, cars have been stolen – our car got stolen ... I tend not to go out after dark on my own anyway, I mean not ... I go by car, but no, not walk, or ... you know, I'd be quite scared to go down to the petrol station at night, after dark.

She mentions a recent incident which had clearly disturbed her:

I mean our neighbours are really good both sides, and there's a lady across the road who's usually sort of standing outside saying her hellos to everyone, so she tends to keep an eye. But we were decorating when my parents-in-law went away and I'd sort of left the curtains off ... you know, the guy across the road came and told me, he said: 'You know while you were out', he said, 'there were some people standing there', and you know, we had our TV in the middle of the room ... he said they were standing there and, you know, sort of just peering in and I said: 'Oh', so that made me change my mind about going out for dinner at night and I just stayed in. You know, it's just things like that.

But the real reason for her dissatisfaction, it soon emerges, is the school system. Asked what she does not like so much, she again answers with hesitation:

I can't say I don't like the schools – I do like the schools, but it's just the intake, I think … that makes it sound really snobbish, but my daughter doesn't actually go to a school in this borough… She goes to a school in Redbridge, but an independent one because we, we're not in their catchment, you know, in the catchment…

So you're paying for her education?

Yeah…

… Ilford – and is that junior, or…

Yeah, infants and primary. I mean I'm not saying that the teachers aren't good here – I myself am a teacher in a secondary school in Newham … so it's not the school or the teachers, the teaching – it's just the workload on them – I mean they have 35 plus students in primary schools … very large, so … and in terms of resources they're not really, you know, well equipped, so yeah, that's why I decided to put her into an independent school. You know, it almost seems hypocritical, doesn't it, that on the one hand I'm in state education, but then I won't put my daughter into state education, but it's for reasons like that – and the intake itself, I mean I … I often see children go by who actually go to primary school at the end of the road, and see children go by with their parents and they're both swearing at each other and things like that, and I'm not very…

Happy?

No, I don't want her to be exposed to that sort of thing, so it's just choice.

She explained more specifically why she was doing it. It was to avoid immigrant children, a paradox she herself found ironic:

I'm actually paying for her to be in a nice, friendly environment, you know, where the parents are, you know, concerned about their children and their progress. I'm not saying the parents aren't here, but you'll find a different type of parent here, especially when you've got maybe – I don't know – refugees, or parents that have recently come over from another country, like India, Pakistan, Bangladesh, their main priority is to survive when they first come here, that is … you know, I mean that was the same as us when we came here 20 years ago, our parents had to think about earning a living so that we could live.

She was agitated, though, because the school in Redbridge had raised its fees, and they were struggling to cope:

… I actually made a comment on that, I said: 'We're still working-class, we send our daughter to your school, but that doesn't mean we have a tree at the end of our garden where we can just, you know, pick off some money and pay you'. I said: 'We do work really hard to allow us to send her there'. The deputy head that I spoke to was very understanding, but I'm not sure how the head would have taken it if I'd spoken to her … I think in general people seem to think that if we've got money to, you know, pay for our child's fees, then we must be earning mega bucks, you know, and it's not like that at all. And I'd say that is the case with most of the parents there.

They are in the process of buying their own home in Redbridge, because of their child's education. So she sees life in the immediate future as a struggle, financially speaking:

I know one thing, I won't be financially better off – it'll be, it will be a struggle … because the last 11 years, I mean we've had it fairly easy, especially since I've started working … been able to take holidays whenever we wanted and just go out as often as we want, and that won't be happening.

But they are making that sacrifice deliberately, moving to Redbridge 'specifically for schools'. She also thinks Redbridge offers much better public services for children:

I tend to compare a lot of the services to the services offered in Redbridge – I don't know why, it's probably because we've got family there and I tend to know about things that go on there more, and they do … you know, they have a lot more sort of summer schemes for young children, and lots of other activities going on during the summer holidays for children, and even sort of general … not just during the holidays, but other – what shall I say – other activities like, you know, they have a huge school of gymnastics…

Otherwise, her family and friends are all close by. But, significantly, she said that there was a general exodus to Redbridge, especially of families with children, for the same reason: the schools:

I've got my own family that live in Forest Gate, they're still there. A few of my friends live in Newham, you know, sort of college friends, but a lot of them have sort of moved out, into Redbridge again. So yeah, it is a mixture, but we tend to have more family and friends in Redbridge… They used to be here, but it's just that they've moved there – for the same reasons, I think – schools.

House prices were higher out there, she said, but were rising rapidly here in Newham:

… at the moment, they're more expensive at sort of Redbridge and Clayhall are more expensive than Newham, but the prices in Stratford are going up rapidly, and Newham's actually had the highest increase in house prices… I think this house will definitely be an investment … you know, if we keep it for a few years…

Dafina

Dafina, one might say, is still on her way in. In her late forties, she is an African lone parent, originally from Zimbabwe, with three children in their late teens, employed and also at college, living in a housing association semi-detached modern house. She came here in 1990:

I came here 1989 to visit and I did visit and I got a job during my visit, and I worked I think for 6 weeks, but because my children, specially my youngest, was small – 10 years I think – I thought no, let me go home and sort of see if I can wait until she's 15 or something. But when I went home I found that my … I had stayed, I overstayed here … my job was gone, I couldn't find my job, because I didn't leave … I didn't take enough notice to say 6 months, I just took a little holiday and… And then without a job it was very difficult in my country to sort of settle in as not working and looking for a job, and I think in my mind I thought it's better if I go back because there is a job where I've been and I couldn't find a job, and at the same time, I think my marriage was very much on the rocks, so it was just, things were not going right. So there was only one way I could look at it … the way out is to go somewhere and…

And start afresh, a completely new start.

A start.

When she returned, she was effectively destitute:

When I came to London now to stay, I didn't have money on me, I just had, I think all in all when I changed it, I had £50 … and I didn't have anybody … at the back of my mind I knew that although this person has been so nice and saying: 'You can stay for as long as you want', I will be out before time, and that is true because I … at that time it was in Hendon in North London and … I used to work with his brother, and that was the other brother, I stop with him, and he had a family – his wife and the children – and it was a packed house with kids – and they offered me the big girl's room and she wasn't happy, she really wasn't – that night she really cried and I felt so bad.

Thus she found a job as live-in helper to an old lady. She did not have any professional qualification, but just drew on the experience of life in her own family back in Zimbabwe:

But what I did was to look in the shops, you know, adverts, little adverts, and you know, for jobs ... job adverts in there, and there were loads – things have changed – there were just loads of jobs, and... And there was this job, a live-in job, for a lady, old lady at Hampstead, and I went – I didn't even phone, there was an address and everything – I went there and the lady was in her room and she asked me if I had any experience, and I said: 'Yes, I've got experience', and: 'How much experience?' 'Well, I used to look after my grandmum, or my mum', and back home for sure this caring is part of ... family life.

And you have an extended family that you live with?

Yes, yes, always been an extended family we live with. I didn't have a grandmother of my own, but there were old ladies, always old ladies within the house. So really issues of helping, were not ... it's not something that I need training for. Of course, knowledge, yes, but to say: 'Hold me here – do this', you know, things that are practical...

Help me out of the bath and that sort of thing?

Bath, yeah. So I said: 'Yes, I've got experience', and she just trusted me because she could walk, but very slow, and the nurse used to come in in the morning, and another carer used to come in the evening, but she wanted someone to live with her...

So she felt safer, not falling and...

Yeah, yeah. So anyway I stayed with her, and she gave me something like £30 a week, and to me that's good money.

Yes, cos you were living in and...

Yes, and earning £30.

And so you didn't have to pay for...

Anything ... well for food, yes, I used to pay my own food...

But after six months the old lady died:

and that was it for me, yeah.

So she went to a centre for Zimbabwean refugees and declared herself destitute. They put her in one-room accommodation in Leyton and got her on to the benefit system, even though she was not officially a refugee. In fact she never succeeded in gaining refugee status, but was given the right to stay and renew every 3 years, and they had just given her and her children the right to stay indefinitely:

Actually, it was not ever official, no, because my papers were in the Home Office at that time, so I was just waiting for my papers to come out and then I would know what category … I was classified into. But at the time, the refugee people just helped me to have … somewhere to live, yes, and they sorted the benefits out for me, which was good. And … although I had that entitlement which they had sorted for me, I still looked for work, I was like desperate for work. And I did get a job at the hospital for the children in Hackney, you know, in a laundry … laundry outside, you know, because of the, you know, white sheets … loads of sheets … I got a job there, and I got a job and then I just stopped the benefits, because of the fear that if I do the benefits and something will go wrong and then, you know…

And what was the pay like on the job with the…

I think – Oh my God – I think it was £3 an hour, it was good money, it was really good money.

And were you still living in the room in Leyton?

I was still living one room and it was really good money – £3 an hour, and I worked I think 5 days, which was really good earnings. And at that time in my mind I was building up, even when I lived with the lady, that £30 I had so much, because I was just putting it, not using it…

Putting it away.

Yes, opening … I did have a bank account because back home we've got a Barclays Bank, so I just opened the bank … I didn't have … I mean those days I didn't have any hassle … I opened the bank, there was no problem. So I used to put my money … I would just bank, bank, bank because I was thinking of the girls to come and join me. So it was the money issue to send home so that maybe they would come.

She worked in the laundry for the whole of 1991, but then decided she should obtain a vocational qualification to become a professional care worker:

I worked the whole of 1991 – yes, I worked the whole of 1991 and at the end of 1991 I thought of the caring job because it has got more money, and then I left the laundry and I joined a training course to do an NVQ, because although I lived with that lady, I felt that there were some issues really that one needs to know when you are handling a person, so this time if I had to look for a job I thought, you know, I'd better do a little bit of training, so I joined this course, it was in Tower Hamlets, caring for elderly people, which I did for 6 months… Then when I finished that course it was really a foundation and I got a job – that was my first job in the care profession then, that's where I still am.

So now she was professionally established – and soon she gained promotion to senior care assistant. But she was still living in one room in Leyton:

I was looking high and low for a house, for a flat really ... I was looking for a flat, because I was thinking of the girls, and I was, I was planning...

She got this house in 1994, and her daughter – by then 19 – arrived almost immediately; she had not seen her for 2 or 3 years:

And I think what I want to mention is just that if one has got an ambition, if you focus on something, no matter how difficult issues are, no matter how difficult settling is, if your plans and your focus ... I want this... It's hard, but you persevere, you've just got to, because I don't know how I managed to get the house ... I just found myself with a new house... I registered with the Council, and the Council ... my points were very low because I was on my own. And this one time, the adviser, the housing adviser, advised me to register with the housing association because they do give houses, but on shared accommodation scheme, if I can pay a deposit. I said: 'Wow!', I said, 'It's what I want', and I registered with the housing association.

She is on a shared equity scheme:

Actually, I pay two amounts – I pay mortgage and I pay rent. I pay rent separate to the landlord, which is the housing association, and I pay mortgage at Abbey National – two different ways ... now I've got only one share that I bought, which is 50 per cent of the ... of the house, and 50 per cent still belongs to them. When I feel like I'm comfortable I can take that share, buy it off from them, then it becomes ours.

Now she is taking another course, but this was a stressful experience:

The course I'm doing now, no, it's a grant ... it's the only one course that I'm doing that I've managed to get funding, I've got my own house, so they refused me – Newham turned it down. And it was very stressful – the college also was like about to put me off and say: 'Now, if you cannot pay the fee, Newham can't pay for you ... you won't be able to'. But however, at the college there is student support services – I went to the lady there and she was ever so supportive – that's how I got to get the funding because she fought hard.

Her other daughters came in 1993 and 1994. One was 14, the other almost 18. Now, she is in the interesting position that she is studying for a Social Work degree at the University of North London while her oldest daughter is completing her English course at the University of Westminster. But the education of her daughters had been yet another stressful experience for her:

... when the girls came here they were like, to me they were like intelligent, if you like, and when they got into this country, I don't know, all that intelligence deteriorated.

They didn't seem like clever at school like they used to get As and Bs – their grades dropped down to really Es and Fs, so I couldn't understand whether was it the school, or was it them children just changed – I didn't know. But I think it was more to the environment, the fact that they changed from the lifestyles that they used to be to this type of lifestyle where people can be in control of theirself and say: 'Yes, I'm all right, if I don't want to do something, I don't have to do it'… I almost had a nervous breakdown. Imagine that – I'm talking about three girls – and one after another, one after another … but then again I should say that I was fighting hard in the sense that I used to tell her: 'Well look, I came here because I thought it would be of benefit for you guys to join me and better yourselves – I didn't realise that I was wrong when I was giving you so much stress, such that, you know, I don't know what to do'.

For her, it proved to be a kind of crash course in confidence-building:

… yes, the difficulty is coming down … I can manage, I can … I think I can put my foot and say when the bills come I can even say: 'Oh' – pick up the phone – 'I will sort you out'. I've got that courage to say, you know. And yet before, Oh God, if I saw a letter I was like: 'Oh my goodness, what am I gonna do?' it was too stressful, I was like under pressure all the time.

Financial pressure?

Financial pressure was the most, then personal pressure like, you know, I didn't have any friends, I didn't have any boyfriends, no men in my life, so that was hard too… All the time really, I've just been feeling like that, but still you carry on, keep going.

Is that still the same now?

It is, yeah, still the same… I do know people in my course, but they, they all got their own little bit of life … they don't, we don't really meet… I was even saying to my daughter the other day that honestly I need to do something to my life because otherwise I will be left a zombie. I need to do something active, something, maybe. So yeah, that bit of life has really gone, it's empty…

And what about meeting neighbours and so on, do you know people…

Yeah, we chat – me and my neighbours, we get on – if we meet we just chat and we chat. And that's all outside, it doesn't extend to, you know, internally to reach out like to … you know, I'm talking about a friend that we can go out for a cup of tea and have a laugh, or maybe even extend to cinema.

Life, she said, still remained very hard for her:

Are there things that you feel as though you do without?

Oh yes, lots of things I do without, loads, yes.

For example?

Well I would love to drive a car, I can't afford a car, I'm so old now … I'm 48 and it's this buses, get up in the morning … I wish I could drive my nice car. I never go on holiday… I'm so stressed out as it is, I feel like … I was itching the other day, I thought maybe I need the sun. I need a holiday and I need a lot of things…

That you just…

Can't have. As long as I can pay my house and that's it.

And do you think things will get better?

I do, yes, I do think with, you know, forecast, ambitious and working hard, I might get there.

And how long … your course is for…

Two years to go now.

And then you'll have your social work qualification?

Qualifications … and that's what my goalpost is now, that's what is shining in front of me… I'm thinking yes, once I reach there I will get a job definitely, and I will shape my life … and that I'm sure.

She said she had never experienced explicit discrimination, but it was rather more subtle and even ambiguous:

If you look – if you become too negative and you see it obvious, but it's there. But I always try and tell myself if the discrimination comes up that … say for example, if I go for … there are times when I have gone for a job and I don't get it and maybe I would have felt that I'd done better, but I would think that maybe I didn't do … it's just to console myself, I say I didn't do well…Yeah, and it's making me feel comfortable because then I don't have that edge of anger, because if I think I've done the job and they didn't give it me, because you get so … and you build up something that you … I would get nowhere with it. So I always find an excuse that will make me feel comfortable and kind of consolation, if you like.

But she felt she might experience it once she tried to buy a house of her own:

I think that's where this prejudice would come, where you ask me because I said to you I haven't experienced it, because some people have told me that, you know, when you are looking for property in some areas you find that even if you would buy the house, it becomes very difficult because maybe it's like white people's area, and you have a black person trying to fit theirself there. I haven't personally experienced it, but I have a friend who was looking for a place, she said she felt like that.

We asked her, were there things she thought were holding her back, stopping her getting on or living the kind of life she wanted. Her answer was very honest and revealing:

... there's a lot of things that stop me from doing things... Financially really is one big one, yeah – you might want to do something and you cannot afford it, and I think social classes as well – you don't fit it, you feel like you don't fit in and you can't do, you know, you can't join in... And maybe colour, like I say, you might want to go West End now, and for instance, I might think: 'Oh, I'd love to be going', but if you're on your own, you are a woman, you just feel that you don't fit in, you can't do it.

And how do you think people identify your social class?

As low really, as very low-class.

Why?

Because of the way I am.

In what way, what about the way you are?

Well language for a start – even sometimes some black people classify each other ... if you can't speak fluent or if you can't do ... you know, the lifestyle like this, you know, for that social class, and then you... Maybe sometimes I push myself to the lower class, because you find that that's where you feel safe ... you know, that's where I belong, that's where this is comfortable.

She thought very little of this area:

... actually really, yeah, it's a black people's area... Like Asian and black...

... and she revealed that for her, this somehow symbolised the fact that she had come down in the world compared with her previous privileged life in Zimbabwe:

Well, the area, to be honest, everybody has got prejudices – I think that's my prejudice myself, because I don't like the area at all. I don't like area, for one, it is very much of a low-class, if you like, you know. Back home, where I used to live, where my husband come, we used to live in a really kind of a nice classes, cos we were working-classes – we had a good house, swimming pool and everything... If I had money I wouldn't purchase a house here – maybe I would, I dunno, but it's really ... it needs a lot of improvement because the people put themselves in a category of low if you like, because it's not tidy, it's not clean, and the children just wild. They wander, they can just play at the end, they throw my ball, the ball over to my yard and they jump over, or maybe if they want they come and put pressure one me: 'I want my ball!' and there's no respect, you know. And those issues I think the higher the class you go people will be disciplining the children in a different way, I hope.

The area was physically depressing and run down, because people did not care for their environment:

I think I'm talking about … you know some areas when you're, even when you're driving along, you could see plants, flowers, you know, and houses are different, and the streets are clean – you don't see it here, you just see rubbish, just people don't care, they just chuck junk in front of the … you know, it makes the place low, it really…

Crime, too, was a problem, basically because there was very little sense of neighbourly feeling:

There is actually, a lot of crime, and my neighbour at one time … not the next door neighbour, the neighbour after this one, was burgled, and my neighbour next door before she moved in, people moved in. If you leave your car they just…

So you don't feel as though people look out for each other round here?

No, they don't, I don't think so really, I dunno. Because I don't look after people myself, I don't know who lives across the road. Well, I do know my neighbours, but I don't have time to be checking on what's happening, you know, my life is too busy. If I'm here I'm on my computer – honestly, my assignment – and if not, I'm at work – and if not, I'm at the gym. So I haven't got one minute of rest here.

But, revealingly, she felt that the basic problem was poverty, which gave the whole tone to the area:

That's why I say to you that the reason why I feel low because it's where you live, everything is just minimum, it's low-class – there's no good shops. Maybe if they could sort of give the shops money to promote their shops, not into second-hand, but into something…

Ian

Ian is representative of the gentrifiers: white, in his forties, married for a second time, employed as a social worker specialising in difficult children, and owner-occupier of a modern terraced house in Stratford. His wife joins in the interview occasionally.

He grew up in Chelmsford but his family came from the East End, so he has roots here. He came to live in Newham 5 years ago, when he divorced, and moved into this house 4 years ago from a rented flat in Forest Gate:

Well, because the … the rent that we were paying, although it was very reasonable, there wasn't much different between the rent and actually paying for a mortgage… And so we decided to … to buy this, em, subsequently it's turned out to be a good decision, because since then, over the past 3 or 4 years, but certainly within the 12, the last 12 months, property prices, particularly in the Stratford area – and I dare say a lot of that's got to do with the regeneration that's happening in this part of the borough – has gone mad, I mean … you know, this house was sixty thousand when we bought it and now, you know, looking at comparable properties, you know, within the borough, you're talking about a hundred at least… So, in … in 5 years it's nearly gone double.

To make ends meet, he is doing two jobs and working a 12-hour day:

I do two jobs, you see – I do an early morning cleaning job before I go and do my other job … that's domestic assistant cleaner, starting at 6 O'clock every morning till quarter to nine, that's in East Ham, so that gives me 15 minutes to ride my bike to my proper – well, not my proper job, my other job.

And why do you do two jobs?

Because I need the money… Like, sending him to nursery and also I've got two other kids that I need to pay for…

And you're still paying child support for them?

Yeah, yeah … to enable me to do that and make sure they've got a good standard living, to make sure that we have a reasonable standard of living, one job wasn't giving me enough income.

So, did you have two jobs before that, or did you…?

No, I struggled … well not struggled, it meant that – come the end of the month, you know – yeah, I was struggling a bit, really, to … to … not to ensure that we have a fantastic standard of living, because we don't now, we're comfortable, and … but, you know, to buy the things that … that, you know, we like to have and to, to eat relatively well, and to give us a bit of money for … for leisure as well, the only way was to do a bit more work, and so that's what I've had to do.

It must be really hard doing a full day's work at – from that time…?

Yeah, it is, by the end of the week, yeah. I get up at just before five, and by the time I've had a shower, take the dog out, come back, it's time to … to ride, so just before five I, I get up and I get home from work at half-past five, so it's a long old day really.

Twelve hours…

And, and what that means is … is that, of course, is that I very rarely go out in mid-week … there are occasions when it does crop up, that … you know, you'd … I'd end up being a bloody hermit like, you know, because offers and invitations come about, and … you know, you've just got to be … pick and choose, really, you know, when you go.

At the end of the day, he felt he was not very materialistic:

I don't say I want great things out of life, I want my children to be happy, I want them to get a fair deal, I want to be able to pursue, or have the opportunity to continue to pursue my, my leisure interests, obviously, I want Jo to be happy, and I suppose to … to enable that to happen, you know, I feel that I've got to maintain some sort of decent income. Em, but it's not the be all and end all and, you know, if I … if I had to, you know, if it was a choice of being content and not having a lot of things, well then I'll go for being content.

But they are finding it hard to make ends meet. Their child is in a private day nursery costing £110 a week, just about to go up to £115 for a full day 5 days a week:

Cos Jo works and I work and … you know, it's the only way really that we could maintain a … you know, a half decent standard of living, really.

They are unhappy about the quality of care, but:

Unfortunately, you would probably say … logically 'well take him out and send him somewhere else', but there's not places around, we were lucky to get him in there and although we're not happy generally with it … the proprietor appears to be accommodating, but … a few staff that really I would question whether they should actually be doing the job, although we're told they're all qualified … but … if you're qualified for something, it doesn't necessarily mean to say you're any good at it…

Like so many we talked to, he thinks that this area has always had a bad reputation: professional people do not want to live here, because they see it as poor and run down:

Yeah, I mean … in, in particular professional walks of life, they're finding it difficult to attract the worker, and I mean … I know the social work department are trying, you know, like Canada and New Zealand and Australia, to get … to get workers to come and work in the borough …there's a shortage of social workers anyway, but particularly, you know, for Newham and Hackney as well, one of our neighbouring boroughs because, you know, it's always … you know, the East End is not always been seen to be the best place to … to work.

The problem is that aspiring younger people had moved out to the new towns, leaving the poor and unemployed behind. And this area, he thought, remained what it had always been: a place with poor jobs paying poor incomes:

… traditionally, you know, young people have moved out… And that's … hence like the Basildons, the Milton Keynes, the Harlows, and places like that, and it's only left the old people, but … you know, they trying not only to maintain young people in the borough, but … you know, to draw people in as well. The unfortunate thing, of course, is … is that, you know, there's no industry … all you've got to do is look through the local paper, and what jobs there are extremely low paid, you know, and if you … if you matched that up against the price of property, well people don't stand a chance, for the ordinary person it's … there's nothing about, em, sort of like labouring jobs in picking and packing, that … that sort of industry.

It is a myth, he thinks, that the East End was once a real community. It is and was a poor area:

Yeah, and another one of my bugbears, you know, you get … you get these, the people like, you know, who … who get on the bandwagon about the Krays like, you know, how … you know, 'Oh they were lovely people, only done it for their own', that's a load of bollocks, they … they were, they were bullies and … you know, you don't get to own a snooker hall when you're 21 years of age by being a nice guy like, you know, they … they terrorised the East End and that's how they got their position, and people that … you know, are unable to understand that, live in another world, like, you know, they didn't get … 'they didn't get involved in drugs', well they didn't, no, because drugs weren't around then. But it's significant that Charlie Kray's put away now for dealing in drugs, like you know, if it was available at the time and it was a way of making money, they'd have been into it like, you know … so the whole thing's a fantasy as far as I'm concerned, and … and, and the stuff like leaving your backdoors open is a load of crap as well, because … you know, although people didn't have a lot to nick, they daren't leave their backdoors open, because what they did have will go, you know.

He is willing to admit that there was once a certain sense of social solidarity in the old extended families, now curiously found only among the Bangladeshi and other Asian groups that have so often taken their place in the streets where they once lived. But among the old white working class, that has long gone, as generations split up and moved out of the old East End into Essex:

So, parents were living close to children…?

… in a lot of cases like they all lived in the same house like, very much like the extended family of the Asian people that have … that live in the borough now, and

… you know, they all live together, you know, a lot of that, you know, occurred in them days, but … but then, you know, the families sort of fragmented like, you know, when … when the younger people decided that for a better life they'd rather move out into, into new towns, and so … you know, the … the community of families living together sort of like disintegrated really.

But, other than that sort of family unit, the idea of community spirit's no different now, you don't think, than from when your mum lived in this town?

I think that now there are sections in the community that, that would … would rather, I mean they … because of their culture, you know, they … they make … they make up their own little communities rather than, than it being sort of like a big community.

In any case, he thought, there was a great deal of false sentimentality about those so-called good old days, the supposed golden age of the East End working-class culture:

… you know … there's a contrary sort of like historical opinion that said that that's just crap like, you know … you know, them days were, were bloody hard and terrible, it's a lot better living today like, you know, so … and I'd rather go with that line of thought than … than the good old days when everybody left their backdoors open and everybody popped in, and nobody would nick each other, nobody was fighting, the youngsters didn't go round fighting – that's a load of rubbish, that is, they did it as much then as they do these days.

There is a drugs problem here, he thinks, but it is simply another expression of the area's extreme deprivation; people traded in drugs because this was the only way they could see to share in the affluence they saw all around them:

… there are a lot of 'have nots', and – you know – I'm not making excuses, but for some the opportunities to be a, a 'have' is … are very limited, and so therefore, you know, they take other channels to, to get what they have got, because – you know, we do live in a very materialistic world, and – you know, a lot of pressure's put on – especially in, sort of the, the teenagers to, to have the things that a lot of other people have got, and – you know, if – if parents are unable to provide, well then, you know, to avoid them being a bit of a social misfit, and you can be a social misfit if you haven't got the right sort of trainers on… Em, there's another avenue to get money, and – you know, whether it be selling drugs or thieving, they – they'll take the opportunity if it arises, so…

Petty crime, he feels is a fact of life here, and always was:

I'm fairly accepting … that, you know, there's … there's a high crime rate, that's part and parcel of living in this area. Em … em, I'm accepting that there's not a great – a lot of opportunity for people to – work-wise, I'm accepting of that, because … you know, there never has been in this area, historically. I mean OK the big industry's gone, but even when the big industry was here, I mean people were never able to really earn a lot of money and all … all the extra money they did earn was on the fiddle, you know, I mean the docks, for instance, you know, was … was a great employer, but you know, people didn't earn a great lot of money there, they used to thieve a lot to make it up, so…

This he can accept, but there are parts of the borough he would not want to live in:

I wouldn't want to live in Custom House, I wouldn't want to live in Canning Town … I wouldn't want to live in Silvertown – no … it seems that particularly … the less savoury people of the community have all been sort of like lumped into, you know, a couple of areas like, you know, which … you know, people have been re-housed cos of various, you know, antisocial behaviour, they've all been re-housed in the same bloody housing estate like, you know, so … I mean Forest Gate's OK, this area's OK, Plaistow's OK, Upton Park's OK, Manor Park's OK, you know, there … I mean there … there is sort of sub-areas of those areas which are not very salubrious really, but … but generally speaking, I mean … you know, the borough covers a vast area … Custom House is, is … is the worst, I think … you ask anybody and they'll tell you that.

Nevertheless, he is happy for his child to grow up in the kind of place that Newham now is: a diverse place, where people of different origins and cultures grew up to live amicably together:

… it's important as far as we are concerned that, that he … he's educated in an environment that is … is … has a diversity of cultures, and I think that's the best way to bring kids up, and of course this part of London is one of the best areas, because it is so cosmopolitan like, you know… And … and, you know, going to school with kids from … from various, you know, ethnic backgrounds is … is an education in itself, I think, and I'd much prefer that than to live in, you know, like a 'Shire where, you know, everybody was….of the same ilk really…

Despite all its problems, he thinks that Newham has a good quality of urban life:

… we've got a cinema in Stratford, Stratford Picture House, there's a Theatre Royal there, that's been done up at the moment, we've got a theatre there as well, and we've got excellent shopping facilities in Stratford, they're only getting better, we've got a brand new library that's taken over the one that's just round the corner there…

I'm happy with that in that, you know, and there's ... there's lots of places you can go to get things to eat, so ... you know, that's not a problem, and you can go at any time, day or bloody night, so ... you're never stumped 'Oh, I've run out of this, where am I going to get it from', there's always somewhere local within walking distance you can get it.

And he would like to see Newham's built heritage preserved, though he senses that it is being lost:

Things ... things I don't like, yes, and it's the ... the old pubs that were built at the turn of the century and before, that ... that are closing down here, in Forest Gate there's loads of them that have ... that were locals to various, you know, the streets around them for years and years and years, and they ... and they haven't been able to hold their own against the competition of ... of places like Witherspoon's Pubs, for example, who can churn out beer at ridiculous prices because they buy it in bulk, if I had the choice, I'd rather pay a little bit extra and ... and keep, keep the old, the old places alive like, you know, but there's so many in the borough that have closed down, it's a damned shame...

He still has roots in Essex. They still have regular reunions:

Yeah, I've got a brother and sister in Chelmsford, I've got a ... my father's in Billericay, my mother's in Swanage, but my mum used to live in East Ham, so ... we're going to see me mum next week, we go on holiday, we go ... twice a year, once in August, once in April, and she comes here once a year for a week. Em, I probably see me mum about five or six times a year, I see me dad four or five times a year, I see my brother a lot more often than that...

His childhood friends, some of whom have become very affluent, also live nearby out in Essex:

... a lot of my friends live in various parts of Essex really, em, and some of 'em have ... they've done very well for themselves ... they've got properties right out in the country like, you know, and one of them's just bought a pub right in the middle of bloody nowhere like, you know, so ... yeah, it's ... it's ... but they're people that, em, I'm told it's fairly unique, I've got a circle of friends, there's about ... about 15 of us who went to the same school... Yeah, some of us went to infant school together, yeah, we've known each other since ... well, I'm ... I'll be 44 next month, and ... you know, for some of them I've known since I was 6 years old ... yeah, we see each other regular like, you know.

If he were ever in real financial difficulty he would have to go to these friends, he says, because his own family have nothing:

I've got plenty of friends who've got a lot more money than what I have, and I've known 'em so long, as I pointed out earlier on, that there is that sort of relationship where, you know, they wouldn't think twice about giving me what I wanted, em, and I'm lucky in that respect. There's no good going to me dad, because he's got bugger all and me mum's, you know, I suppose relatively … she, she's OK, but I'd prefer not to go to her. I can't go to me brother, cos he's got nothing, and me sister hasn't got anything either.

The neighbours are a very varied bunch, and one next-door neighbour presents a serious problem:

Marcella, next door, she's … she's a nurse, we don't really see her because she does shift work. The person … is a French guy, a French family, lovely people … right at the very, the last house, Roy and Kim – yeah, a good couple – coming in from that, there's a lady I don't know … really know, em, and then we've got a young lad and he's alright, Sean, he's a bit of a tearaway, but I get on with him alright … em, next door here's a bit strange, but … you know … she's got a strange personality, it changes like the wind like, and … never had any problem with her, except that … you know, I don't necessarily agree on the way she disciplines her kids, and you might … you might say 'it's got nothing to do with you', you know, when I hear shouting and screaming, I have to bang on the wall for her to shut up like, you know … and the occasion … I haven't seen her since, since this thing, which is about a month ago now, I hear her laying into one of the kids like, you know…

Generally, though, he has a good relationship of mutual trust with his neighbours:

… lots of neighbours have borrowed tools off me before, to enable them to do various tasks, whether it be a small job or a bloody big job … there is a sense that, you know, we're sort of living together, inasmuch as that, you know, people will stop and talk, they will ask you questions, they don't mind asking for help, and they will return the stuff.

Padma

Interviewed with her flatmate, Padma is another of the newer arrivals: you could call her one of the newest wave of gentrifiers. A single young Asian woman in her twenties, employed, she rents a room in a terraced house from a private landlord. She came to London as an 18-year-old first year student at Queen Mary (University of London) in Stepney, moved here in her fourth year, and came back because it was familiar:

I moved from Bedford when I was 18, I'm 25 now so I've lived in London for 7 years, I mean first year I lived in South Woodford, second year I moved down to Bow, third year I lived down in Mile End, then year four I moved to Stratford, yeah, then I moved to North London I've been living in Tottenham. Then I moved back to Bedford for a while and I've been living back in Stratford for about a year and a half... Yeah, yeah so, and then after that I think it was just one of them things I mean I moved, cos every summer I'd go back to Bedford for the holidays, came back the following September knowing that I wasn't studying any more but just didn't want to be in Bedford any more so I came back, moved to Stratford because it was an area that I knew quite well you know I used to come here regularly even when I was living at Mile End. I'd come here to do my shopping and things like that and I preferred it to Mile End you know cos of the facilities and things...

What the shopping centre?

Yeah shopping centre ... you know, you could just do more things in Stratford, basically go round look at clothes and things like that yeah.

She describes how she moved into her present flat – she first, then her flatmates. They work in different jobs and places, mainly but not exclusively in central London:

I was the first one to move in and then a month later Kim moved in who I actually knew from work, then two girls from New Zealand moved in. And then there was a Polish guy in here who had already stayed in here from when I ... he was there before me and the other three that was in when I moved in had actually moved out so, then Kim moved in and the two New Zealand girls and then it was like that till about em ... beginning of February. It was like that and then the Polish guy moved out in about May I think it was, then another bloke from New Zealand moved in and he stayed here till about October, then one of our friends Jo, she moved in for a little while. She moved out when you moved in didn't she? ... about February time, and then Nicola moved in in February and then Marian and Michelle moved in in April was it?

And so even though you've all not been here terribly long in the house you've become friends quite quickly – is that just because you get on really well...?

Yes, I mean it is like that isn't it, I mean I feel as if I've been here for ages and I haven't been here that long really have I ... 5 months yeah ... cos we all spend a lot of time in the house you find that you end up just sitting down together and watching TV together and just doing little things and I cook for all of them ... like on a Sunday we cook a big dinner for everyone in the house you know, and in the week normally if one person cooks everyone else has some anyway so it's just like that ... if three of us go shopping together we just put in like £10, £20 each and then no-one feels bad about eating anyone else's food cos they know they're putting some contribution toward it.

She had to build her own social network in London, but seems to have been quite successful:

No when I first came to London I knew no-one in London, I had no friends here no family, the people I met were through like university… I moved into halls of residence and … basically the people I met in there were my first friends in London and I didn't know anyone but it's good because since then I've got loads of cousins and friends and things who have moved to London to study or whatever, but I was the first one to actually make the move and come over here.

She now has several different circles of friends, the most recent the people she now lives with:

I've got my friends and family in Bedford I suppose, and I've got most of my friends round here, I've got all my work friends, got these flatmates that I live with. Yeah I've got my flatmates and I've got like friends I've made through working in other places in London like where I've worked in the last 4 or 5 years I've always kept friendships from people that I've met at work as well so…

But she confesses that at the weekends she is more or less too exhausted for any sustained activity:

By the weekend I just wanna sit at home and do nothing cos it's … I think it's cos the job I work in … I'm just continuously just talking, explaining things and you're just mentally tired by the end of the week, I'm just shattered you know.

She feels she has just enough to live on, but no more:

Well I don't know, I suppose if there's something I really wanna do I don't really do too badly I suppose but it's like where before I could put aside money for savings and that I can't now really so… Yeah just like the end of the month I'm skint basically so … so really I'm not thinking about long term I mean when I finish my loan payments off next year anyway so, thinking if I can just live out this next year, just scrimp and save and whatever, after that year I should be ok.

She is unhappy about her landlord. When they were going to redecorate the flat:

… Well he said he was gonna come down and buy some … choose … we could come with him and we could choose the paint together… But then he didn't show up so… Yeah I think he's a bit scared we're gonna do it in some garish colour because we suggested we wanted him to do it in a yellow but we're not talking about some really horrible yellow … just something bright and cheery and then we were gonna … and we even said to him there's certain things we're willing to pay for ourselves like put in a tenner each and get like a bit of carpet you know, we're not really too bothered we can do all that, but he's just not very happy about it…

She thinks he will do what is legally necessary and no more:

He is good with that he's … I think everything that he isn't happy about is what he thinks is kind of like above his call of duty kind of thing – do see what I mean, it's like, those things that do need to be done you know, that are a risk factor or whatever, he'll come straight round and do it you know, he's not, he's not funny … it's like as long as the house is safe and it can be lived in he's OK with that you know so…

Theirs is a typically mixed London neighbourhood – perhaps especially typical of this part of Newham. And what is most interesting is that the mixture goes right down to the level of the street and even the individual houses:

I would say the majority of people round here are black yeah but that includes Black West Indian, Black African, Black Other – do you see what I mean – so even though the blacks might be the major group, there's a lot of mixtures as well and then where you get further into Forest Gate and go down to say like East Ham, Green Street it's very Asian isn't it, so I suppose you can't really say … I mean you've got your areas where there's a very strong … but Newham in general is very mixed … especially like our street, if you go to the neighbours everyone's quite mixed you know like lady next door she's white but I think her boyfriend's Indian isn't he. The upstairs man is he a white man?

Flatmate: Yeah.

The couple of the students next door they're actually oriental and then there's like two white people … there's a black girl that lives there and the neighbours after that they're actually Italian and then there's the neighbours after that well they're mixed it's a mixed house there.

And what about the age range, the students are next door what about further up are they all quite young around here or?

Oh OK his name's Mario, he's um, I think he's probably late twenties, early thirties and he lives there with his girlfriend. Then the next house up is a lady who lives with her husband and she's … there's just the two of em, she's just got a few cats and things and the next neighbours from there is like the man lives there he owns the house and he's got a couple of lodgers living with him as well and they're like around the same age … none of them are really family, family you know. It's only further down that way there's a couple of Asian families where I suppose the children are like teenage.

She knows her neighbours and finds this a happy, friendly neighbourhood:

I know all the neighbours in it cos I'm the one when we always have parties or anything I get sent round there to go and tell everyone, all the neighbours, we invited all the neighbours on the street and everything so … they are really nice, like when you walk past they will always say good morning and hello and, or they'll stop for a chat sometimes you know.

So she finds her immediate local area quite safe, but has real doubts about the centre of Stratford:

Yeah it seems to be quite safe, I wouldn't say it's safe because where I work at the job centre I know there's a lot of nutters that live in Stratford … no there is, there's a lot, there's a lot of mad people around in Stratford but you know around here you do feel a bit safe…You know a bit nearer to the shopping centre it's … I think all the weird people seem to congregate around the shopping centre – it's a bit rowdy round there … obviously Stratford has got a high rate of unemployment because if you go in Stratford centre on a week day it's just as busy as it is on a weekend …

And, because of this, she does not feel completely safe coming home at night:

… most times like if I'm really late from anywhere I get a cab, I know it's not far but I normally would rather get a cab to get to my house but I don't feel safe at all… I've walked through there once one time late at night and there was no-one there and some guy came walking towards me – he said, you're a bit brave, and I thought is he warning me about himself or… Cos people hang around there you know, yeah there's loads of little dark corners and things you think, I don't think anyone would even help you to be honest with you.

Christian

Christian is the newest arrival of all, and it is unclear how long he will stay or what will be his likely future. In his thirties and single, he is a French African-Caribbean, whose family came from Guadeloupe. Presently unemployed, he is living as a private tenant in a terraced house. He came to live here from France about 8 months ago. His story is not entirely clear; it does not entirely add up:

I come in London, yes, to learn English, so learn English … I was living in Bournemouth, I came to this house two months ago.

And why did you choose to come and live in this area?

Because I have friends here…

And what do you like about living round here?

What I like … is, the first thing is because I have friends around here, so that can speak together and can exchange.

Most of his friends, he says, live around here:

Plaistow I have friends. I have another friend in Forest Gate, other one in Stratford – not so far, yeah.

He has relatives a long way away; he doesn't say where:

You don't have family here?

Ah, family, no.

He finds life in Newham rough and disquieting:

And what… do you dislike about living round here?

… they're young people that walk around and shout and make nuisance, something. Sometime they destroy the cars … the town, to be quite honest really we don't have many shops… I do the shopping sometime in Stratford, at Stratford, or in Forest Gate nearer the train station – yeah, I do my shopping sometimes at Tesco, Plaistow, so it's far, quite far.

His main problem in London is housing:

The main problem is to have a house and it's not easy to find a house, a new house where you will live … you have to have time to find house – I can't have time, yes, and … as I've told you that I move with some people I know, you know, friends, and if I go far from here I will miss…

Five adults live in the house, two married, one with his son, the others apparently single lodgers. He did not have to search for this place:

… no, just when I came here before I have all the friend here and they already find a house for me so I…

His last job was in a hotel. He got various menial jobs through agencies:

Like cleaning, kitchen porter, that kind of … yes.

He is eking out an existence with the aid of his family, plus casual work:

From the family and from small jobs … till now I've not had great problem of money – yes. Maybe I will have it, but when I will have the house I will turn either on my friend, to see my friends, or to the family.

He could have continued to work in France as a teacher of philosophy, but he had decided that he had to come here to learn English because it was the basic medium of the modern world:

I saw that most of books were in English, yes, and to work with many peoples in the world you have to know English – it's the first thing, that English is like the first language in the world now today... I decided to learn English.

But he will have a problem to find a good job in England, he realises:

When you go you want to do something – they ask you what can you do – you say philosophy ... you have to choice to do like kitchen porter, or cleaning job, or something like that, yes, and that is ... you are not working in the way, in your domain, you know, own domain...

He is realistic about his position; he does not aspire to a lifestyle that he knows is at present beyond his means:

But I do not intend to buy many things that I don't know when I have money to buy it. Now I know that I'm not working and I have not, I don't have good qualification to work, and buy things like – I consider myself that I've not begin my work career – yeah – so that I don't have to put something ideas in my mind, I will sort them after.

He knows nothing at all about the people in the neighbourhood:

I cannot tell you nothing about people that are around me, you know, because when they come they are in the house inside, you see – I don't go knocking about, I've never gone there, not there. Sometimes I don't know my neighbours because you can see some people come inside and you don't know that if they're living there or not.

So you don't know your neighbours like at all?

I've never exchanged word – nothing.

Everyday Life in the Transit Centre

Christian is the extreme case of the newcomer to the big city: lost, confused, friendless, isolated. There are many other former newcomers in Newham, many from other parts of the British Commonwealth, who – even after years of residence – seem equally to flounder on the margins of urban life, hardly able to cope with their multiple misfortunes or the complexities of a bureaucracy they cannot comprehend. Yet, equally, there are others, similarly former arrivals into the city, who have struggled to overcome their problems either through tenacity and hard work, or through exploiting their native wit. Some even manage to find a sense of home here, though many more seem to see it as an alien and even threatening place.

So this part of Newham is poised in an unusually delicate state of transition. Its geography gives it huge advantages. Its history gives it a legacy of housing which is relatively inexpensive. In the language of the estate agents, it is an area with 'great potential'. Already, this has resulted in an influx of households – both white and non-white – who seek bargains near the bottom end of the housing market, either because they are still in the early stages of their lifecycle and their earning potential, or because they do not hope for much better. They can be called gentrifiers, though theirs is a world apart from the classic, high-earning professional colonisation of more desirable areas such as Battersea and Bankside. Of course, many now-fashionable London areas were like this once. But Newham still bears a much heavier imprint of its working-class history; its physical environment, facilities and infrastructure recall the area London forgot.

Yet there are some echoes of the Battersea of the 1970s here, and perhaps of the Camden Town and Islington of the 1960s. The area is mixed, socially and ethnically. The people who live here seem to like the mix, perhaps because they are certain kinds of people – young, more outgoing and sociable, less fixed in their lifestyles. True, some older residents feel – as in Bermondsey – that a traditional sense of community is eroding. But the loss seemed much less catastrophic here.

There is, however, another element in this social mixture. Located as it is, Newham is increasingly becoming an extension of the huge and congested Bengali area of Tower Hamlets. And, where this is happening, locales are evolving their own distinctive quality of life. Here, some people reported a sense of anonymity and little sense of a rich neighbourhood life. And the same feelings were also prevalent in other areas with big stocks of private rented housing, where tenants came and went rapidly, keeping themselves to themselves. Most people reported that crime was widespread and in some cases (especially car crime) getting worse. Some spoke of a past sense of calm and security, recently lost. Others suggested that their own local area was safe, but that Stratford centre was dangerous. Many seemed to think high crime was just part of life in inner London; it came with the territory. And racism was not generally seen as a problem here – though some older-generation Asians were clearly having problems with the very different values of younger people in their own community.

Above all, this is still an area of intense poverty. The stories some of the people tell are ones of multiple misfortune, of a steady but tortuous climb out of poverty and deprivation, that seem to belong more to Dickensian London than to London at the dawn of the twentieth-first century. Many are making it by their own efforts, but some seem to be getting nowhere at all.

Of all the places we visited in our study, Upton Park is the nearest to the archetype described in the classic studies of the Chicago sociologists of the 1920s (Park, Burgess and McKenzie, 1925): the zone of transition, where people come and people go, seeking somewhere that can perhaps meet their dreams and hopes. Those who come in, most of them, are trying to put a foot on the first rung of the ladder of economic success and social ambition. Those who leave have already climbed that first rung, maybe several, and have developed higher aspirations which this place, this zone of the city, can no longer satisfy. So Upton Park, and places like it, may always serve as the city's ever-revolving door.

Green Street Market

Heston flight path

© Bill Knight

Chapter Five

Airport City

Heston

Most people who ever see Heston do so at about one thousand feet above the ground, almost at the end of the 25-mile-long glidepath that brings planes from Catford in south-east London down on to the twin Heathrow runways. And of course they do not know it is Heston, because it does not identify itself. Later on a few of them, using the old A4 as an alternative to the crowded M4 to get into London, may actually pass through the middle of it. But again, since it does not aggressively advertise its presence, there is hardly any way they would know.

And, to tell the truth, Heston does not exactly distinguish itself. It looks and feels exactly like hundreds of other such outer London suburbs, built at speed by speculative builders round the underground stations and along the then new by-pass roads during the 1920s and 1930s: mile after unending mile of almost identical semi-detached boxes, distinguished from each other only by mock-Tudor detailing and variations in the obligatory leaded light window in the front hall. Architects and other enlightened folk mocked them, then as now; but whole generations of Londoners, lower-middle and middle-middle in their socio-economic composition, flocked to live in them because they offered a lifestyle to which they aspired.

Seventy or eighty years after they were built, many such suburbs are showing their age. They have not become outmoded as cars or refrigerators of the same era would have done, because often they are paradoxically more spacious than their equivalents built beyond the green belt in the 1950s and 1960s, and because they proved easily capable of retrofitting with successive waves of technical refinement, from TV aerials to central heating to broadband. But they have aged in style, and the taste for retro design, which has made Victorian and then Edwardian suburbia again fashionable, has not yet rolled out to encompass them.

And they have aged in another way. Their original inhabitants, almost without exception white and middle-class and married, have long since gone through their lifecycles, and almost all have by now died. They have been replaced by new waves of incomers, often – because this is London's story at the end of the twentieth century and the start of the twenty first – newcomers from abroad. They too are middle class, or have middle-class aspirations. They too are married, and are raising families. They too seek more space, a better suburban environment and better schools for their children. In most respects, they have the same lifestyles and the same aspirations and the same values as the original inhabitants they succeeded. But many of them are not white.

This can bring minor and transitory problems of culture and style. But they are seldom traumatic, and London's unsung success story is precisely how successful it has been in absorbing successive waves of newcomers. Problems can arise, though, when successive waves of movement overlap and come into conflict, as when old-established middle-class white and more middle-class migrant minority ethnic groups find themselves challenged by yet a further wave of newcomers, whom they perceive as threatening local social relationships and educational standards.

Nowhere is this more true than in Heston. For, more than any other such interwar suburb, Heston found itself transformed by one of the most important single structural changes that occurred in post-World-War-Two London: the opening in 1946, only a year after war's end, of Heathrow airport. Many of Heston's inhabitants work either on the airport itself, or in a host of airport-related enterprises that cluster all around its perimeter, from hotels to logistics services. More than this: they, or their parents, often came to London precisely because they knew they would find jobs that were freely on offer as the airport steadily expanded. Heston, and similar suburbs all around, are London's Airport City.

That has brought employment and prosperity, but it has also brought its problems in the shape of aircraft noise, traffic congestion and pollution, and a strong sense that the quality of local life is diminished and diminishing. Of course, this sense is quite widely shared in many parts of London – and also in newly-developing suburbs beyond the M25, as we shall see in a later chapter. But here, perhaps, the sense is extreme.

Some History

Strictly, Heston might be called a suburb of a suburb. It is an outgrowth of Hounslow, the place that gives its name to the borough of which it is a part: a small town that grew up as a mail coach stopping point on the old Bath Road – the original route, going back to Roman times, to the west – at a point where it crosses a flat and extremely fertile plain of river gravels. As London grew, wheat fields increasingly gave way to fruit gardens, and then to the beginnings of suburban development. Hounslow was also a significant industrial centre, with traditional agricultural processing – mills, maltings, breweries – as well as Pears Soap, sword-making, gunpowder, potteries, brickworks and turpentine. The nineteenth century saw the extension of the Grand Union canal to the Midlands, the building of gas and water works, and boat-building around Brentford Docks.

But the key agent in transforming the area was the railways, with a line to Waterloo in 1849–1850 and a second twenty years later, followed in 1883 by the Metropolitan District Railway of the Underground. Each extension was quickly followed by a wave of housebuilding: the District served as the trigger for the first large-scale suburban development at Bedford Park, with more sporadic building at Osterley and around Hounslow itself. But large-scale suburbanization had to await the Piccadilly line extension of 1933, which took over the District line and provided an express service to Hammersmith, integrated with local bus feeders. To this day, good-quality residential property follows these rail lines, while a more modest style of working-class housing follows the old Bath Road through Brentford and Isleworth to Hounslow, reflecting the influence of the electric tram service that opened in 1901.

After the Great West Road opened in 1925, major industrial developments followed: Gillette, Martini and Firestone Tyres (the borough's major private employer up to the mid-1970s) were early arrivals in what became one of the largest industrial complexes in West London, still evident along the 'Golden Mile' from western Chiswick through Brentford and Isleworth, which in the early 1990s had no less than twelve trading estates or business parks. There were other significant industrial concentrations in Brentford, Hanworth and Feltham, which helped to make this a major manufacturing area: down to the mid-1970s half of the borough's male labour force and a third of the women worked in manufacturing, particularly electrical engineering, although office development was already occurring around the major shopping centres and the Great West Road.

But, as a result, in the 1970s and 1980s the borough was heavily exposed to the job losses which hit London manufacturing, including these inter-war industrial establishments. Between 1973 and 1988 over 23,000 jobs were lost, reflecting both growth constraints on local firms and closure of major manufacturers, including Firestone and United Biscuits on the Golden Mile. On the other side of the picture, however, first Heathrow airport (on the north-west edge of the borough) and then the M4 and M25 motorways (intersecting nearby) have given the borough enormous new locational advantages, especially for headquarter functions of international businesses. The current Chiswick Park development in Gunnersbury, nearing completion in 2007, claims to be the largest in London since Canary Wharf.

Heston Today

So Hounslow's economy today is predominantly a service economy, though still one-third of all jobs are manual. During the 1990s manufacturing job losses spread to a newer range of industries, including defence-related activities where employment fell by about 4,000 between 1990 and 1996. But manual job losses have been comfortably outweighed by expansion in non-manual work which grew by 31 per cent between 1991 and 1998. This is very much part of the M4 corridor zone of growth.

Oddly, almost all the jobs at Heathrow – 83,000 on- and off-site, according to BAA estimates – are credited statistically to the neighbouring borough of Hillingdon. Even so, Hounslow is a net importer of labour: it has 100,000 inward commuters, two-thirds of them coming from other parts of West London. Local employment includes an increasing number of company headquarters, 200 in all, notably on old factory sites along the Golden Mile and including many multinationals, for whom airport access has been a key location factor. Major corporations represented here include airlines, computer manufacturers and private mail services, together with a range of other industrial headquarters. Since the mid-1990s, high-profile developments have included Samsung's European HQ, Kvaerner (the Norwegian-based multinational) and a new headquarters for SmithKlineBeecham on the site vacated by Samsung after the Far East economic downturn.

Socially Hounslow's population is mixed, with 28.5 per cent of the labour force in professional/managerial jobs, less than the London average, 12.1 per cent in 'elementary' occupations, far higher than the London average, and 21.6 per cent economically inactive, somewhat lower than the London-wide average, in 2005. Compared with neighbouring Richmond, many fewer Hounslow residents are in managerial occupations, reflecting more modest educational or vocational qualification among the local workforce; the area remains what it always was, lower-middle or middle-middle class. And housing tenure is evidence of this: owner-occupiers made up only 60 per cent of households in 2001, in the mid-range among London boroughs, thus a high proportion still lived in social housing.

Reflecting the postwar wave of immigration, Hounslow – like much of outer West London and its near neighbour Slough just across the London boundary – has a substantial Asian population. At the 2001 Census 17.3 per cent recorded themselves as Indian, 4.3 per cent Pakistani. In addition 2.7 per cent were Black African. And 24.9 per cent had been born outside the EU. In terms of religion, 7.6 per cent were Hindu, 9.1 per cent Muslim and 8.6 per cent Sikh. Since 1981 the white population appears to have fallen by about 25,000, while the number of non-whites has increased by about 35,000. There has been a recent inflow of asylum seekers and refugees, estimated to comprise about 3 per cent of the resident population by 1997. As elsewhere, ethnic minorities are more strongly represented within the school-age population: 48 per cent of those in the borough's schools were non-white by 1999, while for 39 per cent English was a second language; 12 primary and two secondary schools had over 80 per cent of their pupils from minority ethnic groups. Politically, when we interviewed, Indians (at least) are now strongly represented within the borough council, with almost one-third of the seats.

Unemployment rates in Hounslow are very modest by national and regional standards. At the 2001 Census 3.3 per cent recorded themselves as unemployed, with a mere 0.8 per cent long-term unemployed. Hounslow lies in the middle of a ranking of boroughs on the IMD2004 index, somewhat more deprived than Hillingdon to its north and much more deprived than Richmond to its south, but very close to Ealing on its north-east. Only three of its micro-statistical units (Statistical Output Areas) fell within the most deprived 10 per cent in England. The one weak domain is housing and services, where 44 (32 per cent) of SOAs fall within the most deprived 10 per cent. But on this index London generally scores badly: it accounts for 43% of such SOAs in England, reflecting the perennial problem of affordability. And Hounslow additionally has an above-average household size (2.5 in 2001) and resultant overcrowding: the index of overcrowding was 16.2 per cent in 2001, high for an outer London borough.

Heston, the area where we conducted our interviews, spans the busy six-lane 1920s arterial A4 Great West Road, just east of Heathrow airport. It is actually two wards of the London Borough of Hounslow as they existed when we surveyed them in the year 2000: Heston Central, south of the M4 and north of the A4, and Hounslow Heath, south of the A4. Hounslow Heath is in turn bisected by the old Bath Road, running from the town centre of Hounslow about half a mile to the east; Hounslow West underground station, where the Piccadilly Line dives underground on its final leg into Heathrow, forms a kind of local town centre for the ward. Southwards is yet another centre of a peculiar kind: the historic cavalry barracks, established here at the end of the eighteenth century. The buildings seem anomalous in the surrounding sea of small semi-detached houses, now uniformly extended at the front with subsidised treble glazing against the constant roar of the planes that seem to be just above the rooftops. The little front gardens are almost all turned into hard standings for cars: multiple car ownership, you sense, is the rule here. The middle-class inhabitants are nearly all Indian except for a few young white people in newer small estates near the periphery. Eastwards, towards Hounslow town centre, are older terraced streets representing the town's nineteenth-century growth, accentuated after the railway came here in 1883. Heston Central is very much the same, but with a slightly more varied layout including culsde-sac and crescents – and even, in one place, a vast central green space on which an extended Indian family was playing cricket when we passed. Here, too, there are some larger and evidently more up-market houses; generally, though, the great bulk of the housing stock is of a kind that represented the bargain basement level when it was built and first sold in the 1930s, and has remained so because of the ever-present noise. Generally, both areas seem otherwise peaceful – though broken windscreen glass on the street tells its own story.

Socially and in terms of housing tenure, Heston is close to the London average, with a middle-class population and a majority of owner-occupied properties. It has exceptionally high proportions of non-white residents, mostly of Indian ethnic origin (in 2001, 52.3 per cent in Heston Central, 47.3 per cent in Hounslow Heath) – as are all but two of the local councillors. As in the borough generally, there is little sign of deprivation except in housing, and here it represents overcrowding which is a statistical artefact of above-average household size: 2.9 in Heston Central, 2.7 in Hounslow Heath, against 2.5 for the borough and 2.4 for England and Wales.

Betty

Betty, our first interviewee, is one of the oldest-established. A married white mother of three, in her fifties, and a homeowner, she has lived within 100 yards of where she lives now for her entire life, and her family have been in the area for five generations:

… my whole life is here, my mum lives round the corner, my sister, five generations of my family went to the local school, you know, I really feel here, this is me. My great, great grandfather, you know, his cottage up here, they used to get their water out the stream, you know, and I, he, he used to meet me from school and tell me about these things, you know, so this is my roots here.

But now, she feels, this is a place in constant motion, constant change:

… a lot of people just come here for a while and move on, you know, a lot of people coming into the country settle here for a year and then move on, get settled, get everything they, you know, where they know where they're going, and then move on somewhere else.

And recently, she told us, the area had gone sharply downhill:

Well, when I was a child, if you lived in that house over the road, you was posh. If you lived in that house over the road when I got married 30 years ago, you was quite probably Asian, or 20 years ago maybe, you were probably Asian but you would have been a solicitor or a dentist or, now you're probably either left here or from goodness knows where and possibly not working, and it's that kind … it's changed a lot in my lifetime. When I was a child, Hounslow was a leafy suburb of London but now I see it as part of the inner-city degradation type thing … there are still some roads, there are still some people, there are some, but there's nothing left of how it used to be, it's not a nice place to live any more… I want people to sweep up their front gardens and not leave their rubbish piled up, you know, but people don't do that any more, it's different like that round here, people don't do that any more … my husband's favourite expression is, 'Will the last person out of Hounslow please turn off the light', it's what he always says, there's not many of us left, you know..

Part of the trouble, she said, was the travellers who colonised local parks and open spaces:

… they dry their washing on the hedges and things, you know, in the gardens, like a third world country. But I don't blame the people, I blame the Council for letting them be like it.

But even without the travellers, the parks had become menacing places that no one would want to visit:

… the dips they put there so that the gypsies can't get in, you know and it's just a waste area, you know, the grass is this high, and it's a nature reserve now, just a good excuse for letting it go to rack and ruin and not maintaining it, nowhere for the kids to play, but it's a nature reserve, nice for the butterflies. Kids are all out their heads over the park on crack cocaine or heroin or whatever, there's a nice nature reserve over there for the butterflies and the dragonflies, just what you need. (*Laughs*)

She conveyed a generalised sense of menace, of fear, though she admitted they had not themselves been crime victims:

It's intimidating there, there's a lot of … you get the feeling that you're not safe, I can't explain it, there's a lot of beggars, well, there's not so many actually at the moment, there were a lot of beggars there last year especially, well, we had them knock on our door … people get over there in gangs, and they sit around drinking and you can't use the parks any more round here, cos they're like, just horrible, they're, apart from, I mean everyone says there's drug addicts, I don't think it is, I just think it's people who don't care about anybody else… You can't go to the park cos it's not nice and I blame the Council for all those things (*laughs*) everyone wants to go there, it's just no-one can, the only people who can go there are horrible people, who go there to get out the way, you know, dodgy people, but normal people want to go there with their nice normal children, we're all still here, we're just shut away indoors, so it's ridiculous. I blame the Council.

And she was clearly sensitive to minor incidents that suggested the place was not what it used to be:

… honestly, other than horrible things like, well, just yesterday, my daughter phoned me, at Abbey National at Hounslow West, there was a man peeing up the wall, just stood there, you know, just horrible things that you wouldn't see unless it was late on a Saturday anywhere else in the country. Well, you would see it in other places in the country but I don't wanna see it.

Speaking as someone from a family where five generations had gone to the same school, she also felt that the quality of the local school system had declined, and is now much lower in London than elsewhere:

No, no, I've got a grandson who's at school in Hounslow now, and my daughter changed her religion to get him into the only school what's worth sending a child to in Hounslow. She doesn't tell you that, but I know it's true, she's, she changed to a Catholic, my eldest daughter, and it's so that he could go to the local Catholic school, because it's very good… My youngest, I've got three daughters, my youngest is 22 now, she, I took her out of that school and moved her to another school which I wouldn't have thought I would ever consider sending her to, and I don't want you to think it's, I'm a racist if I say it, culturally it's changed completely in the space of 2 or 3 years. It went from being an English, a school in England where a lot of Asian children went to, to a school in England that was like an Asian school, if you know what I mean … they stopped having assembly and all kinds of things, you know, and they didn't have a nativity at Christmas and things like that, things that I'd thought were a traditional part of going to the infant school.

And, she said, white children became isolated at adolescence:

… what happens with the girls, when they get to about 11 or 10, whereas I would consider allowing an 11 or 12 year old, you know, let them go swimming or pictures on a Saturday afternoon, because of the way the Asians are, which is fine for them, they, they don't let their daughters … they stop letting their daughters do things like that, so you are then … your, your white girl is then in a minority because she's got no one to go to pictures on a Saturday afternoon with, so what's happening now is people are trying to find schools where there's other girls of the same ilk, so that when they get to about 12 or whatever, they're not going to be isolated…

Everyone, she suggested, was packing up and leaving because of a sense that the place was going downhill and that they should realise the equity on their houses while the going was good:

Well, they all moved away cos Hounslow, everyone laughs about it, you know if you're still in Hounslow they think you're either mad or as bad as the ones who live here, all my friends moved away years ago, years and years ago.

Most of them had however moved not very far – just the other side of the M25:

No, no, I think the furthest one who I knew went to Hemel Hempstead, and I think it's a kind of, you know, within probably the M25 border now almost, not much more of it, some moved out to sort of like Lightwater and Camberley, some places like that where there was a lot of new development, Royston, they're the furthest.

Because so many people had gone, they have very few friends left in the area. Their friends live outside, either connected to her husband's work, or in Dorset where they have a mobile home:

I do know them [the neighbours], but they're not my friends, I haven't got any friends at all in Hounslow, not one … my family are my friends in Hounslow, here still, but all my friends moved away, my husband works out at Stoke Poges … since April when we bought our mobile home in Bridport we've made more friends down there than I've made here in the last 20 years.

They have been contemplating a permanent move to Dorset, which they felt still had the qualities that Hounslow once had but has now lost:

It's still what I want, you know, and it's still, the Council still respond to people, you know, you feel, people still sweep up outside the house and their hedges are cut and their gardens are tended and their net curtains are clean, and even if you haven't got any money, you still got pride. But round here, no one seems to have any self respect.

But then they had second thoughts:

… we're debating now, because we were gonna go completely this year, we were gonna sell up and move miles out and buy, with the equity in the house, buy somewhere cash and then me not work and my husband really downgrade his life, and do that, move down to Bridport, we were going to do that. We got there we thought no, this is too young, no it's too young to do that. So … and then during the winter when we were going backwards and forwards cos we specifically looked in the winter, I was thinking Oh dear, supposing my grandson's not well and I wanna get there, and then one time we were down there and I, I had an abscess on my tooth and I couldn't get to a dentist, within 28 miles on a Sunday, whereas here I think I can pick the phone up, get the Yellow Pages out the cupboard, phone 12 people and see a dentist within an hour. It scared me a little bit.

Donald

Donald is another exceedingly long-time resident: a white married father in his late fifties, employed and a homeowner, he was born here, and his mother moved here when she was young:

I've lived in this area all my life, 57 years. When I was starting in this, my mother actually come to this area when she was quite young, she lived in here 68 years, and when we come to this area, I know what I was saying, yes, when I was born from this area it was sort of a village, it wasn't part of the Great London Metropolis, so I have seen it develop from a, fairly reasonable village...

He felt his own neighbourhood was quite stable and peaceable after a time of upheaval:

Well, when we first moved in, it was 23 years ago, to this house, the neighbours was all very stable, and then they was stable for about maybe 10 years, 9, 10 years and then they all sort of moved, a lot of them moved out the area, wanted to move out, and then the sort of new people come in, this side they're stable again, I've got Chandra here and I've got the Reynolds next door, Hardys have lived here for 25, more than me, so this side of the road is very stable, fairly stable, the other side of the road is settling down, it went up and down a bit, and so yes, really it is fairly stable to be quite honest, it's been one big move the last 10 years and then it's settled down again.

The area worked well as a multi-ethnic multicultural community, he felt. But, like everyone we met in Heston, he became very exercised on the subject of asylum seekers:

I got a lovely Asian neighbours, very very friendly, very nice, but I think, you know, how far can you go with ... er ... with ... taking them in, if that's the word, and that is, you see the thing is ... another thing up the road here they got a big hostel, cos you know, and we get all the refugees come in there, so the refugees flood out and then the trouble is, first of all you had the sixties, you had the Asians, and then you've had the, I don't know, you've had Italians here, you've had Bosnians here, you've got the Africans here, and you've got the Ethiopians, whatever it is in the ... so there's someone coming here all the time, there's a refugee type coming here, but to be fair to them, though there's a real mixture, as far as I can see they are pretty law abiding...

The reason was that a hostel had opened, logically next to the airport, to house asylum seekers:

Now that hotel, funnily enough, was owned by British Airways, it was built by British

Airways to house the apprentices, and then they changed their policies, Oh I don't know, seventies late seventies and they changed their policies from you know, their recruitment and they sold it some Asians, and the Asians have then re-leased it on to Hounslow Council, and Hounslow Council used it for, first of all for homeless, I think it was then, it was for the homeless and people like that, and it's gradually been used for, homeless still but mostly for refugees in the last, I don't know, 10 years, different types of refugees, you've had, as I say you've had Africans, Somalians, Ethiopians, you've had them all there, you know...

But the biggest problem for him, as for many others, were the Irish travellers:

... the only race that isn't law abiding and they're trouble, are the Irish, unfortunately, and you know all these Irish travellers, now Hounslow Council have got a habit of housing them and even down where my mum lived down Church Road, they housed them down there, and they used to burn the house down, so, and I've seen these, and there are a group down here and they were all over the place, you used to get them all over the place... There's a group ... I see the other day, of Irish travellers, you know, and OK they might be OK but a lot of them are causing trouble. You find the kids all over the place, and you know, they're dumping things everywhere, and junk in their gardens and things, you know ...

One problem resulting from the influx was in the local schools:

... when we went to school there wasn't a language problem, you know, obviously with the schools today the kids going into school today, you've got a 50/50 split, you've got half the Asians I think are really westernised, maybe more than 50, very westernised, no problem with English or whatever it is, going to school, but you're still, I think what I hear from the neighbours I know, the problem's growing and growing and growing, that the kids, some certain kids are being held back because the others have got to learn the basic English before they can pick up the general education and I think that is a problem and I think, and you know that's a problem in quite a lot of age levels, if you know what I mean, not only the 4 or 5 age level, I think it's more also the 6 and 7 age level, and it's not all the, sorry, it's not only Asian, to be quite honest, it's Eastern European as well now, cos as the Eastern European comes here and they can't speak English, children are being pushed into schools, now first thing a lot of them want to do is push them into schools, but what they don't obviously understand is before the kid can understand what is being taught, he's got to know the language, so that will hold back others and I think that's been coming up more and more now really.

He too finds a sense of deterioration in the area, with growing crime associated with a collapse of the old bonds of community:

Yeah, Oh yeah, there was an era, no, there was an era where you might not have known everyone personally … but you knew him, you know, the walking bobby and things like that, and you felt safe, and you don't, I tell you what, you don't feel safe now without any doubt, I don't care who you are, you know, we even lock the back door even if, in the day if my wife's here like on her own during the day, the back door's … because of the massive rise in crime, and I think if I had to judge one thing out of my life which I'd like to see changed it would be the stem of crime without any doubt, and it's rising at a fantastic rate… Hounslow West is an area, Hounslow bus garage is an area where there's a lot of violence, and people just won't go there at night, which I thought that was sort of areas like the Bronx in New York, or Harlem, you know, but it's definitely round here as well now, definitely.

The town centre was deteriorating and people were going elsewhere to shop, to Staines or Kingston:

Yeah, people are going to Kingston, Hounslow is coming a real dump, I'm telling you that now, it's a shame really, I've seen it as a beautiful shopping centre, it was really really, in fact it was such a nice shopping centre when we were younger we all used to meet there every Saturday afternoon, or before football and have a walk down the High Street, and they've really let it go down, really, and also, all the major stores, as I say, if Woolworth's, Debenhams and C&A, if they pull out, cos that's a really good Woolworth's there, they'd have a problem, then it would not be worth going to the place at all really.

The old sense of community, he feels, has been eroded because people are out at work all day and no longer meet in local shops – and also, of course, because of the pervasive fear of crime:

… my mother was brought up in the era of the corner shop, and she used to walk up the road and I used to walk up with her, and that is another thing that's killing neighbours, sorry, that is another thing that's killing off the friendliness, see, where you would walk up every day to get a certain items you would meet people, you would talk to them, like maybe your parents and things, you would talk to them 'Oh how are you?', you would talk to the local policeman, to the local guy crossing the road, the road sweeper, you don't see that any more cos you jump in the car, you drive up the superstore, you buy your frozen gear, whatever it is, you get back in your car and you don't see anyone.

And there is a more general decline in physical quality, related to a change in attitude; he blames the local council for a deterioration in service:

The change hasn't been for the better because I think, I've grown up in an era where, not been strict discipline but it's been discipline and, not only discipline from home but discipline from a ways of working and council working and the places, the place, like for instance, I'm not happy with the way the Council has got such a large, large sort of control that you don't get things done anymore, you know, then I've seen dirt in the streets, I've seen you know, rubbish, I've seen foxes running around tearing bags open every night, and there's no control over that now … there's an old cinema at Hounslow West, dead opposite the station, that's now been converted, if you drive round the back of, it's a supermarket, if you drive round the back, all round back there, and the back of car parks, and you'll see sacks of stuff dumped everywhere, and there's rats everywhere, I tell you what, my mother would turn in her grave actually because she used to say to me, you know, how good it was and what ever, and I never thought I'd rats running down the end of your garden, do you know…

The problem, he believes, is that all local services are increasingly stretched to perform more services while facing cuts in resources:

I suppose thinking of the police and things like that, we're a lot larger community now, a smaller community was easier to serve. The trouble is, the major problem today, without any doubt, is this famous word, two famous words and we use them at work as well all the time, inflation and cost cutting, and they go together, and everything is either inflation, when they wanna put things up, like they do regular, it's inflation, and when they wanna cut things, which they do all the time, they call it cost cutting, because of inflation, and that's the two go together, and that's what's happened, you're getting less people what you're, erm, you get less people like on the streets, like from road sweepers, from guys, dustbinmen, policemen, postmen, and everything's cut down and the services are definitely deteriorating, so when you're, when you're a resident and you are paying over a £1000 pound now a month, sorry you're paying over a £1000 a year tax, rates, you wonder what you're getting really.

Everyone, he said, had already left or was getting out:

Yeah, well, everybody, all my friends now, and the last one moved out this area in April, have got out of Heston, they've all got out of Heston, might not be, cos Staines is only 6 mile from here so in the car it's not far, and they just moved across the M25 there, but they're all out of Heston, they are really, they've erm, and I think looking back when you've been in an area you've grown up in and you've seen it change so much, it's not really, you want to remember it as it was, if you know what I mean, and a lot of them they just wanna get out, and they're not all getting out because of any racial problem, or, that might be some of the problems for some of them, or immigrant problem or what ever it is, it's also, this place has got so busy now, the roads and the hustle and bustle, and the dirtiness of it.

And he too has been planning to move out to the coast, taking early retirement:

I've been contemplating moving out, must be the last good few years, 5, 6, 7 years, and every time I've gone to move there's something come up that's blocked it like, kids at school, going to a new school, changing schools and so I've waited till they're ... erm, finished school, and then I'm sure I'll move out ... I don't think we'll get too far, either towards the coast, 10, 20, 15 to 20 mile from the coast cos I'm working it with retirement, early retirement, or maybe a little bit west, past Bournemouth way, that way somewhere, but not miles in the middle of nowhere, no.

Sandhya

Sandhya is a Hindu married mother with one son, in her forties, employed part-time in a launderette, and a homeowner. She has lived in England since 1976 following an arranged marriage to an Indian from Uganda, first in Southall, moving here in 1988. They live on Bath Road, near Hounslow West station. All of the houses on her side of the street are privately owned; she can't say for sure about the other side. Her son is studying for an MA in engineering at King's College but is living at home. All of her husband's family live here, but none of her own family. The area in which she lives has a very mixed ethnic composition, with a largely middle-aged and elderly population. Race relationships, she felt, are complex. Older whites were racist, but so were Asians:

English older ladies, they're completely racist, they don't, they don't want to see any coloured people, and they're always talking about the refugee people, look at the mess there, they don't like ... Asian community is very bad because Asian, Asian community don't like Asian each other, that is a problem.

Like everyone else in Heston, she is obsessed by the topic of asylum seekers, who she says come wearing long dresses and cover their heads and steal from her business. It has happened a number of times and appears to involve different people each time:

... and everyone is coming there is, I'm sorry to say there is some rough people, you know, I mean yeah ... you know, it's all dirty, all messy now and not very good ... we think, we don't feel safe now, I mean when we come out from 7, 8 O'clock, 9 O'clock from the house we don't know, you know, they are stealing with their ... or ... hard time, so don't feel safe much... No, there's so many refugees here now, even I, I got a shop here, still I don't feel very safe ... don't ... I don't feel safe, if I am alone here I just try to lock the door ... yeah?... Because they are nicking so many things ... nick the money or something, they are after the money.

Not only that: their house has been broken into twice. She is very concerned about the effect on her son:

So they just took everything there in my house and, you know … everything … my son got a very nice computer I got for him and they took the computer unit and everything, which one is alright, we are grown up … you know, which one they took other things, you know, some jewellery and videos and … but when they took all his, his personal things then he said, 'It's, it's not fair with us, we work hard with our lives. Six months, one year we make a plan to buy a thing, then we work hard, then we earn some money, collect some money, then we buy the things, and they just come and spend half an hour and took away everything and nearly five, six thousand pound'. My, my son, he work hard in holiday time and collect some money for the computer and later they come just to spend half an hour they took the computer away and everything is gone. He, he is a younger brain, he think that's easy way to earn the money. So that's a … it's crime is a … and they break my whole house and lock inside, all the doors, everything, even I, I can't sleep nearly one month, it's in the night time … me, you know, somebody is coming in night time.

And, like so many other Indians, they have been very disappointed with the standards of their local school. It seems that they may have a higher expectation of the education system than white parents who send their children to state schools:

You know, sometime I ask him, 'Why you don't do that study at home?' you know, he said, 'Nobody give me that. My teacher is all the time is … she's on sick or sometime she's on holiday', and he said, 'I … you know, wasting my time to go there, and sometime there is no any lesson in the school'. So I must say, you know, the school was a worser school, you know, it's my big mistake to put my son in *** school … it's not only with my son, it's all the children. If you give the private study, tuition or something so that you are alright, otherwise if you just leave on the school study the children is not happy with their … because there, there, there, you know, there is not enough study anyway in the school, teacher not well…

Everyone, she says, is trying to move because of the feeling that the area is going downhill:

That's why … like us, you know, living from long time. Everyone wants to move from here now… Yeah, yeah, the Asian people like us, you know, I live here 25 years and sometimes we are thinking, my son said we should move from here, it's not safe area now… Yeah, we are thinking to leave, we go on the side, you know, where there are not many refugee people there.

The white population are moving out, she thinks:

Yeah, they are moving, you are right, they are moving now (*laughs*) … if any sort of house on the sale it's all the coloured people coming and English is going. Maybe they're going because of the area is not good, you know.

But the Indians feel exactly the same:

So we are like English people, we know how to live, because we have grown up here. So ... our living standard, our thinking, everything is like English now because it's a long time we live, but that people is completely different. We never give the harm anybody, we never ... we work hard in this country, we never try to steal the money and nick the money to give somebody and stolen everything in the stores, anywhere, we never try this one? We are different, yeah?

Jalil

Jalil is Indian-born, in his sixties and now retired. His wife works in a pharmacy in Hounslow, and they have three daughters all living at home. He has lived in this area since 1977:

Because when I came from India my all, my friends were living in this area, so I came in this area.

They originally rented this house but then bought it under the right to buy scheme in the 1980s. They have spent some time in Essex, but they felt isolated there, compounded by the fact that he had developed a problem with his knee, requiring two operations:

Essex is a very ... again, isolated area, then in these circumstances that if I'm going to be ill the whole of my life then I would like to stay in Hounslow, where I can have lots of acquaintances and er ... that's why. So, then this is why in '85, '86, '87 we bought this property, '85 or '87. We bought this property after my second operation, actually, we thought that ... that we should have somewhere.

This was very largely an Indian, specifically a Gujerati, area:

Yeah. The total neighbourhood area is a mixed area. On one side of this ... road you will find all Asians, quite prosperous ones, and the other side are all, this is council area, so they're predominantly white again. Same if we go little bit further, all the houses, private houses are occupied mostly by Asians and especially from Gujarat province, 24 councillors, Asian councillors. Asians and, when I say Asian – Muslim, Hindu and Sikh...

But generally, he saw the area as a very well-established middle-class Gujerati neighbourhood:

Gujarat, people from Gujarat are very strongly associated with business. There are lots of business, rows and rows of people after, near Hounslow, Rosemary Road and

Rosemary Avenue and the other, there are two or three roads ... where residents are from Gujarat mostly, about 70, 80 per cent. And they are very well established... Some of them have business in Wembley, some of them in Harrow, some of them have businesses around the er ... in London and still they come here, same as with Osterley, we have lots of ... business people living in Osterley. It's a posh area and, you know, very big houses and jacuzzis and all these things and so ... yes, these private areas are beautiful areas actually.

He felt he knew the area and its people extremely well:

(*Laughing*) So, it's, yes, I know lots of people in this area, as I said, and erm ... but whether they are friends? We have a few friends, yes, about seven, eight, nine, ten, we could call them friends, but rest of the people I know, almost whole community over here, and I know their ... childrens and their even children's children.

Another factor was that his children had got a good education here, he felt:

... at least I'm satisfied that I manage, my children's got good education, two are, one is already a practising barrister, the other girl, a daughter is a barrister, qualifying, qualified just, you know, almost qualified now, this year...

But that was no longer the case:

Recently they have neglected, in the last 10, 15 years ... I thought Hounslow was a very good education authority, but in the last 10, 15 years they have neglected education altogether... Actually I would rather, if had I been the inspector I would call some (*laughing*) extraneous body, somebody to take over the education from the Council ... some two, three schools you just don't have any A levels... Because it is admitted fact that people from subcontinent, India and (*phone ringing*) and in Pakistan, especially India and Pakistan, they are very intelligent people, given ... opportunities or given proper education and proper incentive and ... er, little bit encouragement they can do wonderful, wonderfully well, but they are not being encouraged, and this education is going down and down, down drains ... predominantly white school, they have better standard, which are predominantly Asian schools the teachers just give in and they just don't do anything.

He thinks that there is a particular problem of bullying of Indian by black children in Hounslow schools:

In Hounslow all the schools are like this, the bullying is just, just, just and ... endemic or epidemic? (*laughs*) I don't know which word to use ... usually it is ... more so between, actually, black and Asians, there's more bullying, actually, black and Asians.

He reported that there had been racial problems in the past. But they had subsided, he thought:

.... not to that extent, once or twice our window was broken, erm ... but the only crime we suffer from, we get lots of bullying, as I was told, talking in the beginning, that there was lots of problems, and these people just get together and they were, some these, some of these families they created some for ... one summer it was just living in a hell, and that was neighbours from hell. It has ... subsided, it has, things have changed little bit but still at occasions we do get, but I don't know now for last 20, 15 days there are, there's some movement going on through the Dole centre...

The area was going downhill, he felt, because incompetent councillors were allowing the creation of lower-class ghettos:

Yes, these ghettos are being created, actually, knowingly ... all these councils they are ... I personally feel they are responsible, they're ... all these things what is happening to people, they just don't consider them as people ... and the other thing, we have twenty ... of these people all old ... in Council, hardly educated, some of them even can't spell a letter, I mean, most probably can't spell the ... name of their own street ... one day they do one thing and then next day they break it because the planning has been so defective and then they go again...

He intends firmly to leave the area, but not to leave London:

I would definitely now. Once I ... the children now, when my daughter finishes her education I would definitely think that if I could get rid, go away somewhere from here, I would take the first opportunity... I won't leave London... I'll leave London only when I'm ... when I'm either in grave or in cremation. I won't leave London. London is the ... I am, I am just in love with London... I wouldn't leave London not at any cost, so long I'm alive. Erm ... definitely not Hounslow, I'll leave Hounslow, but not London. There are lots of other beautiful places in London.

Surjit

Surjit is a representative in our sample of the younger Indian generation: in her case, a second British-born Indian generation. A single Sikh woman in her twenties, a student living in her parents' owner-occupied home, she was born here and so were her parents:

My dad used to work in the airport about a year ago, in the control tower, but now he just works local, just works down the road, Hitachi building. It's really nice quiet area, that all I can really say. Friendly people.

They moved here from the Harlington area of Hayes, another locality, mainly for family reasons:

Just moved here from … we living down Harlington area, down Bath Road. Erm, we moved here because it's local for my travelling to university and also because my aunt lives down the road and it's sort of like family, close knit area… My aunt live down, just down the road at 68 and she's been living here for about 12 years, we used to come to visit her and then one day we were just driving down and we was, you know, we were thinking of moving from that house and we saw a for sale sign here and then we just decided, Oh, this is a nice house, nice area, close and … try and get this house. So…

She described the archetype of a middle-class area:

It's a stable area, yeah, everybody's in good jobs, I think. Next door is an accountant. That's on rent so I can't really say much about them, but the person who owns the house, he seems like a stable guy, he's got a couple of houses down this area and he rents them out.

But it was also more Indian than their previous locality:

… there's more Asians, you'd find more Asians here, that was more erm … there was a couple of Asians and it's more a white area.

But she mentioned the existence of a 'bad' estate:

I've heard the *** estate area is, and we don't usually walk down there by ourselves. Erm … there's quite a bit of racist behaviour gangs down there, I've heard this, I haven't experienced any of this, but I've heard this from my aunts and other ladies that go and drop their children off at *** School, I've heard that they've had a few bad experiences.

She herself could recall only one minor racial incident:

I haven't … I haven't experienced any racism here but I have experienced racism in the area I used to live, in Hayes. Once we did have a nasty experience, it was just a lady just being abusive. That was my first racist experience. Yeah. It was like just general stuff like her getting mad and then just saying nasty things like going back, go back to your own country, sort of … I was just down the street, it was this little misunderstanding. I think we was, my mum indicated her car and she just thought that, you know, she didn't give way, and then she came out of her car and she started throwing abuse, so that was my first real racist experience and it wasn't very nice. (*Laughs*)

Sewa

Sewa is another representative of the new Indian generation: a single Sikh woman in her late twenties, employed as a desktop publisher, living at home in an owner-occupied house on the busy Great West Road with an extended family and young child (not hers). She was born in London but her parents are originally from India. They moved to this area from East London, living first in Southall and then in Hounslow where they have been for about 8 years. They always had stronger connections to Hounslow than to Southall, even while living there; she went to school in Hounslow, her parents would go shopping here.

She does not feel particularly Indian or Asian:

Me personally, no, not really. Cos I was, you know, maybe cos I was older when I'd move there, if I'd grew up there perhaps I would. I grew up in more of a white area, when I was younger.

She also had very little consciousness of racism:

… a couple of times when I was younger, in my teens. But not much. Throughout my whole time in London there hasn't been much, but say on (*child interrupts*) … the total amount in my whole life is probably (*laughs*) (*child interrupting*) probably not more than about seven or eight. Total amount of racist incidents throughout my whole life is probably not more than, you know, as I say, seven or eight... It's not bad. (*Laughs*)

She went to university because this was the Indian middle-class norm:

There were lots of, no, there were lots of people who went to university but I think it's more because they come from Asian families and their parents expect them to go to university rather than the fact that the schools are very good here. The schools are rubbish. And … but there are a lot of people, I mean, going to university is definitely the norm in this area, I would think. Out of my class of, say, thirty students, I would have thought that 75 per cent of them ended up at university. Even though they might not have been particularly bright, or, you know, exceptional, it's just because it's expected.

Educated as an engineer, she got into her current job, desktop publishing for an investment bank, by chance after responding to an advertisement in the *Guardian*:

Just a fluke, as I say, just an advert in the paper. It was just basically cos I was temping and it was good wages.

She is very happy with her work:

My job is fabulous. It has, I have no stress whatsoever.

She only works at the weekends, because she gets paid more money for this and then she has five days free. For her it is important that her life does not revolve around work:

I have five days free. And so ... you know, I might be looking after him or ... just, you know, doing whatever I wanna do. I like to not be tied down to a job, you know. Not to feel your life revolves around work. Life can revolve around whatever you wannit to do.

This area, along the Great West Road, was unusual in having a mixture of Indians and elderly whites:

This stretch? There's a lot of elderly people here. Er ... unusually there's mostly white people who live down this road, which, I don't know, you've obviously seen Hounslow, it's a lot of, high Asian population, so ... that's quite unusual.

It was not, she suggested, a particularly friendly or neighbourly area:

I don't think so. Not in this bit of the Great West Road really, not as far as I know. I know there are some streets where, you know, everyone knows everyone, but I don't think there's any sort of, there's not very much, I mean, we talk to our neighbours, obviously, but erm ... no, we don't really know people that well. And we've lived here, as I say, for 8 years.

The area was changing, and not for the better:

... it's just more, more rental accommodation and it's just ... every surge of refugees that comes in seems to come into this area as well. When there was all that stuff about Hong Kong going on, you saw like quite a rise in Chinese people, though they seem to have moved on, and now there's a lot more people from the Bosnia Serbian area, although I couldn't identify which was which, you know. And a lot of Somalians as well come in. Over the past few years really, it's been more noticeable. You know, prior to that it was more just Asians...

Though relatively crime-free, it seemed that the area was becoming more and more a kind of transit camp:

Er ... it seems to be coming a bit more ... a lot more rented accommodation and less people who've lived here for a long time, more people who just seem to be passing through. And it just changes the character a bit.

Now her parents are moving further out of London, mainly to get away from the noise and pollution:

Just, it's … cos of the main road, airport, it's all quite polluted and dirty, isn't it? It's a nice area for other reasons, you know, to get into London and things like that, but it's just … it is really polluted.

Rajiv

Rajiv, British-born of Indian origin, represents the newest Indian generation of all. In his teens, he is a sixth former. His parents were East African Asians:

… my mum came over from Kenya, I don't know when, and my dad came over from Uganda somewhere, and I don't know when.

For him, this is a harmonious enough place. And racism is not a problem at all:

Racism, no way, I haven't had experienced it at all, I don't think. Only … no, I think it's only like really really minorly if I have, that's not even a word, but still, no, I haven't experienced it that much and I don't think that there is much racism, but everyone says that in … they state that there is so, and it's always in the newspapers, the local newspapers and stuff, and on the local radios that there is racism but, I mean again I'm like totally sceptical about that, and if you see any other Asian young guy round my age, they'll probably tell you that there is a lot of racism and stuff. But I don't see that… I mean it hasn't happened to me, so, and it's only a couple of cases which they tell me about and it's only like hardly ever that it happens to them. I mean it doesn't happen on a, like a regular basis or anything, but I mean it's happened once or twice here and that's about it, and so I wouldn't say that is that much of an issue.

His friends from school are drawn from every group and every area:

… most of my mates are white and black and yeah, just mainly white and black, and there's a couple of Asian friends as well, but I mean I don't know, it's nothing to do with area really, I mean I just got to know them through the school and yeah, just through the school and that, and so it's not to do with the location really.

But life here, he feels, is also boring:

I think the people round here are all right, yeah, but I mean in terms of like everyone getting along with everyone, like the ideal type, it's not that I think. It's like close, like each and every person has their like friends and type of thing, but I mean life round here is dull. Right, I would say that, I mean I've like been living here all my life and so you get bored of it.

One problem is the juxtaposition of respectable middle-class Indian areas and estates that are very much the reverse:

Along here, I reckon you'll probably see mainly Asians and that, and, but down the road, it's just like really close here, about the round the corner literally, it's, there's an estate and there's … estate and it's quite rough and so, and there's like whites and that, but it's like, it's mainly a mixture, it's not mainly whites down there, it's just like total, like … there's like a whole mixture of people round here.

Asked what he means by 'rough', he answers:

I mean it's known to be rough, I mean by the police and that, there's always trouble going on around there … I don't know, like kids bashing in cars and like bashing in windows and like stuff like that. Cos there's always police cars going, driving down there like, with their sirens blaring and stuff.

Linda

Linda represents a new white generation, drawn here – like so many others – by the need to live near her job at the airport. She is a mother in her late twenties or early thirties, living with her partner in a privately rented house:

… I moved here 18 months ago. Previous to that, I'd … grown up in Buckinghamshire, and always lived in there or Berkshire around and really, it's just through meeting Martin really. So I'd always, I'd worked for British Airways for, until March this year, nearly 10 years. So I said, 'I don't mind moving in, move towards London', so that's how come. We rent this house because we're not sure where we want to go eventually and that's how we came to be here.

She feels the area is quite stable and quiet:

Well, in terms of … people, it's predominantly Asian, so … I think it actually has quite a peaceful effect because they generally … in, if it's predominantly Asian, as opposed to Afro-Caribbean and Asian, it, they're, they're quite, they're very family orientated, they're quite respectful, well, they are very respectful, you know, within their families and I think that rubs off on the general area itself. So we don't really get any like … violence or anything and then, there's a lot of white people who have obviously lived here for about 50 years, a lot of old white people and so really, I think the mix is quite good.

Hounslow in reality is much better than its reputation, she thinks:

'Oh, you know, God no, I don't want to go and live in Hounslow'. And I think it had,
I think it does have a reputation, outside of Hounslow, of being quite a rough place
to live. But actually having, now living here … I wouldn't necessarily, if I had to put it
on a list of five places to live, it probably wouldn't make the list, but I actually quite
like living here, in terms of like the shops are nearby and … there's, you know, quite
a lot going on really, so it's not that bad.

She goes up to Central London a lot, but also enjoys visiting Chiswick,
which is nearer, with her son:

Yeah. A lot, my brother lives in London and like one of my closest friends, they live
in London, so I just like going to London, I always have done since 17 year old,
whatever. We do go up there for entertainment… I like going to the theatre and just
going out for meals, or it depends if it's in the day time, then I like going to museums
and galleries, but Martin's not really interested, so, but I do go and do that… I go up
to Chiswick a lot … not so much now but if I want specific things, but then that's only
down the road. You forget sometimes that you … although you say go into Central
London, you actually feel like you're slightly outside London, but you're not really.
Cos if you … Chiswick's only up the road and that is London, so… It's just that me
and my friends used to go after work, so I guess we liked the atmosphere, like the
different wine bars and restaurants, but now it's got a really good Baby Gap (laughs),
so I don't really go to … the wine bars any more, I go to … I take … they've got
Gunnersbury Park, which is like at the end of Chiswick High Road, so … I go there a
lot with Sam and so and then I might pop into the shops or whatever … a really good
park for young children.

But she, too, recognises a downside in life here:

I suppose the only negative thing I … is the amount of traffic, like here, it just seems
like, with the planes and the cars, you're just surrounded by pollution. Because of the
proximity to Heathrow, and so for people who are coming in, the immigrants coming
in, who are waiting to have their … what do you call it, visas or whatever processed,
to see if they can actually stay, this is one of the areas where they're housed. And I
don't have a problem with that, but I do have a problem, I was like threatened, when
I was walking out with Sam and that was in the daytime and it was just like, sort of
like hustling more than anything, and they were, I'd say Eastern Europeans from the
language they were speaking. So, I didn't like that, that's the only thing. Because, you
know, it's not their fault, they haven't got any work and they just have, all they've got
to do all day is walk around and, you know, it's while they wait to hear, but that's the
only bad point, I would say.

And, though she wants her child to have a multicultural education, she is concerned that in practice that will not happen here:

I would like him to go to a school where it's multiracial, so there's ... Asian, black, Chinese. But this school round the corner, they had, it was ... reception class for 5 year olds and they had the month of the year all round the school, all round the classroom with everyone's birthdays and what month. And there was one Western name and they were all Asian... I don't want him to be the only white child in an Asian class, cos if, yes, if I went to live in India, that's what I'd expect, so that's why I wouldn't necessarily want him to go here. But there's another school, where he goes to playgroup ... and that looks really good, they've got a complete mixture, they've got everything, Asian, black, white, everything, Chinese. So, in terms of thinking about school it's like, if we were here, I'd say I'd want to try and get him into that one.

She and her partner are concerned that they will not be able to afford to buy a house here:

Housing definitely (*laughs*). I mean you know, it's ridiculous. If you wanted to buy a property now, you need to either have a whole stash of money saved up, or earn an absolute fortune which you know, the average salary does not add up to what people need to buy a house... So yeah, I do think housing is way too high.

So they are actually contemplating a move abroad:

We might actually be going to live in France. Initially, it will just be for 5 months, for a ski centre, and it will be working as a, Martin's a massage therapist, so it's actually a job for a couple, one to be a cook and one to be a massage therapist, so I'll be cooking in a chalet.

Adeola

We found it almost impossibly hard to interview the latest wave of arrivals: they could not be found because they did not have regular addresses, and perhaps because they did not want to be interviewed. But Adeola is an exception. A divorced Nigerian mother in her thirties, she is employed casually through an agency, and is a housing association tenant:

Yeah, well, I got married, we had a flat in Chiswick, and then ... I got pregnant again, I got ... when I was bearing my second child, we decided to get a bigger place, cos we had a flat then, and then things sort of fell apart, my husband and I, we did buy a place in Hampton actually, but then I think things fell apart, though I did manage to get this place, so I moved in here with the kids.

She had mixed feelings about Chiswick:

Chiswick is nice, Chiswick, yeah, it was ... nice to look at, well, I have to say, sometimes I did feel like, I dunno, but I did feel a bit poor living there, I will say, when I first moved here that was one of the things that was a relief in a way, you could sort of, you know, knowing that people are in the same boat as you, yeah, in Chiswick, like people opposite us, you know, had like ... lawyers, and they had a Mercedes estate, and you know, stuff like that, and you know, always going on holidays, and most people around there, yeah, so, yeah, I did, you know, and you know it's, do you know what I mean, 'Oh we went away' and stuff like that, 'Oh yeah, you know', and I went 'Yeah, I don't know', (laughs) so I mean it was nice, that was one of the first things, when I moved here at first, I did like that, thinking you can say to somebody 'Oh God, I don't know what I'm gonna do next week', and you know they know where you're coming from...

But she did not feel particularly comfortable here either:

Lots of Indians, I don't like it very much, it's just, I don't know, I just find Indians are, ones that are nice, I mean it's not nice to put people in er, in er, in er sort of category, or what ever, and say, you know, I hate it when people do that, say 'this group of people are bad' but you know what I mean, generally, you know, the ones that are nice are very nice, and the ones that aren't are terrible.

She had one experience which suggested that some whites were racist towards black people:

... where I was working I was always in tears, about 3 weeks ago this, it was a day centre, this older woman, and she was ... typical English woman and she was very nasty, cos I had my hair braided then and it was very long, and ... Oh she said some horrible things ... she was very nasty, she says, you know, 'That black girl think she's doing? Get that muck off your hair, and she's touching my food', and things like that, you know, I was very upset, and it was interesting because the two managers there, there's a black one and there's a white manager, and the white manager was saying 'Oh she doesn't know what she's doing', and all that, and the black manager was saying 'She does know what she's doing, it's not, you know...'.

She has one good neighbour, but with others there seems to be no relation at all:

I'm very lucky, my neighbours, there's Simon, he's fabulous, very nice man, he's been, he's really helped me, he does things for me, I didn't talk to the other, my other neighbours, we didn't fall out or anything, it's just, we just never spoke, and I don't know why... I dunno, I would find most people that live on estates and council properties, they seem to think not having money is an excuse to behave badly.

She suggests that some Indians are racist:

I think they're more racist, almost as if, it's almost like, you know, when they say people who are uneducated are the ones that are racist, and things like that, not knowing any better, I find Indians are, Oh gosh, I mean because as far as I'm concerned I would expect white people to be racist but not Indians, oh yeah, they're really funny.

And, like almost everyone else we interviewed, she complains that the area is visibly going downhill:

Oh it's changed for the worst, this estate, I think, we were the first, it was brand new when we moved in... It was really nice when we moved in and everything, just, you know, the park, it's just... Oh ... the kids, literally, they've been digging out the bricks, literally, just, you know, big holes in, and you wonder, and, Oh my car was, one day I came back and the windscreen had been smashed, it wasn't an accident, Simon came and said 'A little boy just...' not a little boy, one of the kids over there, they were smashing, they literally came out with a, things, bat, and went smashing, they smashed the windscreen.

She has family here in London, but they do not seem at all close:

Well, I've got my sister, I've got, I've got two sisters, and two brothers around, but they're not near me, like my sister lives in Finchley and the other one lives in Gypsy Hill, down in South London, my brother lives not very far, actually, Twickenham... No, we just, you know, we talk on the phone, and stuff, or your birthdays and stuff like that, we get together as much as possible and that's it really, everybody's so busy doing their own thing.

Nor does she seem to have many friends here, either locally or more widely in London:

Very few, very very few, because this is so far from (pause), yeah, very few, most people who I was, went to school with, because my husband was, maybe I dunno, maybe because my husband was white, so it sort of ... I don't know, I don't what it is, I sort of, I, I didn't keep in touch with a lot of my friends from before, I didn't have many... I'm not very good at keeping friends, people call me and I never call back, I mean to but I just...

Partly, she claims, the problem is that Hounslow is too remote:

I never spent more than a tenner, £8, £7 to get to the West End, but here it's like miles away from everywhere, it's too … no, I do not like Heston.

Currently she has casual work in the kitchens of an airline catering firm:

… it's an agency I'm working with, so I go to different places, because of the children I can't take anything permanent, you know, cos I just never know, you know, which week I can work and which week I can't work. The plan was to go back to college this, this er, cos my youngest child has started full time, on Monday, so my plan was to go and get, and go to university or something and try and get some sort of qualification, but it's easier said than done.

It begins to emerge that hers is a case of downhill social mobility: she is deeply embarrassed by her present menial position:

I'm not quite sure what to do at the moment, to be honest, I don't like what I do now, and that's another thing, my friends are very sort of, a lot of them are well off, cos in Nigeria, my father was, he was in the Army…

In fact, she tells us, she grew up in a privileged position in Nigeria:

I as you can see I'm very idle, you know, gosh, at home you walk through the door and 'What you going to eat?' and clothes get washed, and everything done for you (sighs). Oh dear.

Her great fear now is of being recognised at work, because other Nigerians might work there and might leak the news of her menial position back home:

… and we had, it's hard to explain this, you know, it's the way things have changed… I said to her 'British Airways, do you know they've merged with Nigerian Airways, British Airways…'. You can't go, you can't go,' I say 'I'll go for one day, I'll go and see, and if there are any Nigerians there or anything then I'm not going'.

She likes the work, though, because it gives her flexibility in caring for her children:

Well, like I said, the good thing about it is that you can have days off, and you know, cos I, but the bad thing obviously is that you don't get paid if you're sick, or whatever, which can be horrible because, you know, but I don't like to mess people about, and you sign a contract, you're supposed to start work somewhere, and I just never know when I can work because I need to, the kids, you know, need me to take them to school, and most catering jobs start early, about seven, they like you to be there at seven or something like that, which is, I got her nan doing that, and she got really sick one time, cos she was coming from Chiswick, she was leaving home at six to get here, you know, I said to sleep here but she wouldn't, and she had her thingies, her medicines back home, she's a diabetic, and the poor lady almost had a stroke, you know, so it's just, I said 'No, it has to be anything after ten', and right now I'm doing this ten to two, I've been doing that for about 3 months now with the same company, they have asked me to stay permanent but, I thought about it cos I thought that would be nice, but then, I don't want, it's so easy to get stuck, you find yourself, you know, look back 5 years from now I'll still be there, and it's not what I want, I really don't.

She seems rather bizarrely to have retained her former affluent lifestyle, at least in her shopping habits:

... Knightsbridge, yeah, I like Harvey Nics, that's where I go... Yeah, buy myself something, I like to go to Harvey Nics, I like Knightsbridge, that's where I go to shop, I couldn't, oh gosh, no, you see the things I like, I like designer stuff you see, so, when I go out I like to look nice, (*laughs*) I'm not saying you can't look nice (*laughs*) oh gosh, what must you think of me?

But she recognises that despite all her advantages, her life has somehow gone wrong:

I used to go to Gucci every day, and then all of a sudden I find myself in a... The only thing I regret really is dropping out of school, you know, not taking my education seriously, everybody ... time. Plus my father always reminds me he spent a fortune, you know, big fortune.

Yet she plans to send her daughter to Roedean:

Nice posh school, yeah, so she can talk nice and posh.

She has converted to Catholicism in order to get her child into the best school in the neighbourhood:

So are you Catholic at the moment?

Yeah. At the moment, and the big thing was, I had to go to church, to be honest with you, they wanted me to go to church a few times and all that before Yasmin could go there so, so we ended up in Springwell, she's quite happy there, it's a good school...

She likes the school for its multicultural quality:

I like that fact that it's a multicultural, you know, I do like that, I suppose I thought to myself, you know, cos I mean the Catholic school, you know, there's only like one or two black faces there, and you know, I suppose I thought that would be good for her, and you know, but it's nice, I really love the way she pronounces all the Indian names and everything very well, she knows about Hindis and stuff, things, saris and you know, it's so multicultural and I really like that.

But she is clearly very unhappy with her Housing Association flat, and even more so with her neighbourhood:

I thought, my first thing was do it up, but every time I keep saying that, I want to be out of here, be out of here, be out of here, and you know, and thinking maybe I should do it up, just make it more, I just can't stand the place, I can't stand, it's not so much the house, but where it's at, I don't like it at all. I could be very happy in Cobham or Leatherhead, or Winslow or somewhere, I wouldn't even mind moving out a bit... We lived in Cobham once, I remember I was so miserable then because I was younger then, and I used to be 'Oh, I want to be in London', but now I think I've matured, yeah, even Reading, say. (*Laughs*)

But she seems to be suffering from a kind of terminal inertia:

I'm not very organised, I'm not, I don't, it's like that letter, I don't like opening letters, I'm … that is my biggest fault, I say to myself that I will do things, then I forget things, I'll come in … and … my husband 'Oh God'. You know, like in the kitchen he's got things written on the door, 'Tamara, Jade goes to school', big letters, you know like a to z he's marked it, you'd think I was a kid, you know, but I used to get annoyed but I know why he does it, I don't mean to be. I think it's the Nigerian in me, in my country, you know, people just don't take time seriously, you know, 'oh well, you know, so what, I'm 2 hours late, hey', you know...

Airport City in Holding Pattern

Heston is clearly a suburb in a state of massive transition. Until very recently whites and Indians have lived together in a stable, sociable and secure community with a good quality of life. In this sense, Heston is the archetype of what London has done so successfully over the last half-century: the creation of a peaceful, contented, middle-class multicultural way of life. But we found many people, from different ethnic and cultural groups, now very discontented: they told us they wanted to move out because the area was going downhill and wanted urgently to realise the equity in their houses. And some, who remained, saw this as a sign of failure. Again and again, they cited the arrival of asylum seekers, whom they blame for rising crime and harassment. But some mentioned Irish travellers. They were deeply anxious about the impact of all of this on children, both directly in the streets and parks, and indirectly through what they saw as the decline of the local school system. Change, they clearly thought, had got out of hand – at least, out of their hands.

It was a potent reason for choosing the exit option. They were also disparaging about what they saw as the poor quality of the local physical environment, especially the pollution and the noise and the dirt. But these views concealed the fact that others were quite content: it seemed that some areas were seen as deteriorating, while others were holding their own. People saw the town centre shopping and leisure facilities as reasonable, and were satisfied with their local council services.

The newest arrivals were in a way the most contradictory, the least consistent. There were young professionals who were working hard and who clearly just found this a convenient place near to their work, without any longer-term commitment to the area. And there was one downwardly-mobile arrival who was obviously unhappy and very isolated, living with dreams for herself and her children that she might never be able to fulfil. This was, we felt, a community in danger of ceasing to be a community: that community might well rebuild itself elsewhere, beyond the M25 in Surrey or Berkshire, but Heston's future lay in the balance.

Well Hall estate

© Bill Knight

Chapter Six

Garden Suburb Challenged

Eltham

Eltham is yet another of those interwar suburbs that sprawl along and between outer London's bypass roads – in this case the old A2 Rochester Way, built in the 1920s to relieve the old Roman Dover road, a mile or two to the north. But it is unusual in two ways. First, much of it is rented public housing – or, at least, housing built for public renting, for since 1980 most of it has been bought by its sitting tenants under right-to-buy legislation. And second, much of it is of unusual architectural quality: it is the 1200-house Well Hall estate, designed for Woolwich Arsenal munitions workers in 1915. Built in an amazing 10 months and one of the great triumphs of the garden suburb movement that stemmed from Raymond Unwin and Barry Parker's work at Letchworth and Hampstead Garden Suburb, it is in every way a worthy rival to them.

Renamed Progress Estate by the Royal Arsenal Co-operative Society when they took over the management in 1924, it began to sell houses to middle-class buyers and the area became a colony for creative people like the actress Sylvia Sims, BBC producer Dennis Main Wilson and Dame Mabel Crout – a quality it retains to this day, a kind of South East London answer to Hampstead Garden Suburb. Now, though the Co-op tradition survives in a big store close to the train station, most of the 'Progress Cottages' are in owner-occupiership, still commanding a premium when they appear in the local estate agents' windows, and clearly cherished by their proud owners. The Co-op sold the estate in 1980 to the Hyde Housing Association, which works energetically to maintain the area's Conservation Area status.

But Eltham is unhappily known for more than architecture. In 1993, it became notorious as the site of the murder of Stephen Lawrence, a talented black student. In consequence, it was widely represented in the media as a crucible of white working-class racism. That was of course a caricature, deeply resented by many residents. As we discovered, much of Eltham remains a stable and coherent community, settled by people – many from inner-city locations like Bermondsey – who have moved from their parents' homes a short distance down the railway line, and who use good transport links to maintain close mutual contact with their parents. Most are white, some belong to minorities; all have come here in search of a good physical environment for their children, and better schools. Many told us they 'fitted in' and felt psychologically comfortable here, and this was equally true for older white and younger ethnic minority members. But there were stark exceptions, especially in some of the council estates.

Eltham lies in the London borough of Greenwich, and thus on the margins of inner and outer London, about 5 miles downstream from Bermondsey and Peckham on the south side of the Thames. It occupies the southern half of the middle part of the borough, with Woolwich (and its huge Arsenal, now closed and redeveloped) to its north. Technically they now count as part of outer London, though before 1965 Greenwich as a whole was included in the old London County Council area and its social characteristics remain closer to the inner boroughs. Indeed it is a very mixed borough, both socially and environmentally, ranging from very desirable middle-class housing – especially near the royal parkland further south in Eltham – all the way to other working-class areas – as in Woolwich near the river – which are physically rather squalid. Unlike those inner boroughs, and indeed unlike most of London, this is also an area where large, stable employers (notably the Royal Arsenal) once provided a social base for organised labour – including the Royal Arsenal Co-operative Society and Woolwich Council, a flagship socialist borough in the 1920s, as well as the strong community spirit which had typified Well Hall. That economic base has now gone. But to the west, on the Greenwich peninsula, the now empty Millennium Dome and the next-door Millennium Village are tokens of the ongoing efforts to regenerate this area, part of the government's Thames Gateway scheme, through massive physical investment.

Some History

There were two very different, even contrasted keys to the development of this part of London: heavy industrial development on the banks of the Thames, and suburban expansion along three commuter railway lines which run in parallel west–east through the borough. These lines initially brought high-class development, including clusters of villas and developments such as the Eltham Park Estate where the substantial houses had servant annexes.

On the waterfront, in contrast, the Royal Arsenal grew from the seventeenth century to encompass large industrial buildings, and an artillery testing ground which was both noisy and grossly contaminating. Effectively, the Arsenal workers constituted a separate, isolated community, in many ways like the dockland communities across the river in Silvertown. They lived within walking distance of their work, historically in sordid housing. From the mid-nineteenth century, Woolwich also became the first seat in Britain of the new electrical engineering industry, when the great Berlin firm of Siemens established a factory to exploit the growing market for undersea telegraph cables, with heavy materials and products shipped in and out by water. Thamesside became the national centre for the industry, remaining so into the 1950s. All sorts of other basic, often polluting, industries set up along the waterfront – including paint, plaster, glass, chemicals, tanning, and milling. These firms also were typically large, and at its peak the local manufacturing base employed some 150,000 workers. As in Newham, this was generally industry that the rest of London did not want.

When the London County Council was established in 1888, these were among its outermost areas, and Eltham in particular was among the new housing areas built on electric tram routes to accommodate the working-class poor whom the LCC sought to move out from inner-city slums. This compromised the private developers' vision of the area as a series of superior bourgeois suburbs, leading in the inter-war years to an uneasy relationship between areas of speculative semi-detached housing which spread along the railway lines, and the LCC and borough estates along the tram routes. To complete this set of juxtapositions, in the late 1960s the newly-established Greater London Council built the Ferrier estate at Kidbrooke in North Eltham. Grim, neo-brutalist, instantly unpopular, it deteriorated rapidly and came to be used only for the most desperate and uncomplaining tenants – most recently, refugees and asylum-seekers; it has long been slated for demolition, which at long last was beginning when this book went to press.

Woolwich suffered particularly badly from London's deindustrialisation over the past 40 years. Between 1960 and 1990 its manufacturing base simply collapsed, a process highlighted by the closure of both the Arsenal's Royal Ordnance factory and Siemens (then the dominant employer) in 1967/68. Total employment in the borough continued to decline right through to the 1990s; a mere 9 per cent of jobs were in manufacturing in 1999. Today, as elsewhere in London, the economy is dominated by the service sector. But the borough has not really developed a strength in financial or business services, and so – comparable to Newham, but to an even greater extent than in other parts of east London – it unduly depends on public services: 35 per cent of employment is in health, education or public administration. Most of these jobs are concentrated on the Greenwich waterfront. With major development projects on the Greenwich peninsula and the Royal Arsenal, the borough now pins its hopes on retailing, leisure, tourism, and construction, with administrative, service and light industrial employment following in the longer term.

Eltham Today

So Greenwich is now more a dormitory suburb than an employment centre: 56 per cent of residents worked outside the borough in 1991. At the borough's extreme west end, public transport connections to central London have hugely improved with the 1999 opening of the Docklands Light Railway extension through central Greenwich and the Jubilee Line extension through North Greenwich, to be followed early in 2009 by another DLR extension to Woolwich Arsenal station. But the central and eastern parts still rely on the three commuter lines which provide a slow and sometimes uncomfortable journey to the centre. House prices remain below those in western suburbs or in more central areas.

In fact Greenwich remains predominantly what it always was: a working-class borough. At the 2001 census, just under 4 per cent of the population were unemployed but another 4 per cent were recorded as 'permanently sick or disabled'. Greenwich has a significantly larger-than-average social housing sector; under half of all households in the borough are owner-occupied. Educational achievements reflect the social class profile, with just 17 per cent qualified to degree level or above, while 21 per cent have no qualifications, and Greenwich school results are conspicuously below the London average. In terms of household composition, the significant features of the Greenwich population are a relatively high proportion (36.6 per cent) of single person households and a fairly high incidence of lone parent families (14.1 per cent).

Greenwich is however unusual for London in its ethnic composition. In 2001, 77.1 per cent of the population was white, above the average for a London borough: the largest minority group was Black Africans with 7.1 per cent, followed by Indians with 4.4 and Black Caribbeans with 3.2 per cent. The borough has an unusually low proportion for London of people born outside the EU, 14.7 per cent. Within local maintained schools 29 per cent of pupils in 1999 came from ethnic minority backgrounds, with 19 per cent having English as a second language. But, as in other parts of east London, the general perception is that it is young white males from poor backgrounds who are the under-achieving group, with problems not only of school performance but also of motivation and self-esteem.

The recently arrived asylum-seekers have distinct problems. By 1997, estimates indicate that they formed about 3 per cent of the borough population. They come from a wide variety of origins, including many Vietnamese and Somalis, but also Iranians, Tamils, Ugandans, Kurds and Eritreans. A local survey reveals a high level of isolation and exclusion among younger refugees, with few feeling their home culture was valued, a majority (particularly of girls) experiencing bullying, 80 per cent reporting that they felt unsafe in their local area after dark, and a quarter saying that they or a family member had been physically attacked. Some groups with high proportions of women and children (such as the Eritreans concentrated in Kidbrooke, including the Ferrier estate) seem to be living in near-total unemployment, experiencing severe poverty and isolation – while others (such as the Tamils) with more family units and mobile single men, and better education have good networks of community support and little unemployment. In the case of the two largest groups, the Somalis and Vietnamese, there is evidence of entrepreneurial potential, though currently they seem to experience barriers in realising this. Data on racist incidents (from the Policing London project) indicate that the risks of victimisation among the local black and Asian population are a good deal higher than in most parts of London – though this is a characteristic shared by other boroughs with a relatively small ethnic minority presence.

The IMD2004 index of local conditions indicates that Greenwich is the tenth most deprived borough in London and the 41st in all England. Unemployment remains well above the Greater London average, even if not as high as in Southwark or Newham. Local studies of the young long-term unemployed show that many have never worked while others have occupied only a series of short-term jobs, with many still being mentally oriented toward the lost industrial economy of the waterfront. However, average earnings among taxpayers are on a par with those in most of the case study areas. In fact conditions vary greatly between different parts of the borough: 30 per cent of the population, concentrated in a line of wards running north–south through the centre of the borough, figure among the worst 10 per cent of wards in England.

Our interviews took place in North Eltham, in the middle of the borough about 2 miles south of the river, comprising two wards with somewhat different character: Well Hall (already mentioned) and Sherard. (Their approximate 2001 Census equivalents are Eltham North and Eltham West.) The quality is sylvan, arcadian, a model garden suburb. Or, rather, two: the great Well Hall estate, and the much more modest, frankly dull, Page estate designed by the Woolwich Borough housing department in the years immediately after World War One. Well Hall (or 'Progress') is an urban design lesson: the infinite permutations of what were supposed to be only four basic designs give it a quality that is almost unsurpassed. Page, inevitably, is glummer: the uniform grey pebbledash casts a kind of institutional pall on the estate even on the brightest summer day, and the design, semi-detached houses around huge elongated open greens which have been partially and insensitively infilled with later development, seems oppressive. But both estates look south on the lively and beautifully-tended local park, Well Hall Pleasaunce, and back to the north on to the wooded slopes of Shooters Hill: an ideally arcadian setting.

Well Hall's higher-quality housing is popular and now mostly owner-occupied, with a small proportion of housing association-sheltered housing. Unemployment is low and residents appear to be relatively prosperous, often commuting into other parts of London to work. Sherard provides a sharp contrast: most of the housing is less attractive 1920s brick-built houses, on the Page estate still owned and managed by the local authority, and cut into four by major roads. In 2001 56.1 per cent of Eltham West residents lived in local authority housing, an exceptionally high proportion, against only 11.3 per cent in Eltham North. Here and on other local cottage estates, adjustment to the post-industrial economy has been slow, and currently Sherard is amongst the most deprived 10 per cent of wards nationally. Rates of unemployment (7.0 per cent in Eltham West in 2001, against 5.4 per cent for the borough as a whole and 3.4 per cent in Eltham North) and teenage pregnancy are higher than for London as a whole, and participation in formal education training and work among 17- and 18-year olds is among the lowest in the capital. These wards have particularly low proportions of non-white residents: their 2001 equivalents showed 18.6 and 6.9 per cent respectively, and one study of racism among local adolescents, in 1997, described them as 'at the front line of the white hinterland'. Like Bermondsey, this is an area where kith-and-kin housing allocation policies have maintained rather inward-looking local communities, although here there is a much stronger tradition of upward mobility.

Zoe

When we interviewed her Zoe, a white married woman in her twenties, employed and a homeowner, had been living here with her husband Steve for a little over 2 years. They had come here because they wanted to move out of the inner city; she was from Elephant and Castle, he from Deptford:

So what made you want to move out?

He: Well we both come from council estates. Not that there's anything wrong with that.

She: There are some nice people there, and stuff like that, but you just want to get out.

But they wanted to remain close enough to visit their family and have fairly easy access to their place of work. Although their friends and family are scattered they are all 'Within driving distance basically'. And that is what is important to them:

He: And now we've got the car and all that, we can see your mum ... we're then in 15–20 minutes, so she knows it's ... it's only like a phone call if she needs us and we're there in 15–20 minutes, so. And that was part of the consideration when we moved here, that we didn't want to be too far away … I mean, probably although we like the area, if parents weren't a consideration, we'd probably gone out further.

Really? What kind of area?

She: I really desperately want to go to Australia.

They found the area a big improvement on where they used to live in many ways:

She: I mean, compared to where we lived, this is so quiet…You can actually hear the birds chirping and things like that.

He: Yeah.

She: And foxes crying, you know.

He: When our parents come here, they say it's like being in the country don't they?… Because I don't know if you know about this little estate. They built these for the armoury workers in the First World War, so there's a lot of history. And they've all got quite nice features and character. So the house itself attracted us.

They also feel safer there:

Is crime and safety an issue for you around here?

She: I would feel 100 per cent safe walking round here in the dark on my own. Back home, I wouldn't have done, even though I knew the area better than I do here.

He: I would never feel unsafe here.

She: No, I don't.

He: The only thing I probably wouldn't do, as I say, unless I was going down there drinking myself, the High Street on a Friday or Saturday night can get a bit rowdy when it's pub turn out time, you know. If you're half drunk yourself, you probably don't care.

The services are better:

So in terms of quality of local services there seems to be some substantial differences?

She: Definitely.

He: I think Greenwich is pretty good. Although Greenwich is probably one of the most highest council taxes in the country, which isn't very good, the services are quite good.

It appears to be quite a family-oriented area, with many different age groups living there:

He: Yeah, you've got a lot of families. Like young families with kids. I mean, out of the people we talk to are like all ages. We've got a young couple who are younger than us, who've got a couple of kids, we talk to. And we've got the lady next door we talk to and she's sort of like 70. And then the guy next door is in his fifties, so it's all different ages really.

They found out about the area because they knew some people living in it, but having friends here did not actually prompt their move. They have in fact made many friends in the area since they arrived. They think the reason why people in the area are so friendly is because there is a lower turnover of people than they used to find on the council estate where they lived:

She: We've got lovely neighbours… we know more of our neighbours here than we did back where we lived… And I'd lived in a tower block for like… well, I'm 28. I'd lived there all my life and I've never known so many people as I have since I lived here…

He: In tower blocks, people come and go – quick turn over. Yeah, we've got quite a few friends. I don't know, I suppose like because we work and that, we're only here at nights and weekends, but you do… It's very friendly isn't it?

She: Yeah. I mean, people round here I find are quite friendly anyway. Well, most.

He: This side of the road. It's really weird. It's like there's a this side of the road and that side of the road… They're a miserable lot over there, but everyone along here's alright, but it's only because we don't know them probably.

She: Yeah, but they're just not very talkative so to speak.

He: They're the sort of people they'll look out for, you know, if you're at work or anything, they'll keep an eye on the place and they notice things. They're really good you know. Our neighbour's away at the moment and like you're feeding the cats and I'm watering his garden.

So you help them out?

He: As I say, we've never had so many neighbours that we've spoken to have we?

She: Because where we used to live, we didn't … wasn't no-one literally.

He: It was one big churn of people. You never knew from one day to another who was coming in and out.

They came back to the contrast with the estate on which they used to live:

He: And the thing is … estate cultures where if you, you know, you've got to be tolerant or you're at each other's throats with your neighbours all the time you know. So…

Is that just through lack of space or…?

He: It's lack of space and I think as well like, it's sort of … you know, the walls are thinner and you know, you've got to be tolerant of people.

She: You could hear every noise and things like that you know.

The other big difference they find is that this is not an ethnically mixed community. This they see as having its negative side: a lot of racism in the local area which they really don't like:

He: The obvious thing that Eltham's got a bad bit of … is probably going back to the Stephen Lawrence thing. So it's the sort of the racism thing.

OK, is that something you've found?

He: I've not found it personally but then I suppose I'm not going to find it because I'm not black, but I think a lot of people who moved out of sort of like to Eltham, Bexleyheath were people who originally lived probably where we used to come from like Bermondsey, Rotherhithe, Deptford area…

She: We come from quite a big, if you like, black community really.

He: Yeah. And a lot of people moved out this way, have got like, you know, racist views because they've moved out probably because a lot of black moved in where they lived. And I think a lot of people have got this preconception… I wouldn't say they sort of racist, but they have got a…

She: I think they sort of hold grudges…

He: Yeah.

She: … against a lot of them because a lot of new houses went up. Because where I used to live was near the Thames and it's really an up and coming area now. Like people are paying like hundreds of thousands for houses round there, even flats, you know. And whereas the Council had obviously bought a lot of houses and they were doing them up, a lot of them went to … I know … he's going to say I'm racist, but there's no other way of putting. A lot of houses did actually go to the black people. And I mean…

He: A lot of the local residents resented it didn't they?

She: Yeah. There was my mum, you know, for instance. She's been stuck in the tower block and been trying to get out for like 28 years of my life, and she's not succeeded. I mean she's actually moved now, which is the funny thing, but, I mean, saying that, we've got lots of black people and…

As well as the racism itself, there is the area's racist reputation since the murder of Stephen Lawrence:

He: It's not a problem for us like racism in the area and I've not witnessed it, but the problem is when you say I live in Eltham, they automatically link it to the Stephen Lawrence thing.

… What do you find people's reaction to be?

He: They say, Oh wasn't that where Stephen Lawrence was killed and like literally, I don't know if you know, but it's sort of just a hundred yards a way, you know. It's down the top of the road.

She: A lot of people do link it with that don't they?

He: Yeah. And that I suppose as a reputation, that's probably Eltham's downside. It will never live that down I don't think. As terrible as it was, it will never live it down.

And does have an impact on you or not really?

He: I wish it wouldn't. But obviously… I wish for his parents and everyone else, don't you. It's a terrible thing to happen. It's just very unfortunately … I mean, where it happened is such a, you know, a busy main road, it's beyond believe that no-one even saw it, or you know, what went on, you know.

She: I think people … they don't turn their nose up … they don't sort of think, Oh you know it must be a rough area.

He: But I know like black friends I've got, you know, would say, Oh no I wouldn't go there…

The other thing which seems to affect the reputation of the area is the Kidbrooke estate, also known as the Ferrier:

She: I'll tell you another thing people associate with Eltham as well – Kidbrooke.

He: Kidbrooke's got a terrible reputation. It's a big estate up there.

There appears to be a lack of local facilities; the local cinema closed down, and the pubs are not really their scene. So when it comes to going out they stick to the places they know:

Yeah, that kind of thing. I'm just wondering if you spend a lot of your spare time locally?

He: If we go out drinking or something like that, we don't really go in Eltham do we?

She: No.

He: I suppose I go back to sort of where my parents live and go out there a lot there because I know the area and our friends are sort of scattered around as well, so I probably can count the times on one hand I've actually been out drinking in Eltham. Eltham High Street on a Friday night isn't the nicest place to go. It's full of sort of 15 year olds who want to fight the world, you know.

They are both working and seem to be fairly contented with their jobs. The only thing which really seems to mar their quality of life is the dreadful journey to work:

What do you think of the train service?

He: Well, when we first moved here, they were pretty reliable… But for the last 5 months, it has been absolutely disgraceful.

She: It's been horrendous.

He: My train home. My normal train home has been cancelled because there's been a landslide at the Strood Tunnel, something like that. They've cancelled my home for, I think it's 8 weeks out of the last 12.

Really?

She: And I mean, we buy season tickets. I pay over £700 and most mornings you can't get a seat.

You're not quite far enough out?

He: No. You can just about get on the train.

Fortunately her boss is very understanding about the train problems, because it affects many other people too.

Perhaps because they are both working, they feel they can cope financially:

So are there things you feel that you go without?

He: No, not really.

She: I can honestly say that, not really. I mean, our days of clubbing are over anyway.

He: I think it's part and parcel. When you've sort of, I don't know, when you've sort of been together or you get married and settle down, you know, you do it when you're ready and you've done all the sort of… We've done all the holidays. We've done … I mean we still go away and that, but we've done all the things like that.

She: I mean, we're quite happy just to sit here and watch the telly really. We're happy with our own company.

He: ... well I bought the car before we got married, so the last two and a half years have been non stop, you know, it's been one big pay out.

Overall their feelings about the area are very positive; it is a place where they would like to stay:

He: I think so. We'd like to stay here for as long as we can wouldn't we?

She: Yeah. If we could find another house as this was when we first came in here, but may be more bedroomed, like when we decide to start a family.

Alan

Alan, an employed white divorced father in his fifties, has only been living in his owner-occupied house for 12 years. But he has lived in Eltham since the early 1970s. Twelve years earlier, he and his wife decided to move – unusually, to somewhere smaller. Alan is also unusual in that many who choose to live in Eltham assume they will commute, seeing it as a residential area rather than a place to work. But both he and his wife were teachers who got jobs in the area, and that had triggered their original move here:

... in the early seventies, teachers in London, it was like it is now. Teachers in London were very few and far between. So they were just glad to grab anyone so I thought Oh well, you know, good school, prestigious school. First job. Start earning there. So that's how I came to live in Eltham. And I think you'll find that there's a little bit of syndrome in fact, that a lot of people that trained and qualified at Avery Hill at that time came to stay round the area, got jobs in the area. We've got the jobs here so we'll stay here. No real need to move out. And although we're separated now, and have been for 10 years, my ex also still lives in Eltham.

But it would seem that over the 30 years, the area's basic amenities have declined. Shopping, for example:

I think what you notice about Eltham, but it's going it's going to be true of all places like this, is that there's been a decline in the High Street ... measured by the number of town shops and charity shops and cheap shops and it's absolutely no doubt that the High Street itself has declined as an amenity.

So you do kind of most of your food shopping in the High Street?

If they want to buy clothes, I drive over to Lakeside. Why do I do that? Because there's no clothes shops in Eltham. And because it's so close isn't it? I mean, you know, just go straight down the motorway. It's actually quicker to go to Lakeside than it is to go to Lewisham, which is the nearest big centre.

Leisure facilities, likewise:

And there was a Lido. Brilliant. But that developed cracks in it. It closed and there was no money for improving that. The Coronet Cinema which you walked past, an example of an Art Deco cinema, that struggled and struggled for years and eventually that's given up the ghost. The same if you go over Woolwich Common down into Woolwich. There's another Art Deco cinema down there. That's now closed. There's a swimming pool, there's a municipal swimming pool, up Eltham but that's going to close because it's … the cost of refurbishment or something so dated you know, the golden era of the thirties when they bought the… That's closed.

Like Zoe and her husband, he and his daughters (who live with him) don't go out to drink in Eltham.

So would either of you I mean, would either of you drink in Eltham?

But if we really wanted to go, we'd wait until the weekend and go to Greenwich, Blackheath or even if we had enough money, up to London. Occasionally, they've got a nice pub in Bexleyheath.

Crime also appears to be a problem:

We've been burgled here, this place has been burgled. But interestingly this area does not figure prominently on insurance companies' areas of vulnerability. I find that quite interesting. And I think like everyone there is this sort of fear of crime that it's not actually met by the reality. And that parade of shops that you walked up past when you came off the train, yeah alright it's stereo-typing, but there is this council estate behind there with lots of problem families and I think every single one of those premises has been broken into and it's a steel shutter kind of place now. And I know that people have moved out there because of that. And it's usually the same kind of bunches of kids and they do drugs there. So I think when people think of crime round here they think of vandalism.

Alan has reached the stage where he would quite like to move:

Whereas, and I know through experience, that the grass is always greener on the other side of the fence. But it would be nice to live somewhere leafier and greener and with a prospect when you look out of a window, which isn't just a prospect of a house opposite.

But looking at things realistically, it seems quite unlikely that he will make the move. Put simply, he has put down too many roots here:

… you can't live in an area for getting on for 30 years without your network of friends actually being in the area. So it's like anything else isn't it? The longer you're there, the more people you know, the greater the wrench for moving. It's not family because we've scarcely got any family. So it's nothing to do with family. And it's inertia. If you're going to choose to move, you'd have to make a very sort of radical choice. And all the time you're sort of bogged down in trying to be good at what you're doing. You sometimes sort of forget all those other things. Again it's a personal thing isn't it? I mean I'm quite old now, you know, I'm in my fifties and I'm a head of faculty which may be as far as I'll ever get, but I'm surrounded by younger people with very, very clear career ambitions and very careerist in mentality who choose to move, you know, my immediate line manager's just moved down to Ilfracombe. And so I'm surrounded by people who have that kind of mentality. I never have. And I suppose that's the kind of thing that stops you staying in one area and moving to another. You've got to have that kind of careerist mentality. If it's good for my career, I'll do it and then come back here when I've, you know, got a headship or you know… I suppose that there is nothing particular about Eltham that would make me want to stay in Eltham. Nothing particular about this place at all. In fact, in many senses it's quite a dreary place.

Although he says that his decision to stay here has nothing to do with his family, this does not appear to be strictly true:

You mentioned you'd like to move … have you ever actively thought about moving out or not?

No. Not actively. I think it's this thing, you know, like most people in my position, most people of my age, that there are family ties. You can't … if you're going to move, you probably have to do it when your children are young. But you know, but probably I shall actively be thinking of that in 2 years time, you know, when Laura's degree finishes. Because I'm the person she has to live with you know. Students can't afford to … by and large can't afford to live away from home these days.

As head of department in his school, Alan has achieved a senior position in his profession. So he has what might seem to others a well-paid job, but he feels that nonetheless money is rather tight. This is partly because he is supporting one daughter through university while the other is a single parent who lives at home. He is also a single father and, although he gets some kind of help from their mother, things are always more difficult when there is only one salary coming in:

By any standards, my salary is good. By the standards of having to … and I largely do … they do get some help from their mother, but by the standards of having to support a child through university and to support … Debbie's on benefits, and they're both girls right. So this is totally sexist of me, but if you have girls, there is … the washing machine's on the go all the time, because girls cannot have a bath without using three towels – I don't know – some sort of in-built you know … and cannot go through a day without at least three changes of clothes. So there's a heavy cost in all of that. You know, plus whatever costs were left as a result of the relationship break up and everything and the cost of living in London. You know, London is an expensive place to live. And you know, in all kinds of terms, I don't think a teacher … you will find that most teachers have to have two incomes to have anything approaching like a decent lifestyle if you live in London. Although my income to some people might look like two incomes, it doesn't feel like that. And it's not like that. And I mean that's … you know that partly counts for the lack of holidays – big bone of contention. They have their holidays. They have their holidays, I don't. But…

So that's something that you go without type of thing?

I mean even cheap holidays are expensive aren't they? So that's one of the things which reluctantly I've gone without.

And are there other things you've felt like you kind of gone without as such?

You do. I mean I can't deny it. I can't deny it that in irrational moments you say, I really resent this, you know, I resent this. Aren't children supposed to leave home when they go to university? If children go away and start a family, aren't they supposed to stay away and not come back? Because that's what the eldest's done. She came back with him 3 years ago. But you have to balance up your irrational moments with your rational moments and you say, that boy has been the absolute delight and joy, you know, of my life in the past 3 years. He's a phenomenal child and I love him with an immense passion. And you will also say to yourself, you know, it was your choice to bring those children into the world and if things don't work quite as they should, well tough you know. You've still got the … responsibility doesn't go away even if things aren't working out quite as well as they should. Responsibility doesn't go away. And there are people who have much, much worse lives. Much, much worse lives. And it's sort of … almost like a 'Thought for the Day' on Radio 4 isn't it? You don't take the times of resent with the times of saying, well hang on, it's really alright, you know, really, you know.

And, although his job is well-paid, it is very demanding in terms of the hours he has to put in:

I would say it would be a good time to retire now because I don't know how long these things are going to stay at bay and there's no point spending 6 days a week, 12 hours a day – I'm lying, it's not 12 hours a day, but whatever it is, a very large number of hours a day – there's no point just doing that to … until such a time as you can't do anything. That's not a life. It's not a life for anyone. And I work because I need the money to keep all this going, but I don't get any sensation of working in order to forget other things. In order to sort of put other things into the background. But I think there is a danger of slipping into that you know. So you have to keep in your mind, this isn't the only thing that exists in the world and sooner or later … see as a teacher, as a committed and dedicated teacher, you can't do both at the same time yeah?

The workload with the job sounds really hard?

It's phenomenal but if any of your other interviewees are teachers in positions of responsibility you find them … you find worse situations in life.

Really?

But you will talk to people who are driving themselves into breakdowns over their workload in teaching. Well again it's already been quantified hasn't it? And it's not just union propaganda … it's, you know. A lot of people I know they go to their GP and they say, what do you do? I'm a teacher. Well there you are then.

His workload also appears to eat into his social life:

Friends?

Teachers… They're all teachers… Almost entirely. Almost entirely, except for neighbours and I'm not sure you know, I mean neighbours are neighbours and they're friends to a degree. But teachers. I married a teacher. Her friends were teachers and are teachers… I think you will find it's true with many, many teachers that they do know teachers and it's very, very typical. I get out my tweed jacket in a minute with the leather elbows.

How much contact would you have with your friends say?

At the moment in the week time, in the week days, I do not socialise at all in the week days. I don't socialise in the week days because I work a 12 hour day and when I come home there's always stuff to do here.

So how much contact would you say you have with people locally?

Well I have long conversations with my hairdresser. But that doesn't count does it? He's a nice bloke. And with the people that repaired the TV and the VCR. I see them quite a lot. But in all honesty, I mean I think this is true of modern society. I mean this isn't a personal thing. It's very true of modern society. But big demands are made of you in your job. I cannot do my job if I don't get there at 7.30 in the morning. If I don't start at 7.30 to be ready for my group coming at 8.35, I can't do the job. I can't do the job if I go at 3.30. And I suppose the people that I know best at school are the school keepers because they kick me out, sometime between half past six and quarter to seven. I like campuses because you do that. But you actually don't really catch up and what you do tend to do is fall back on the old friends. You see them a lot more and you go out for more meals and you know the cinema and everything else. But they're just like me. I mean to say they come and they're exhausted and they say, well I'd like to have gone out tonight but I'm shattered, I'm going to go to bed.

How about with your neighbours then? Do you help each other out or...?

I've got an awful memory. The bin men come round on Wednesdays. I always forget to put the wheelie bin out the front and Bob does it for me. And like all neighbours, we lend each other things and talk about football and that kind of stuff.

And he does find his job quite rewarding, paradoxically because it is so demanding and responsible:

... increasingly what I do like is the problem solving aspect of it. That every day, in one way or another, there's going to be millions of problems coming at you. Some of them big, some of them small, some of them you know very, very trivial. So although, I mean some people ... would drive absolutely crazy, Oh it's terrible, Oh this is awful, Oh look what's happening, Oh this is terrible, you know, doom and gloom and I say, well hang on, you know, you're a manager, you're not supposed to think like that. You're supposed to think now here's a problem, how am I going to deal with it? How am I going to get the best resolution of this? If I can't get the best resolution, what's the second best resolution I can get? And I actually, you know, I actually enjoy that kind of you know ... OK that didn't work, I'll try this way, you know. And there's a real danger in your life whizzing past too quickly before you notice it you know? So, I suppose what I should say is I feel very, very grateful that at least I'm in that position because I know so many people that aren't, but you know job satisfaction comes from thinking that you can make a difference in some kind of way isn't it?

Rob

Rob, a white married father in his forties, chose to buy a house here because it was where he grew up and his parents still live here. He is satisfied with the area where he lives, because it isn't 'council':

How do you like it round here as a place to live...?

As far as my particular house is concerned, it's good because it's on a main road, so it's not inside a council estate. So you're not surrounded by noise, etc. You get traffic noise, but you don't get so much noise from people... Greenwich Council's a reasonable council.

But in terms of the general quality of life here, like others Rob notices that the area seems to have gone into a decline. Crime, he thinks, is a problem:

There could be a lot of improvements. There's a lot of vandalism and trouble, especially at the weekends in the Eltham High Street.

You mentioned the vandalism and kind of trouble. Is that something that affects you or not?

My wife's had problems. Been attacked.

How much does it impact on your behaviour as well?

And you just walk round it. You avoid it.

And is that a common experience round here?

It is yeah. The second time I was burgled, in the row, there was 26 houses broken into in the same street. That was about a year ago.

He also sees a decline in the local shops and entertainments:

… is there any change in the area? Has it got better, worse, stayed the same?

In my opinion it's got worse. That goes for most places at the moment. The cinemas have gone. There used to be a good cinema. The improvement on it is there's more shops. Supermarkets – we didn't use to have them.

So what do you think … how about like local services? How do you find those?

… walked past Pleasuance and it would be all nicely trimmed, the plants looked nice and looked after. Now they're growing through the railings, all the way, you know.

He has been working in a plant hire shop for 17 years, but doesn't seem to be particularly keen on his job:

I don't particularly like it. I don't think anyone likes their job do they? But, you get some job satisfaction, but, you know, don't particularly like it.

So you've always haven't liked the job and have looked for other things?

Yeah, that's right. You know, you have a couple of years, you get bored. You know, just like that. Uninteresting. So you try to find something more interesting. But it's never worked out.

This is mainly because he feels he is under constant pressure and because he gets little appreciation for what he does:

I like to get job satisfaction, you know, doing a job well. In this particular job I'm doing now, it's a service industry and you're constantly being complained at by the customers. And you're constantly being complained about from your bosses because you're not hiring enough equipment … pressured.

Yeah. Quite pressured ... in that kind of sense that you've got like targets?

Again I think it's probably throughout most service industries. You reach your target and they're happy. The following year you've got another target to reach and they think it's ... constant pressure.

So do you think there were any barriers to getting like a good job do you think for you?

Yeah, I think education obviously. You know, qualifications, it hard if you haven't got none these days. Although I'm 47 years old, whether that'll make a difference. If I was educated now, I don't know.

Is that uncertain...?

Well again, you know, we're told/advised at work that no job's for life any more. So you've got to sort of keep on your toes to keep in work. And you've got to make money to keep the shops open, keep the work going like, you know. Constantly being told that if you don't hit the targets, you know, they have to close the shops down.

He has family living locally, and they are obviously quite important to him:

And so, whereabouts are your family?

The majority of them within the Eltham, Greenwich Council area.

How often do you keep in touch with them?

Very, very regular.

How often are you talking?

Some of my family at least weekly. And the rest probably monthly. ... if I had a serious problem, I'd go and see my dad ... again, it all depends what problem it is, you know. As I said, sort of contradicting myself really, saying I go straight to my dad, it all depends what problem it is. You know, if there was ... certain problems I'd go see my dad, certain problems I'd see my brothers, do you know what I mean? Or my brothers, if it was something I didn't want him to worry about, do you know what I mean. If it was for like personal, sort of things you want to keep quiet a bit, you obviously go to your family;

He also has very good relations with his neighbours:

.... very good. The direct neighbours have got a good spirit, you know what I mean. We look after each other. Look out for each other. Things like that. Very caring ... I do their gardening. Odd jobs they want done. Look after them, especially the older people. Been doing that for years. I think it's a good thing to do.

Do they help you out? Do they do things for you in return?

Oh yeah. You know, whatever you ask for, they do it, you know, generally, you know. Bit of shopping. Things like that. You know, if you needed it, get you a pint of milk. If you've been on holiday or something like that, always get a pint of milk when you get home. Loaf of bread, you know, things like that.

Is that important to you to have that?

I think so yeah. Community spirit, you know, neighbourly spirit. And you feel safer. For instance, I was speaking earlier about the burglary. If it weren't for my neighbour, if he hadn't been sort of vigilant, I could have had a lot more problems … a lot more stolen because they've had more time to steal it.

… how about beyond that like within the road and within…?

No, I must admit there's direct neighbours, but along, say within six houses either way, we really don't know them.

Nonetheless, in an ideal world – like many people here – he would like to move. But he recognises that in practical terms this would be impossible:

Would you like to move somewhere else?

Yeah. We'd all like to move, but again you're tied to your employment.

So is moving something that you've thought about?

Yeah, I've thought about it. Again it … because you're tied to the area where you work, it's the travelling. Move out in the country where most people would like, move to the seaside, something like that, you've still got to travel into London. That's the problem.

Where would you like to go?

A number of places. Kent coast. Most people recommend … right out of London.

Margaret

Like many other Eltham respondents Margaret, a white married mother in her fifties, working part-time, has lived here for a long time. When they were originally allocated their current property by Greenwich Council they had been living in Greenwich for 3 years and had three young children. Now they were owner-occupiers; clearly, at some point, they had taken advantage of the right to buy. Although they had been given no choice about the house originally, they were very happy with it – mainly, it seemed, because this was the place in which they had brought up their five children and which had provided them with a happy home:

How do you like it?

Love it.

Really?

Yeah.

What's good first of all? What are the good things for you?

The good things, that we brought five children up here. We've got lots of good friends. Lots of good neighbours and if we could move, we would. But we'd take our house with us.

How did you find this area as a place to bring up children?

I think, what it was then, you were just happy to have the house of your own, you know? And the house they first gave us, it was nice, but it was so tiny. And I don't know, there was just something not right about it, and the thing is, they say, that if you've got to go into a house, when you take a child with you, the child will pick up and sense whether it's going to be happy there. And personally I think that's very, very true. And we lived at Lee for about three and a half years and then they offered us a big place, which was this place, and when we walked in it was horrendous. All the walls were cream and you know. But to us, all them years ago, it was wonderful. The garden was like a wilderness, but it didn't matter. But the kids were happy and I mean we had another … well we had another little boy, but he died unfortunately. So we had another two children while we was here. And the kids adored it. And there was so much freedom for them, you know? The generation today's so different and I accept that because I've got grandchildren. There's never enough money. They always want this, that and everything else obviously. I mean their home's aren't happy without a computer and you name it, they've got it.

She also seems to play a pivotal role in her local community:

Well, let me put it this way. I went out with my grandson yesterday and he's 12, coming up 13. And we were up the road. Went to the local shops. And he's quite … and the others have often said it to me, Nan do you know everyone in the street. I said, no not everyone. He said, what about the children, because every child that walks past you, knows you. I said, well, they're my friends or my neighbours' children, grandchildren. It seems, I know it sounds strange, but it seems as if, since we've been here, there's not been a lot of people that actually moved out. So all our children have grown up together. The grandchildren. So our children have been friends with their children and the grandchildren are now friends with their grandchildren. I mean, I've got a friend over the back here, about three doors up, and I was actually born with her in Plumstead. And she actually moved the same day as I did. I've got another one down the road. Done exactly the same thing. Another one in Fernington. Done exactly the same thing.

Many neighbours had become very good friends:

And how do you know them?

A lot of my friends are neighbours and there's still quite a few in this area, but we've been neighbours for many, many years. Wonderful neighbours. A lot of them, yes, I've met through work. A lot of them I've met through work. Even when I've packed up, they all still keep in touch. Prod me, meet them in the street or whatever.

Do most of those live local as well?

They live in Bexleyheath, Welling, Charlton, Woolwich.

Perhaps because she is so well integrated into the local area, she seems far more enthusiastic about it than most other people to whom we spoke:

So what you like is more to do with the house rather than the area?

No, we love the area very much. We like it as well. Never had any problems. Can honestly say that. It's very quiet. As you can … I mean, there's children all over the place, but it's so quiet. Certainly where we are any way.

Is there anything else particularly good about the area for you?

There's the hubby. Because he's disabled. So if he wants to get to local shops, probably takes him about 3 hours, but he can get there. And as I say, we don't get any problems. We just don't get any problems…

However from what Margaret says, it seems clear that the area has become much worse. The worst aspect is security:

Over the time you've been here, has it changed a lot?

Oh crumbs yeah.

How has it changed?

In many, many ways. For a start off, when you moved in, you had no carpets, no nothing. Just plain painted walls, which everyone's back to now. The kids could run in the street, but now they can't run in the street. You know, you could leave them out, and they'd play in the street literally. Go to the park. But they can't do that now. There's, you know, there's no way they can do that. They just … well you wouldn't be able to trust them any way. Traffic. The motorway obviously. Shaking problem.

The park was beautiful, but it's now wrecked, which is sad really, because they keep rebuilding it. I mean it had a lovely paddling pool, but that was all wrecked.

Do you think it's got better or worse then would you say?

Over the period of years we've been here, it's got worse. Traffic wise. Safety wise, yes. I mean when ours were little you could go to Redbridge, we quite often did some times, and leave the front door wide open. Leave the windows wide open.

The biggest problem seems to be the young children who live locally:

And I think it's the rudeness of the kids these days. They've altered so much. I mean, so rude. I don't know. Hyperactive, whatever they are.

This meant that she couldn't let her grandchildren out to play without watching them as she could her own children when they were younger:

When they come round to you, would you let them play out or not?

No way. No. Even if they went to the front garden. I would be out there with them. Or if they wanted to go up and down on their bikes like they do. The little ones, we're talking about the little ones. Then I would stand out there with them. I certainly wouldn't leave them on their own. There is a lot of rough little children about and I think if you're sort of that more … then you do worry, you know. It's like playing football in the park. Sometimes you go over there and you know they all join in with the other children. There is some lovely little kids about. Another time you get the one that's f'ing and b'ing and … I mean 6, 7 year olds sitting smoking and drink and… It makes you wonder. It really makes you wonder.

Are they from … are they local?

Oh yeah they're local… I think the naughty ones are the ones that are smashing in … now, smashing phone boxes at 11, 12 O'clock, 1 O'clock in the morning.

Does that happen round here?

It does yes. I mean, it was actually about 11 O'clock. And again, they're not so much teenagers, but the young ones.

What kind of ages are you talking about?

I'm talking about 6, 7, 8 years old.

Right, so that young…

Oh yes. I mean … last week, a little one come up to me and I put him [at] one of our grandson's age, I'd say 7, and he said to me, excuse me lady, have you got a light? I said, no darling I haven't brought one out with me. And the other one said, you haven't got a pint of lager have you? And I went, no I don't carry cans of lager. And I think, are they joking? But they're not. They're smoking cigarettes at that age, you know?

Like others she also felt that the publicity which surrounded the murder of Stephen Lawrence had impacted negatively on the local area:

So do you feel that you can't say what you want to say sometimes?

I've got to be honest, since Stephen Lawrence died round here, which was a terrible tragedy, I think that's when things have got worse. And that is where people sort of bite their tongues. But they [*the houses*] was boarded up for reasons because they had something to do with the Stephen Lawrence case and again, there was two over on the other estate.

So the effects have been long lasting?

Too long. Too long, you know? ... And then only 2 years after he died, there was the young boy of 17, a white fella, killed up on Westbourne Avenue. One of the nicest blokes you could wish to meet. He was knifed to death and clubbed about the head. But that doesn't continuously go on ... and on ... and on ... and on. And his home wasn't boarded up, or no one else's home was boarded up there.

Although she likes where she lives, she realises that in the eyes of others it doesn't seem such a nice place:

... you mentioned like the break ins and stuff, so that isn't something that worries you?

But I'm just one of these people that will quite easily walk out and leave my doors and windows open. But the children, no. I think because they was brought up here, and they live in different areas, like Bexleyheath, Lee Green and that, they know exactly what goes on. And in their eyes, Eltham has got ... not a very nice place to live in. And that is the way they feel about it.

She had actually considered moving because of the problem of crime in the area:

In terms of, looking to the future for yourself, I mean just like you personally, how do you think things are going go?

What for me and hubby you mean? I don't know. I think in a lot of ways, they're going to get worse. I think it's going to be a case of bars and bolts on windows, I think it will be case of let's move on.

And this would also benefit her husband who is becoming increasingly disabled and finds it difficult to live in a house with stairs:

We have got to think about it obviously in the next couple of years, you know. If he deteriorates that much, then we have to move.

However when asked where she would like to move to, she replied 'Eltham'. So, even if they do move, she doesn't plan to go very far.

Heather

Like so many other Eltham residents, Heather – a white divorced mother in her thirties, employed part-time, and a homeowner – was born in the area and chose to stay here when she got married. And this is despite the fact that she is highly critical about the area and the people who live here:

How do you like it as a place to live? What do you think of it?

I preferred where I used to live to round here. This is a bit... We're right on top of the Ferrier so I don't like that. I'm very aware of people's attitudes in Eltham... I don't like people in Eltham. I think a lot of people have got like a real problem. They're very narrow minded. Very intolerant. And I don't think that's a really good thing. I really would not choose my kids to be brought up round here for the people's attitudes. They more racist. It's like at Louis's school there's no black children. I think that's really wrong.

Is that something you really notice ... people's attitudes I suppose?

Yeah. I've just been brought up with it. My mum and dad were really good, but from my friends' ... from my friends' parents, I've always been around there, always. Especially, you know, the Stephen Lawrence thing, that really gave Eltham a really bad name. But it's true. And there's a lot of people that aren't like that. But there's a hell of a lot of people that are like that and I hate that.

Like other residents, she is shocked by the behaviour of the young children in the area:

So what are the bad things? You mentioned being near the Ferrier... How does that impact on you?

Well the night before we moved in, we were burgled, so it wasn't a really good start and it's just like a lot of kids hanging around the street which just drives me mad.

... you mentioned crime, as an element, is that a issue for you or not really?

There are a lot of sort of kids that hang around these streets and little gangs and things and I can stop them now, but I'm not always going to be able to stop them, so.

And one of the other things that you mentioned was the other children in the area…

We're really near *** School and a lot of the kids around this area, around our house, go to that school. The kids swear and, you know, they're just, I don't know. Just feel a bit uncomfortable about it really.

And is that the impression that you get round Eltham that it is quite a problem?

Yeah. You hear about fighting and … it's just the way they talk you know. There's some kids across the road … just you know … it's just appalling. It's like 'int' instead of 'isn't' or, you know … and he's picking it up just by playing with them sort of outside for 10 minutes. I don't know. I'm just an old worrier.

Perhaps the bad behaviour of the children is linked to the other factor which residents noted: the dearth of facilities in the local area:

This particularly area – no parks. No decent parks. And the tiny crappy park they have got which is full of like teenagers … and you know, another thing, they took all the swings out the parks because there was some sort of… Some sort of accident and they took all the swings out the parks because some parents were suing like the council.

One of the good things about living in the area is that she has found a decent school for her children:

Well, the number one good thing at the moment for me is that I've got them into a really good school. A nice school round here. I can really say that. My mum and dad … my family and friends live round here. It's just quite a nice sort of safe area. I'm not sort of scared to walk around.

But what is most important in keeping her in the area is that she has good friends here:

Most of my friends are… I've got three … like my best friends … well I've got two sets of friends. But my best friends are from school that I've known since I was 11…So I'd say generally you know like from way back just from school and stuff.

And do they still live locally or…?

Yeah. It's funny actually. Because we always said you know like … we always took the piss out of everyone living in Eltham because we said that people live and die here and they do you know.

What do you think draws people back? It's interesting that…

I think a lot of it with my friends is families. Because their families are here and because they're families we're friends with them as well so that is my reason that I moved personally. Not the area at all, but the people.

However people seem to be more friendly in the council estates than in her immediate area:

It's there. And a lot of those houses there are like council tenants but it's really … I mean I didn't always like that. It's like a really friendly area. Everyone sort of knows everyone and they're the kind that do anything for you know. They sort of helped out a lot when I had babies and stuff, whereas round … this road seems to be more half and half and it's definitely not as friendly. It's definitely not as friendly. But I mean our next door neighbours they're a bit funny.

In financial terms she appears to be in an extremely difficult situation:

No, no. It's about money, how do you think you are getting on money wise, do you think you've got an adequate income?

Adequate would be the right word to use. Just covered. [*Interviewee begins to whisper*] I can't tell you anything about it but we … he left me like in March with a 10 week old baby and we were in loads of debt. He was just sort of staying here until he … leave. He moved out with somebody else. Woman or whatever. I didn't know where he was, so. And it was just at the time when I got a job, so I now like support all of us on my two days a week and Family Credit. I mean it literally covers… I've got no spare money. If he didn't give me a bit of money as well then I would. you know. I would get behind with the mortgage and stuff. I've got a mortgage to pay, but yeah… Oh God, this year's just been absolutely a nightmare year it really has.

However she has a job and appears to be coping with things as well as she possibly can:

So you've been there 6 months, how do you like it?

I really like it. The job's … it's not like a job for life. The job's actually quite boring. I have to deal with the wages and I'm absolutely crap at figures, but it's just a laugh.

What other things have you done?

And I'm just doing this part time really like (1) for the money and (2) just to get a break from the kids you know. It is hard work and it was really sort of monotonous. Every day's the same, so.

Do you see yourself staying there or not?

So I'm going to literally do this part time until the kids go to school and then I'm really going to think about you know ... and then I'll leave ... just do something purely for the money like be a legal secretary or I'll re-train to do something I want to do and not have the money. I just want it to be something where I'm really getting benefits from it rather than just you know sort of plodding along.

You made the distinction between like a job where you get job satisfaction and the money, do feel as though that's the choice?

For the things I enjoy doing, I don't ever think will ever make me a lot of money so I'm going like have to get to the point where I have to choose whether I need to earn a lot of money and then not really, you know, not have my dream job or go for my dream job and then be able to afford to do it.

Which way do you reckon it way pan out?

The money.

Yeah?

And you know, the way things are going money wise, I just think you know, you're going have to sort of go for the money that you can get. And I just want for my kids to have holidays and ... so I should imagine it would be like the money. The money route one day.

But she also recognises frankly that she may find difficulties in trying to get a better job:

I think if ... you know a good 10 years where you really worked at your career and you got something then you know you've got your house, you've got your nice house and then you can afford to ... kids. Whereas if you do it this way round you know you're not starting your career until like ... well it depends what age of course you have them, but for me it will be like the mid-thirties and that's not like a really great time to actually start on a ladder.

Do you see that as being a bit of a barrier?

Yeah. I do. It's hard to sort of go and train and start at the bottom in a job like any job I think. You better being a trainee or something in your twenties than you are in your thirties.

Most of her money comes from Family Credit, which she finds a tremendous help:

Yeah it really does. Because I've got a mortgage. If I was Income Support they don't. They really help with your mortgage when you just basically get behind. With Family Credit, they just top up your money to £240 a week ... whatever you earn. Say you earn like £30 they'd make it so you earn £210. Like an extra... It's just the same live on and therefore you can pay your mortgage then. You've got the money to pay your mortgage. And they pay your child care and if they didn't… I wasn't on Family Credit then I wouldn't get that paid. That would come out of you know. It's really good. It really suits me in my circumstances. Probably not everybody but.

Nonetheless it is still extremely difficult to cope on one income:

So in terms of … so do you ever feel as if you go without things or is that something…?

I think it's very hard in this day and age unless somebody's got a fantastic job to live on one income … two incomes you know you can afford holidays but I think one income you literally … sort of cope… before I started this job, and we sort of again had one income so we never really could afford things like holidays. Especially because we'd bought a house and we've had the kitchen done and we had to buy a car.

So you're supporting all three of you on that, how's that?

It's fine. The thing that bothers me is when they go on school journeys and when he started school. I've never had to buy school uniform and it's like so expensive, and computers and things like that. Which is why you know I say that when I get a proper job it'll have to be money, I'm sure that'll be the deciding factor.

But she still thinks things are better than they were before:

I think better. Because I was like miserable you know like … he was self-employed and now it's for me … although I haven't got a lot of money, I know where I stand in money.

She would like to be able to move but due to her financial situation she cannot afford to:

Although … you've only been here for a little while, do you see yourself staying here…?

I should imagine we will stay here, but if I had the money, I would move. Particularly away from this street and this estate for the sake of the kids. I'd like to be nearer their school and I just, I don't know, it's me being a bit snobby probably, but I'd just rather be somewhere where they're not going mix with, you know, the wrong sort, like swearing and all that sort of thing. There's also there's a lot of older kids that hang around. They're only little and they're just picking up all sorts of you know.

Where would you like to go? Where would you be thinking of?

May be somewhere like Avery Hill or Eltham Park. A little bit further south really I suppose.

... So that's not something you could do?

Not really because of money. I just don't think we could afford, you know, particularly at the moment to... It would be like another £30–40,000 on our mortgage and it's just not an option at the moment.

Tracy

Tracy, a white mother in her forties, now separated and unemployed, used to live on the Ferrier estate but moved to her current council accommodation here 7 years ago after an extremely nasty mugging incident. Although she got the better of her attacker she was very traumatised by the incident and required psychiatric treatment. The person who had mugged her had also continued to follow her and was making her life impossible, so she decided to move to another estate.

Did you go to the police?

Oh yeah. They didn't want to know. They kept saying, Oh is he black, is he black? And I kept saying, no he's not black, he's white. You see, like people kept saying, he probably tried to mug you for you jewellery and whatever and all that, but he didn't even attempt to get my jewellery. He didn't attempt ... I mean, grab the stuff out of my hands or anything, do you know what I mean? Just asked me the time and ... I thought it was my mate's son as it goes ... and as I looked and thought, you ain't him, but before I could... I don't know, he just sort of ... throat ... knife and pinned against a wall, do you know what I mean? And I just thought, what's going on? Just everything sort of passes. And everybody says, Oh I'd do this, or I'd do that ... you don't. You just freeze. And then I sort of ... and I thought he ain't stabbing me. That's all I kept thinking. He ain't stabbing me. So I just brought my knee up and I head butted him and ... cos I mean I've got big brothers. There's ten of them in the family and I mean when my boys fight, I have to break them up, do you know what I mean? And I thought, I ain't having this. And I really beat him. And I had this shopping trolley and I had the stuff in it cos I'd like ... people's toys and that. There was watches, walkmans and all that. And as I've gone to swing it round, the bag's fell off and I'm just whacking him. And he's... He's crawling away from me, screaming and everything. I'm just whacking with this ... the metal bit of this trolley ... trolley. I was going mad. And I kept say, how dare you. Who do you think you are? Why do you think you can get away with it? And all this, you know. Do you know what I mean? And he's punched me, but I can't feel it. And I thought, that's alright. So I've turned round to try and hit him hadn't I, and of course like three ribs are broke, but I was doing it ... at this time, I don't know. I'm just thinking, he's hitting me. Do you know what I mean? I fought him off once, I can hit him now. Do you know what I mean? I could still hit him. Anyway, as I've turned round, and I've really gone to town. Like I really, really lost it. And ... cos I've got a bad temper any way, but it's the shock.

However since moving to this new estate, if anything matters appear to have become worse:

... so I come down here anyway, but I mean it's true all what they've said cos they reckon that it's a curse this road. Cos if you come in, you're happily married, you'd be divorced within 3 years. Well it works. It happened. Not divorced, but I've been separate for 4 years, but...

And it seems she may somewhat regret having left the Ferrier:

So do you keep in contact with people ... from the Ferrier?

Yeah, yeah. My best friends are mainly all over there, but I don't ... I mean, I've got a sister over there, but I don't really go over there.

You don't?

Cos when I go over there, I know I don't want to come back here ... I was always laughing and joking and whatever. Do you know what I mean? I loved it on there. Shouldn't have ever moved off there.

In fact she doesn't seem to think there is anything good about the area where she now lives:

OK. You've mentioned quite a lot of, not so good things about this area, are there any good things for you?

No. None at all.

First, there appear to be very serious problems with crime in the area. As all our other respondents noticed, the main culprits appear to be quite small children:

So crime's quite an issue then you think round here?

Oh yeah. I don't go out shopping longer than an hour.

Why's that?

I don't go to Eltham or near by, because if people see that I'm out, I know that I'm going to be burgled.

... you don't to go to certain places.

No, I don't go out at all. It's just like I'm prisoner in my own home.

So it had a direct impact on you..

Because I used to have pick Gary up at half past three. The bigger ones would come home on their own, but it's that time, that you used to get burgled. When you was taking the kids to school or when you was picking them up. That's how they work, you know. And they were burgling. They were doing it while you was picking up the kids.

The only consolation is that a couple of the older burglars are in prison at the moment:

Well, a couple of them are prison at the moment, so it's not too bad, you know.

Couple of the burglars?

Mmmm. But you see, it's their little friends that are around and about. Like over Christmas there was loads and loads of burglaries. I mean, I didn't even put my presents out. Cos normally they're all round the tree and I have me tree there, but no. I don't even go out at that time.

In fact the children are not even afraid of the police:

Well, nine times out of ten, it's the park police that come, not the proper police. And when the park police do come, they've got the dogs, but the kids face up to them. They say, let the dog go. And they go up to the dog and they go to kick it and bark and all that, but they know that them park police can't let them dogs off. They can't let them bite them. So it don't matter who turns up. Even to the police. The only reason they sort of go away when the police come is cos they know that they can get nicked, but they know, that nothing can be done to them because they're too young…That's why half of them phone the police. Cos they want to go for a ride in the police car and they want to be in the… So they come out, and, Oh yeah, I'm big, I've been in the police station, blah, blah. Do you know what I mean? You don't scare them. And then as soon as the police of gone, the other lot all come back. It all starts up again. So you can't keep phoning the police. Oh soon as you left, they come back. The police ain't going to come back. But they don't come back and recheck. Do you know what I mean? They just … it's a waste of time anyway calling them. They don't do anything. Don't take none of them away. Just turn to go away. And what they do, they come straight over and talk to you, so then you'll caught … you'd get called the grass. So that's why you get all things coming through your windows cos the police come straight up to you in the front of the kids. They know who it's been. So you can't win.

On top of that, medical facilities appear to be very poor:

And the doctors won't take me on.

Really?

Yeah. Because of I'm from the Ferrier... OK. I did go to... I went to this thing and they said ... cos he was just round the corner, where ... Lynne's. That's where the doctors was before when I first moved around here. And I went to this thing and they said, yeah I can have a doctor and they allocated me him... He gave ... my son went round there for his acne and he give him slimming pills. I went there with a cold shoulder and he tried to give me an injection and I wouldn't have none of it cos I don't like them. And then he ended up going to prison and we lost the doctor.

The doctor went to prison?

Yeah, right? So, I've ended up having no doctor for about 4 or 5 years. Going down the new one that's opened up, now I've lived here 7 years, Oh no, sorry, we've got all that we want. And half of his patients are off the Ferrier or Westbourne Avenue or Middle Park or wherever, yet I live here, and can't get on there.

She has had terrible problems with her neighbours:

We was going to do different to this house and what have you and all that, but it just didn't work out, but it seems like everything I put my hands to, it goes wrong. But the thing is, I ain't racial. I mean yeah I was near enough done for racial, because of the woman next door, but she was white. But cos her husband was black, which she did it on purpose to get out. She did it when she lived on the Ferrier. She told me all about it. Told me what she was going to do and everything. She made my life hell, you know, and they moved her. I was here on my own, had no phone, she used to get men come throw bottles at my windows and kick my doors down and all that, you know. And she got moved. She phoned the police, said it was me doing it all. And when the police did come one day, I did lose my temper and I did go in there and she had a broken swing in the front garden and I'd just had enough, so I smashed the BMW up. After what she put me through for 2 years solid. She got the kids to throw bricks over and one hit me in the head. Cut all my head open, right? And she reckoned it was a can. A can of coke. She reckons I threw it over and it hit her baby. And it was her... She had the baby and it was all shitty nappies in my garden.

Drugs appear to be part of the local scene:

And the other week there was boys over the park. Beginning of the holiday. My little boy come in and he went, mum? I said, what? He went ... because he was due to go to my sister's like for a week, and I said, what? He said, there's men over there. He was putting a needle in his belly. I said, do what? Well I've gone over there and he's standing ... he's out the car ... he's standing at the front of the car and he's what the name ... he was injecting himself ... into his belly.

In fact the area seems to be so dreadful that even ice-cream vans will not go there:

… are there any good things about this area?

No. Only that you've got Lewisham that way and Eltham that way and Woolwich the other way. That's the only … nothing good at all. You don't even get an ice cream man down this road.

Why not?

Nowhere else. I mean, you get the cars speeding down here all the time, like little boy racers, and you've got the old men racing down here and all that. The amount of people that have been knocked over down here is unbelievable. Cos as they're coming out of the Meadowside you see. That's forever being burgled. Do you know what I mean? You get the travellers up there. Settling in the park and everything. The Council don't seem to bother. They don't seem to care what goes on as long as it's nothing to do with them I think.

However she has managed to establish a certain local reputation, and that means that she is less likely to be a victim of crime:

But they'd never ever attempt, because they call me the mad lady round here, they say Oh no don't attack that lady because she hits kids. But I do. And I do own up to it. If they're cheeky to me, I will hit him, cos my kids … mine ain't cheeky and I've got three teenage boys. They don't smoke, they don't drink, they don't swear, they don't hang about street corners. See what I mean.

Have you been burgled yourself?

No. Wouldn't dare. Not with the dog. No. But they tried to burgle me once, but this door was shut and obviously they look in the windows. And didn't see my dog in here and they'd bashed the thing up, so it was blocked up and they got through that like window to open the big one. They've come in and they're trying to unplug the telly and video and all that. And I had Sky and everything. And my dog's gone up my stairs, jumped out my Ricky's window, cos he didn't have no lock… Come round the front. And she got him. And she bit him seven times. So he let everybody know about this mad dog, breaks out the house, you know, to get you … there's a woman up there. She's got three Alsatians, so they know they can't burgle her. But, they just make a mess. Like they tried to feed the dogs. And they spray paint through your letterbox and just like … just smash your windows and … I don't know, just mess your house up. Do you know what I mean?

But after that you haven't had experience?

No. Cos I know them and I like faced up to one of them. And I said him, I'll do it to your mum's house. Cos his mum's a little old lady. I said, I know it's you, I said, but I'll tell you, if it happens again, I'm going to do it to your house. Whether it's you or not. So let them all know.

She sees herself as very different from the other people in the area: while they are happy to live on Income Support, she has always attached a great deal of importance to working:

I don't know if they're working or on the dole or what, but they seem all to be in the same category, like they don't really want nothing better for theirself see. Quite happy plodding along daily. Waiting for their Giros and things like. Do you know what I mean? Where, I'm not into all that.

She has done many different types of jobs:

… when I was on my own, I tried to keep jobs. I was having part time jobs. I had three kids at school then. But I was doing party plan. I was doing Ann Summers and all things like that, but rather than go out, I was inviting people to my house from the estate who I knew and here and if they had parties, cos they're my friends, I had to take my kids and they'd go up in their bedrooms and play computer or … because it was all to do with my friends. Do you know what I mean? I'd never sort of go somewhere without the kids. Oh and my husband, he'd always like walk me home or bring me home if I was over there or whatever.

You mentioned that you'd done a lot of other things. What other things have you done?

Pet shop cos I always wanted to be a vet. I worked in the vet's as well. I worked … I was head cashier in a shop called… It was years ago. You had to memorise the prices. I was a Blue Coat…

So you've had quite a lot of jobs?

Yeah. Worked in a bingo. I was a caller. I always worked even when I had kids and I lived at Gravesend. I used to go pea picking and potato picking, but I used to take them with me. So … because I couldn't work in a shop because of the kids, you know. And then I started doing cleaning… No, I don't know. I like trying different things. Do you know what I mean?

She has also done many caring jobs and describes that as being her favourite kind of work. However in her last job she became very attached to the person she was caring for and took it badly when she died. She doesn't appear to have done a caring job since then.

She feels optimistic about the future because she hopes that shortly she will start working again:

But you think things will get better?

Oh they will. They will. Cos I know I'm going to work again… And like me health, because of me thyroid, I've got inflammglitis [sic] as well. That's hereditary in our family. But I won't go and have like an operation or do what they've done with my family. Because… But … it's weird, because I can't eat what I want to eat and I can't work cos I can't at the moment. I can't move. It's every … I can't … I can't … Do you know what I mean?

In the face of considerable odds, her children appear to be doing quite well.

And how important do you think education is for them?

Oh well they all seem like to do well. They don't bunk off school or anything like that. But Ricky wanted to stay on at sixth form, but he was doing engineering, so he had to go to Eltham Green. And that's another thing. Like a kick in the teeth for him really. Because he started there, but because there was only nine people in it, they stopped it. And my Rick was on like … he didn't know what to do with himself. Cos he really wanted engineering. Do you know what I mean?

One of her sons was recently diagnosed as being dyslexic but is struggling on to do as well as he can.

So you've been pleased with their progress then?

Oh yeah. Tony's … he don't like reading and writing and that. He's not into that side of it. He's more into… He's art and drama and, I mean, all that sort of stuff. But, the thing is, what he wants to do, he's got to get certain grades, like in English and maths and things and all that. He's really trying. I mean, he's coming home … he's asking for extra homework … the maths and things and all that. Do you know what I mean? And he's really pretty … but you can see it's taking its toll cos he's sort of, 'I can't do it, I can't'. I say no, you don't say you can't. There's no such word as can't. You say, I can do this if I try hard enough. I can do this. And like we would muck about with it. But then if Gary knows something or Gary do it and he says, it's so easy for you. Do you know what I mean? He gets right cross with it. Tony don't want to be in school at all. Cos he's so arty. I mean he does loads of things with his hands. And he's a brilliant painter. He draws pictures. Plus he can sing and dance and all. And he … if he can't do animations, then he wants to be on stage and whatever. I mean, he's waiting to go into the BLA Academy. He used to go the Bob Hope Theatre, but that got expensive and his dad said he couldn't go anymore. He was doing rugby as well as Thai Quando and that. He's the one that's into everything really sporty. Ricky was into like into the running and all that. I mean, he had loads of chances to be in different football teams, but he's not really into that … at the age that he was, he was too shy. And now, he says, Oh I wish I'd gone. Charlton Athletic wanted him to run for them as well.

How have they got on there?

Oh brilliant, yeah. My Gary's probably the highest of his … in the whole year… Brilliant he is. Don't ask me where he got it from. He's really, really clever.

Financially she finds things difficult:

Cos he's a big boy and he sweats more and… I mean with trainers… I mean, I wish they would have to wear shoes, but if they wear, they're going to be the odd kids. Do you know what I mean? Cos everybody wears trainers, but you're talking like sixty pounds for Gary. I mean, my Tony's a size nine. That's like hundred and odd quid. Do you know what I mean? So I'm still pinching pennies trying to… Do you know what I mean?

She had problems with her Social Security:

Ricky started work. I sent my book back, but they didn't read the letter properly. So they didn't know that he started in May and they still gave me money. So I owed them a hundred and seventy pound. So I've had to send the book back and then take five pound week, so that's like I'm only getting eighty pound a month … I was getting a hundred pound a month. And now I'm only going to be getting eighty. Nine times out of ten, I mean, that pays for like … well, used to pay for the phone, but I haven't got a phone now. It used to pay for Cable. I haven't got that any more.

But she has developed means of getting by:

I go to the cheap shop, I go to the butchers… Buy big thing of potatoes… They like salad with everything and they like dips with everything, you know, like yoghurt and mint and those sort of things. I make them myself now, where I could just buy before. I don't know, I do lots of pasta things… Often like, when I went to the butchers the other day, yesterday I think it was, I bought two packets of mince. Seven trays for ten pound. Two lots of mince, pork chops, chicken, sausages, burgers. Do you know what I mean? But, I already had a bag of sausages from Iceland. Buy one get one free. So I do do that as well.

She is also helped by her sons:

Like we had so many hopes and dreams and things, you know, and it just sort of all went wrong. Now like people say, Oh it must be a hard life with three boys and that, but it wasn't. Cos they'll help. Like if Ricky's got any money and I ain't, I mean, like the other night, Gary heard the ice cream man and Lynne wasn't in so the kids had come back round here. And I only had like two pounds. Ricky give me the other pound to get them all an ice cream. Do you know what I mean? He's quite sweet like that. But

I could have done without it because the other two pound could have been for their school dinner for the next day.

She would love to move from here, and is actively trying, but finds it incredibly difficult to do so because her location stigmatises her:

I've been trying for 4 years now, but no other council will accept me. I've tried … like I buy the *Loot* and all that and whatever, as soon as you [say] Eltham, people don't want it.

Because of her vulnerable financial situation she is keen to remain a council tenant as she knows she can afford the rent. She feels that if she tried to get somewhere privately the outgoings would become too large and she would have to go on to the Benefits system, which she would hate:

And I went up there like Hillingdon way and all that, but I don't know, it's just … people say the only way I'm going to get up there is by going private, but I don't really want to. I want to stay on council really. I haven't got that sort of money to put down for private. Do you know what I mean? And I don't want to sort of have to live on the Social and them to pay all. Do you know what I mean? Too much kafuffle for me. I'd rather just do a straight exchange and that's it.

However it is very difficult for Tracy to exchange her flat because no one wants to live in the area. This is because the area is so strongly associated with racism. Yet she has not witnessed racism herself:

They never get anyone that wants this area. They want round about, but … cos nine times out of ten, as I said, there's mainly Indians or anybody, whatever they are. They don't want Eltham. Because there's been such a big thing to do with Stephen Lawrence. Do you know what I mean? And it's just… I think it's just scared everybody. I mean I've never ever like experienced it. I mean, my boys, most of their friends are black boys and they've never experienced none of it. Do you know what I mean? And it's like … just like a one off. I mean it can happen everywhere … it happens everywhere. Do you know what I mean? Notting Hill Carnival there was two black boys killed by a black boy. Do you know what I mean? And it's like that CJ and all that. It's just… Do you know what I mean? So it happens wherever you go, but I think cos they … it's just classed as a racial area.

Even if she were offered a flat from a practical point of view it would be very difficult to move:

I've got three teenage boys. Do you know what I mean? And I can't just up and off and everything. I've got no money for vans or anything, you know. I mean, it's easy to say, but it's hard. If I was gonna move, yeah, then you've got time to ... like, if you were doing an exchange, nine times out of ten, you pay half for the van because it's got to come here. It's got to go back to pick their stuff up, so it can take two lots. Do you know what I mean?

Her family have offered to help her out, but she is reluctant to accept their help:

So they offered to lend you the money for that kinds of stuff did they?

Oh yeah. If I was to say I was going to move or whatever, they'd offer yeah. But, I wouldn't accept it.

Why not?

I'd never be able to pay it back, you know. My brother, like he offered me eight hundred pound to go to the ... two hundred pound deposit and six hundred pound like for the first month. And, cos I'm not working now, I said yeah it ain't only the deposit I need. I need to like ... for a van and you know, all different things and like when you're moving, it is costly and all that and it ... like he said, I don't want it back. But I think, yeah but you've got your own house. You work all hours God sends. You've got four kids. Anything could happen to his house tomorrow. Touch wood it don't. But... Do you know what I mean? And, you know, he's sort of ... I don't know. He don't... To me, he hasn't got the time to help me. Do you know what I mean? But, yeah, he can give me the money, but that's why he's offering me money, cos he can't help me any other way. And I ... well, I wouldn't be able to pay it back. And I'd just keep working to try and pay him back and then... Do you know what I mean? Cos then I think, how long am I going to be employed. Do you know what I mean? And I've got to work to try and get that then as well and... Do you know what I mean? It just seems to be more than a hole in the head than, you know. No, I'd rather sort of wait to do a council exchange. At least that way, you know you're still on the council and you ain't going to be chucked out at the end of the month or, you know.

Trouble in the Garden

Eltham often seemed to us an outer London equivalent of its inner-city cousin Bermondsey: in some ways, a deeply troubled place. Here, the trouble seemed to be of two kinds. First, many of the inhabitants were individually struggling to survive: theirs was an all-too-familiar litany of unstable relationships, sudden descent into near-destitution, balancing precarious casual jobs and welfare. Their personal troubles were compounded by their problem neighbours and by what they saw as the precipitous decline in their quality of life, threatened by the petty crime and vandalism they found all around them, and by a general sense of menace that made some of them virtual prisoners in their own homes. Add to this a general lack of basic shops and services, and concerns about the education their children were receiving in local schools, and the outcome was a potently problematic mix. This in turn was causing a rapid churn of population: some were coming here from places like Bermondsey to find a better quality of life; others, equally, were exiting to find that life in places like Greenhithe further down the road.

All in all, these stories told us that the remnants of the old London blue-collar working class were deeply afflicted by the economic changes that had undermined their traditional modes of making a living, and by the deep social transformations – some consequential, some contingent – that were causing the breakdown of old-established patterns of communal life. In particular, they were deeply shocked by the apparent collapse of law and order they saw all around them, and by the rampaging activities of children who appeared out of control. What would be the final outcome, no one was able to say.

Again, as in Bermondsey, it was not all like that. We also found some people who found the place fine, who were secure in their personal lives and family relations, who were happy in their jobs and comfortable materially – even if they occasionally suffered from strained finances. Some told us that the area was a great improvement on where they had come from – typically, a nearer-in part of south-east London. And quite often, they quoted rich networks of friends as one reason for their attachment to the area. Everything seemed to depend on detail: precisely where you lived, who were your immediate neighbours, whether the local children behaved.

Perhaps that is true of any area of any city anywhere. But here, it seemed rather more extreme. There were 'bad areas' and bad people living in those areas, who could bring havoc to a whole neighbourhood around them. And there was a powerful sense, among many, that these 'bad areas' were expanding outwards in a kind of contagious process, bringing down formerly respectable and pleasant neighbourhoods. Perhaps this sense was exaggerated, and certainly some interviewees seemed consumed with almost paranoid fear of the world immediately around them. But, as the phrase goes, just because you're paranoid doesn't mean they aren't out to get you. Their sense of menace affected their entire perception of the world, closing it in and leaving them in a sense of semi-fortified fear. This is certainly rare in London, at least in the areas and among the people we interviewed. But for some of those we talked to here in Eltham, it was an ever-present reality.

Eltham Swimming Pools

© Bill Knight

Gants Hill

© Bill Knight

Chapter Seven

Arcadia under Shadow

Gants Hill

The average Londoner might just recognise Gants Hill as a place on the Tube map; specifically, a passing station on those Central Line trains that advertise themselves on the display screens as 'Hainault via Newbury Park'. Or, perhaps, as an often-gridlocked roundabout where the A12 Eastern Avenue meets a road that used to be the North Circular, but that got demoted when that road was extended a decade ago. In the stationary traffic, this car-bound Londoner might idly notice the remains of a typical 1930s outer London shopping centre, now clearly fallen on hard times. Beyond it, there is row after row of semi-detached suburbia: the kind immortally described by the cartoonist Osbert Lancaster, half a century ago, as By-Pass Variegated – which, quite literally, these are. And, beyond those, glimpses down side streets of reveal somewhat more desirable residences, detached, on tree-lined roads; leafy outliers, as estate agents might call them.

Suburban arcadia, in short: the kind of place where, ideally, nothing much ever happens. London's story is very much the story of successive such arcadias, inhabited by ever-increasing numbers who sought solace here from the grime and stench and noise of the city: Belgravia and Barnsbury, Ealing and Eltham, Greenford and Gants Hill. For decades, these suburban refuges have been colonised by new recruits to the middle class, who settled in them in search of comfortable lives for themselves and semi-rural backdrops for their children. Most lives lived here recall George and Weedon Grossmith's *The Diary of a Nobody*, where Charles and Carrie Pooter ('The Laurels', Brickfield Terrace, Holloway) 'can manage to pass our evenings together without friends. There is always something to be done: a tin-tack here, a Venetian blind to put straight, a fan to nail up, or part of a carpet to nail down'. Here, families keep themselves to themselves. Some have close family ties, others not. They may have local friends, especially through their children's school, but often their friends have moved away. They like to feel neighbourly with people very much like them, but there are well-defined limits.

Like most people anywhere, they care very much that they live in streets where they do not feel threatened – by crime or the threat of it, by physical intrusion, or by the arrival of new groups who might disturb their peace and their established way of life. Their local physical environment, and local facilities such as schools and shops, are a very important part of the package that makes up their quality of life. But in Gants Hill, and many other similar places in London, we found that people now feel overshadowed by change and its effects on their locality. They sense a physical decay of their neighbourhood: a decay that is partly the inevitable effect of ageing, but accelerated by a sudden decline in the quality of local facilities. Many in Gants Hill have been deeply affected by a much-publicised 1998 Civic Trust report, suggesting that the area was showing signs of incipient decline and decay: an 'unattractive, highly congested and polluted environment'. They are also powerfully conscious of new residents who they perceive as not quite fitting in, and who – so they believe – are compromising the quality of local schools and neighbourly relations. It would be easy, too easy, to dismiss this as simple racism. In fact, as our interviews showed, it is much more complex than that: it affects people from widely different ethnic groups, different ages, and different socio-economic groups. It is, as much as anything, a question of different lifestyles.

People react to these changes with varying degrees of anxiety, concealed from the outside world – including their neighbours – by layers of dissimulation and artifice, even plain hypocrisy. They maintain the veneer of good neighbourly relations, even if there are tensions underneath; this is the land of the twitching lace curtain. These, after all, are the London middle class – a class that now includes the great majority of the population, and embraces many different races, creeds, cultures and lifestyles. So it is often difficult, even for those involved, to know what exactly is going on. Sometimes, it becomes explicit, as with noisy or obtrusive neighbours. More often, it may be something so subtle as to be unclear, and even over-interpreted.

Gants Hill might almost be called the archetype of such an area. Located in the outer north-east borough of Redbridge, and centred on nearby Ilford, it was originally settled by Jewish and other white inhabitants, whose families moved from the East End in the 1920s and 1930s when the area was being built. In the 1980s and 1990s, they have been supplemented and in part succeeded by waves of arrivals from the Indian subcontinent, now in the second or third generation, whose families also started in East End slums – indeed, in many cases, the same slums – but who have moved in search of a better quality of life. These new arrivals share similar beliefs, and live the same family-oriented lives, as the older generation they are replacing. They delight in the quiet, the arcadian quality and the high standards of the schools. But relations between old and new inhabitants are not always smooth, as we can see from the stories they told.

Some History

Until after World War One, this remained an agricultural area with scattered gentlemen's residences, some of which survive as listed buildings and public open space. Ilford was a village, with brick works and lime fields that added working-class and artisan housing in the early nineteenth century. But real urban development came only from the 1890s, after the Great Eastern Railway was compelled by Parliament to offer cheap fares as a condition of their extension into Liverpool Street. Speculative builders ran up dense terraces of houses which were bought by clerks, skilled workers and officials, and a few better-paid shopworkers, most of whom commuted into the City. Soon after 1900, they were joined by small villa estates for the professional classes in Woodford and Wanstead, to the north and west. But even after a branch railway opened from Ilford to Fairlop, in 1903, the rail journey into central London remained slow and uncomfortable, so development was slow.

Then, in the 1920s, new arterial roads – Eastern Avenue, the North Circular Road – were followed by bus services which opened up Gants Hill for development. Estates of semi-detached and detached houses sprang up, stimulated by demand from the upwardly-mobile children of the Jewish refugees who had settled in Whitechapel during the 1890s. Whether through inheritance of businesses built up by their parents, or by moving into professional careers via the great East End grammar schools, this second immigrant generation left the dense slum streets to seek new homes in areas like Gants Hill. Soon, it had the standard appurtenances of any London suburb of the time – the Odeon cinema, the shopping parade, here with its kosher shops. But it continued to suffer from poor transport: the Central Line, planned in the mid-1930s, was delayed by the war and reached there only in 1947. So this became a rare case where transport followed London's spread rather than guiding it.

Gants Hill Today

Ever since, the area has remained what it was from the beginning: middle-middle class. Redbridge as a whole has an extremely high proportion of owner-occupation (75 per cent of households in 2001, the fourth highest proportion in England and Wales) and very little social housing. But the proportion of professionals/managers is significantly lower than in an inner London borough like Wandsworth. At the 2001 Census 36.5 per cent of

Redbridge's population was from non-white ethnic origins – a huge jump from 12 per cent 20 years earlier; just over half of those were of Indian or Pakistani origin. In the schools, no less than 47 per cent of pupils were from ethnic minority backgrounds, with 36 per cent having English as a second language. In 2001 nearly 12 per cent of people recorded themselves as Muslim, nearly 8 per cent Hindu, against 6 per cent Jewish. But the social composition has changed hardly at all, because the new arrivals have mainly come from a middle-class second generation among the large Asian communities to the south, in the terraced streets of Forest Gate and Upton Park, following the trail beaten by the East End Jewish community 60 years before; refugees and asylum seekers have been much less significant here than in inner boroughs such as Newham. In response, the older Jewish community has tended to move on, though concentrations remain, particularly in Gants Hill.

The area remains pleasant; there are a large number of parks and much open space, while the borough's schools – including a range of independent, grant maintained, single sex and faith-based secondary schools, as well as mainstream coeducational comprehensives – enjoy a high reputation both locally and more widely across East London. In 1999, the borough's secondary schools as a whole achieved the fifth best GCSE results among English LEAs. Redbridge is a borough with generally low rates of lone parenthood (13 per cent), low absenteeism from school, and rates of violent crime which are low by London standards, if still above the national average. Overall this still appears to be a rather comfortable area.

The centre of the area is still recognisably Gants Hill Cross. Until the mid- to late-1970s, this was a thriving local shopping centre. But it stands at the intersection of two very busy dual carriageways, requiring access via a subway system, which is widely regarded as unsafe. This has clearly affected its viability: it has suffered closure of all the banks bar one, the post office, the clothes and shoe shops, and many food stores. All that remains is a small convenience store, newsagents, estate agents, two furniture stores and a cinema; the area looks run-down, though the Council has encouraged 'night-time' uses and this has brought a number of new restaurants and a small night club. Two large office blocks remain occupied but the council is concerned about their future.

Within Gants Hill, which covers four wards, our study focused on Barkingside, which is rather more affluent and less deprived than average. It fans out northwards from the Tube station: an architectural gem, one of the last and finest fruits of Charles Holden's great architectural collaboration with London Transport's Frank Pick, with staggering platform furniture under a barrel roof, escalators up to a brilliant underground circulation system to multiple exits. But outside is anticlimactic: despite sterling efforts by the borough to spruce up the shopping centre, it remains run-down and partially vacant. Away from the roar of the traffic on the A12 Eastern Avenue, Gants Hill falls neatly into two halves: slightly older and grander semi-detached houses in a subdued Mock Tudor on the south side towards Ilford, along tree-lined streets framed by the vast Valentine Park; and extremely modest terrace houses lining interminably long roads in Barkingside ward to the north, with only the rare appearance of the occasional semi and even rarer detached house or bungalow. Here, though there is every evidence of tender loving care on the part of the residents, parking problems have caused almost every front garden to be cemented over to make a car port – with the occasional London taxi making its appearance. Eastwards towards Newbury Park come older terraces, presumably built immediately after the first railway came this way in 1903, behind the chaos of Eastern Avenue: older shopping parades replaced by an incongruous melange of filling stations, huge tin sheds and brand new developer's apartment blocks.

Most housing is owner-occupied, with prices averaging about £232,000 in early 2006, slightly higher than in some other parts of Redbridge, though still clearly lower than in London's western suburbs. There are variations within the area, with one neighbourhood of substantial pre-war semi-detached houses or bungalows, some more modern blocks of private flats, a small council estate, and another neighbourhood of smaller post-war semi-detached housing with some more recent terraced housing. The area still has a predominantly white middle-class population, but with an increasing number of middle-class Asian families. A significant Jewish population remains, though the more affluent have moved north-west to Woodford Green or out into Essex. Although there are some younger families, the majority of residents are in their late thirties and forties or older, including many over retirement age. Most residents work outside the borough, commuting on the Central Line from Gants Hill into the City or West End.

Now the residents can tell their own stories. First, the older-established ones, who are white.

Sheila

Like the vast majority of Gants Hill residents, Sheila is the owner-occupier of a semi-detached house. In her thirties or early forties, she is married with one daughter. She is taking a part-time college course; her husband is between jobs. She moved to this house 16 years ago when her husband inherited it from his parents who had lived here:

His mum and dad bought it, and when they died, he was – obviously he was the only child, he inherited it.

But she has always lived in the area – earlier, also in Barkingside. She likes the area:

I mean living here we're central to Ilford, Barkingside, we've got the Tubes, we've got the buses running just outside … so I think it's quite a nice position to be living in, because it's so well connected to – to other places.

Her main headache was the choice of secondary school for her daughter, because it was fiercely competitive:

… you have to appeal, and even appealing doesn't guarantee that you're going to get your child into the school that you want … you have one choice, unless you did your 11 plus and passed, and then you could go to Woodford… I think of 70 girls, or 70 people that took their 11 plus only two passed, so it's very, very hard… I didn't think that she would pass it, and I thought it was a lot of stress.

And unfair to put her through that if she wasn't going to pass?

Yeah – yeah… And even the children that had the tuition, you know, they had people coming in every week to tutor … tutor them on the 11 plus, none of those passed either, so… (*Laughter*)

She was acutely conscious of the different qualities of the schools on offer:

And you said that though *** is nearer, you were quite happy with her in ***, what … what, is there a difference in the schools?

I don't think so, I think if you look at their results in the newspapers when, you know, the schools' things come out, they're very, very similar. Em … the children that I've spoken to that go to *** are all very happy there, but I think *** tend to push them that little bit further than *** do.

But she prided herself that she was not going to push her child artificially to become an academic high-flyer. She was relaxed about her daughter's progress after her GCSE:

Em, I think if she had a job that she really wanted to do, then yes I'd be happy for her to leave, but I'd totally leave that up to her, I wouldn't push her in any way, if she wanted to stay on then, you know, that's fine, but if she wants to leave then … as long as, I think, she's got a job at the end of it, if she didn't have a job then I'd try and talk her into staying, just just to get something else.

Qualification?

Yes.

Pam

Pam, in her mid to late forties, married with one son and employed, was joint owner-occupier of her semi-detached suburban house. The family were united in a common love of sport:

Well I'm a tennis coach, my husband's a PE teacher and Simon's mad on any sort of sport...

But this was a relatively recent development:

I used to work in the Stock Exchange, no I've gone well away from what I used to do. I trained as a secretary then ended up in the Stock Exchange on the market floor, I was the only woman on the market floor, and then I left when I had Simon and didn't work for, well years, until he went to infant school and then I did riding for the disabled voluntary only when he was at school cos I'm one of these horrible old-fashioned people that think that if you have children you should stay at home and look after them, so I haven't really started working until I took my coaching exams 2 years ago and I became a tennis coach.

She was doing a great deal of voluntary work as well:

I work Tuesdays and Fridays at the riding for the disabled and then I do varied, cos it's self-employed work so I can do sort of as much as ... I've just done a big, a lot of work with schools, I've been working in about five schools each week, going in sort of doing the youngsters so I end up working about, well must be about three days a week tennis coaching... I want to help people I suppose at the end of the day. I don't want to earn big money and be unhappy any more I've come to the stage of life where I want more out of life. And it's about the reward of seeing people develop...

Like Sheila, she had lived here for 16 years but had lived in the same small area all her life; her move to this house had hardly been a move at all:

Just about 200 yards up the road and my mum and dad live 200 yards up the road that way!

They lived a classic suburban life, keeping themselves to themselves and maintaining a low-key existence:

I mean we don't have flashy holidays, we don't go ... we didn't go anywhere when, until Simon was about 5 years old, I mean we would only go away for a weekend cos I didn't want to so we probably didn't, cos when I left work and for sort of 2 or 3 years we really struggled cos we were only on one wage and we found that quite hard... Both of our houses we've done up ourselves, we do all that ourselves so that's our entertainment if you like you know, and we don't sort of go out, we're not drinkers we're not ... our socials is round our houses and that, so er, so I suppose at the moment we're probably the most well off we've been but because we're contented I don't have to go and spend it, isn't that sad but...

She too was obsessed with her child's schooling, but had distinctly dim views of the local schools. Of her chosen school she said:

... it's very good for music and sport, so obviously sport was my main thing, but you sort of look at the school and they are different the children, you know you stand outside most schools cos I've been round em all and I sort of ... they all come out and they've got this horrible look, they're very calm at ***...

You mean they're quite aggressive in some of the schools?

Yeah, they hang around in gangs you know so er, it's very different round there... Now *** is our catchment area and I actually know a teacher that teaches there, she said don't let Simon go there (*laughter*) and ***, *** had so many Indians in, the Asian ... and I mean let's be honest we are white, I want him with the majority of ... yeah, so I know it's awful but that was a big factor and in the end actually we got him to ***. Now *** is out of our borough but it's not far away it's down, you know where *** is, so that was, we actually got him in there but because *** came up we didn't need it .

The area in general had changed, she thought:

... definitely has changed they're moving in so, and they're such big families this is the thing, they don't have one or two they have four or five or six so that's why, and the Asians don't wanna give anything back to schools I mean they, they don't go in and help.

She expressed very conventional middle-class aspirations for her son:

To be happy in life and hopefully to have a job that he enjoys and you know basically that as long as he's got an all round education and he's a kind boy, I don't want him to be a job hunter or a you know someone that's a high-flyer, as long as he carries on happy and you know able to hold down a job.

She thought he would stay on and go to a university, though she doubted the value of the experience:

I think yes, definitely yes. I don't know whether he'll go to university, he says no but I think he's coming round to that, I don't think that's always the be all and end all I really don't, cos I think nowadays everyone's going to … well they're not even universities half of them are they, colleges and at the end of the day they're coming out with these qualifications but they've got no practical experience and I think still if you get into a job and work your way up it's just as good if not better than university.

She clearly felt somewhat uncomfortable with her neighbours, both old and new:

Neighbours yeah, got nice neighbours but not… They're Jewish, lot of Jewish people round here and they're very nice but they're not the same as us and actually we now, there's a lot of families moved in with younger children so we're the oldies now… This road is changing, where when we moved in it was more like our mum's and dad's area and they were saying well how can they afford a house like this and now it's changing again we're the older ones and it's the younger ones coming in.

She did not regret that her son had lacked other children to play with, because she clearly had little to do with her neighbours:

… we're very friendly but we wouldn't have them into our house, you know we'll talk over the fence and I'm sure if anything happened yes you … but we're not that, you know we're not that close I think we've had them in once for a meal when they first moved in but they're not that friendly you know.

She described her Jewish neighbours as:

Very money orientated … very yeah. When we moved here this guy next door had a chauffeur every day and it was just a standard joke cos he used to have this chauffeur turn up and Richard would go off on his bike you know so I mean it was just really hilarious and I mean I think they've got four cars over there, they've got two cars there, two cars there, these have only got one car but you know we were, we always were the (laughter) … he's just quite well off and he moved to Chigwell after that you know so, and these, I mean if we do something in the house they'll go and do it but they'll cook one better you know… Really they look at what you've done and they do… Absolutely we've had double glazing and they've had double glazing and it just goes on up the, and Jewish people seem to be like that.

She described the street as:

Very Jewish … we still haven't had the Indians in here yet, they'll come but I, not just yet, this is quite a sought after road for er, cos there's *** School up the road which is the Jewish school … and the Jewish people are … a lot of them are self-employed and they want to be on top of their work, you know like the work in London so this is close enough, taxi driver, he's a taxi driver over there. They're taxi drivers down there so we've got a lot of taxi drivers in the area, so they all belong to the Lloyd centre you know it's… (Laughs)

What was happening, she thought, was that some Jewish people were still coming in while others were giving way to Asians:

… well that was all very white I mean that's changing isn't it, yes. There was always Jewish people I mean when I went to school there was always Jewish people in my class but there's more and more and I mean they say the Jews move out and the Asians move in, that's definitely how… Definitely from Redbridge roundabouts they're coming up from there cos the houses are slightly cheaper, they're the slightly smaller so they're getting in there and then they'll creep up here…

And you think that's what's happened with the Jewish population, it's moved up from Gants Hill roundabout up to Longwood and…?

Yeah and then they're going to Chigwell, you know they go to Chigwell and er, yeah definitely.

And do you think it's got better or worse?

Worse I think in that way, I think people are so, they just look after themselves and life has changed so much.

She saw the area coming under increasing pressure from new development:

… they're building a lot of houses by Clayberry Hospital you know all round there. Well I think that's going to make an awful difference round here and up by the new Jewish school, at the infants, junior school you know where they're building there, well they've built loads of houses round there… I mean it's gonna bring so many more cars and people into Barkingside that that's not going to be good … parking is gonna be horrendous, more and more people in the area, probably the crime and everything else.

So she was clearly contemplating a move:

I'd like to think I would yes, I would like to think I'd move out a little bit… Um, out Essex way if possible but that determines … I mean mum and dad are now getting old and they always moan cos I haven't moved so they didn't move so, so it depends where Simon goes to and there's so many things isn't there, but I wouldn't like to think that I'd still be here when I'm 60 when I retire, but at the moment everything is so available and until Simon goes to university or what then I wouldn't dream of moving cos I know he wouldn't want to go into the country and then you've got the thing that when you get old you might not be able to get about so you can't.

She had not even contemplated a move earlier on, because of the complication of her son's schooling:

Well no because we knew we wanted him to go there and Richard being at Forest Gate if we moved out to Essex it would cost us a lot more cos we'd have to have two cars and then it goes on and on and on so, and he's one that, because his job is unsociable hours if you like, cos it's always after school the matches, he wouldn't, I mean sometimes he doesn't finish till 8 O'clock in the summer with a cricket match and then another hour's journey.

And she felt that she had to stay within easy reach of her parents:

Oh yes, yeah absolutely yeah, so I mean mum's 73, dad's 76 so they're getting on now so at the end of the day if one of them died I don't think they'd be able to manage in that house so then you, you start thinking, ah, what do you do, don't you, and I'm an only child so it's down to me.

Jenny

Jenny, a mother of twins in her mid to late forties, is in unpaid part-time work and is owner-occupier of a semi-detached house. She came here 16 years ago from Walthamstow:

… Walthamstow was the first step, em up the ladder and then obviously we got a better house by moving into this one. Just bettered ourself really… We looked at, er, em, Collier Row to go nearer to where my husband came from and we looked at Woodford and we looked at Chadwell Heath, which is actually where he comes from. Em, decided I didn't really want to go that far. Woodford was a little bit more expensive than here so, er, we sort of plumped for this really. Right on the underground. Mm, thought it was an ideal position.

She seemed satisfied with the neighbourhood in a kind of low-key unenthusiastic way:

What other things are quite good. Well the houses are fairly nice. I think the houses are nice, they're, they're spacious. We got quite a spacious back garden, which I think is nice. I don't like new houses, so I wouldn't like to move out. I like it because it's central. You've got everything around you. You can move out one side, one way you can go out to the country, Hainault or somewhere like that and go inwards you can go into London very, very easy. Em, what else do I like about the area? I wouldn't want to move, let's put it that way. I don't know why, I, I can't seem to find any more words to why I like the area, but I wouldn't want to move unless I won the lottery and then obviously, you would, you know, you wouldn't live in here then would you? But, no I wouldn't want to move.

Part of this lack of enthusiasm, it appeared, concerned her neighbours:

Em, you know, it's, it's a shame, my neighbours one side are quite nice though they're both working, but they, you know, they're very nice people and they always say hello, but the … it's not a friendly environment here at all you know, I don't think.

People don't talk much...?

I've got a friend down the road, Laura, who she … her boy used to go play school with Caroline. If I need anything at any time I could always call on her. Yeah, and vice versa … and the children, if ever they need anything, either one of them, they would always call … just a couple of doors, that you could rely on. But other than that it's not a friendly area as such I would say. Not like it was years ago when I lived in North London or even Walthamstow.

She liked the area because it was accessible to central London:

… having a family, I wouldn't want to bring my children up into, in, in the middle of the inner city. Em, even to where I was brought in Islington, I wouldn't want to bring my children up there now… I just think this is probably a better area. The schools are probably run better. I think if, if you're in the middle of, say Islington, you're probably lucky if you're Catholic because the Catholic schools are generally quite good. Or the Church of England schools are generally quite good, but I don't think the schools are run so well as what they are in the Borough of Redbridge.

Her daughters were at a local school:

… generally I think it's quite a good school. Em, they've done, one of them's actually left now. She's a hairdresser. She's in her first year. She's done a whole year now and she's doing brilliant. She didn't, didn't like authority much. She's done good, really well in her GCSEs at ***.

She had personally rejected the option of force-feeding her children to push them into a highly selective private school:

… from 5 years old they're drumming that into their children's heads to get them extra tuition each week to … and, and don't get me wrong I was exactly the same with the twins. And you know, I thought this is silly. I grew up a bit probably and got my head together with Caroline and thought well this is stupid. I put them all through that and they're doing just as well at ***. They was happy there... I wouldn't, I wouldn't struggle along like some parents do. You know, scraping by just for an education for the children because I do honestly believe if they're going to get on in a school, they'll get on one way or another.

In fact, she thinks that one of her daughters seems to have been wasting her time at school:

... she's doing A levels at the moment and she'll go in and the teacher don't turn up. And em, a lot of the time she might have to only go in for a lesson first thing in the morning and last thing in the afternoon... It's supposed to be private study time... And I find she ... I think a lot of the time she feels as if she's got no achievement. You know, she's just laid out on the couch asleep when I come in and things like that and she'd go through a bad spate where she wasn't em ... she felt tired all the time and I think she was slightly depressed because I just don't think she had any oomph in her, any go in her whereas the other one, she's learning to be a hairdresser, she's going out to work every morning. She's bubbling.

But the problem could have been that she was misplaced in school:

Em, what do I want for Caroline when she finishes? I just want her to be happy. Yeah. As long as she's happy, as long as they're all happy, that's the main thing. Its em, yeah, we was laughing the other day, actually she ain't got a brain cell in her head ... I think she'll have to be a topless model!

One notable feature of Jenny's life is that her family is relatively close by. Her husband's parents and his three brothers still live in Chadwell Heath and hers in Islington; she has a sister in Hainault and a brother in Rainham, Essex. They are such a close-knit family that her in-laws actually go on holiday together, and it is common for both sides to come together for Christmas. She sees her sister around once a week, sometimes twice a week, even five times a week; she sees her mother in Islington every week:

She always comes to me every Saturday. Most Saturdays there's a meeting here. Whereas my mum and dad will come over and either my brother and his girlfriend will come or my sister and her husband now. Or his mum and dad will come over, or one of his brothers and his wife and, you know, there's always something going on here on a Saturday night.

But she is concerned about her ageing parents:

I don't know how we're going to get on with my mum and dad when they ... because being in Islington's going to be a bit awkward. We really wanted to try and move 'em this way. It's not an easy job though… I mean, we've been up to the Town Hall and asked and they said that you know, they'd have to come down and put their name down … they're actually in a tenants association house, with a tenants association, so literally to get a council place they have to be thrown out physically.

Nonetheless, she is well satisfied with life where she is:

I've said that to Bruce many a times, you know. It's either going to a mobile home or a mansion, but I would rather just stay here.

She still likes the area, though she has seen some things she does not like at all:

… at one stage they said some em people were buying in, a lot of ethnics were buying the houses and renting them out to Newham Borough Council, and we was getting people, homeless people moving in into the houses around here … we had a spate where we had three in this little vicinity.

But, in general:

… you know generally I think people are quite polite and, and nice round here and they, you know they look after theirselves and you know I don't think, I always people into serpective, into perspective and I used to say to my friend, she had a really rogue boy, really horrible sod he was, but I used to say, you know, he's not one of these if he'd see the old lady on the floor, he wouldn't nick her handbag, he'd pick her up and dust her down. You know what I mean? Whereas I think most of the people round, I mean I don't know, maybe there are people out there that would nick the handbag, but I think most of the people would pick her up… I don't actually walk the streets. It's quite a nice area. That's why we moved here because it was a nice area. And I still think it is.

Stratford, she thinks, was a different kettle of fish:

Stratford? Well, er em, it's not so nice there, no. Not so nice, em there is, where he is, they've got a big er, gypsy site there.

She has a philosophical view of life and its prospects. Asked what she expects, she answers:

I think that's a very difficult question to answer because I come from nothing and if I go with nothing, it doesn't really matter. You know, if, if we're doing well, we'll go and see a show. If we're not, we don't. If we're doing well, we book a holiday. If we're not, we don't. You know it's, that's the way I'd look at life.

Leslie and Miriam

Leslie and Miriam are a Jewish couple in their early sixties, retired but doing paid casual work, owner-occupiers of a substantial semi-detached 1930s house. They moved here in 1978 from Chadwell Heath:

He: Er, reason for the move, er, my wife will probably tell you more about that, but er Friary was a smaller house, and she wanted a bigger kitchen, em, I think possibly she felt that the, our daughters should be in a more Jewish area where there were more … not that it made any difference in the long run, but they did go to the Jewish school… And that, I think was her … as it happened I would have been quite happy staying where I was, but I'm a stick in the mud, er I was in the same job for 42½ years, working for the government… We looked at this area when we got married cos of … but we couldn't afford it at that time, now that put you in the picture? … Combination of a bigger house, more facilities, and also a more Jewish area, so that the girls possibly would have a chance to meet people of their own faith and plus, as it happens, my older daughter's partnered up with a non-Jewish chap, and he's a lovely lad, so and we, we've got nothing to do with it. We're not in any way prejudiced at all, we're not over religious or anything like that.

In fact they were not particularly Jewish in observance:

Do you go to synagogue?

He: Only on high holy days, and that's what she wants.

But the area had changed hugely over 20 years, he thought:

He: Well, it's got more ethnic, you know, for, for Asian and the er Indian.

Asians were moving in, while the old Jewish population was moving out:

He: Yeah, oh yeah, I mean nearly all the houses that are sold, nearly all go to ethnic er communities, it was largely Jewish when we, er at the time we moved, wasn't it?

She: … but now it is more Asian people who are moving in… And the Jewish people are moving a bit further you know, Chigwell…

He: Out, as they become em possibly more er what's the word 'opulent' is it no, it's not the word, er well get more money, I've forgotten what the word is.

She: I think it's wonderful really to have you know, to, to have that mix.

He: Oh yeah, and we've got Asian neighbours, they're Ugandan, are they Kenyan Asians, but they're really lovely people, you know, we get on with … we, you wouldn't know, you don't er sort of aware that we're different ethnically, we're just like neighbours, that's all.

Yeah, and do you see them?

He: Oh yeah, often, all the time.

> They help each other with neighbourly chores:

He: Well, I mean silly things, like I mean if you wanted to borrow a lawnmower or something like that and … you know, we're just quite free or silly things like oh, we feed their cat, we used to feed their dog…

> Their friends were mainly in the local neighbourhood:

He: Mostly local, aren't they?

She: Mostly local, we've got, we've got a, you've got a couple of friends over in north, north London.

He: North London, my old school friend, Leo, lives in Barnet, Maurice lives in Mill Hill.

She: And Shirley lives in em Edgware.

He: … and Shirley, in Edgware. So, we have a number of friends.

She: We've got a few friends over there, but mostly they're local.

Mostly in sort of Gants Hill, around this area?

He: Yes, yeah, in Gidea.

She: Oh, Woodford.

He: Woodford, that's right, yeah.

She: Some around Chigwell.

He: Within a few miles.

And you still know people you were at school with?

He: Yeah, yeah

> They saw their friends regularly, once a week on average, and spoke on the phone between times. They saw their families, too, on a regular basis:

She: Yeah, sister-in-law, I see my brother's er widow.

He: Yes, we see her fairly regularly.

She: And that side of the family, his children.

He: They live over in Edgware.

She: My nieces, I've got two niece, he had two girls, I've got two, you know, they live over there, as where Les said, Edgware and Boreham Wood way, we visit each other, you know, they were here recent.

He: Though the older relatives there's not many left.

She: Not many left now, no, they're rather…

He: But we, we have a family gathering twice a year, on Jos… Yeah, the religious festival you know.

She: …Yeah, and then we have a big family gathering, you know, what's left of us so.

They felt the area was quite safe, but was going downhill, due not to incompetence on the part of the local Redbridge Council, but because of the behaviour of local people:

She: Yes, I think it is, I think Redbridge is a good borough for most services, you know, the libraries and everything are good.

He: But we're suffering now from what the, the lack of responsibility of the of population, like leaving old cars along the street and using areas as rubbish dumps and… It's a problem with the occupants, it's not the Council's fault, although er because they're going to have to put more resources into clearing up the mess.

But they could not see themselves moving from the area where they had lived so long.

She: Not really.

He: Well we've given it a thought, but decided not to, I would say.

When, when did you think about moving?

He: Oh, when I get, when they carry me out in a box. No, it depends on what happens.

She: Yeah. Understand we're very happy here.

He: We're happy here.

She: I wouldn't move out from the area.

And you think it's a nice sort of friendly…?

He: Well we find it is, yeah, yeah.

She: I think it is, and I think it could be a big mistake, when a retired couple…

He: Move out into the country or somewhere…

She: Move away completely, I think that can be a big mistake.

And you'd lose the people you know?

He: And it's not easy to make friends at that time of life, is it, you know, it's not so easy.

She: You know, who people think 'Oh, nice to have a cottage'…

He: In the country, yeah.

She: Yeah, in the country or in the seaside, you know, Clacton or somewhere like that, and then inevitably one partner's going to die and then the other one's left out, you know, out, out…

He: All those things to think of.

Ranjit

Among the Asian population in Gants Hill, two we thought were representative: Ranjit, a Sikh in his fifties, employed for nearly 30 years at Ford in Dagenham, and owner-occupier of a terraced house; and Ajit, a Sikh mother with two children, employed in a professional position with Newham Council, and living in an owner-occupied semi-detached house.

Our interview with Ranjit begins with an interesting cross-cultural misunderstanding:

Can I start by asking you when you first came live here?

What, in this country, or … in this world?

Well, this country then.

Yes, I've been living here since '66, er 1966.

He lived first in Canning Town, soon moving to East Ham, living there until about 1993 when his children moved from primary to secondary school and his daughter took GCSE and secured a place in Redbridge Sixth-Form College; she now has a degree and has qualified as a solicitor:

I should have moved earlier because er this education was doing better in this world than what it was in Newham. So, er, it was always there when the children were having the fights in the school and all that … that's why my er eldest son never got anywhere… I thought he was doing A levels, but he wasn't. He was messing about.

He was seeking a bigger house, and he was concerned about an influx of refugees into East Ham:

… the house I had there was in a very quiet area, but it was a bit smaller than this, although it was three bedroom house, it didn't have a kitchen extension. The kitchen was small, the wife was moaning, always moaning about the smaller kitchen, so I said, well instead of building an extension there which would have cost me £12, £15,000 at the time, maybe £10,000, so rather move, there was er so many factors like, never just … it wasn't just one. Because I wanted to move as well because er I was getting er a lot of er refugees in that area at the time especially er from Africa and er all the people in all the houses that were being sold, there was people who were actually buying them they weren't buying them to live in, they were buying them to rent 'em out. So that was a deciding factor, as you understand so they were lowering the tone of the area and all that. As, er, well as I said there was just many factors, there wasn't just one.

And he is well satisfied with the move, but he still looks forward to buying the bigger house which he has always wanted, perhaps in the country:

… you know it's er been fine up to now. It's just a lovely area like. You know, it's, it seems to me a bit better than one where we had [been]. I'd had more money to spend so I want to move up like er and I'd still now like to move out to the countryside somewhere, if I could, if I could buy a bigger house, or a newer house like, not recently built ones about this em age, I want one, the house I had in East Ham was 1932, throughout, this is 1930 really quite old and by then I mean I should be retiring next year hopefully.

On retirement, he plans effectively to give the house to his extended family:

I'll probably be going to India for a couple of years. Yeah, leave this house to the children. My daughter should be getting next married next year, so she'll be moving out, so then all that leaves my son, daughter-in-law and the child, er my grandson it should be sufficient for them unless they want a bigger house, then it's up to them… I'd leave them the house and they can do what they want with it.

It emerges that he has an ongoing problem that has taken him back to India and will take him there again:

… I have a problem over there that's … it's going to take quite a bit of time. I normally go there every couple of years for four weeks and it's not getting anywhere. So the Court procedures over there is very bad… I just have a problem with the relatives now like there, they're, they're squatting on my land and er I want to vacate it.

His idea is to pass this land on, too, to his children as a holiday home, or to live there himself and invite his children to stay.

He came to London at the age of 15, and went to school for about 8 months but could not really understand English, so an apprenticeship was out of the question. He worked on a building site and in a bakery before making oil drums in a Canning Town factory and then Ford at the age of 21:

… soon as I got, became 21 I was started working at Fords. They wouldn't take you on unless you were 21.

He has worked at Ford for 29 years, in a 'not very skilled job now these days'. He is looking forward to leaving.

I want to be made redundant but I didn't have the chance last time round because I'm not quite 50 yet, I'll be 50 in April, so er I wouldn't be, they wouldn't pay me any pension until I'm 50… Hopefully next year, that's what I'm saying because they want to get rid of more people now … the package the company is offering is to me it's quite generous.

He believes he has suffered discrimination in his job:

Well, I, yes, yes, true is there's discrimination in all walks of life. There's no getting away from it… Er, I mean I haven't been er physically or verbally abused. But I know when someone's a bit … say the foreman or the manager might wanted to talk to you and all goes on like you know regarding your promotion or job prospects… And half the management you know it's they only get the job because either they're related to one another or they're, they're white, their colour's white. I may know more about it than them but I've got no chances.

He lives peaceably with his neighbours. On one side:

Yeah, she's a women er in her er late eighties, 86, or 88 I think. She told me she was 82 when I moved here so she'd presumably be 89 now. Yeah, she's quite active. Lives on her own, on her own and er time to time well when I would see her outside or in the garden, see how she is, if she needs anything, she's got my phone number if she needs any help, she can always ring me up.

And on the other:

... they moved from Stratford. Mm. They say, yeah, they like the quiet, they like the area as well.

His mother-in-law lives locally and they see her at least once a week. But his father, mother, sister, and elder brother are all in India – hence his regular visits.

He feels well off and is looking forward to a comfortable retirement:

I don't have money worries. Never have since I've been working because since I've been working I've only been unemployed since I, since once when I went to India for 6 months, came back, I didn't work for about 4 or 5 months, that was the only period I've been unemployed. Well, since, apart from that, I've always been in work.

Life has got even better over the last 5 years, he thought:

Yeah it has. It will be even better once I've got my redundancy! ... nobody has any money worries in my family ... if I did have money worries, well, I'd probably be divorced by now because that's the main cause of a divorce in this country these days or anywhere it's money isn't it, lack of money. I've been married, what, I can't even remember how many, 29 years?

His only worry seems to be the cost of his car, which he needs to work night shifts at Fords:

... If I had a better transport here I would like to sell my car because it's costing so much money.

It emerges that there are three cars in the family: his, his son's and his daughter's.

Ajit

Ajit, a married Sikh professional woman working for Newham Council, living in an owner-occupied semi-detached house, is joined from time to time by her husband as we talk to her. They moved here from Dagenham, 3 years ago, and are still trying to sell their old house, which they are renting out while paying two mortgages:

She: ... we didn't have enough savings to pay off the negative equity but we had – you know, on our salaries we could get another mortgage.

He: We've always had the income but never the savings.

They knew they wanted to move here:

We knew we wanted to move here. I think we drove around a lot didn't we? We drove around Ilford, Goodmayes. We didn't particularly want to move out, because in Dagenham most people move, that move out from Dagenham move out to Romford, Upminster, that way. We don't want to move there, mainly because we think it's a lot of the old white East End people who are racist move out there. I'm very conscious of (*hesitates*) – and here it's a bit more – it's more mixed here. You've got a bit of everything. There are quite a few Asians here. It's still close to Asian shops etcetera... I think it's a nice area. I like it. It's a nice area. People are friendly. The schools are nice. It's okay.

Particularly, they came here because of the reputation of the schools:

It's one of the reasons we did move here, was the reputation of the schools wasn't it. I mean we didn't know too much about what the infant and primary schools were like, but we know that the secondary school, ***, has a very good reputation, even though things could change by the time she goes there, but it was of a concern to us that it was decent schools. Also when we were looking at houses a lot of them would say *** catchment which is her school so it obviously had a reputation as well.

She thinks this is a better place to live than Newham:

Unfortunately, even though I work for Newham Council – don't tell them that. I did. I told the leader that, because he said – the leader of the Council, he dislikes Redbridge because all the affluent Asians from Redbridge move out ... from Newham to Redbridge.

This is partly because the schools were better than in Newham, though:

I mean it is improving. Newham is the fastest improving in the country. Did you know this?

They talk openly about the problems their child encountered in her Dagenham school:

I wondered because there were a few times when she'd come home and say that the kids had been saying you've got dark skin. Even other Asian kids say you've got dark skin. She's a shade darker than a lot of Asians. She'd be very upset. We made a pact once and she'd asked for something – she'd asked for something quite soon after she'd had a cry about being dark skinned, and she said, 'Mummy I wish – because without the sun I'm a bit lighter than this', and she said, 'Mummy I wish I was light skinned like you'. And I made a pact with her when she asked for something. I said,

'Namjot I promise I'll get you that if you promise me that you won't get upset and won't think that you're any less because of your dark skin, and what matters is in there'. She started crying and saying, 'Mummy I love you'. And touch wood, since then she hasn't.

It's not just white children then that are being difficult?

No, it's other Asian kids who are fairer skinned. I mean culturally, in our culture, you know, white skin is preferred.

Amongst Asians as well?

Yeah, fairer skinned. Is this news to you?

The fairer you are the better it is?

Yeah there's plenty of – what's that cream Sangat you can get in India? Fair and Lovely? To make your skin fairer.

I've heard about this, but I thought that was just like a teenage thing and it was coming from the Western influence.

No. Even when there's matchmaking going on for marriages, arranging marriages and stuff, it's all, she's a bit dark isn't she, or, she's nice and fair. It's very much embedded in our culture. You try and argue with any of our lot. They think we're weird … if I try and say you know, look you're no better than the racists out there, they just don't see the connection.

Fellow Indians, they say, defend their attitudes, especially towards the latest immigrant arrivals:

That's different you see – we came over here and we worked – haven't you heard this? We worked, and the refugees and asylum seekers that are coming here now are coming here to scrounge off the State, and we're paying our taxes, and we came over here and we slogged our butts off. That's the argument. I've heard it so many times. We just shut up now don't we… We were in the minority and there was about ten of them screaming us down, so we just said, okay, and we shut up.

Here, they found, Asians were everywhere moving in:

It's very nice. I'm never quite sure what people think of us, but there are more and more Asian people moving in. It's funny cos our neighbours are selling their house, and every time we say to them – because they've had quite a few offers that have fallen through, and every time we say, so who's buying your house, they say, it's a nice Asian family. (*Laughs*)

But this had caused a misunderstanding that still hugely rankled with their son:

One lot that came round to see the house were a Sikh family, and we're Sikhs and Sangat used to wear a turban, but about 6 months after we moved here Sangat had his hair cut off which was a big deal for us… But this guy, when he had the Sikhs coming to see the house said to him, 'Don't worry, once you've been living round here for 6 months we'll have your hair off!' And he told Sangat this, and Sangat looked at him and said, 'If you'd said something like that to me, even just before I cut my hair off, I would have smacked you one'. They just hadn't realised… Sangat said to this guy, 'You have no idea how you've insulted him and me. You just don't know'. I think people are nice, but I think it's because their backgrounds are that they've been taught to be nice.

Perhaps there was racism here, they thought, but it was implicit:

I'm not sure what people think of us. But it's not in your face. I know some people say they prefer in your face rather than subtle, but give me the subtle any day. (*Laughs*) I don't want my windows smashed in.

She mentions another incident, apparently trivial, concerning remarks by a white neighbour who looked after a boy of Indian parentage in her son's school. It caused her to reflect on a certain ambivalence in her own attitudes:

This boy… He's noticeably behind the rest of the class. And she wondered whether that was anything to do with the fact that the childminder doesn't communicate very well in English. I think she's fine. You know, she's got an accent and everything. And that did, you know, it got to me. And then I thought, hold on, this is just a bit of shit basically … although she's not outwardly racist, it's just the odd comments like that that make you think… Like when she talks of moving out of her old place it was because all the other kids in the class were not fluent speakers of English and it was possibly holding her child back. I've heard that elsewhere and I do wonder. Yeah, that's a valid enough reason I guess. I wonder whether I would say that to another Asian person. Do you know what I mean? It's like (*pauses*) – anyway…

Back in Dagenham, they thought, it was much more explicit:

When Namjot went to nursery there, there was another couple. The woman is Asian who's married to this white guy who's a lot older, although that doesn't mean anything. The girl was ostracised by her family basically. They're both teachers. She still sees her mum, but in secret type of thing. She doesn't dare come to Ilford because that's where her family live … they still live in Dagenham, and I wonder why, because they're got a history of racism you wouldn't believe. Well you probably would. I'm sure you're heard it elsewhere… Plus there's an added factor there, which is a weird one, because they're teachers. He teaches in Dagenham, and people in that area don't seem to like authority... There's a lot of racism in Dagenham. I didn't like it when we lived there. I didn't experience it much but you could sense it...

Is Dagenham sort of white, old East End?

Yeah, white, old East End ... when Saroj was 18 months or less than that, under 2, they had a petrol bomb through their window. They had their house set alight. They've had the troublemakers coming round and having fights on the lawn with Brian – broken his nose. I mean they've had so much. They've had their tyres slashed, their car regularly trashed. And they're still there!

They find themselves in a strangely ambivalent position. Though their native language is Punjabi, they speak English at home:

We're in a weird situation where – I mean we don't know what white people round here think of us, but we know that our family think we've become white... So we can't win really. We're not white enough for the white people. We're not Asian enough for the Asian people.

She begins to try to explain. His parents are in Heston, West London. Hers are nearby in East Ham:

One of the problems immediately was that in our culture, when you get married the woman is supposed to live with her husband's family. We lived there a month and then moved out this way near my parents, which is like really frowned upon. His parents tried to get us to move over there for ages...

These customs are governed by fairly strict Sikh traditions:

... I mean it's either the eldest or the youngest I think traditionally. But I think the situation when we got married was that his eldest brother was living away. He'd bought his own house, not on the same road at that time. The second eldest, who's married to my sister incidentally, they moved to Canada. So we got married and we would have been the ones that should have looked after them at that point in time, and the youngest one wasn't yet married. So we moved out at a time when there was no daughter-in-law to do the cooking and stuff. So yeah, it was a bit – I don't think they appreciated it...

Now, there is less and less contact:

We probably go about once a month now, whereas before we'd probably go ... after we got married, all those years ago, 12 years ago, when we moved over here, we'd go every weekend. And now it's just gradually dropped off. We don't even feel we have to go once a month. It's whenever. If there's a need. If his mum rings up and cries about her other boys not being good to her, and then we go over...

Her parents, she explains, would have preferred them to live with them because they could take the blame, so to speak:

… Oh it's her parents that are making them live near them, type of thing, so it would have suited them if we'd lived there too. But they didn't ever pressurise us. They just said, wouldn't it be a good idea if we lived there and saved all our money, type of thing. Because we rented a place for a year, and everybody in our community thinks that renting a place is a waste of money. With that money you can buy a place and it's yours… They thought we were mad to rent a place because we really struggled for a year. But we were determined not to crawl back so to speak.

Some friends and relatives have dispersed worldwide, but others remain close:

Well, my best mate from uni, from Essex, she's in the States… My sister's in Canada. I've got other sisters. We've got a big family. I've got a couple of sisters who live in Ilford. I've got a sister who lives in Chelmsford. I think I see the oldest one who lives in Ilford the most. She comes round here quite often. Our friends in Dagenham are very close. We've got other friends from my old work – there's some friends in Charlton, who we don't see very often. And another school friend of mine, very old, who now lives in Swindon. She's just had a baby, a few months ago, and I haven't been to see her yet.

Caste, she thought, is becoming unimportant:

It used to be. I mean I was totally ignorant of caste. I didn't know anything about caste until I went to university and somebody said to me, 'What caste are you?' I said, 'What's that?' Then I suddenly realised when my Dad used to sit down and talk… It suddenly clicked to me what they meant. But I think it's slowly becoming less and less important than it was.

But religion still matters among some young men, who are using it as a justification for violence:

There's a lot of rivalry between Sikhs, Moslems, Moslems and Hindus. You know, there've been gang fights and all sorts. These horrible young men…

She sees a very open future for her children:

I'd like to say I want them to do what they want. [*Laughs*] But we'll see how they get on… Namjot goes to drama and singing and dancing. I don't know if anything's going to come of that. But from a very early age when we'd see anything on stage she'd say, I want to be up there, can't I do that. She'd done this for about a year and I thought, we've got to find her a drama school and then she can do that. And it's not one of those schools that ... well I've not heard of them getting kids any major parts up the West End or anything... I think as she gets older if she's serious about, you know, being a star then we'll think again. But like the neighbours, their – Charlotte goes to a specialist dance school – she's had stints in the West End, Les Misérables, and Spend, Spend, Spend, and she's been invited up to the Edinburgh Festival and stuff. That's probably a tad too serious for me.

Sharmaine

Sharmaine, in her fifties, is an Afro-Caribbean from the island of St Lucia, with a white husband; she is a social worker and counsellor, who commutes daily across the capital to south-west London and is making a major career shift, helping young people who have not been able to access counselling and people with depression; they moved here from Scotland some 9 years ago into their owner-occupied detached house, because she had earlier lived in Barkingside and thought she knew the area. Their children are grown up and in professional positions. They have friends:

All over the place really, Oh gosh when you think of it – I've got a sort of a few close friends in London, I've got friends in East Sussex and I've got a friend in Scotland, they're all over the place really and abroad.

Financially, she describes their position as:

I don't know ... I suppose one would say we're in the middle but ... I don't know, yeah, I suppose in the middle... I think, yeah, yeah, there were difficult moments when our children went to university because we both were in sort of full-time and professional work, children didn't get grant or anything like that and it was very costly to see them through that cos they chose very costly subjects...

Interestingly, she feels that she suffers a certain kind of reverse discrimination from black people because she married a white man, because she is educated, because she has a good standard of living. She recalls talking to fellow Caribbeans:

They were all Jamaicans, no from the Lewisham [area] ... the way I experienced this was that they all were talking about not achieving at school. So I suppose the experience that they had, as now they're grown men and women, was that it was very difficult for them ... to get through their schooling. I'm trying to understand that because my children, they were okay. (Laughs) ... but you know, every person's experience is different and that I myself was in the system at 16 and there again they all say to me, what do you know about it because I live in Chelsea in Sydney Street, so it was a lot different to somebody who comes from Brixton or something.

> She remarks immediately that she feels the quality of her neighbourhood has declined:

Well it's suddenly not as quiet, it's certainly not so suburban any more and there is – well more cosmopolitan I would think in a sense and it's funny saying that coming from London, but it was sort of different, quieter, more country-like and so all that's changed and values change, it's not so small, you know, considerate kind of community any more.

… why do you think that is?

… while I first lived there, there was sort of a high proportion of Jewish community which has now moved on and people from other places are moving in. So I suppose that kind of … the sentiment of close knit community and wanting it to be a kind of superb outlook it's not, without sounding snobbish, it's not there any more and I think I'm quite a down to earth person but because of the work I do and the work my husband does, when we come home we like it dead quiet and I miss that.

What's made it more noisy?

… what's made it noisier I think is change of people and change of values and I suppose at the time maybe it is fair to say that many people who lived in – generally speaking – embrace the environment and that kind of suburban quietness, but it's not there any more.

> The problem, specifically, lay with one of their neighbours:

… approaching to the property I think, to my right, I couldn't wish for better neighbours in a sense, I mean there are times, you know, there are special occasions if one having a barbeque for example and things like that, one expects this kind of stuff, but … it's unfortunate to my left it's … it's awful, it's very noisy… I think maybe it's because it's a very large extended family when I came here it wasn't so extended and now it's so extended and it's very noisy, and I … you know, I work with children, I love children, you know but … it's … it's just screaming, you know, at times.

Have they got babies or young children?

A mixture I think…

A mixture – and teenagers as well?

Not quite yet, God forbid, no! (*laughs*) The thought of it!

The family is Asian, an eight- or nine-person family, with another baby on the way, living in a three-bedroom house:

You know, I … I get so upset over it, I've been really upset and Bob's really upset … because you know, I love socialising, I love people, but I just don't like that screaming all the time. It really upsets me and that is mild to what … you know, when they're screaming it's almost like, everybody let loose, no management of the children, everybody just … just a hopeless … and I'm a mother, I've had children and I don't … I'm not empathic with it.

The problem, she concedes, was one of clashing cultures:

… they've shown courtesy towards me and I think the only problem I have is because I suppose our values are so far apart… I think it's maybe they can't see the problem but I can see the problem and I have and they know it annoys me but it doesn't mean to say it stops… And I work at home, I do counselling at home.

On top of that, the neighbours have embarked on unauthorised building work:

… the bottom of the garden, no planning permission and this dreadful view, cos … it's a beautiful view when you look over all the gardens but they're building this great big stuff which actually came over the boundaries, my husband was furious about, really furious about that … it's a great long thing, I don't know what you call it, some kind of place where you put junk, children or whatever!… I can see it and it's dreadful, it spoils the scenery, it's awful and it oversteps the boundary and I think that when the time comes to sell the property, it will be problematic, I mean although the wall is built, but that bit of the wall will have to be maintained by them because it overstepped the mark. So a lot of things has happened since…

More generally, she felt that there was a subtle decline in the quality of the area:

I don't know how to quite answer that but there is a different set of people for different sets of values … there doesn't seem to be much in common. I think without sounding really horrible and snobbish, there is nothing in common at all, I'm just brain dead, there's nothing apart from one colleague that lives about three junctions from here, I go to at times and she writes sort of little bits and I'm thinking perhaps we could join and do some stuff together.

So they seriously intend to move:

Oh as soon as possible, it's just a matter of finding somewhere … preferably because Bob works in Stevenage and will be coming from more North London, maybe Muswell Hill and … Swiss Cottage or places like that.

Suburbia in Transition

Gants Hill, we wrote at the start of this chapter, is in some ways the archetype of what is happening to London's semi-detached suburbs. The same processes, of what the Chicago sociologists of the 1920s would have called invasion and succession, are happening all over the outer suburban ring – in Ealing and Kingsbury just as much as in Gants Hill. Older generations, almost exclusively white, are dying or leaving; their children are seeking new lives in new homes in other parts of the country, or – increasingly – in other countries altogether; their places are being taken by second or third generation descendants of the waves of immigrants who have settled in inner London during the 1950s and 1960s and 1970s. Logically, as inner London becomes quite distinctly unlike any other part of the United Kingdom – even any other British city – by reason of its exceptionally high concentration of ethnic minorities, so must this very fact lead to continuing out-migration into the suburban ring.

The outcomes will provide material for scores of dissertations from sociologists and social anthropologists. One key question, which we do not try to answer here but they will surely attempt, is to what degree differences in religion and culture may modify an all-pervasive (and, perhaps, all-persuasive) middle-class lifestyle. Earlier migrations, notably the Jewish movement that preceded this one, may provide some clues. Perhaps the most intriguing one is that cultures, especially those with a strong religious and ethical base, can prove quite resilient and robust over long periods even while outward lifestyles remain very much in the English mainstream. That, one would hazard, is the most likely outcome we are already beginning to see in places like Gants Hill. But time will tell.

Gants Hill houses

Queen Elizabeth Bridge

© Bill Knight

Chapter Eight

Edge Suburb

Greenhithe

Kent Thameside is a place known only to a few planners and officials in the Department for Communities and Local Government and in the Kent County Council. They would dearly like everyone else to hear about it, because they are trying to build thousands of new homes there to help meet a mounting shortage in South East England, but they may not succeed until someone invents a more memorable name. In the middle of it is a name and a place almost everyone has heard of: Bluewater, the largest shopping mall in Europe, which attracts visitors from not only all over England but from across the water on the European mainland. The rest, in 2007, is a bizarre landscape, almost surreal, of huge old chalk quarries separated from each other by vertical white cliffs. But all that is changing, and about to change even more radically.

For this is a key part of Thames Gateway: a 40 mile long corridor stretching from London Docklands through East London and beyond it into Essex and Kent, which the government has determined should produce hundreds of thousands of new homes and jobs over the next 30 years. Change, frenetic change, is what this area is all about: everywhere new housing, new roads and new shopping centres. It is Britain's answer to Edge City: the term, invented by the Washington journalist Joel Garreau, to describe the instant mega-suburbs, complete with their own centres, that are springing up all around the big American cities. Edge City English-style – call it Edge Suburb – takes a subtly different form from its American cousin: not quite instant city, but a form that wraps round and eventually engulfs much older country towns, on a model that became familiar and even notorious in the 1930s when George Orwell described it in his novel *Coming Up for Air*.

Kent Thameside is strung out between two such places, Dartford and Gravesend; it includes old villages like Greenhithe, main focus of our interviews, Northfleet and Swanscombe. But they are rapidly disappearing as recognisable places as they are eviscerated and twisted by earth movers, construction lorries and seas of mud. This is an area in the throes of major transition, where the visitor experiences a real sense of shock at the juxtaposition of opposites. The brand new elements – the retail park, the new warehouses, the hotel, the executive housing – contrast starkly with the surviving chalk quarries and industrial plants and with small-scale pieces of industrial urbanism, recalling the Black Country or Yorkshire much more than the traditional vision of Kent, now embodied on its car licence plates, as Garden of England. And these superficial signs reflect a deeper economic and social reality: this was an area of heavy industry, which is being rapidly transformed into a new and special part of South East England.

Everywhere is disruption, diversion, noise, congestion, pollution where once was calm. Many older-settled residents feel a profound sense of loss, as they told us in our interviews. But many newcomers are too busy just coping with busy lives, earning two incomes to survive economically, juggling work and commuting and child care, to pay much attention to their immediate neighbourhood or their quality of life; though a surprising number have older family members nearby, they seem barely to know who lives next door. People living here, like those in older suburbs such as Gants Hill, have often moved out from London or from nearer places in search of space, and Arcadian calm, at a price they can afford. But older-established people complain about losing just that quality; they would like to move farther out, but are very often constrained – by commuting time, by family or school ties, and by the cost of housing in more attractive rural parts of Kent.

This extraordinary 22 square mile piece of southern England stretches from the Greater London boundary in the west to the North Kent Marshes in the east, in the weakest segment of the London Green Belt, between the Thames and the A2 London–Dover road. It encompasses half a dozen places with a combined population of about 180,000, together with large tracts of land around these residential areas. Its entire development has been dominated by the river, by the parallel lines of road and rail that followed its south bank, and by the industries that grew up around these two great lines of movement. Its economic story is one of growth, decline and spectacular resurgence.

Some History

The Thames, widening here to half a mile or more across, is the key to Kent Thameside. It carried an endless passing stream of trade from the entire world into what was for centuries its greatest port. And, down to the nineteenth century, there were regular passenger services along and across the river, while Gravesend was a key point for barges carrying goods for markets in London and beyond. Logically, the area was the Merchant Navy's training ground, with a naval college in Greenhithe and training ships moored offshore.

On the land side, the London–Dover road – the Roman Watling Street, Britain's main land link to mainland Europe – was crucial; Dartford, a bridging point on the tributary river Darent, was already an important market town by Tudor times. But, from the eighteenth century this became an area of heavy industry, with the river used to bring in materials in and ship products out. Here were the country's first commercial paper and iron-splitting mills; here too Portland cement production, using lime from the local chalk and clay, was also pioneered to serve the vast London market. During the early nineteenth century, paper making and cement manufacture in particular expanded along the Thames shore, further boosted by the coming of the railways. Almost immediately, their noxious character – including airborne pollution from thick cement dust – discouraged the better sort of residential development. But employment growth brought people: Dartford grew eightfold during the nineteenth century.

And the railway, then as now, was slow. Although there was some ribbon development in the inter-war period, the local towns and villages remained small and quite isolated, little related to the wider London economy only 20 miles away, separated from each other by the huge chalk quarries, and – until 1963, when the Dartford tunnel was opened as a single two-lane bore – lacking any direct link to the Essex side of the estuary. But in the 1970s the local heavy industries started to shut down, with big job losses; unemployment rose, peaking at 10.7 per cent in 1993, while local people increasingly were driven to find work in London. Even more significantly, the area was left with a large number of derelict industrial sites, both on the river front and in the cement industry's vast chalk pits. Much of this land was owned by the Blue Circle cement company, whose immediate reaction was to exploit them as landfill sites; the rubbish lorries, converging on the area from across London, did nothing to raise the area's image or to encourage inward investment.

But then came a dramatic turnaround: in 1986, completion of the M25 London orbital motorway, with a doubling of the Dartford tunnel and then (in 1991) the Queen Elizabeth Bridge to produce a fourfold increase in capacity on the Thames crossing, from two lanes to eight. As the intersection point of the M25 and the main freight route to the continent, the area suddenly found itself attractive for distribution and logistics activities – notably in the new Crossways Business Park, which attracted £30 million investment – and a viable location for decentralised back office functions, especially for financial services including Woolwich PLC.

The new bridge also gave the area a huge potential market as a service centre, with some 10 million people within 60 minutes drive time.

Developers were not slow to grasp the opportunity: close to the interchange, the Australian Lend Lease company developed Europe's largest regional shopping and leisure centre in a 300 acre disused chalk pit at Bluewater. The local Gravesham Council reacted by obtaining government Single Regeneration Budget money to regenerate Gravesend's attractive high street.

But even as the new bridge was opening, the government took a major decision: to re-route the high-speed Channel Tunnel Rail Link through this area, and to use it as an instrument of regeneration for the entire Thames Gateway corridor downstream of London Docklands. A passenger station on the new line at Ebbsfleet, opening in 2007, will serve both international and domestic services and will cut rail travel time to central London from an hour to just 15 minutes, and will put both Paris and Brussels within 2 hours reach. In addition to a huge mixed-use development around the station, dense city-scale residential development is planned for the surrounding area, serviced by a new public transport system, Fastrack, not by car.

The Thames Gateway Planning Framework envisaged that by 2021 50,000 new jobs and 30,000 new homes would be created here from a combination of the station development with other ongoing projects including a new University of Greenwich campus and science park; a new privately funded hospital; further development of the Crossways Business Park; a new urban village in the Eastern Quarry; environmental improvement on the Swanscombe peninsula; and redevelopment of industrial sites on the Gravesend waterfront. The plan has been progressed by a public-private partnership, Kent Thameside Association, which brings together county and district authorities, property developers, the CTRL rail company and the University of Greenwich – rather than a single centralised structure as was used in Docklands. With the benefit of concentrated land ownership and active support from Kent County Council, anxious to divert development pressures from the neighbouring 'Garden of England', the process moved rapidly: by the millennium there was a master plan, encompassing a major new town and business park, and development was beginning to break out all over the area.

Residents generally have welcomed this vast development, because it brings a boost to an area that needs it. But, in an area where house prices remain low by London standards (averaging £214,000 for a semi-detached house in Dartford, £207,000 in Gravesend in early 2006), there are fears that a stronger economy will raise rental levels and hurt residents on low and fixed incomes, including the long-term unemployed, sick and elderly. Local authorities are committed to securing affordable housing through planning gain, but it is unclear how far this is achievable here given the high costs associated with developing brownfield sites.

The Area Today

The Kent Thameside economy still includes a substantial manufacturing element: it employed 17 per cent of local workers in 1999, one of the highest proportions in the London region. And it was still concentrated around traditional heavy industries including chemicals, even though mergers between Wellcome, Glaxo and SmithKlineBeecham have brought a loss since 1999 of no less than 1500 jobs, including closure of the Wellcome factory in Dartford.

Most distinctive, however, is the concentration here of transport and storage activity, employing some 8,000 workers, 12 per cent of the total. For obvious reasons the area also has an above-average share of construction jobs. The balance of employment is thus still quite strongly tilted towards manual employment (37 per cent of jobs in 1998), very high for the South East. Other private services – finance, business services, catering – are relatively under-represented. The area enjoyed average employment growth in the 1990s: manual jobs suffered only modest job losses, as a result of quite strong growth in road transport activities, compensating for declines in manufacturing and public utilities. On the non-manual side there was a very healthy rate of growth in business services from a rather low base. So, between 1991 and 1998, total employment grew by 8 per cent.

Logically, like so much of the Outer Metropolitan Area (OMA) around London, this is middle-middle-class territory. At the 2001 Census there was relatively high employment (60 per cent in Dartford, 62 per cent in Gravesham). The labour force showed a higher-than-average concentration in administrative, secretarial, skilled manual, personal service and sales/customer service jobs. So it is unsurprising that the rate of owner-occupation (74 per cent in Dartford, 72 per cent in Gravesham), was higher than the England and Wales average, almost certainly because access to owner-occupation is easier on this side of London. In household composition, the distinctive features is the high proportion of couple-based households (nearly 50 per cent in Dartford, 49 per cent in Gravesham) with few working-age single-person households (28 per cent, 27 per cent) or lone-parent families with children (just 6 per cent). Nearly 95 per cent (Dartford), 90 per cent (Gravesham) of the population is white; the only notable non-white group is the very old-established Gravesham Sikh community.

So in character, Kent Thameside is ambivalent: with some roots in an industrial past that has almost disappeared, but in many respects part of the Outer Metropolitan Area OMA, rather than of Greater London. In part, this reflects the fact that it has long been an important dormitory for people working in London, and that there is self-selection of those who choose to live outside Greater London: they choose to trade off long commuter journeys for a combination of high London wages and more affordable living space outside the city. Typically, the out-commuters from this area are secretarial, clerical occupations and other junior non-manual workers – while those commuting in to the area from further east in Kent tend to be manual workers.

As in other parts of London's OMA, school standards are good, with above-average GCSE pass rates. Under Kent County Council's Conservative control, there is a selective school system in North Kent including six grammar schools, which are popular with parents both locally and in the neighbouring London boroughs – so much so that they export significant numbers of pupils here.

Though this is one of two case study areas that we deliberately chose outside the London boundary (the other, Reading, does not feature separately in this part of the book), in terms of affluence and deprivation it is more comparable with a London area like Hounslow than with areas in the western half of London's OMA. In October 2001 the (residence-adjusted) claimant unemployment rate was just 2.2 per cent, down from 10 per cent in 1993. As elsewhere, falling unemployment brought an even larger reduction in long-term unemployment, yet more persists here than in Hounslow, with one in six of the unemployed out of work for a year or more – though this proportion is still lower than in any of the other case study areas within Greater London. Average earnings here are also lower than in most of the other case study areas (including Hounslow), although this has to be seen in relation to lower housing costs.

On the IMD2004 deprivation indices, the two Kent Thameside boroughs were right in the middle of the range of local authorities, with not much concentrated deprivation. Local crime reports suggest that race relations are harmonious, with very low levels of reported race-related crime, although stories in the local press give a different impression. Overall crime levels are low by national as well as London standards, particularly for violent offences, though rates of car crime are above the national average.

Our household interviews focused on Greenhithe: an area around an old riverside village on the Thames shore between Dartford and Gravesham, and located on the Dartford side of the boundary. Socially the area spans the mid-range of local wards, although it also includes some of the areas of educational deprivation, and has a somewhat greater proportion both of council tenants and lone parents. But their common feature is that they are on the cutting edge of residential development – including one ward in which the population rose by 12 per cent between 1991 and 1997.

Thus, we found, Greenhithe is really two bits. The first is the old riverside village, with some surviving old village houses plus a heavy infill of crescents and closes, some on the river, others behind the old village street, and on a new parallel road behind, with a mixture of detached, semis and some terrace housing. The other, Knockhall, is an eclectic mixture of interwar and postwar housing, with a few pre-World War One terraces; interwar and postwar terraces and semis, generally quite small but with a view at the back on to open countryside, up the hill just off the main A226 road; nothing very special, but quite a good villagey feel.

There is a third Greenhithe too, just starting construction when we interviewed: the huge Ingress Park development by Crest Nicholson, showered with awards and commendations for its high quality of design, an importation of the concepts of the American New Urbanism movement into Kent Thameside. Here new luxury riverside houses have been built on former factory sites, in close proximity to – but relatively segregated from – the older Victorian housing stock and newer social housing built in the 1950s. Exactly how these communities relate to one another, or not, was a major question for our interviewers as they went about their work.

Harry

Harry is one of the oldest-established residents we interviewed: a married man with three grown-up children, he is aged 69 and now retired. Though he owns a new semi-detached house in Greenhithe village, he has lived in the area for nearly 60 years:

I came to live here when I was 10 years old and I am now 69. So, it's 59 years.

But, like so many others, he felt that it was no longer the same place:

Well, there's no place like home and this isn't really home now. I'll give you an instance, about 18 months ago, my wife and I went into the Pier Hotel with one of the locals in the village, for a beer on Saturday night. The place was packed and I didn't know a soul, they were all local people that have moved in and not only did I not know any of the customers but I did not know any of the bar staff. Yet 30 years ago, not only would I have known all of the customers and all of the bar staff, I would have known about their families and where they work and how old their children were. This is how it's changed and its not changed because I'm too old really to change in that sense, I don't enjoy it.

Even in his local street, he reflected:

… there's a cosmopolitan lot now, something else that has changed in Greenhithe, if I am to put my hand on my heart and swear this … some of them I would not even recognise on the street, there is no neighbourliness in this area now.

But he could see some good things that had come out of change:

Well I suppose so... I was anti-Dome and I was anti-Bluewater but Bluewater has brought improvement to the village. There's employment now, good roads, good railway services, which we did not have in the past, so that's an asset I suppose but I still, if I could turn the clock back, I would say no to Bluewater.

This was in part because the village shops he had known had disappeared:

... generally speaking whatever one wanted to buy you could buy in Greenhithe, this was the thirties but you could buy clothes, get your hair cut, go to the chemist, grocery shopping, bakeries, butchers and cafés but there is nothing.

The point, he recognised, was that Bluewater:

... has brought prosperity to the area because ... the cement factories have closed, the paper mills have closed, the shipyards have closed. The river which was our livelihood packed up and so Bluewater and all these new estates they're building on the back here they call 'Crossways' have brought prosperity.

Nancy

Nancy is a mother in her late thirties or early forties, recently separated, with three children (two boys, one girl) living in an owner-occupied terrace house in Knockhall at the top of Greenhithe. She works in a local school as a learning support assistant. Life has been a struggle since her separation, she told us:

I was really struggling. I was really struggling. But then somebody told me about the Family ... what's it called ... Family Credit. If you go to work, they help you. And I've started claiming that... I don't like anything like that. It's not everybody's fault that I'm on my own with three children and I don't expect everybody else to pay for that, but this is different. Because I'm working, they just ... they help you...

She is one of the old-time residents:

I've lived here all my life in Greenhithe. Thirty-eight years on Friday. I moved out in 1984. I emigrated to Gravesend for 6 years. But didn't settle, so I came back.

Even Gravesend, to which she 'emigrated', seemed a foreign land:

Yes, it's only 4 miles the other side, Gravesend. It was only sort of 4 or 5 miles. But I just found it so unfriendly...

She never even considered moving away:

All my family here. I've got my brother lives in a house there, my sister's opposite, my mother's down the road, and my father's down the bottom. And because, it isn't as much now, but it used to be really a real community place…

But, as an old-time resident, even more than Harry she felt the place had changed very much for the worse:

Because I've got emotional ties, I suppose, it's home for me. But it has gone down hill. This part, Knockhall, years ago used to be the posh bit and the bottom end was for not quite as posh, but it's completely turned now. And I've noticed recently you get the rubbish on the streets. Last night, I don't know who it was, but there was some people screaming and shouting. It has gone down in that sense. But it's still not as bad as a lot of areas.

She also bemoaned the lack of shops:

No, there's no shops. Years and years ago there used to be so many shops down the bottom of Greenhithe. Dozens of shops down there. Everything that you wanted. And now we're left with the corner shop there and one down the bottom…

Asked what she would like if she won the Lottery, she replied:

I'd like the … yeah, I think I'd like the area to come back up to where it was. Because it has been going down and I wouldn't… It would be sad if it carried on going down… I think it's just this generation of teenagers to be honest. I really do … I'd like it to look a bit nicer again rather than the rubbish and the piles of rubble and what have you everywhere and just to have a nice feel about it again.

Dorothy and Bill

Dorothy is a school secretary, Bill an ambulance driver. They are both in their late fifties, married with three grown children, two boys and a girl. They live in a flat in a council block in Knockhall at the top of Greenhithe. She was born here and has lived here all her life. They moved once to Gravesend, 5 miles away, but moved back here again. Two of their children live close by, another on the far side of London, but they contact each other daily:

She: We've got one son that lives in Northfleet, which is a couple of miles. And we've got the daughter that lives in Gravesend, which is about 5 miles. And our other son lives at High Wycombe, so that's quite a long way, but that's it.

And how often would you see…

She: The daughter… The daughter rings every night at 6 O'clock just to make sure that everything's OK.

They too feel overwhelmed by the scale of change. Immediately, they felt that the quality of life in their small council block had fallen sharply. Partly it was the traffic:

She: The noise of the traffic can be horrific and we've got double glazing, but you can still hear it. And if you open the windows, you can hear the traffic, you know, quite a lot.

It was even undermining the physical structure of their block, they thought:

He: I'm looking at the crack. That's the traffic that causes that. There's a big crack going across there. We plastered all these ceilings when we moved in here. And it's all breaking up again through the traffic. But what can you do?

… effect on the structure of the house?

He: [*wife talks over husband*]

She: Well, we think that, that actually is what's happening, but you'd need to have a proper survey and that to make sure.

… *the effect of the traffic, it's a very easy thing to underestimate I suppose?*

He: It's the heavy traffic. It's not the cars. It's the heavy traffic.

Just as problematically, the close sense of neighbourhood had been lost:

She: I should think it's a really vast mix, you know, especially the new people. I mean, they're mostly people that commute to London or something on the train I would say. I would think there's probably very few of people that have been born here and always stay here. I would think that there's not many of those families sort of left.

In particular, their neighbours in their small block had changed completely:

She: … there's only twelve flats here … twelve maisonettes. And there's one or two of them where they've had single mums with either a baby or two children and it's like a stopgap until they move them on and things like that. So they've become a little bit of a stop gap, although the people downstairs, down there, I mean they're intending to stay. But I do think a lot of them move on.

He: Their gardens don't get tidied up.

She: These used to be really nice, you know, this used to be a really nice block. There's just the three blocks like that. And they used to be really nice. Everybody look after them.

He: … rubbish … rubbish accumulates and I mean, they'll walk past it. I mean there's a bag laying there, been there for months and months and months. And on the end, there's bits of carpet left in the garden. There's an arm chair down here in the next … they never think about taking it to the tip. You know, they seem to walk over it and can't see it. Or, it's not my responsibility. The Council will move it. That's the sort of thing that gets … that I don't like. But then there's nothing I can do about it. There's nothing you can do about it. It's just the way some people live and other people don't live like that. So it would be nice if…

She: I think it becomes, you know, you can put up with things for so long and so long and then you say, right, enough's enough and you've got to stand and do something. And I think a lot of people are like that. You know, you put up with things for so long and that's when people get really angry. They should actually, as soon as soon as something happens, they should be on the case immediately and then it wouldn't get to that stage, you know.

But it went far wider than that. The place they once knew had gone for ever:

She: Immense change. Immense change. From a little village with… I mean the street I was born in probably had just over 100 houses and there was probably another 150, 200 houses just dotted around, all round the area. I mean where Bluewater is, was just woods. I played in those as children. That was all there was. That was before they dug the pit.

As a result, the quality of life she enjoyed as a child has gone:

She: I think, when I was a child, it was wonderful. There was so many places to go and, you know, and to be out and about all over the place. But, I mean, in this day and age, children can't do that sort of thing. They just cannot be allowed to go off all day with a packed lunch, you know. But … and life is more difficult. And I should imagine parents have a lot more difficulty with children, I mean … because of main roads. There wasn't all the traffic when I was a child and just the sheer fear of, you know, letting children out of your sight.

More and more, they felt, they were ceasing to be a distinct rural place, and were becoming swallowed up in London's amorphous growth:

She: I think London itself...

He: Is moving this way.

She: Where there used to be green spaces in between, it's all gradually coming this way. And because of the good communication, and there is definitely good transport, you know, I mean we've got a station there, which a lot of villages haven't got. We've got coaches that come past here every day. You know, a good bus service that goes up there. And obviously the good roads for cars. So people are going to move out here because of the cost of housing in London. I mean it's relatively cheaper out here.

They both talked about the loss of the village shops that had once given life to the place:

She: I just feel it's a shame that our ... that my village, as I knew it, is not the village that I knew. But ... because there was shops there. It was bustling. It was absolutely alive in say the 1940s, '50s and '60s. It was, you know, there was... It housed three butchers. And there was probably...

He: Bakers and everything...

She: Yeah, housed two bakers...

He: ... a cobbler, a hairdressers...

She: ... ship's chandler...

He: ... three pubs...

She: ... you know. Oh, more than three pubs.

He: In the village there was three pubs...

She: Well, yeah. Well, in the length of the village, there was three pubs. But, you know, it's just so... I just feel it was a lost opportunity, with all these little villages, little village shops, now that would be, I mean we've just been to Manchester and they've actually built a custom built village on the side of a hill with all these little things, and we had it. You know, we had it.

He: And it's gone.

She: You know, in the little shops, you know. I can still smell this smell of the ice cream that was in Moss's shop, you know. As you went down the steps, the smell of the home made ice cream there...

What kind of things would you like there to be more locally for yourself?

She: I would like more shops. More local shops. You know, as it was. You know, more like sort of bakers, that sort of thing. Because you've got to go to the various...

I mean short of going along a garage ... along here and having sort of a processed loaf or something like that, you know, there really isn't any shops. You've got to go to the shops. I mean, I think they just missed this opportunity in Greenhithe itself to retain the parade of shops that there was. And I'm sure that with all the houses there are now, that they would all still be able to make a living.

Oona

Oona is a divorced mother, probably in her late fifties, who rents a house in a mid-terrace in Knockhall at the top of Greenhithe. She has five grown-up children and describes herself as a psychic. She has lived here for 28 years, she explains:

I escaped from a sad marriage in the Midlands and a ridiculous husband that decided to chat up all my best friends and then move on to their best friends. So I left him... I'm Kentish-born anyway, so came back to live with my mother, to a cottage that she had in the country near here. And met a ... man ... a foreman, he lived here. That's why I'm in Greenhithe.

Like almost everyone we met, she was passionately unhappy about what was happening in the area:

It's all getting gobbled up and it's all build, build, build. So there is no Greenhithe, just Brownhithe! ... I mean any direction I go now, with my dog on the end of a lead, I can no longer find the places where I could take him. They've gone. One by one they've gone. That also applies to people that like country walks. People that like flowers. Places for children to play. My children growing up, right, it was come home from school, have their tea, get changed, have you done your homework? Yeah. Right, OK. Can we go out up to Sandy Banks? Off they went. Sandy Banks is now a housing estate. There were woods down there. There were woods over there. My children liked to go out and play. They'd watch Star Trek and you weren't allowed to speak a word...

She explains how the rot started with the local company that had employed her second husband:

So when I married the worker from the shipyard, actually first we got a house on the river front, which ... are still preserved. But they wanted to knock that down. Everards started the destruction of the village. They knocked down the Catholic church, knocked down the Priory which was a lovely old building. And the Brown Bear... Everards started gobbling up the village..

She feels secure enough in her own local corner:

We've got a quiet little cul-de-sac and everybody watches everybody out the lace curtains. It's not an area that attracts crime.

This was like a refuge from everything that was happening outside:

Here, in this little bit, in this little cell, is like a little old world and it's great. You put your nose out the door and they'll come up and they're cuddling the baby…and everybody is … it's just like a little family. Apart from the rest, we don't even know who they are. Where they come from. Who are they? We don't know. They live their own little lives. They're all new people. They are people that are in new houses, you know? We don't know who they are…

But, like other old-time residents, she found herself in a small minority:

I mean, like, apart from us little old timers here, everybody else is new because all the houses are new. So they're all people from God knows where. We call them yuppies.

Sharon

Sharon is one of the 'people from God knows where': the newcomers. White and in her early thirties, she is married and mother of three children (two boys, one girl), all below school age. She is employed part-time as a shop assistant and is owner-occupier of an end-of-terrace house in Knockhall at the top end of Greenhithe. She was a Londoner, born and bred in Bermondsey, but, she told us, she fled the city:

I hate London. I hate London… I don't like the hustle and bustle and the crowds and the… I'm a Londoner. I come from Bermondsey. But I wouldn't ever, ever move. I get scared when I go to London…Yeah. Being mugged. I mean I used to work in Lambeth and I got mugged. I only worked there for a week and I got mugged like twice. I worked in Woolwich and I was mugged. And that's sore to think of…

Besides that, they came here in search of affordable housing:

We lived in Sidcup… We had a flat and just couldn't afford to buy a house in that area.

They moved first to Stone, then here:

Erm, just wanted a bigger house and we wanted to stay in the area…

But that was not the only reason for moving from Sidcup, it emerged:

I know it sounds really silly, but my husband's mixed race and we had a lot of racism and that in Sidcup... Yeah, a lot of people didn't talk to us. Where here, I suppose cos it's lower market, and there's more council places round here, people are easy going and talk to you a bit. They're more friendly. Not so snobby. We've never had any problems with... We've had no racial thing here at all since we've moved here. .

Otherwise, her husband had experienced no real problem – at work, in fact, rather the reverse:

With my husband, his colour's actually done him a favour. Because they aren't many black salesman ... he's mixed race. So, in old days they used to call it half caste... Erm, but people see him as a black man. Because he's got the Afro hair and everything and he's brown skinned. Erm, so no. I think it's helped him because erm... Probably if he tried to get a job... I mean... Because he's the only black salesman, people know him. And he gets recognised because he's the only black one up there. So it's just like Oh yeah, Danny, the black geezer, so ... although he gets racial taunts at work, it's all just jesting and ... I mean it's like water off a duck's back. It's nothing serious. It's just the way people are really...

He had been a market trader who lost his job; finding another well paid had been hard for both of them:

So erm with my husband, he's only worked on the market. His mum got him an interview first off. When he got made redundant, there was no jobs about and it was really worrying for a bit, but I mean he just put the word around and got a job. I mean, he did go to all the agencies. There's loads of agencies and that in Dartford and that he went to... But they were offering money like fifteen grand a year and he was on thirty-two and a half. You see, so it was getting real hard. We'd be better off on the Social you know... Oh, Oh it was awful. Awful, it was. Terrible. Really, really. I didn't know. I didn't know. I was just like a robot, do you know what I mean? I just didn't know what to do. I was thinking God the house. And I love my house, you know. And I'm like Oh God the house. I've just decorated it all, so. It worked out that he got two grand redundancy money and we could do the kitchen and the bathroom. And he went straight into another job. So it worked out better...

But now, because he sold wholesale fruit and vegetables in the market, it made for a difficult family life:

... my husband works erm goes to work 12 O'clock at night... Then he comes home 12 O'clock during the day. Has a couple of hours sleep and then he goes up and I go to work. I come home, he's in bed... Brilliant marriage because we don't see each other! So Monday, Tuesday and Wednesday we don't. It's only phone contact really and sort of hello, goodbye and then Thursday, Friday, Saturday and Sunday we spend sort of time together.

She freely admitted that they both needed to work, not to survive, but to enjoy the standard of living they had got used to:

Erm, I think you're always struggling. I think you erm … we live to a high standard of living… I mean I couldn't give up work now. When I first started work, I worked because I needed to work for my own sort of satisfaction. Now, I couldn't give it up even if I wanted to … because we need the money. We're not struggling on a daily basis, but it's hard to save for holidays and things. Yeah. We have luxuries. I mean, there's always lager in the fridge and you know and stuff like that and if the kids want sweets, they have sweets… And if they need clothes and that. It's things like holidays and that, that we find hard to save for. We're not very good at saving.

She clearly worked just for the money. She saw her future in terms of her children:

I've got no ambition. No ambition at all. No. I just want to be happy. Got no ambition. Just as long as my kids are happy. That's my ambition. My kids do well and are happy. (*Talks to child*)

But she did not have higher ambitions for her children:

Erm, they could be sweeping the streets if they want. As long as they're happy, that's all I care about.

Her view of education was that the first priority was for her children to be happy at school:

I mean it's not the best school in the world because it's not top of the league tables, but my children are happy there. And they're both doing really well so… I looked at the league tables and I read the OFSTED reports.

She threw her emotions and her energies into a rich local social network:

I'm murder. I've got love written across my forehead. Erm, that's why I'm on all the PTAs and everything. I just… Anybody. If I were chatting to one of the mums and they said Oh no I'm really tired, I've had a really bad night, I'll offer to take their kids for the morning. I used to be registered child minder but I don't do that any more. So, people are happy to leave their children with me. I've always got somebody else's kids.

But this did not extend to any wider civic engagement, on which she was cynical:

I think it's all planned and sorted and I don't think they'd listen to us... They have meetings but I never go... Because they're in the evenings... But during the day I'll do anything for anyone. Evenings are mine.

Though a newcomer, she too thought the area had changed:

Erm, it's changed in the last year... When we first moved here it was lovely. The road's really quiet because we're opposite the school. So although at 3 O'clock and 9 O'clock it's a nightmare, during the day it's really, really quiet... And when we first moved, we didn't have any trouble. It was really, really nice. But in the last year we've had loads of trouble. We've had cars nicked out the front constantly... We've had kids going down the back alley... They throw stones over in the garden and stuff... I mean, touch wood [*knock-knock*], we've had a stop to that cos the headmaster sorted it out. Gangs of youths on the corner, drinking and erm one 11 year old kid down the road was chased from the park with a knife... I mean, I don't... It's not like Lewisham rough... I'm not frightened to go out. Whereas I would be if I lived sort of in London. I come from Bermondsey originally... If I lived there now, I wouldn't step outside my door after sort of 5 O'clock. So it's not like. It's not that bad. It's just kids. But it's got worse.

Most of the trouble originated from teenage boys:

But, this year we've had sort of eggs thrown up our wall and, and what they do is, you know the top of your wall, there's usually like a bit on the top? Like a big concrete bit. They've been taking them off and putting on the cars and things like that... There's kids on motorbikes go up and down with no helmets on. They're not insured or anything and they go up and down the back alley as well ... and that's really annoying because they're really loud. The throttle's really loud and they're zooming up and down the street. They're just showing off. But, erm, some of them... The parents don't give a, you know, so there's nothing you can do. If you went to their parents ... I wouldn't. I wouldn't chance it. I wouldn't be like, you know, beaten up by one of the parents.

But in particular, she thought, it came from a local community of travellers:

There are some really rough people around here... Yeah. I'm saying bikers but most people say travellers... Erm, if I had the choice, it's ... there's too many travellers round here... It's not the council places. I got no problems with that. But, erm, we get a lot of people, caravans and I mean I hate using that word partly because it's racist isn't it? But, it's that sort of people that I don't like and we get a few sort of at the school and they have problems with the children and because the parents aren't interested, they can't do anything with them, so...

And there's lots of erm dogs, stray dogs and that. So ... erm the cats and stuff. I mean, outside there, if you look, there's poo all up and down this road. So I think that affects it as well. Because they're not as caring about the environment cos they don't live here. They don't give, erm, a toss basically. And they litter. And... I sound terrible don't I?

Emma

Emma is a married mother in her mid-forties, employed as a classroom assistant, living in a detached house in a new owner-occupied estate in Greenhithe village, with two daughters aged 10 and 13. They too are newcomers to the area, but – like Sharon and her husband – they have moved only a short distance:

... my husband's from Barnehurst. We were living at Welling. And so we wanted ... he plays rugby at Erith ... so we wanted somewhere that's not too far. We were looking for somewhere convenient to a station, not too far out, and we were lucky at the time with the house prices. We'd made fifty thousand on our house. My husband was doing well at work, so we just ... we did look at new houses around and about, but we didn't want to go too far down the line. So we just chose Greenhithe.

And she is content with the area:

It's nice and quiet. It's nice to know we've got Bluewater, although the traffic sometimes is a bit horrendous. But yeah, it's sort of building up as well, you know, it's sort of coming on a bit. We like it cos it's quiet. And sort of quite close to the river if you want to go down for a walk and that... It's only the traffic. I mean you can sit there for about 10 minutes...

Apart from that she could find no faults with the area:

Well I haven't really come across any. No. Because, I mean, if you think about it, we're local for ... we're handy for the Tunnel, we're handy for the motorways, going up to London, and that was one of the reasons we chose this area...

And she was not really concerned about the pace of change:

You see that doesn't really affect me, because I feel... I think that's more the locals. I don't myself as a local girl. And I think it's the older locals...

She was obviously concerned about her daughters' education and the effect of Kent's selective school system. She told us about the ferocious efforts parents made to get their children into the grammar school:

What they tend to do, is that last year of schooling, they will have a tutor to push them and to bring them up to the standard where they will pass the tests. But what I'd like to see is every child doing the test. Not just selected ones. I would like to see every child doing the test and then perhaps the local authorities turning around saying, well these are the children who have the ability, these are the children who haven't. And doing a selection that way and saying to parents, your child is of this level, these are the schools that are available to you, because I know a lot of parents who have come … it's come to July and they still haven't got a school … secondary school for their child to go to. Because everybody wants the grammar schools and the way the selection process goes. If you put certain schools, and it's not the first one, you then don't get a choice. If you don't get in the first school, the second one doesn't want to know you because you put another one in… So that's another reason why I opted for the Catholic school, because I knew that she would get a place there … guaranteed place.

She did not feel closely associated with the area through a network of friends, partly because everyone was too busy to be neighbourly:

Well obviously because as I said earlier I'm not from the area, so I haven't got any old school friends or anything like that or no old family friends. My friends are associated from school with the girls, because that's where you pick the contacts up. I haven't really got any friends from when I used to work in London, because you tend to sort of drop off over the years. You can stand and have a chat, but it's not, you know, Oh come in for a coffee, not like the olden days, you know, or what you see on the telly, like Neighbours, you know, where they're all popping in each other's houses. I think you tend to find nowadays that most couples are out to work.

With the contribution she made as a classroom assistant they were comfortable financially, she thought:

Well, nobody's going to say no to a few extra thousand. But, touch wood, we do do all right. Basically because I just get my little bit extra. I mean I only get £500 a month but that's enough to cover me and the girls so that we can live, paying the bills, the mortgage and just have our holidays really. I mean, we have struggled. We have been through financial, you know, dire straits. But we've come to a situation now where we're just … we plod along, you know. We have a bit of savings and we have a bit put away, but I would say really that we just live, you know. We're waiting for the lottery win. But, no, we're OK.

But for the future:

Well, there's a question. My husband's job is in banking and the banking world, I don't know if you know, is very up in the air and you could go in tomorrow and they will turn round and say, pack your desk up, you're going... And unfortunately the area that Steve's in at the moment, his bank has now merged again. I think this is the second or third time that they've merged. And each time they merge, obviously his job gets a little bit more insecure and... I think if he did lose his job, then we would struggle.

Like almost everyone we asked, she had little interest in local politics:

Nil. I don't feel ... no, no. I mean you do your voting and stuff and we have the Greenhithe and Swanscombe, what are they? We have a local paper come through and if you've got any complaints you can always put in... That's it, yeah. You can contact those people, but... No. I've got too many... Can't commit myself to any more. But I don't think really, as a resident, I don't think you have a lot of say in what goes on. I think it's all done up at the council at that level.

Richard

Richard is another of the incomers: white, in his thirties, married with two children, living in a detached owner-occupied house in a newly-built estate in Greenhithe village. He is unusual only that he is not a commuter: a printer, he works locally. But, though he likes that, he gets no satisfaction from his job:

I've been at that company for 5 years but I've been a printer all my working life... I absolutely hate it but it's a steady job and err that's what you got to look at it ... when I say I don't like it, err it's a career. It's a job where er you are not ... it's not a problem solving thing, you do things in certain ways, there's certain operations and there's not too much change in the job, emm ... it's procedures basically, you go in do it and come home, that's as much as I think...

He works from 6.30 until 2.00 every day, which for him is the main benefit of the job:

It's an early start but an early finish, that's the main benefit of the job that I finish early, sort of twenty past two I'm home which is great.

He finds it less stressful than working in London. He used to work in Peckham, but:

I detested it in the end, absolutely detest it, who wants to work in a ghetto full of crackheads.

The job does not pay particularly well, but it is enough – and:

Yeah, middle of the road, I could earn more money elsewhere but err I'd probably have to go up town, up to London to earn more money which involves more spending on travelling. For me the convenience of working there and the convenience doing the shift that I do is good for me now... I've worked up London. I detest it, absolutely detest it, yeah, I worked up there for 10 years, I can't stand the traffic, you know it's just a nightmare getting to and from work every day, you know especially if you are working say eight til four you're hit all the traffic both ways...

So his job satisfies him at some basic level, despite his protestations:

If someone could guarantee that I would have employment until I retire that would be it for me, not just any employment, employment of a reasonable standard, I think it's what everybody wants really. No one wants to have to go to work but it's something you've got to live with really, so until you get to a retirement position, yeah I'd like to have employment. I mean there's too much trauma involved in not having a job. I've been there, all right I got employment quickly, but it is quite traumatic...

He recognises that his job as a printer is very vulnerable to technical change:

I mean, the particular industry I'm in it's quite a mechanised industry, there's a lot of new technology coming in that's gonna cut back on manpower... I mean it's only 5 years old that you had artwork, with motorbike couriers with artwork ... here and there to the various print companies, now it all comes down the phone line, ISDN, floppy disk and stuff like that, we've got all computers that just download everything. You just stand there with a mouse, it's changed so much and you've got to know it.

But, underlying all this, he seems to have an unsatisfied yearning:

I'd like to do something a bit more scientific, err a marine biologist or something like that you know, something where every day it's different, which at the moment isn't the case.

Like many of the newer residents, he and his wife have moved only a short distance:

She knows it around here, you know she's from local, I'm Bexleyheath way, so I don't know Greenhithe as well ... we didn't want to move out of the area but wanted a bit more space, a slightly bigger place and so we moved in here.

His parents live near Bexleyheath, hers near Dartford. He sees his parents at least once a week and his wife's parents quite regularly because they go bowling together.

They like the area, despite the evident problems of growth:

Well we liked the area before Bluewater, it's not something that attracted us to the area. It's more of a hindrance the traffic, but er, it's the right sort of houses that we were looking at and the right sort of people, it's just a nice, nice friendly area, we really enjoy it here…

He characterises the area as:

… definably more a blue-collar area, not all but the ones that I know…

He knows most of his neighbours, and gets on well with them:

Yeah lovely people we've got both sides.

But, like everyone else, he feels that:

There's far too many houses being built I think, which is probably general for the whole of the South East.

So we hear him repeat the usual litany of old-timers and newcomers:

… it's lost the village community atmosphere in the place … you tended to know all your neighbours and stuff like that you know and there was quite a community spirit, a lot of people using the local pub and stuff like that, but not so much, it's new faces now.

Despite that, they have plenty of friends:

Some work related, some family, some people I know from the pub, some people I just know. I know a lot of people… Friends that I see regularly live local…

There are many other friends who lived far away, but:

… you're friends and that's what matters, the distance, to me er good friends don't live in each others' pockets, you know, you've always got that bond, whether you don't see someone for a year you're still mates, you know that to me… I think you have in your life, you have a lot of acquaintances, but you only have half a dozen real friends that are real mates, you know but you have a lot of people who you get on with, you know, you enjoy their company, but they aren't real mates that you would trust implicitly.

So there are a very few people he could rely on, for instance if he got into financial difficulty:

I wouldn't hesitate to ask to people who could help me if I needed but that would only be people I know well, close friends and family, that group, I don't know really, then again I've always tried to know a little bit about everything so that I do things for myself.

With good friends, too:

… it's just a more relationship thing with those friends. I mean it's not a case of Oh I've lent him a lawn mower, err you just enjoy one another's company I suppose… Yeah, it's an emotional thing with real close friends, as I say I mean I know a hell a lot of people that I get on with but other than the fact you know them, that's it, there's nothing else. There's no bond. I mean my very best mate is my wife's ex-husband…

Jill

Jill, running her own carpet and furnishing shop, remarried with four sons, is 59. Asked what she would like to see change, she confesses:

I tell you what, if I could change anything, I'd like to be a bit thinner … you know so I could get about a bit easier.

She has lived in a new detached owner-occupied house in Greenhithe village for 8 years, but is locally-born:

I've always lived in… I was born in Dartford, so I've always sort of basically lived around the area, other than about 3 years, we went to Gillingham, but that's all.

She is not happy in the neighbourhood, which seems a nest of contention:

… to be absolutely honest, is not the area, it's my next door neighbour. You know, we don't talk… Her children are absolutely awful to my grandchildren.

Part of the trouble seems to be the lack of space for children to play, which is an obvious source of conflict:

… there's nowhere for them to play to be absolutely honest. And, I'll be absolutely honest with you, there's a woman across the road that is moving because of all the children down here playing football on the other corner. And I'll be honest, I can understand why she's moving.

She is also concerned about the future of her own shop:

It's quite frightening because of the area now, because it's really run down to be absolutely honest and it's getting worse and worse and worse. I mean, most of the shops are now closed. So we're just waiting to see.

Nevertheless, perhaps inconsequently, she finds a good atmosphere in the area:

When I'm home Saturday and Sunday, I suppose I speak to all of them, with one exception. But yeah, I mean, we all … we don't go into each … although saying that, Linda sometimes comes in on a Saturday if I'm here for a coffee or I go into hers for you know … very rarely I go to her, but I'm not that way inclined, but Saturday I did. So, it's a nice atmosphere and it's always been that atmosphere here, but you just say good morning and as I say, if you wanted anything, you know that they'd be there to help you, you know. It's a good environment in that respect.

They do things to help each other out:

… I used to have their kids while they went shopping or I could leave the boys here when they were down weekends while I popped out if I wanted to. Linda's boy, if she wants to pop to Sainsburys, she'd say, 'Oh Margaret I'm going to Sainsburys at ten. Can you keep an eye'. So yeah, I mean in that respect… I mean, we don't mix that much, but you know if anything went wrong, you could knock on somebody's door and say, you know, can you help or … and yet, we would.

The need, she felt, is:

To improve the local area. Well, they're doing it really. I mean they're putting … I don't know if it's going or what, but I mean you're going to have a little shopping precinct over there, which to be honest, it needs. It could do probably, and they are building one up the other end, a nice restaurant perhaps, but they are supposedly being … there's a new development going up there. They are supposed to be doing that, so it does need that. Yeah, I mean, the situation is, they're doing something about it.

But even then, she is apprehensive about what the new development will bring:

Whether that's going to improve it or bring it down because you're going to have an awful lot of people, boys and girls coming and congregating at night because there's going to be a little precinct there, with shops, so that could be a down, but we've got to wait and see, so, but apparently, Asda are having a security guard out there, but whether that is … you know, materialises or not, I don't know…I think they could have done something probably, as I say, because the children haven't got anywhere really to play. I think they need an area that is a bit of grassland to kick a ball in without having to go too far away so that you can go outside and just walk down the road and say, look come on it's time to come in. But I think that's the only thing really that it lacks. I mean you've got down by the river there's a little bit of grass down there that they can, but you get an awful lot of people from the pub where … and they are drunk because it's an all night and day pub, so you can't really send them down there, so you know, it's … that's the only thing that it is quite bad I can honestly say.

James

James is still in his twenties but already divorced: a financial adviser, he lives in a new owner-occupied semi-detached house in the Persimmons estate at the top of Greenhithe. He came to live here when the house was built, about 10 years ago. Like many of the newcomers, his parents are not far away in the Kidbrooke/Blackheath area:

At the time I was working at Woolwich. I couldn't afford to live round where my parents were and this seemed the sort of area where a lot of people that I worked with moved out to. It wasn't so far out that it was a completely different area, but it was close enough and the prices were a lot cheaper, so. But there wasn't a great deal in Greenhithe at that point. It's been made much more residential over the last few years.

It helped that his friends moved out too. And he sees his parents fairly regularly:

Mum and dad, I don't know, whenever I need a free meal I guess. Once a week, once a fortnight maybe. Brother, because he's kind of 50 miles away, as and when. Perhaps more during the summer when you might go and … you know barbecues and things like that. But less during the winter; perhaps once every couple of months on average.

But he has no particular attachment to the place:

I have no great desire to leave it but apart from the accessibility of things from here, I've got no fantastic desire to stay here either. If I found it … if traffic … driving to, say to work got so bad that I would need to live closer to Bromley then I would move to Bromley. It's a place to live. It's quite nice but if I had to leave I'd leave…

One reason could be that – unlike so many others who had moved here – he basically preferred the more urban lifestyle he had known in London:

Well for me personally, going back to where I was brought up, having somewhere a bit more social like somewhere like Blackheath village, even in Bromley where I work, we've got a lot more restaurants and bars and things like that, yeah that would be an improvement for me.

Karen

Karen is in her thirties, married for the second time, with one boy and one girl, working part time as a salesperson, and living in a detached new owner-occupied house in Greenhithe village. She is yet another of the newcomers:

We've lived here coming up to 2 years in October. But in Greenhithe, I moved in about 1990, so I've been here from the onset really ... when we first moved into the area, we bought a house in Saxon Court, which is the top end of Greenhithe. And we were there for 7 years and 2 years ago we wanted ... a slightly bigger house, but we were worried about Bluewater and the amount of traffic that would bring, and because it's literally down the bottom on the road, then you've got that main roundabout that takes you into the centre, we decided to move away, but we still liked Greenhithe and we still wanted to stay in the area, so we looked around and wanted one of these four bedrooms here. We wanted to stay in the area, but not so close to the centre, we wanted to be a little further.

As with so many others we interviewed, however, it emerges that they both have local roots:

Well, my husband originally comes from this area anyway and I come from Bexleyheath, so he quite likes it round here. He liked it. But ... that's why we moved here. He had a flat on the Persimmons Estate, so that's how it started off.

She describes the neighbourhood almost in terms of a sociological archetype:

The type of people are quite nice in the area... Let's say they're middle management type of people, quite a lot of them. In and around the new estates anyway, so, we quite like that environment... And it's quite near the station, which we like. What else. It's quite quiet really.

She makes another attempt to identify the quality of the area, interestingly, in terms of what it categorically isn't:

Well, I just want ... sounds snobbish doesn't it? You just want to make sure that the environment you live in is a nice type of environment for the children to grow up in, so … but they're not street corners or … just generally the type of people and their children and how they behave and all that type of thing really. And from that point of view, I don't want to be in an environment that my children are going to get involved and get into trouble or get into the wrong … get involved with the wrong type of people.

She has aspirations that she knew they could not hope to realise:

Yeah. If I had lots of money, you know, I'd probably move right to the heart of Kent I suppose. Country type of house. But I'm not in that league.

Having lived in London, she sees this area as relatively safe and secure:

Yes it is. But I think … I think of it, but I don't worry about it as much as maybe I would have done in others areas if you like, so, yes, it's on your mind. And we've got an alarm system, etc but I don't worry about it as much as I would if I lived somewhere else … if I lived in Plumstead, for instance, where I used to live before. I mean, crime's quite high there. Bexleyheath, I think. Anywhere where there is … you're quite near shopping centres and sort of big places like that, there's a lot of crime and things. But, we're in between Dartford and Gravesend and I know that sort of… I think Gravesend is probably worse than Dartford for crime, but, yeah, I'm sure it's Gravesend, but we don't … we tend to stay away really.

So it's not an issue for you as such?

No. So, I'm not involved in it. But yeah, we're aware of it and it can happen anywhere can't it? But, I think we've … again I think it goes back to the type of house you're buying and the type of people in the area really.

She is quite content with her part-time sales position, because it allows her to spend time caring for her children:

No, I wouldn't go back to full time, not if I can help it. Yeah, I'm quite happy doing part time, so, providing … yeah, I want to stay part time. I think, if I come out of sales and do something completely different, maybe I might have to think about it. It just depends. But I'm quite happy at the moment … When Joseph's a bit older I might go back and … go back to college or something like that. I don't know. I haven't really thought about it.

She might have had a managerial position in her old job, but they would not let her stay on a part time basis:

I wasn't allowed to stay in the position I wanted to stay in for instance on a part time basis. They said no. If you're only doing part time, then you can't be a manager, which, thinking about it now, if I'd have fought it, then you know, would probably have won. But I just thought, well it's just easier… I think I just needed to get out. I just needed to go part time and spend more time with the children. So I'd had enough of it. But I would have liked to have stayed where I was, but I just wanted to do part time, so, it wasn't a possibility.

Her husband is a director of a publishing company in Middlesex, and commutes a long way, right across London:

It's a nightmare… Absolute nightmare. And he's said over the last 10 years that the traffic has just become worse. It's just horrendous. It's just a journey he has to do. The other side of Uxbridge. It's just a nightmare, but he does it.

They were comfortably off, she felt, with their two incomes. They lacked not money but time:

I think we're in a fortunate position that we can make … that we are financially OK. And if I was to give up, I could give up. From my husband's point of view, I think he would like more free time and he would like to do his own things. So, from his point of view, he's restrained a bit. But, you know, I'd be alright to give up work. We're quite OK really, but everyone wants more money don't they? Or to do more things.

So the one thing she would really value is simply more free time:

I think that goes back to having more time just, you know, the working environment takes such a lot of your own time … all those types of factors, less of a working week, so more time for the family.

The overwhelming problem here was her husband's commute:

Four hours a day driving. He's done that for 7 years and I know that he's itching to get out.

But he would not want to work locally:

No. He doesn't want to do that. Not in the line of business he's in because, it sounds funny, but he doesn't really want to see the people that he works with at weekends… We like to go shopping or to the park or whatever.

So you like to keep that quite separate?

Yes definitely.

The people she calls 'friends' are scattered:

All of them are scattered about actually. I've got close friends, probably half a dozen, locally. But there's quite a few that are ... you know, some in Sussex, one in Lincolnshire, Yorkshire ... so they're scattered about. Everyone's sort of moved on and ... so yeah, but they're all close friends. But we don't see them as much, but they're still very good friends.

But in fact she has a set of fairly close acquaintances, through her children's school:

One of the reasons why I like to stay here was because we've got some very good Catholic schools, which we use...

What do you think the reasons for the success of the Catholic schools are in your experience?

Because it's family orientated and the local community is involved. So, if you go to church and your children are at that school, it's almost like one big family. So you're brought together as a family and you do things together and everybody helps each other. And I think that's why it works well... They make you feel very welcome. I'm fairly new to this school, so ... and I don't go to their Catholic church because I went to the other one connected to my daughter's school, but within a week, you know, they rally round you and if you need any help, you know ... for instance somebody will pick up my little boy after school because I'm working, or that type of thing. They don't leave the children out on their own. Somebody is always there to look after them. It's very much like an extended family really. So, you get to know them from school. And obviously church you get to know them probably.

As a result, she finds herself increasingly involved in the life of the school:

So I help out... I will help... I'm going tonight, for instance, with the school. And I've got friends, that if they need any help, they can give a call and I'll help out with either the children or that type of thing. My immediate neighbours that I ... no, but I don't really have time to speak to them all, you know. If they need anything, I always say like I'm more than happy to help, but I wouldn't ... not really. I don't belong to any clubs or anything like that to be of help that way.

Like so many of the older residents, she too felt a profound sense that the old rural quality had gone. But she saw it as lost even before they had arrived:

The quietness has gone. But ... the village environment in terms of what Greenhithe was when we first moved in, we actually saw the old derelict buildings and the little shop all being sort of, you know … they were all evicted and like they were all pulled down and, you know … if you go along the High Street, there's two pubs there, nothing either side and all of a sudden there's houses and … right across the river. And it's very nice, don't get me wrong, it's very nice, but it's just becoming more and more built up, so I don't want them to build any more. I want it to keep that sort of village…

They shouldn't expand it any further?

No. Not really. But we know it's going to happen, which is why, sort of in 7 years, we're going to find somewhere else.

Old-Timers and Newcomers in the Gateway

So, sadly, it seems that virtually no one likes the Greenhithe of today. Those with long enough memories mourn the passing of a real village community. Those more recently arrived share their sense of loss, even though they remember the village only when it was already in sharp decline. We had a strong sense from the old timers that nothing would compensate them for the loss of their rural idyll. The newcomers, though they almost without exception have local roots and have moved only a few miles from their parents' homes, are less sentimentally attached to the place, or not at all; they are too busy either at work or with their families to care very much. They have established themselves here, they have made many acquaintances and perhaps a few real friends, but when the time is ready they will move out, probably just a few miles down the road towards the remaining green fields.

We found the same sense in Lower Earley, a very similar instant suburb of a slightly earlier generation, built during the 1970s 60 miles away on the edge of Reading. Places like these are almost bound to evoke the same reactions wherever they get built. Everything happens at once, everything gets built at once, everyone moves in at once: these are instant places with instant populations. Not, perhaps, the best way for cities to grow; but, given the housing shortages which have plagued South East England since World War Two, it is difficult to imagine a practicable alternative. Indeed, given the pressures of growth that inspired the government's February 2003 statement on *Sustainable Communities*, it looks as if many more Greenhithes will be built, not just down here in Thames Gateway, but all over South East England, for fully 20 years from now.

Greenhithe: keeping up appearances © Bill Knight

Rush hour at Farringdon

© Bill Knight

Part Three

London Lives

In Part Three, we turn the emphasis around: we attempt a more complex, less direct exercise in comparison and contrast, a contrapuntal exercise combining different voices. Here we seek to understand the common themes, and also some of the differences, in the experiences of different Londoners across this vast city.[1] These are London Lives.

1. Here, we also use material from a further set of interviews, not utilised in *London Voices*, from the east side of Reading.

Battersea old and new © Bill Knight

Chapter Nine

Making Ends Meet

In Putney, then a Thames-side village 6 miles outside London, Cromwell's army officers met in October 1647 to hold a great debate on the principles that should govern an ideal Commonwealth. It was there that Vice-Admiral Thomas Rainborowe coined the phrase that has resonated for radical thinkers ever since: *The poorest hee that is in England hath a life to live as the greatest hee*. Yet not far from Putney, in the London Borough of Wandsworth, three and a half centuries later, there are estates that give point to Rainborowe's assertion. Many of their inhabitants are female, struggling to bring up children on minimum incomes; barely getting by, certainly not getting on.

Fundamentally, though, in our hundreds of interviews we found a basic distinction. Very many Londoners reported to us that they were struggling to make ends meet; that it was a constant battle to keep their heads above water, or that they had only just got into the position of being able to breathe freely. But for a significant minority, especially the lone mothers, it was almost a nightmare struggle for existence.

Keeping Heads above Water

Many of the people we spoke to grumbled about the high cost of living in London, and said either that they were having to cut back, or had only just reached the standard of living to which they aspired:

I don't know. To be quite honest, I think our standard of living's gone downhill since Labour's been in. I really do. Prescriptions for a start. You know, they've all gone up… And look at petrol? That's … my brother can't believe it. Because out in Spain they pay 30p a litre. And generally the cost of living has really rocketed since Labour has been in… Use to go to bingo twice a week. I can only afford to go once now … I … used to take the kids at least once – we'd go down the beach for the day. We haven't got the petrol to do it any more… Used to be a tenner, you know. The motor's got older, but ... as I said, we haven't had a holiday for 2 years because just can't afford to do it. And there's things you've got do. He's got to fix his car and that. I think it's gradually getting worse. The general situation, 10 years ago, we were better off.

Deidree, married mother, fifties, employed, white, council tenant, Greenhithe

They often came back to individual items, like house prices or rents or the cost of the petrol they needed to get them to work:

Yeah, I mean, we're both working, I mean, together we pull in a pretty decent amount of money ... but we're still struggling ... to, you know, meet the mortgage, which is just crazy because it just shouldn't be like that. But that's the way it is, and if there was just one of us who had an income and the other one didn't, there's no way, I mean, there's no, you know, we'd have to rent.

Rochelle, female cohabitee, twenties, employed, white Australian, homeowner,
Newtown, Reading

The price of petrol, vital for the daily commute, seemed to be a particular concern for many respondents, especially those in outer London and in the new suburbs of the Outer Metropolitan Area:

Life is expensive or ... not in this area, all over England. Wherever you, and the petrol, charge 84 pence per litre, it is everywhere in all England, so the life is very costly all over England, not in Hounslow, everywhere is. The petrol is not 20 pence litre in Reading. Still you are paying 79, 80, *(laughs)* everywhere, you know, your life is not easier, so all over England the life is very difficult, expensive.

Saqib, widower, sixties, retired, Pakistani, council tenant, Heston

Yeah, I think if they brought down the price of petrol, that would improve my life... I'd be able to go out more... I mean, my little one, I can't take her up to her cousin as I used to, because I can't afford the petrol, you know.

Deidree, married mother, fifties, employed, white, council tenant, Greenhithe

Some, who had enough experience to make the comparisons, referred to the cost of London living as compared with other parts of the country:

I'd say it's expensive, I mean ... I mean, I've lived up North for quite a long time, previously, and coming down here, you notice a huge difference, just, I mean, just going out to the pub, you know. I mean, the price of a pint, it's ... extortionate, but, yeah, I definitely would say it's expensive. And I mean, even though we probably got this for quite a cheap price compared to others, and what they're going for now, I still think it's a rip-off for what we paid for it and there's just no way, for what it is that it should be worth that amount of money really.

Rochelle, female cohabitee, twenties, employed, white Australian, homeowner,
Newtown, Reading

Poorer respondents told us that council housing was no longer available and the new housing association flats were beyond their means:

Yuppies are all round here in the new flats that have been built that we can't afford to rent and I get annoyed that they've knocked all these things down and built all these housing association places and they are the only ones that can afford to move in 'em. Our children can't.

Patricia, widow, sixties, retired, white, council tenant, Bermondsey

They told of the constant struggle to make ends meet, the worry that some key support prop – a car, a second job – would be knocked away, their inability to afford the little luxuries that would give them pleasure. Here are a student and a recent ex-student:

Oh well, as a poor student, I'm struggling with financial things cos this room is so expensive. But apart from that great, yeah.

Seung-yun, single woman, twenties, student, Korean, private tenant, Heston

I left in ninety-six which is like 4 years ago and still paying off big debts yeah. I got so financially unstable that I ended up taking out a bank loan to try and consolidate some debts and paying them off and things like that, but now I'm paying off the bank loan which is a big chunk of my wages every month you know so.

Padma, single woman, twenties, employed, Asian, private tenant, Upton Park

The Two-Income Minimum

A repeated theme, among those in employment, was that they needed two incomes in order to make ends meet:

Originally us both working, we purchased more and more things and loans etc. So once you've committed yourself, you've committed yourself within the framework of two incomes. So obviously it means both of us have to work to pay off the loans etc.

Rob, married father, forties, employed, white, homeowner, Eltham

I think it's very hard in this day and age unless somebody's got a fantastic job to live on one income. I think generally you sort of need two incomes, you know to afford holidays but I think one income you literally you sort of cope ... before I started this job we sort of er had one income and we could never afford things like holidays.

Heather, divorced mother, thirties, part-time employed, white, homeowner, Eltham

Some, living on low incomes, found it particularly hard to survive:

Well, no. We struggle... We struggle, but we get along ... well, we both get disability money. And that's about it really. We survive … I feel like I'm surviving, not living, just surviving, yeah. I've never bought anything. Really have to scrimp and save. Yeah. But I mean we eat well. We've always got plenty of grub. If anybody really wants anything, you know, we'd obviously get it, but there's nothing really I want.

Deidree, married mother, fifties, employed, white, council tenant, Greenhithe

Working and Juggling

For many, this made the work/family balance particularly difficult. This was especially for families where both partners were often working, while juggling child care responsibilities between them, or using informal carers to avoid the high cost of child care in London. Long commuting times were also significant here, especially in Greenhithe.

So is time the main thing that you'd want more of do you think?

… Yeah. It's time really. You know, it takes 2 hours for my husband to go out to work, 2 hours to come back and it's a long way. So, we can't really do anything in the evening, because by the time he gets home, it's like gone 8 o'clock… So, it's very difficult.

Karen, married mother, thirties, part-time employed, white, homeowner, Greenhithe

Women's access to employment is very much determined by their child care responsibilities, still far more onerous than men's. They deal with this by taking local jobs, even if they find them unattractive:

But when my Christine was like 11 and she was going to grammar school I had to give up the office cleaning because I couldn't get home to get her up of a morning so I went into the school meal service then I was there 22 years. So I was at home when she was at home.

Rosemary, married mother, sixties, retired, white, council tenant, Bermondsey

I like to work close to home, because of the kids, obviously, like, I don't want to be too far away. If I can't get to the school, they've not got far to walk home and so … obviously, that sort of location. So, really, travelling, because of the children mainly.

Cheryl, married mother, thirties, employed, white, council tenant, Bermondsey

Well I've had to look for a job that ties in with that. Because I was working for a play group, which was quite handy, because that was nine to whatever. Nine to one I used to do and then nine to three certain days. But obviously you've got to find something that's school hours. So I couldn't go and get myself a shop job. I couldn't go and get myself a job in the bank or anything like that. But I'm lucky, I've just had a break and I've got a school job now. But yeah. That sort of impact.

Emma, married mother, forties, employed, white, homeowner, Greenhithe

Emma talks of realising her ambitions in the future, by going back to college. But she is torn between her desire to improve her qualifications and her urgent need to earn money:

I have never done teaching, but that would be my ambition. I'd like to be a teacher.... (but) I'd have to pay for my course. And if I went to college full time, I'd then have to give up my job you see. So I would end up paying out and we wouldn't have our pocket money... But it's something I've got at the back of my mind again for the future perhaps. Not too old, I don't think.

Emma, married mother, forties, employed, white, homeowner, Greenhithe

And of the barriers she finds as a mother in getting worthwhile employment:

I feel … personally … because I've got the children, I do feel that perhaps the financial institutions didn't want to take me on. Because obviously you've got holidays. You've got family commitments. I feel they do worry that you have got to find something for that, you know. And obviously if they're not well, they're probably frightened you're going to take days off here and there. And the 6 weeks summer holidays are quite a long time, I think because you know. I mean I can sympathise with them … it is hard to get child care and whatever, but at the end of the day, they've got to take that person on trust and say, well, they're the sort of person who's not going to take time off …

Emma, married mother, forties, employed, white, homeowner, Greenhithe

One respondent – Selina, a married Asian mother, in her forties, employed and a homeowner in Gants Hill – told us that she is happy enough, she feels quite comfortable, she doesn't feel that there are things she has to go without. But, of course, if they lost their jobs – they are both working – then 'it would be a nightmare'. They need two jobs to be able to pay off their mortgage and 'for the whole thing'. The same theme was repeated by another Gants Hill respondent:

And as the kids get older, they cost … they're … they cost us more money. When they're young it doesn't make much of a difference, but when they start wanting the trainers and the tracksuits, they're the ones that cost us more money.

Rachel, married mother, thirties, part-time employed, white Jewish, homeowner,
Gants Hill

They have increased their mortgage living here, but she would rather live here and sacrifice the occasional holiday than live in an area they found problematic:

No, not really. We did increase our mortgage, and since we've been here we've had, we've put an extension on the kitchen, so we have done quite a lot of work to the house, but I suppose I'd rather be living here and do without one thing than staying in Newbury Park and going on nice holidays.

Rachel, married mother, thirties, part-time employed, white Jewish, homeowner,
Gants Hill

For those in certain stages of the lifecycle – a student loan paid off, children growing up, finding better-paid work, paying off the mortgage – life might become less difficult:

… the only thing we really pays our gas bill, and electric bill, and the water and the, you know, and we can manage with that, so you know, and I don't buy clothes every day, you know, I have plenty clothes. I don't drink, I don't smoke.

Roland, married father, sixties, retired, Afro-Caribbean, homeowner, Upton Park

… it's sort of recent that we've been in the financial position to have the car and the motorbike but that comes as you get older and you haven't got the big expense of when you first buy property sort of thing when all your money goes on bills and mortgage, so we are a bit more comfortable in that respect now. I mean we both work full time and we haven't got children, that's why I suppose.

Richard, married man, thirties, employed, white, homeowner, Greenhithe

Life on the Margin

These were the people who were struggling to get by, and just succeeding. But there was another substantial group of Londoners who were barely making it at all. For them, life was a constant battle to survive: a battle with bills that could not be paid, with bureaucratic rules that governed what they could or could not do to earn more money, with conflicting demands for living and working and bringing up children.

One such group, who might be described as intermediate between the struggling-to-be-comfortable and the near-desperate, were those living on the basic pension, who could find themselves slipping. An older couple told us that their savings were dwindling:

… well we as a couple we don't go without at the moment but our savings are dwindling and dwindling 'cause you are not putting nothing away but you are taking out all the time. So sooner or later we'll have to be looked after. Les still works but he's in a position he could pack it in tomorrow if he wanted… But I do think they could make our pensions a little bit more. Cos I only get £51. See cos I only paid the last 10 years. Up to then I'd only paid the small stamp. When the government say £75 pensions it's not, I only get £51 'cause it's a proportion of the when they say the pension is £69, I don't get £69 but (*talks a lot about pensions and how you don't get enough money*).

Rosemary, married mother, sixties, retired, white, council tenant, Bermondsey

But those who found life most difficult were single mothers bringing up children on their own:

Well I would love to drive a car, I can't afford a car, I'm so old now – I'm 48 and it's this buses, get up in the morning – I wish I could drive my nice car. And I wish I could eat out, and really, like I say, the reason for moving that I like to be special really, you know, somewhere where you feel like I just said, you don't have to fear anything – not really fear anything, but people are – they respect themself, they respect their – they respect other people's private lives, and they are, you know, there, and they eat out and go on holiday. I never go on holiday – I'm so stressed out as it is, I feel like – I was itching the other day, I thought maybe I need the sun. I need a holiday and I need a lot of things … can't have. As long as I can pay my house and that's it.

Dafina, single mother, forties, part-time employed/student, African, housing association tenant, Upton Park

… they never stop needing things, they never stop needing finance… I mean, I haven't asked Davinda to contribute to his food, although he eats … about 6 foot and I can't believe the amount he eats, it's like three big dinner plates … just so … Oh gosh. So the shopping bill in Sainsbury's this week shot up from about £46, when it's just Prem and me, to £85, because it, he largely eats that much more. And so he does have to give me a bit when he goes to … but he does find…

Carol, divorced mother, fifties, unemployed, white, private tenant, Battersea

He hasn't increased his maintenance, but he does pay his part of the mortgage. And, you know, if I need anything for Ewan, and it's only been the last year, I could say to him, look, I need something and he'll, no problem. He's now got himself a better job, which is better paid which helps. But, financially, I am struggling. That's only because they've cut my hours down at work. I used to have two jobs and I've lost one of them… So that's been taken away and financially things are very tight. They are very tight. I live from day to day basically.

And when you said that money was tight, what sorts of things do you feel as though you're doing without?

Probably holidays. Decent holidays. You know, sort of trying to grab a bargain or whatever. Um, going out and buying clothes…

And that's because you've got, not got, you've got to watch the budget all the time?

Well that's right. That's right. You know I sort of put myself away £45 a week to go to Sainsbury's shopping and that's what I have to spend … I'd like to have take away meals more often. You know, can't be bothered to cook. Ewan, let's go out to the Chinese. And, or, go out for dinner or, those kind of things. I do miss out on that.

Sally, divorced mother, forties, employed, white Jewish, Gants Hill

For Sally, a low income also meant that she didn't have much of a social life:

So you don't tend to go out in the evenings or at weekends or whatever?

Not very often. Getting baby, I say, getting baby sitters in, it's expensive. You're not only doing that, you're paying to go out and because things are so tight, it's very difficult. I've lost a lot of confidence in myself as well since the divorce. I've lost my own self esteem, of going out and meeting people. And I've let that consume me a bit, I would say. Which is wrong. I know it's wrong. I can't do anything about it...

Sally, divorced mother, forties, employed, white Jewish, Gants Hill

It was those on Income Support, many of them single mothers, for whom life was perhaps the most difficult of all:

And in terms of income do you feel like you've adequate income?

(*Laughter*) Do you know anyone on the Social who's got adequate income? No I must say it's a struggle but it has to be done... If the government would let one parent families and parents with multiple children, and poor little children at all, get away with all the tax that they're trying to pile on them it would be fine, plus the petrol tax which is just outrageous.

Angie, single mother, twenties, unemployed, white, council tenant, Battersea

The same sentiment came from Janice, another single mother, in Bermondsey:

Do you have to live completely from Benefits and stuff?

Yeah.

That must be quite difficult.

It is, because, like, none of them see their dad, so it's ... everything's sort of all left down to me. And, like, my cooker blew up at one stage, and I asked for Social to help me and that, and they said, because I wasn't an elderly person, they couldn't help me. The only way they could help me was by giving me a grant... I ended up having to get it off the catalogue which... I just used the Child Benefit to pay for it.

Janice, single mother, thirties, unemployed, British-born half-white, half-Afro-Caribbean, council tenant, Bermondsey

Janice ironically felt that she could cope because she had low aspirations:

I suppose if you had people like … like upper class kids, or people our age, and they wound up on the floor with no job, living in a gaff with no electricity and all that, they wouldn't be able to survive, whereas we would… But, I mean, it's only a question of what you're used to, I suppose. You know, like I've got no aspirations to be a millionaire.

Janice, single mother, thirties, unemployed, British-born half-white, half-Afro-Caribbean, council tenant, Bermondsey

Work to Welfare – and Back

But, despite this, once on Income Support it was often simply not worthwhile to try to go back to a full time job. Val and her daughter Joan recorded what happened firstly when their friend, a single parent, moved into employment from Income Support:

Val: Well that was because of Housing Benefit. She had to keep taking time off … because Housing Benefit continually got her claims mixed up so she was always having to take a day off work to go down to the Housing Benefit offices to sort it out over and over again. Because she'd been threatened with eviction.

So she didn't have a high, a high enough…?

Joan: She had a high wage, but by the time she'd paid her rent, by the time she'd paid to have her child minded…

Val: Her child, child fees definitely and fares to work and I mean it got to the point where she wasn't seeing her child.

Joan: You have to pay for the doctor, you have to pay for the dentist.

Val: She was poorer than she was before.

Val, fifties, unemployed, white, Battersea, and her daughter Joan, a homeless single mother

Val told us of her own experiences as a single parent of moving into employment from Income Support:

Val: I was working where my husband was, sometimes.

Joan: And it was a disaster money-wise.

Val: It was a disaster.

Joan: Money-wise.

Val: Economically I just went down and down and down and down…

Joan: Yeah, it's really a question of just, just keeping your head above water all the time, just, what is it not waving, drowning.

Val, fifties, unemployed, white, Battersea, and her daughter Joan,
a homeless single mother

Others also explained why getting a job was often the poorer option:

She: Well you take the cost of our bills as we just said, Council Tax and all that, and the jobs are on offer for about £150, £180.

He: You're going to work to get the same money as what you'd get...

She: They're claiming on the dole, and they get all the extra...

He: ... what they're doing they're making money up to what you would be getting on the dole. So they want you to work 40 odd hours a week to get the same money as what you was earning on the dole. I'm not making that right or making that wrong, but that is a fact because of the way the work is. But I mean in this area, that over there which is a big industrial, like all those little units, that was Peek Freans used to employ thousands of people...

Gary and Dawn, married parents, forties, employed, white,
housing association tenants, Bermondsey

A housing officer in Bermondsey explained to us why this was the case:

We find that a lot. A lot of people say that 'what's the point of going out to work' and we can understand it. People say the nursery fees, the childminding fees are so high and they sort of think 'if I go out to work, it's a low paid job, I'm not going to get much money if I'm employed' and if they are on Income Support it's even better. Income Support is the key word because unemployment benefit might not be as much but Income Support opens doors, no Council Tax and there's a lot of things you don't have to pay. Income Support you get your Housing Benefit your water rates. So some people might be inclined to say what's the point in doing that, I might as well wait till the children grow up and when the children grow up its too late. They can't get a job then because they are not skilled to do anything and they perhaps don't want to retrain. So a lot of people think along those lines.

Debbie, Housing Officer, Bermondsey

The reason why moving from Income Support into employment entails such difficulties is because people find themselves paying all kinds of bills – for example Council Tax, service charges, water rates, and other taxes – which they had not had to deal with before. So even for those who were not single parents the basic question, in such circumstances, was whether it was worthwhile to work at all. Many had faced it:

Kenny: Well, a lot of people gave themselves that question, didn't they. And they're using that as an excuse... Well, I'm better off not working, because I can't find a thing that'll pay the actual ... a living fucking wage, you know... And basically, I was clearing, after tax, after I'd paid me fares as well, I was clearing 23 quid a day. And that's eight to five... It was basically treading water. I weren't getting no ... I weren't getting no further forward, but ... I had the choice. I could've done that, or I could've gone, 'No, I'll go on the dole', and waited 6 weeks with no money... Anyway, I went to work as a road sweeper, I was getting up at half past four in the morning... So anyway, I ended up in court over that, because of non-payment of rent, and all that shit. Do you know what I mean?

Del and Kenny, single and divorced father, brothers, thirties, unemployed/employed,
white, council tenants, Bermondsey

Tiffany explained how it was difficult to get an education while on Income Support. This again made it less likely that people would be able to move into employment:

I mean my friend was going to college, yeah? And she got, what you call it? A grant, but it's a grant towards all her books and stuff, and her fares and stuff and they're telling her that they're stopping her benefit because she got a grant from them. Now she's getting a grant for her books and her thing, it weren't even that much, it was like £80 for the, well, she was there for, she was there for a year and it was like three £80s she was getting and they're stopping her benefit because she's getting that. That is stupid, and that was for her books, they say it was for her books and her fares... They don't know what they're doing. They stop giving out free bus passes to anybody, they stop doing anything for ... to actually help you really, so you ... they keep you in a rut, don't they?.... They give you in one hand but they take it out the other so there ain't nothing, you go back, you actually go back to where you start from... That's why a lot of people just give up because ... they really need to go out and find out, you know what I mean? Cos they're sitting inside the offices and they're making all these decisions and they don't know nothing.

Tiffany, divorced mother, thirties, part-time employed, Jamaican-born
Afro-Caribbean, council tenant, Battersea

And those who did manage to get into full time employment found themselves disadvantaged in ways which they would not have done had they remained on Housing Benefit:

They are then interviewed by the housing association ... they go through all their money what they have got and everything else 'cause they are paying rent. I had a family who lived on my estate they needed an extra bedroom and they built flats up by Peckham Rye, beautiful they were ... ːlooked at it and everything put their names down ... a woman come and see them, put them through it and she said you haven't got enough money coming in to pay for the rent, your Council Tax, and your water rates, she said you'll be living on baked beans all week. There was her money, her husband's money, and her son's money. That put together she wouldn't be able to afford the rent with that money. She turned round and said if you were Housing Benefit we could accept you. And that is what I keep turning round and saying. If you were on Housing Benefit and you were charged so much the government puts the difference to make that rent up.

Patricia, widow, sixties, retired, white, council tenant, Bermondsey

Juggling and Struggling

For some on the margin of existence, dependent on the vagaries of the welfare system, life is a near-nightmare of juggling to make ends meet and to deal with the ever-increasing intrusions of officialdom:

Joan: I was trying to help my son onto, off of the Social, so he had nowhere to live so I said: 'Well stay with me'. They took 46 pounds away from me and he was only earning 30 pounds and I said he wasn't giving me any rent but they took no notice. As a result of that, I got into rent arrears … and I had a letter of eviction and I was really quite…

Val: Panicked. (*Talking together*). Well most people would, I mean I panicked when I got an eviction notice… Do you know anyone on the Social who's got adequate income? No I must say it's a struggle but it has to be done.

Val: They tax that, everything.

Joan: And even if you're an Avon Lady, you have to declare it…

Joan: So they're cutting away every form of little extras so we never go on holiday, we never go to the cinema, we don't buy wine, we don't, we just barely exist.

Val: We just get by from day to day.

(The interviewer knows that Joan does some freelance work on the side. However she won't admit this.)

Joan: And I live on a book, I have a book, I'm one of the only … there's only two customers they allow and, so I'm not really supposed to tell anybody but I, I pay on Monday and by Tuesday and Wednesday I'm getting on tick again and that, in my whole life I've never been on tick.

Val: We can never get ahead.

Joan: I've pawned my wedding rings, I've had to pawn my wedding rings to pay the electricity.

Val, fifties, unemployed, white, Battersea, and her daughter Joan,
a homeless single mother

And this experience was far from unique:

Because once you're poor, you just don't want to care – you don't care, you say: 'After all this rubbish, why should I clean, it's dirty anyway'. So everything is like I don't care – once it's I don't care, it just becomes rough and it will just drown. Whereas if people care for whatever they have, they will improve it, so children would improve from that point of view, they would sort of, you know, everybody go on the same line.

Dafina, single mother, forties, part-time employed/student, African,
housing association tenant, Upton Park

Rule Books and Tax Traps

Many of our respondents were dependent on benefits, and this could leave them in a vulnerable situation. The welfare system is hedged around with complicated rules and regulations, and often appears to be managed rather inefficiently. So, all too easily, many of its recipients could accidentally break one of the regulations or an official could make an administrative mistake – as witness the stories in the media, in mid-2006, of overpayments followed by attempts to reclaim the money. This could leave them in a situation where they stood to lose everything – even the roof over their heads. Val and her daughter Joan, in Battersea, described an acquaintance who had lived through a nightmarish existence:

Val: And this gentleman had the same problem as Joan. He thought he was paying his rent. He insisted he was paying his rent and they said they weren't getting it... Now this gentleman was eventually evicted by the bailiffs, they took everything. (*Talking together*) And because it was cold he had winter clothes on. He became so distressed, so distraught, he couldn't see a way out, he went into the Housing Office and set ... poured petrol over himself and set alight to himself, now that is not an English thing, that's normally Asian thing, this is not an English thing. (*Talking together*)

Joan: That's not something we do.

Val: Because he had all his winter clothes on, he, they were able to save him. They put him into prison for 18 months for damage to the property from setting fire to himself. (*Talking together*)

Joan: That would really make him cheerful wouldn't it, (Talking together).

Val, fifties, unemployed, white, Battersea, and her daughter Joan,
a homeless single mother

Part of the reason why people felt so vulnerable on Income Support was because many of the informal mechanisms which had enabled people to get by had been chipped away:

Val: Yes, they've, they've cut down all the little, the little, you know what women used to do for pin money you know. Folding envelopes, things you used to do at home, you cannot do those things.

I mean when you say you, you cannot do them anymore, they, this is because they're trying to…?

Joan: It's illegal, it's illegal not to declare it.

Okay, but is it the case that…?

Joan: And it's taxable, and your, and your income and your Child Benefit is taxable now.

Val, fifties, unemployed, white, Battersea, and her daughter Joan,
a homeless single mother

However there were some other mechanisms in place which enabled people to get by:

Val: A lot of the local, a lot of the smaller local shops realise that there's a lot of people like pensioners, a lot of people that are on Income Support who, before the end of the week their money's gone and so they allow them to get milk or bread or whatever and they pay the following Monday so you are continually in debt. Always … they're doing a service, because without that, a lot of people would go hungry or would go without, until they get their money and so you're always living just that little bit above your means.

Val, fifties, unemployed, white, Battersea, and her daughter Joan,
a homeless single mother

For many in this position, there was a key dilemma: whether to commit fraud or to profit from the underground economy, evidence of which was all around them:

And they're £50 a pop, or £25 a pop, and I know people who, like, can afford to go out and buy one out their dole money. It makes you wonder, don't it… But all these things I see people getting and wearing, and all the clothing and everything else, I mean, honestly, I can't afford it, and I go to work. I wouldn't… I'd like to know their secret, to tell the truth! … you just gotta wonder, you've just gotta wonder why wide screen TVs are available round the pop, I tell you, if you do a survey round here and see how many people have got them, and when it comes to it … like, the adults in them families don't go out to work to pay for that thing, they sit in front of it all day long. Work that one out! I can't.

Del and Kenny, single and divorced father, brothers, thirties, unemployed/employed,
white, council tenants, Bermondsey tenant, Bermondsey

You can go into any pub and buy cigarettes that, duty, duty free cigarettes, you know, however much they are, you know, and you'll save … £1 a packet, whatever the hell they are, you know, I don't know what they sell, 200 cigarettes, whatever they are. But, you know, if you bought them in a shop they'd cost you 40 odd quid.

Gary and Dawn, married parents, forties, employed, white, housing association tenants, Bermondsey

A Peckham respondent laconically described his dilemma:

Have things been getting better or worse, with your financial situation?

Worse.

Why is that?

Because I have given up the fraud.

Why?

Because crime doesn't pay and it is bad.

Kosey, single man, twenties, student, African, lives with family (council tenants), Peckham

Shelter: The Search for Space

The first essential after money is a roof over your head, and at this point there is a fundamental distinction: between the council tenants, dependent on the whims of officialdom, and the owner-occupiers who are exercising freedom of choice – albeit a constrained one. This freedom to choose where you lived was an absolutely essential difference between those in public housing and the rest, and for those who had very little freedom of choice, many other restrictions arose. Young professionals had actively chosen where they lived, while for others it was the council which decided; they could not feel that they had any choice at all. The presence or absence of this choice seemed to influence those aspects of the area which would be seen as important to the person living there. For those who had chosen where they wanted to live, facilities seemed most important, with a pleasant local community providing an additional advantage. They often had less attachment to the area; the three Bermondsey young professionals we interviewed had already made arrangements to move, not because they disliked the area, but again because they were exercising their freedom to choose. Toby wanted to be able to spend more money on what he described as 'toys' and other 'little habits of his', and since Henrietta could not afford to buy the kind of flat in Butlers Wharf which she wanted, she had got herself a job and accommodation in Sydney and decided to move out of the country altogether. For her the only cost of moving to Australia was that she would see much less of a grandmother she was very attached to, but she was clear that she would never let this influence her freedom of choice.

The tenants in public housing tell their own stories, and they are stories of lives that are totally constrained by the arbitrary boundaries of the local authorities in which they happen to live – in fact, in which they happen to have been born. These people are tied to their local plots almost as rigidly and as arbitrarily as the Russian serfs of old:

I've come to live in Eltham is because my parents live here … and I'm on the housing list, you know? The council gave me a place in Eltham … you're sort of stuck to that council. That area where you live in.

Rob, married father, forties, employed, white, homeowner, Eltham

It was chosen by the council.

Cheryl, married mother, thirties, employed, white, council tenant, Bermondsey

Wandsworth council, cos my parents are on Wandsworth so I've always had an address with them.

Barry, married man, forties, employed, white, council tenant, Battersea

Yeah they just gave me a transfer and I had to come down and view it and I had to say I liked it, otherwise I don't know what would have happened but I had to take this one so…

Susie, single mother, thirties, unemployed, white, council tenant, Battersea

… I had a few choices … it's just that because I was brought up in the community I just wanted to live round here, not that necessarily the other choices were bad… I wouldn't have liked to live in Peckham anyway but it was one of the first places that came up.

Rafi, married father, thirties, employed, British-born Afro-Caribbean, council tenant, Peckham

… It's just what I had heard people say about Peckham, I just didn't want to live there.

Azizi, single man, twenties, employed, African, private tenant, Peckham

For many Newham residents, particularly, it seems that life there does not appear to have been a conscious choice; rather, it was the product of a fairly complicated chain of circumstances involving access to council, housing association, or other cheap housing. This respondent moved across London from Newham to Battersea, simply because a flat was available there:

… when you are on the Peabody list you do not have much option, well you ring your circle areas and I was an organist round the corner anyway and I knew the area

... you can circle preferable areas where they might offer you somewhere, and the more areas you circle the more chance you will have a quicker offer of a flat ... you have to be desperate at the time ... I knew, I didn't mind, I come from south London so I didn't mind.

Sandra, single mother, forties, employed, British-born Afro-Caribbean,
council tenant, Battersea

Many described the endless years on the waiting list, the compromises that had to be made, the total lack of choice:

Eleven years, eleven years on the list to get a one bedroomed flat ... and they said 'Take it or leave it, you won't get another one'. So that's how I moved to Battersea.

Barry, married man, forties, employed, white, council tenant, Battersea

... we have big family, so they ... they made it two ... tell me, if you are waiting for a big. house, or a house in the one place for the two families, you have to wait for a long time... So, we know ... we stayed together. I mean, we live independently, bathroom and the kitchen, everything together.

Seema, married man, thirties, employed, Bangladeshi, lives with brother
(council tenant), Battersea

But, it seemed, some would like to go elsewhere if they only could. This rather laconic Peckham resident explained how he would like to get away to a leafy suburb like Kingston:

... I don't know ... just to get away from this place ... this place they call ghetto ... really... I can't really explain it... It's just what people say... I feel it is the wrong impression really ... but ... you know...

Eze, single man, twenties, student, African, lives with family (council tenants), Peckham

Many of those we interviewed told us stories of quiet and not-so-quiet desperation: the struggle to live on low – or, in some areas, moderate – incomes; the sheer inability to find any housing in the privately-rented sector, let alone owner-occupation; the inexorable operation of points systems that left them for years on the waiting list, or even permanently denied any possibility of getting a place of their own; and the nightmare experiences of those left literally on the edge of life. Their incomes made it inconceivable that they would ever graduate into owner-occupation or the private rental sector:

... basically, anyone who wants to buy one has got to have a combined income of what, thirty-five thousand? Maybe forty? Do you know many people who've got that?

Paul, married man, thirties, employed, white, homeowner, Newtown, Reading

James: … my income's only £10,000 a year … if you go in for private accommodation, the cheapest private accommodation you would be expected to pay at least £550 a month and if you earn £1,000 a month you pay a lot of tax, you pay a lot of… How can you survive because of price. So I decided to change my shifts from work, start at 3.00 am and finish at 3.00 pm, twelve hours away… I work twelve hours a day now.

Juliette and James, married couple, twenties, employed, African,
living with council tenants, Bermondsey

Joan: So I was trying to get somewhere to live before he came out *(before son came out of prison)* so that he had somewhere to go but it was just impossible. It's, it's not that I can't find a flat or a house, it's just that I don't have the funds to put down the rent and deposit it involves because it works out to over a thousand pound.

Val, fifties, unemployed, white, Battersea, and her daughter Joan,
a homeless single mother

Others spoke of their endless battles to balance expenditures and keep their heads above water:

… your main priority is your rent and your Council Tax. Now even if you're working you can, if you're on a low income you can still claim Housing Benefit to help with your rent, cos very few people can afford the full rent as well as the full Council Tax but because of the, the slowness and the incompetency in the Housing Benefit system, if you miss a week you, you then get an eviction notice or a possession order so your first priority is that, so all your money goes to making sure you have your home, your gas, your electricity, your home. After that, your main priority is the children, if you have children, if you're a working mother for instance or even a working couple, your, your next priority is you getting to work and your children getting to their, their school.

Val, fifties, unemployed, white, Battersea, and her daughter Joan,
a homeless single mother

Val stressed that it was not just a matter of income: with children, one was at a permanent disadvantage in the housing market:

… apart from the financial aspect, it's very hard to find someone who will take someone who's on Housing Benefit or on Social Security, Income Support and difficult to find somewhere that will take children, even though mine are 12 and 14 at the moment, they … they prefer professional people because obviously there's, there's less risk of them having noise in the place or anything broken and usually because they're worried that if you're a mother with children, you might end up not being able to pay them, so it's almost impossible.

Val, fifties, unemployed, white, Battersea, and her daughter Joan,
a homeless single mother

Others talked about the severe lack of council accommodation, the long years of waiting, and the endless arguments about the rules:

I am here am waiting this ten years this I'm renting places I could not get this council flat ... but they can't give, say no, you are not... High enough for points that's I not feel happy.

Nahar, married father, sixties, employed, Bangladeshi, private tenant, Upton Park

... the big problem in Reading is the lack of council accommodation as well. I mean, you've literally; I mean, my sister got a council flat after I think she'd been on the list for, well, probably since she was eighteen and she moved into that flat three years ago... And the only reason she got that was cos she had two kids and was living in a converted garage that was damp.

Paul, married man, thirties, employed, white, homeowner, Newtown, Reading

I ended up with three kids over there... In a one-bedroom, in a one-bedroom. They were rude, I found them very rude, because she come up to me, and I don't know what she expected to find, the council woman, she went, I told her to come and she went, 'it's lovely and clean here'. I thought, how dare you; just cos I've got three kids in a one-bedroom, it doesn't have to be, you know... I've been in here now ... just over 12 years, I mean there was nothing in here, there was, the fire was, and they knew I had three kids... So they come down and chuck us out, the council man come down and told me I had to go up the office, and within 3 days like I signed papers to ... mind you I left my youngest, she was a baby at the time, I left her at the council. It wasn't very ... a bit stupid, but they were ever so ... I gotta admit at that time they was ever so nice and that's when one of the women come up, she went, 'come and get the baby because social services will be involved', and she said, you know, 'go and squat over there'... at the time you didn't know, like you don't, and the damp was unbearable. My, my youngest daughter, Laura, was in hospital with pneumonia... I'd been here about, we couldn't use one of the bedrooms, that's how bad it was, the water was coming through the floor, and I moved out, I went to Citizens Advice and the Ombudsman, and anyway they moved me out, but I said I wanted to come back because I liked it here. They moved me in another grotty old place right round the back.

Liz, divorced mother, thirties, unemployed, white, council tenant, Bermondsey

Some told stories of sheer desperation, like this homeless family man who was moved to bed and breakfast accommodation in a town distant from the dialysis that kept him alive:

And homeless that time, I'd been there since 9 o'clock they call me, I am waiting, waiting, waiting, you know, all day. The evening, 6 o'clock, they called my name – yes, yes ... before I explain everything and letter, everything, and then one day, you know, 24th, move the house, you come there early morning, 9 o'clock there. OK, hand over key… This is on the day we vacated the house, 9 o'clock in the morning we had to go… All things I put in my son house… I went to there – went to there, me and my son. All day I wait there – so many people… And the evening, 6 O'clock only the officer call me: 'we've got a hotel arranged'. So I said: 'Where – hotel', I say, 'is it somewhere here – we want to live here', you know (*Makes groaning noise*) 'Southend'…

> *Kamal, married father, fifties, unemployed, Indian, private tenant, Upton Park*

And one was driven to near-suicide:

Joan: I rang them, I said: 'I am on the beach front with my children in my car and I have enough petrol to gas us all'. And they said: 'Well there's nothing we can do about it'. But even the number for the Samaritans, nothing… I was … and I kept thinking, all I kept thinking to myself was, I can go to my mum, I've got my daughters and my mum and my family, if I had nobody, I would have been dead that night, I would have killed myself.

> *Val, fifties, unemployed, white, Battersea, and her daughter Joan,*
> *a homeless single mother*

Others, not in such dire straits as some of these, felt that though they might exercise their right to buy their council flat, it would do nothing for them:

… if you did, say, bought this place and sold it for, say, £100,000, you would then have to move right out of London, because you wouldn't be able to buy anywhere within Central London at all, and you wouldn't be able buy anything else in Rotherhithe just further down the road, you're looking at £150,000–£200,000. It's like what I was saying earlier, you'd then have to end up moving into Kent.

> *Simon, male cohabiteee, thirties, employed, white, council tenant, Bermondsey*

Nonetheless, council housing did represent a basic level of security. Tracy, a single mother of four, was highly dissatisfied with her location in Eltham, largely because of her experience as a victim of crime, and her fears of repeat victimisation. Although she was clear that moving house was the key factor which would most improve the quality of her life, she was not prepared to trade the security of her social housing tenancy for the risks of the private rented sector in her preferred West London location:

I've been trying to move over to like my dad at Hounslow cos he's really and my sister's really ill. And she's got the only kid, so I'm always quite a lot up there. And I've been trying to move to there… I've been trying for 4 years now, but no other council will accept me… No, I'd rather sort of wait to do a council exchange. At least that way, you know you're still on the council and you ain't going to be chucked out at the end of the month or, you know. I mean going private is too much of a risk.

> *Tracy, separated mother, forties, unemployed, white, council tenant, Eltham*

Previously we had been living in another part of the estate ... North Peckham Estate ... and I was newly married and it was time for me to find new accommodation in we had been living as a family on the estate prior to me moving here, in 1971.

Rafi, married father, thirties, employed, British-born Afro-Caribbean, council tenant, Peckham

That example illustrates the point that one effect of borough housing policies was to weaken family ties. This couple, who had moved out to Gants Hill, told us of the problems of their aged parents left behind in Islington:

We really wanted to try and move 'em this way. It's not an easy job though ... I mean my dad's what he's 78, 77 and my mum is 67. And they was petrified and when they went up the council and said you know, like can we put our name down they said no, you have to be homeless, literally on the street, as soon as you've got that order to get out, you can come up here then and we'll put you in, you know, accommodation just for now until we find you a place.

Jenny, married mother, late forties, white, homeowner, Gants Hill

Getting By, Barely Getting On

Evidently, for many of those we interviewed, life in millennial-year London was a constant struggle. They felt they had their heads just above the water line, but in constant danger of dipping below it. In particular, they stressed the need for two incomes in order to achieve a decent standard of existence. And those who for one reason or another lacked this second income – in particular, lone parents with small children – found life a never-ending battle to balance commitments.

And this was compounded by the problem of housing. For many on low incomes, some kind of social housing was essential. But the rules for access to it meant that many were waiting for years, making no perceptible progress – while even the successful, who got housing because they qualified, too often found themselves in unsuitable accommodation, or accommodation they disliked. So, for those on the margin, living in social housing, life was a constant battle to survive. Getting somewhere to live could mean a struggle; finding a place often meant lack of effective choice, and condemnation to a marginal life with difficult or even impossible neighbours. How precisely this affected the quality of their lives will be the theme of the chapter that follows.

Property market, Newham

© Bill Knight

Chapter Ten

Finding a Place

What is important to a good quality of life will mean different things to different people. In particular, it will depend on their lifestyle and their stage in the life cycle. For those in full-time employment, although the qualities of the home area may be important, work-related factors such as commuting, job satisfaction and job security are likely to have a bigger impact on quality of life. For people who spend more time at home, the character of the area or its social networks will seem more important. If children were asked, it might be schools which have the biggest impact. Very evidently, the more time people spent in the area, the more aware they became about the different factors which affect quality of life.

Nonetheless, for many people their home and their local neighbourhood will constitute something very important for their lives and something that most directly shapes the quality of their lives. Everyone has to live somewhere, and for many the result is a tradeoff between the ideal and the possible, the dream versus the reality. People have very different reactions to their neighbourhoods, depending on where they have come from and how long they have been here. Tiffany, who grew up in Jamaica and lives in Battersea, likes the local community but remembers her childhood spent roaming freely and feels particularly conscious of constraints in the big city:

I missed the freedom mainly ... the freedom to go and come, you know, it was different over here cos you couldn't get up and go. Like back home you'd get up in the morning and just disappear and go, everybody's neighbours are there, you know, you know everybody ... and over here it's just, everybody's just closed in... Yeah it was, it's free, you know what ... more freedom is because there's so much can't do this, you can't do that, you can't go there, I mean, I can't send the kids outside without keeping a eye on them. Back home they could just run around and play ... nobody worry, you know what I mean? And nothing happen, just come home when they feels like it, yeah, and all the neighbours, them looking out for you or somethin' like that.

Tiffany, divorced mother, thirties, part-time employed, Jamaican-born
Afro-Caribbean, council tenant, Battersea

A person who has lived in Greenhithe for a relatively short period of time and who used to live in London thinks the traffic not too bad, but for those who have lived there all their lives it has become pretty unbearable. Likewise, the 40-year-old who has lived in Greenhithe for 10 years does not really mind the new housing:

… that doesn't really affect me … I think that's more the locals. I don't see myself as a local girl. And I think it's the older locals… I think it's, you know, those who have been here years and years, sort of 15, 20 years. But I mean I'm all for progress. The land's there and as I say, I feel it's improved the site. I mean this particular side anyway, 'cos this was just all quarries and factories and sort of derelict land really. So, it doesn't bother me. I'm quite happy with that…

Emma, married mother, forties, employed, white, homeowner, Greenhithe

While the 70-year-old, who has lived there most of her life, very much does:

Yeah, many many houses where fields were, up the top of the road, Knockhall road there used to be a wood, it's all pit now. We used to walk from Swanscombe through them… I think it's a big shame, you can't live around buildings I think you need open spaces, I worked down in Greenhithe, in the village, in the sea school college, it was a magnificent building, I think it was the happiest place I've ever worked but it was pulled down for houses again.

Ann, widowed mother, seventies, retired, white, homeowner, Greenhithe

Age and lifecycle, but also social class and residence, are very important in determining attitudes to change. Many of our sample neighbourhoods were undergoing change: some were seeing social and ethnic transition, with the arrival of new groups; some huge physical transformation, in the form of large-scale development or redevelopment. And this had a whole range of impacts, both positive and negative. That was particularly evident in Greenhithe, which was perhaps the fastest-changing area of all. Here, some saw new opportunities in the form of new stores or better service:

And the train service, I've been told, has improved. And that because of people getting to Bluewater. We've got a new Asda being built just down the road… When we first… I don't know if that was Stone, but now I've noticed they have started to stay open later. It's getting more like, almost like London innit? Erm, and Bluewater's just brilliant. It's there 'til 9 O'clock at night... I mean, if say like 8 O'clock you think Oh God the kids get ... a fever or something, you need Calpol, just shoot down to Bluewater. It's just brilliant.

Sharon, married mother, thirties, part-time employed, white, homeowner,
Greenhithe

But she also saw the attendant problems, whether these were high prices or higher crime:

It is very... I find it very expensive. But then that's because they only got erm premier shops, they haven't got like Argos or Woolworths or anything, so...

Sharon, married mother, thirties, part-time employed, white, homeowner,
Greenhithe

Now since Bluewater's been there, we've obviously had a lot more people come in to the area, but a lot people... It's been built up. I mean I've been here to near 5 years and it's like doubled in size – housewise. And they haven't got the police... They haven't got any extra police to cover that... I mean, erm, Craig down the road got chased by a gang of youths with knives and it took the police over an hour and a half to get here. Of course the kids had gone and they couldn't find them. But, for an 11 year old boy to be chased with, you know, you'd think they'd be here straight away.

Sharon, married mother, thirties, part-time employed, white, homeowner,
Greenhithe

But in Battersea, a gentrifying inner London area, people also saw the positive side of change:

Joan: It's a lovely atmosphere, it does make a nice atmosphere. And safer as well. I, I feel safer in Clapham Junction than anywhere else I've been and a lot of that is to do with the market ... and the restaurants now. Because the restaurants have the tables outside and they don't finish till eleven/twelvish, you've always got people on the street, it's a very, it's a nice atmosphere as opposed to walking down a cold dark road...

Val, fifties, unemployed, white, Battersea, and her daughter Joan,
a homeless single mother

Yeah. But ... in a sense, that's good for us. Not because we don't have nothing to do with them, but it makes the price of your property go up.

Cheryl, married mother, thirties, employed, white, council tenant, Bermondsey

Yet there was a strong sense here that gentrification also brought negative pressures, above all in the housing market – especially felt by older-established, lower-income residents:

Joan: Oh it's dreadful around here you know it really has, the property values have just shot up, ridiculous and what happens when that happens, when this happens, they want poor people out. They do not want poor people in the area, they don't want poor people parking their naff looking cars everywhere, they don't want people on Income Support, lowers the tone of the area and so rather than actually come out with it and say: 'We don't want you poor people any more, get out'. They out-price them, so they put the parking up, the, the bus fares, you name it, everything shoots up in price and, and people like myself, or pensioners, are literally squeezed out cos they can't afford to live there any more.

Val, fifties, unemployed, white, Battersea, and her daughter Joan,
a homeless single mother

The Council Tenants: Community and Solidarity

Some people, when they say what they like about an area, talk about the other people that live there: the local community. That was particularly true for council tenants, 'allocated' to live in an area without any real choice on their part, perhaps for life. Partly this may reflect the fact that many of them were mothers, who tended to spend more of their time in the area and have much stronger networks through the school gates, tenants' associations, and other aspects of social life. Many council estate respondents had also been living longer in their area, had moved far less, and had roots in the area, as compared with their middle-class equivalents. Some, who had left, might even express a desire to return to their roots. This Bermondsey resident explained that she and her husband were both born very locally and that most of her family lives in the area:

You'll laugh, I said to Les I want to be cremated, me ashes down at Elvins so I end up where I begun. In Bermondsey. I've still got that instinct that I belong. Yeah I was born in Paradise Street.

Rosemary, married mother, sixties, retired, white, council tenant, Bermondsey

Here, in Bermondsey, others display a sense of territory that is almost tribal:

… where I was born, in Forest Hill, my mum's still there, my brother, my sister is still there, I've got aunts and uncles and cousins, all still around Forest Hill, Sydenham area, area, but they kind of leave home and then just move up the road, virtually. They've all stayed in that area, and it is … it's like generations after generation… And various friends … but then Lorna's aunt used to live here before her, she lived here for … Oh years.

But you say she's from Ireland, because that was…

Yeah, she was Irish, yeah.

> *Simon, male cohabitee, thirties, employed, white, council tenant, Bermondsey*

This British-born black resident displayed the same deep attachment to the area:

I actually want to stay in Southwark … because all my family, well, part of my family is still in Southwark… My nan used to live in Old Kent Road, so, as a little one, I've just grown up, and I've always been in Old Kent Road.

> *Janice, single mother, thirties, unemployed, British-born Afro-Caribbean,*
> *council tenant, Bermondsey*

These people's ties to their community may also to some extent represent a kind of compensation for a lack of other opportunities. While middle-class people looked first to the facilities that would give them the quality of life to which they aspired, for council tenants the general stresses and strains of everyday life made this kind of choice patently absurd. For many of the Southwark mothers, either facilities were simply not available, or available only at a cost that made them inaccessible. But, where facilities were available, they were much appreciated, and played a bigger role in people's lives.

For some longer-time estate residents, there was a feeling, too, that the old sense of community had been lost and that neighbours had become strangers. This sense of loss could be profound, as here in Battersea:

And they, they, people used to take notice of their neighbours. If they saw someone's milk wasn't taken in, they'd be concerned or, and I find that kind of community atmosphere is still going on here. It goes when you, especially on estates, you find although people know each other, there's a fear of, of allowing people to get too close, because you never know, you never know what's going on really. People come and go. It's not, my children, when they were living … on the estate they had an estate mentality, they continually bickered, they were, they were never really happy, I wasn't very happy. I moved here, within a week the change in my children's attitude was unbelievable. They literally, they were sleeping in the same bedroom and not arguing. I couldn't believe it because when I was at home they were arguing through the walls … when you're on an estate you feel like a nobody really, you're an estate person. People who can afford to go to work and haven't got children, they go in, they live and they come out.

> *Val, fifties, unemployed, white, Battersea, and her daughter Joan,*
> *a homeless single mother*

Val and her daughter Joan felt that life in public housing too often created a sense of dependency and despair, partly because successive public expenditure cuts had removed many of the facilities that had contributed so powerfully to their local quality of life:

Val: What I'm saying is the people themselves create a community themselves because they have everything in common. They're poor, they're trying to get by, they've got nowhere for their children to play so the people themselves come together but there is a mentality on the estate that grows up with the children so you find that in one area.

Joan: They don't have sense of worth.

Val: Yeah they don't, they don't have any self worth, anything to feel good about themselves and they don't project it onto anyone else so, you find that if someone goes onto an estate, after X amount of years they become isolated and secluded and demoralised, the community projects that used to be there have been taken away, the children's community centres have been taken away, so the things that used to bring the people together, have actually been stopped because of lack of funds and it breaks up what little community spirit they had, and feeling they had, and it becomes harder and harder for them to fight to get that community feeling back again. So … the feeling is there that they want to be a community but it's just thwarted every which-way they turn. When you've got a property like *** where to go up and down in the lift is, is so disgusting you don't even want to go outside your front door.

Val, fifties, unemployed, white, Battersea, and her daughter Joan,
a homeless single mother

Peckham was a particular source of grief. Southwark Council had lost much of its stock through right-to-buy policies – which it had enthusiastically supported as part of its campaign to diversify its population. At first working-class people were reluctant to participate, but this was changing. At the same time Southwark was engaged in a huge rebuilding exercise, demolishing the problematic North Peckham estate and decanting the residents to other parts of the borough, some into the hostile territory of the former Docklands. A housing officer graphically described the consequences:

It has because of the right to buy, because of the restrictions from central government, local authorities are not building any more, we're not building. All the new properties which have been built have been built by housing associations. The right to buy has eaten up a lot of our properties. And because we're not building we haven't got the availability of properties. There are so many more people needing accommodation and we just can't provide the accommodation that we need. Before it was easy to, we had the only sons and daughters that was brought over from the GLC so that people living on an estate they could ask for inter estate moves, they could say I would like to live here because my daughter lived here or my mother lived here. It was quite easy. We, while we try we can't really sort of... Things change, those schemes are no longer in existence and the only way perhaps a son or daughter might get on the same estate is if they need to give or receive medical support and that would have to be tested ... and they would have to prove that. So the restriction really is from central government. We're not building, people are buying properties.

Wynette, British-born Afro-Caribbean, Southwark Borough Council official

The tenants, faced with a *fait accompli*, described the consequences:

We never had a choice because they were knocking down the buildings, unless we were to stay in there! ... we did not have a choice; we got allocated because it was a bit too late that's why we ended up here.

Kosey, single man, twenties, student, African, lives with family (council tenants),
Bermondsey

It's totally arbitrary the way they allocate flats I mean I had the other flat for 7 years and then after she was born I mean it was the top of a tower block and it was really dangerous you know we put a transfer to here ... you know its like a lottery.

Shaun and Katie, married parents, thirties, self-employed, white, council tenants,
Bermondsey

... the actual system of putting your name down, and then they offer you one, and if you don't like it, they sling you off. You have to wait, wait, wait. And if I'd have turned this down, I'd have been still waiting till another one come up. Do you know what I mean?

Del and Kenny, single and divorced (father) brothers, thirties, unemployed/
employed, white, council tenants, Bermondsey

And in Wandsworth, which had pioneered the process of decanting long before Southwark took it up – here with the objective of rehabilitating and selling off the units – a former tenant describes the result:

We was living in an estate called ... it was called Winstanley estate and it's just before Clapham Junction... So they took out a lot of people from there and moved them onto another estate and they refurbished the whole estate and moved in the yuppies ... now when a lot of people go through the new estate, it's not called Winstanley no more, I can't remember what it's called, when a lot of people do go through they see the difference. And so a lot of people knew that they, they were kind of like conned and it was a scam... So when I walk past there now and I see my old flat, my old mum's house, it's really done up and it's really modern and it's really nice. But that's okay, you know, but erm ... I get good memories, I get good childhood memories from that estate, but it's okay now.

Daniel, single father, twenties, employed, British-born Afro-Caribbean, council
tenant, Battersea

Many respondents, both in council and housing association units, described their frustration and rage at problems of maintenance and repair. Some of their stories were horrifying:

Yes, they sort of really fight for money and I think that sort of pulls it down. I know we had no heating once and we waited 3 months for it to be fixed.

Seriously. Five children and no heating, and you had to wait three months.

Yeah, and it was winter as well. It was the pump, that's what it was, the pump wasn't pumping round. We have got a gas fire so I suppose they thought 'Oh well they've got a gas fire' and there's just one gas fire in the front room. The rest is centrally heating so it was freezing, you know.

So what did you do for hot water, could you use it on the immersion, on the electric?

No, we just used to boil kettles.

Gary and Dawn, married parents, forties, employed, white,
housing association tenants, Bermondsey

These tenants felt that there was nothing much to choose between the council and the housing association, because both were chronically short of money:

I think they just struggle with money like the Council do. It's more like a little charity this housing association.

Gary and Dawn, married parents, forties, employed, white,
housing association tenants, Bermondsey

But others felt that despite their financial constraints, housing associations gave a better and a more personal service, so that transferring units to housing associations, or to tenant management, had brought real improvement:

I've found being on the housing association for 6 years if ever there was a problem and it's dealt with straight away. So there was a big difference in how a housing association deals with it and how the council deals with it.

Theresa, married mother, forties, part-time employed, white,
housing association tenant, Bermondsey

Mind you it was longer than that when I was in the Council … the same thing happened to me when I was in the flat and I waited 6 months there, and in that time they sent three people round and each time they brought the wrong part and you had to keep on chasing them, chasing them, and get someone else to come round.

And they go away and say they'll be back the next day, but didn't turn up...

Anonymous respondent in Bermondsey Focus Group meeting

The real problem, one respondent explained, lay with owner-occupiers who were in danger of being repossessed for mortgage arrears, and so had let their homes to irresponsible tenants:

So a lot of them was doing that, you know they was renting out part of it or whole of it while they live with a friend or whatever, whatever... The most problem it create is like noise and music, they have parties cos they're mostly youngsters from Spain and France and things like that ...

Ronnie, male cohabitee (father), fifties, employed, Afro-Caribbean, homeowner, Battersea

The Basic Problem: Change and Instability

There is an underlying fear, among many public housing tenants, of change that they cannot control and that will bring chaos and unhappiness. People, we were told, were on the defensive whenever a place becomes empty: they were terrified that they would find themselves with bad neighbours, or that people would move out without anybody knowing:

... problem is cos there is such a shortage of available housing in Southwark whoever gets to the top of the list is the most needy person they just get the next available place which isn't necessarily suitable to them or their neighbours. And where you used to have like whole blocks ... that were residential blocks for the elderly that's gone now. Families were living in there with young children, there's young couples living in there and its not conducive for everyone's sake. Its not conducive to put old people and young families together because it just causes a lot of hassle... Elderly blocks move families in and that causes a lot of tension with tenants having a go at each other 'cause they are used to the quietness.

Anonymous respondent in Bermondsey Focus Group meeting

One tenant, a white married woman, movingly described the results on her estate:

It used to be lovely ... it used to be quiet, it's very noisy now. And obviously, you ... I mean, you can't pick and choose the people you live next to, but, I mean, there has been people who've moved round here who, idyllically, I wouldn't like to live here! But, I mean, I can't choose that!... Everything. Noise, fights, cars ... rubbish. I mean, I'll be honest, what I'm basically talking about is, like, the new flats that's just been built there. Since they've been here, it's like ... I think they're Church-owned. And I think they're all like ... problem people ... not problem people, but they're all single parents, or there was overcrowding... People that don't help theirselves, basically.

None of them go to work, they just have loads of kids and just get on with it. They get the new ones, and we get the old ones. So … it's quite annoying, really. But, there you go… But certainly asylum seekers I have got no problem but I think that they shouldn't be given a better standard of living than people who have been born and brought up here, I think that is a bit wrong. But that is just my opinion.

Cheryl, married mother, thirties, employed, white, council tenant, Bermondsey

And this was compounded by the irony that many people found that once they had been moved from a block scheduled for demolition, their new flats were inferior to the old ones. Those in social housing found that their quality of life was greatly affected by intangibles like community, but also by a very tangible effect: lack of space. Time and time again residents complained about it. Lack of space directly affected the quality of life of individuals, causing them to feel claustrophobic, trapped, or cramped. But it also had an indirect impact on many of their other complaints. Limited space amplified the noisiness of a neighbours' music or their playing children, increased the possibility of a football going through a window, increased the likelihood of children being naughty and the possibility for cars to get in the way. It also meant that uncollected rubbish and dog mess were more likely to cause offence. Life in high-density housing raises difficult questions: what should be a person's level of tolerance, right to choose, or duty to exercise restraint:

… if you are comparing a three bedroom on the North Peckham estate for one in the regeneration, the real sizes here are actually bigger. This is one of the main gripes, that the former tenants say that they don't want to move to the new properties. Because it involves also getting rid of furniture, carpet … the local authority or should I say Peckham Partnership are not compensating for, and a lot of people are not happy with that. They have spent a lot of years making the place look nice, carpet to fit etc, etc … got a nice big table in the kitchen and when you are finally moving, you have got to get rid of your table and no-one is helping, and you are not going to be compensated on a lot, and people are not very happy with that.

Rafi, married father, thirties, employed, British-born Afro-Caribbean, council tenant, Bermondsey

… really, the bedrooms are too small. I prefer big size bedrooms, where, at least, I can put wardrobes and hang clothes up … that's its downfall. And the bathroom's really small. We seem to be quite squashed all together.

Janice, single mother, thirties, unemployed, British-born Afro-Caribbean, council tenant, Bermondsey

But it was not only a matter of size: people simply could not afford the new flats, one respondent explained:

It is mind boggling how they have got themselves into this situation where they have got people who don't want to move into these new places because ... its nice and new but size wise, and you have things like water meters etc ... the cost of living plus the council tax will be a lot more. Because a lot of the people here are either unemployed or just normal working class, the cost of living will go up for some of them. Those who can afford it will be alright, but there will be those who will find things difficult.

Rafi, married father, thirties, employed, British-born Afro-Caribbean, council tenant, Bermondsey

What mattered too was privacy, especially for those who lived in flats:

... because these converted houses, you're so close to each other, they've got timber floors so you can hear absolutely everything, so just one load of rows, absolutely appalling. You see we're just like a load of rats, we were all on top of each other and if you get a load of anything on top of each other then you get on each other's nerves...

Carol, divorced mother, fifties, unemployed, white, private tenant, Battersea

... this place is thin, you hear the next door neighbour when they are beating their kids ... umm, if any anything drops by the wall its going to make a hole.

Kosey, single man, twenties, student, African, lives with family (council tenants) Bermondsey

A particular complaint, from Battersea this time, was that flats were unsuitable for families with small children. This could be compounded because people felt that there were inequities in the system. And, in the particular case of Lambeth council, there was an allegation that officials could be bribed. This, we were told, was common knowledge:

There's a lot of backhanding things going on ... if you know people you get moved to where you want.

I've heard, I've always heard this about Lambeth Council...

Yeah, yeah, I gave her about £500 .

Amir, single father, forties, employed, African, council tenant, Battersea

The Owner-Occupiers: Space, Peace and Money

The owner-occupiers we interviewed lived in a very different world, and had a very different view of it: they consciously and freely choose their location, constrained partly by the length and cost of their journey to work, by the price they can afford, and sometimes by family ties. But others, especially these younger inner-London residents, talk straightaway about the facilities:

It's generally a very good area to live in, very safe, haven't had any problems. It's about 50 yards from the river with good views and generally relaxing on a good day. There's a park close by which is fairly small but is still a good stroll if you want to have a bit of greenery. The walks along the river are very entertaining, generally St Paul's [Avenue] is still quite safe, and the view, pubs along the way.

Timothy, single man, thirties, employed, white, private tenant, Bermondsey

But some ethnic groups are more affected by particular changes than others, as in the case of this Afro-Caribbean family:

Well Somerfield is, it doesn't really cater for the ethnic minority, you know. Kwik Save was a bit better... Somerfield's product is dearer and also it hasn't got the range, but I think there's an Indian manager now so he understands and it's a bit better. But it's still miles behind.

Ronnie, male cohabitee (father), fifties, employed, Afro-Caribbean,
homeowner, Battersea

I mean Northcote Road, don't know if you know Northcote Road, that, the trading up there it was one of the best places, especially for me from the ethnic minority or something like that, where you can't get things in supermarkets, you could go down there and buy stuff. You can get like fresh thyme, I'm not talking the one that grow in the greenhouse, that just grow with electric heating and you know what I'm talking?

Ronnie, male cohabitee (father), fifties, employed, Afro-Caribbean,
homeowner, Battersea

The approving statements came from younger Londoners, but the same sense came from a Reading resident who had deliberately chosen to live in a mixed area near the town centre rather than what he saw as the kind of soulless suburb he had experienced as a child:

Well, what I like about it is it's quite close to town. There's plenty of nice sort of local pubs around the area; you've got the river just down the road, you know, which is, which is quite nice. You know, I do a bit of fishing now and again, so that's quite handy. The Junction is quite good because you've got a lot of shops and you've got restaurants there, and that sort of thing. There's Palmer Park over the road, which is nice... I go to several of them [pubs] round here, but the reason I prefer going to those rather than going into town is they're more like, sort of local type pubs, you know, more traditional, I guess. Whereas, you know, they're more individual, whereas the ones in town are more sort of all these sort of chains. So, I mean, I can remember, you know, a few years ago there never used to be hardly anything in town. It was only really about 8 years ago that they started opening up new pubs and that down there. And now…

Paul, married man, thirties, employed, white, homeowner, Newtown, Reading

He did not find much sense of community in his local area. And yet the pub provided a source of informal services as well as sociability:

… as an example, I have a problem with my roof. Last year, some time, and some of the tiles got dislodged in the wind and that. And, you know, and it's difficult to get someone to do little jobs like that for a reasonable price, but I just went down the local pub and said, does anyone know a roofer, and someone said yeah, gave me a number, and I got a guy round who sorted it out for me. You know, things like that. I do, I'd rather pay someone local to do something like that than go to some sort of like big sort of building firm, or something.

Paul, married man, thirties, employed, white, homeowner, Newtown, Reading

Facilities seem to be better in an inner London area like Bermondsey – or, now, inner Reading – than in places like Greenhithe, where you need to have a car to get anywhere:

Well, I must be honest, I've never found it a problem. We've got small corner shops all round us. There's two chemists within walking distance. I've never really found it a problem. I mean, Surrey Quays is a bus ride away, which will take 15 minutes, and then you go up there, there's restaurants, there's pictures, there's bowling, there's, like, the big supermarket, like a sports hypermarket, so, no, I think…

Do you use that quite a lot, Surrey Quays…?

Yeah, yeah. I mean, I shop at Surrey Quays, do me, like, the house shopping. The boys go pictures up there, or we do, or bowling. So, you know, yeah, we do use it. Bingo, I go bingo now and again!

Cheryl, married mother, thirties, employed, white, council tenant, Bermondsey

The Search for Roots

Many of our interviewees demonstrated deep roots in their local area: they spoke of staying in the place where they had been born, or of continuing family ties to ageing parents which would keep them there. This was true of traditional working-class inner-city areas like Battersea and Bermondsey, as we have already seen. But it seemed equally true of owner-occupiers in the London suburbs, and – perhaps most surprisingly – a boom town like Reading:

I was born here on the other side of Reading, in Southcote, which is the west end of Reading. I've lived most of my life here. I've spent a few years overseas working and travelling, but generally, I've lived in Reading all my life... I used to think that I wouldn't mind moving away from Reading, but I'm getting a bit older now and me dad lives here, and my sisters and that, and most of the people I know, you know, live around here. So I'd quite like to stay living in Reading, I think.

Paul, married man, thirties, employed, white, homeowner, Newtown, Reading

My mother's family came from Caversham went to Australia in 1914. I was born there a generation on. Came to England in 1960 at the age of 25, you know, the way young people travel to Europe, but I always had it in the back of my mind that I wanted to stay because it was always referred to as home.

Margery, widowed stepmother, sixties, retired, white Australian, homeowner,
Earley, Reading

In consequence, many had simply moved from their parents' homes just a short distance down the railway line:

I originally come from the Elephant & Castle and Nick from Deptford, so our parents are still in that area, so we wanted to move out but we wanted to be close enough to get them you know.

Zoe, married woman, twenties, employed, white, homeowner, Eltham

... my parents when they were alive they always lived in Eltham. And my wife, she comes from Bexleyheath, which is only what 2 or 3 miles down the way. Erm, yeah I suppose all my family live, you know, not necessarily Eltham, but not far out, you know?

Joe, married man, sixties, employed, white, homeowner, Eltham

I know the areas around this area. I know Charlton's more expensive, Greenwich is more expensive. I know what Lewisham's like. I didn't want to live in Lewisham more because it was ... and this part of Greenwich, this outer part of Greenwich, has got a lot of greenery attached to it... I used to live in New Cross for 7–8 years and I wouldn't want to go back there either, because it's too cramped, there's no open spaces for children... It's just the road noise. If I was living over there, it'd be fine. Everything would be hunky-dory. Because I know the area. I know what it's like. I've lived in south-east London all my life. I know exactly what the area's like. I don't want to live in Bromley. It's too far out. Too conservative.

Jeff, divorced father (living with partner), forties, employed, white,
homeowner, Eltham

We found the same in Heston on the other side of London:

... because of my parents cos they live in Osterley and I used to live in Central London and I was just looking for somewhere, further out, not here actually, I didn't want to come over here, further out, but because I was pregnant with the little one, they wanted me to be near them. So, I'm stuck here… I really don't wanna stay here, I'm just staying here for my parents. I would love to move to Ashford, Egham.

Layla, married mother, forties, part-time employed, Egyptian parents,
homeowner, Heston

Others felt attached to London, though not necessarily to the area they happened to live in. They would thus be prepared to move – but not very far, to what they saw as a more desirable area to live:

No…I won't leave London… I'll leave London only when I'm .. when I'm either in grave or in cremation. I won't leave London … I am just in love with London … definitely not Hounslow, I'll leave Hounslow, but not London. There are lots of other beautiful places in London. Once my daughters decide where they want to settle then there are places I have in mind. Place like Richmond, place like Kingston, beautiful places where everything, though education may not affect me now but my daughter's children will definitely be affected … they would be last people to have their education, children's education in Hounslow, the way it is going now, unless it is taken over by some. (*Laughs*)

Jalil, married father, sixties, retired, Indian, homeowner, Heston

This seemed particularly true of younger people with a busy active lifestyle, including one respondent with a passion for bungee jumping:

… in the centre of London means you're not far away if you want to go and bungee jump, you can go down to Chelsea Bridge, which is about 20 minutes away, and throw yourself off a crane. If you want to go and blast someone away with a laser gun or a laser … you can do that at Piccadilly Circus…pubs, clubs, everything else, cinemas, pretty much anything you want to do you can get to within half an hour whereas if you're living in the country … more difficult to get to… Apart from it being more expensive, it's … the access is fantastic… In the long term getting older I don't think I want to throw myself off a crane or a bungee rope or blast someone away with a… The speed of life involved will catch me up quite fast. Premature ageing I suppose.

Timothy, single man, thirties, employed, white, private tenant, Bermondsey

Similar sentiments came not only from younger residents in Bermondsey, but also Heston in the London suburbs:

… at the moment, it kind of suits us both down to the ground, at the moment, where Lorna works and I work, and if we want to go out into town, like … we're both still at the age when we go clubbing and stuff like that, so it suits us at the moment. But never say never! Maybe when we're older, we'll see. But at the moment, no.

Simon, male cohabitee, thirties, employed, white, council tenant, Bermondsey

I don't like the boring type of lifestyle, like I don't know, countryside and that, it's not me, yeah, I just like to have a busy lifestyle like you have in London, yeah, and you associate within London, but yeah, I reckon I'd wanna live like closer to London or somewhere, just away from Hounslow and just like move away and start afresh or something.

Rajiv, male teenager, at school, Asian, tenure not stated, Heston

Moving Out Here…

But very many of those we interviewed, especially in the outer areas, were seeking arcadian calm, and some complained of the loss of it. Many would like to move further into the country, but felt constrained by the resulting commute or by family or school ties. This Greenhithe family for instance have lived there for 2½ years. Before that they lived in Stone for 3 years and before that in Sidcup. They left Sidcup basically because they could not afford to buy a house there:

We lived in Sidcup… We had a flat and just couldn't afford to buy a house in that area … as an estate agent, people who couldn't afford Sidcup, we sent to Dartford. So it was just automatically for me to come here as well.

Sharon, married mother, thirties, part-time employed, white,
homeowner, Greenhithe

Generally, people in Greenhithe had lived in the same general area before, and were moving out in search of more space at a price they could afford. These Greenhithe respondents were typical:

Well, my husband's from Barnehurst. We were living at Welling. And so we wanted … somewhere that's not too far … mean, obviously we looked within the vicinity that were looking where we lived, you know, Welling, Sidcup, Barnehurst. But we did actually go out. We went as far as Rochester. But, a bit too far for travelling really.

Emma, married mother, forties, employed, white, homeowner, Greenhithe

The same stories were told in other parts of London: in Upton Park and in Heston:

… we were living in a council property before, and then we wanted to buy our own property and we just found out that, you know, it was much cheaper in Newham than Hackney … because I work in Hackney and the kids were at school in Hackney, so it was just convenient.

Nadira and Coffie, married parents, forties, both employed, African, homeowner,
Upton Park

… we wanted a larger house, maybe something with a garage.

Faizah, married mother, thirties, employed, Malaysian parents, homeowner, Heston

Once they had made the move out, many were well satisfied. In Gants Hill, many people referred to the quiet and the suburban quality, which had drawn them there and which they deeply cherished:

Quiet, tree-lined, nice style houses – these houses are Smith built and they're nice style houses, near the park … where we [previously] lived was a quiet as this is. It's just like a step upwards, that's what it really was.

Rachel, married mother, thirties, part-time employed, white Jewish,
homeowner, Gants Hill

One Gants Hill respondent moved there from Newham because of the housing quality and the schools, both of which they found better here:

'Why did you move out?' I said, 'Well Newham doesn't have any semi-detached with garages'. I mean housing stock is mainly terraced. I mean apart from the education we did want space. We wanted bigger rooms and a garage and space around the house… Unfortunately Newham was short on those… They do have a conservation area. They've got some nice double fronted houses in Forest Gate – the Woodgrange Estate I think it's called. But they were quite expensive. I remember saying to Sangat at the time, and I think they were similar prices to houses round here, and … I said, 'Why don't we move there, because they're nice Victorian houses?' He wouldn't have it because of the area's reputation and the schools. He said, no way, I'm not moving there.

Ajit, married mother, thirties, employed, Sikh, homeowner, Gants Hill

I love this area, I don't want to move anywhere else, I think … I come in from North London in Islington and my partner, or my husband now, he comes from Romford in Essex, we tried to pick something that was sort of in the middle. So Walthamstow was the first step em up the ladder and then obviously we got a better house by moving into this one. Just bettered ourself really.

Selina, married mother, forties, employed, Asian, homeowner, Gants Hill

This last comment comes from a working married Asian woman in her forties, originally from Bangladesh, who married and came here 26 years ago, now living in an owner-occupied semi-detached house in Gants Hill. They have been living in this area since the 1980s; this is their third house. As they had more children they moved to bigger houses in order to have more bedrooms; she now has three children. In the most recent move they have just moved a couple of streets down the road. Having chosen what general area she wanted to live in, she had a clear idea about the kind of house she wanted:

I have looked at a lot of houses also, I like the setting of this area, whatever I want, quiet road, a reasonable big garden, actually I wanted always good family houses, and I have found they're quite – I like – the one, I like it.

Selina, married mother, forties, employed, Asian, homeowner, Gants Hill

Others – one Bangladeshi, the other Sikh-Punjabi – described a similar search for more space in and around the house:

I mean in this area but to a bigger place maybe end of terrace or a semi with you know, so it's got a garage I can put things and also something with the side entrance I prefer you know when you put the dustbins outside you don't have to drag it through from the back garden in wet and snowy weather.

Shirin, married mother, thirties, Bangladeshi, homeowner, Gants Hill

I wanted to buy a bigger house, like four bedroomed … with a garage and all that… The kitchen was small, the wife was moaning … I want to move up like er and I'd still now like to move out to the countryside somewhere, if I could, if I could buy a bigger house, or a newer house.

Ranjit, married father, fifties,, employed, Sikh, homeowner, Gants Hill

Some Gants Hill residents seemed remarkably content. They were older people who felt quite comfortably off, partly because they had paid off their mortgage, so that apart from paying the bills, as one put it, 'the money's ours'. Others spoke of moving to the Essex countryside. But they were constrained by the cost of travel, or by schools, or both.

The Importance of Schools

That last point proved significant. Many had moved out, or were contemplating moves, to put themselves in the catchment area of a better school for their children. We heard this strongly expressed in Gants Hill, but it worked in two directions. Some were coming from places they considered much worse:

So the schools have got a poor reputation relative to Redbridge?

She: Yeah … Newham is the fastest improving in the country. Did you know this?

Yes.

He: But we haven't heard about that!

She: Don't you dare! They're saying that if you start at a low enough base of course you're going to be the fastest. But you could choose to stay there couldn't you, or you can choose to move.

Ajit, married mother, thirties, employed, Sikh, homeowner, Gants Hill

But the same sentiments were expressed elsewhere, in Eltham:

We moved out of Lewisham to here because it was nearer their school basically.

Mick, married man, fifties, employed, white, homeowner, Eltham

In Heston, several respondents spoke of moving out because of what they perceived to be the poor quality of the local schools:

… coming and going because of schools. Yeah, the lady that I bought this house from had only lived here about 4 years before she moved and it was because of schools. Er and we were talking to the next door neighbours and she goes 'The people before that, in this house, have only stayed for a while'. And all of them are moving out for schools… A lot of them are going up to Egham, Staines, Ashford, there are better schools up there. And there's grammar schools up there, there isn't any grammar schools round here.

Layla, married mother, forties, part-time employed, Egyptian parents,
homeowner, Heston

But in Earley we talked to a family that had moved in the reverse direction, from the countryside into the suburb, to reduce a long commute:

It was the Caversham school which influenced my grandson and his wife to come and live in Caversham. He, they used to live in Cricklade and he works in London at the *Guardian* and works journalist hours, you know and drove 90 miles a day and all that and the children were miles away from anybody to play with and they decided, well, all right they'd come and live a suburban life and he was saying it's taken 10 years off his age not to have to commute all that far. He rides his bike to Reading station and rides his bike to go back again and life's a lot easier for them.

Margery, widowed stepmother, sixties, retired, White Australian, homeowner,
Earley, Reading

Another Reading family want to move to a bigger house, but to stay in the area mainly so that their son can still attend the same school.

…it's just a nice place to live. I mean the fact that we've lived here 10 years says it all really I think.

Tony, married father, forties, employed, white, homeowner, Earley, Reading

Fitting In and Feeling Comfortable

A very important consideration, for many people, was their sense that they 'fitted in' to their area and felt psychologically comfortable there – or, of course, did not. This was equally true of older British-born people as of those who had very recently come to London from abroad:

First of all it's security. You like to know where you are. Again the idea of fitting in. And also just like to feel part of the place, so you like to be recognised and you know say hello and just to be ... yeah just like to be recognised and feel that you fit in with the local area. Yeah, that'll do.

Jeff, divorced father (living with partner), forties, employed, white, homeowner, Eltham

I have friends around here, so that can speak together and can exchange, I can talk to them, is the first thing, and I feel that is the more important thing that brings me to area.

Christian, single man, thirties, French African, unemployed, private tenant, Upton Park

One Gants Hill resident described how traumatic it had been to move from her home in north-west London to Gants Hill, how a friend had helped her, and how she now felt very differently about her new home:

North London is a lot different to where we are now... Now I love it. I mean, this is my home and that's how I think of it... I remember the first day I cried my eyes out. Because I didn't know anybody. I had his friends and his family, but all my friends were all down in Edgware... I think I would have died if I didn't have anybody up here... Edgware is a lot more snobby. My mother's still a snob. And she admits it and says she says she's proud of it. This sounds awful because people say I talk very posh for up here. And that was it. I think the difference was because I was so out of sync because I was so, this was so new to me.

Sally, divorced mother, forties, employed, white Jewish, homeowner, Gants Hill

Part of her sense of isolation, at the start, was that she had no easy access to a car and so felt trapped:

... when I first got married I didn't have my own car. We shared a car, my husband and I. And he used to use it so I was very isolated. I used to work but I was, I just couldn't get myself in the car and just go. You know.

Sally, divorced mother, forties, employed, white Jewish, homeowner, Gants Hill

Social networks seem to be important, we found, in determining where people want to live. In the Newtown area of Reading, for instance, one young woman told us that she was quite keen to leave, but stayed there because of friends; if she had moved, it would have been within a 30 mile radius, because she would want to be near her friends:

I don't think Reading is at all a wonderful place to live, and I've recently been looking for a new job, so I've definitely been considering whether I'd move away. I didn't want to move away from Reading because of my group of friends.

Kate, single woman, thirties, employed, white, private tenant, Newtown, Reading

But others expressed a sentiment that they did not fit in and felt uncomfortable. Clearly this was associated with a sense of social class – as for Jeff, an electronics technician, living in Eltham:

If I had the money, I don't think we'd live in West Greenwich because it's too it'll be full of professionals and I'm not. I don't want to live in an area full of professionals. I want to live somewhere where I feel comfortable. I just can't find where my niche is…

Jeff, divorced father (living with partner), forties, employed, white,
homeowner, Eltham

Battersea in particular seemed to arouse feelings of hostility:

… we've lived here more or less since he's been born, or since he was a year old… No, I don't like Battersea … I would have preferred to live in Putney.

Carol, divorced mother, fifties, unemployed, white, private tenant, Battersea

When people did not fit in with their surrounding community, as in this case, they had a greater fear of crime and appeared to be worse off financially, whereas for those who were well linked in to the community, that seemed to be the key from which many other good things stemmed. Carol lived in a housing association property in a street where all the other residents were wealthy owner-occupiers. She felt that the way people looked down on her was almost tangible, she would get told off when her boys were making too much noise in the garden, she had no one to share school runs with (because the other children got dressed in knickerbockers and went to private schools) or to turn to for any kind of help advice or support. She seemed to struggle much more than other single mothers on the estates: she was very anxious about crime, and the worst thing about her situation was the way in which she felt totally and utterly trapped:

They're the sort of people around here who look down their nose at you if your child doesn't go to prep school. I mean, Raj goes out in his old jogging bottoms and sweatshirts and trainers … And I get into my scruffy old 2CV and … single parent, urgh, you know, tatty old… You can feel it, it's, it's almost a tangible thing.

Carol, divorced mother, fifties, unemployed, white, private tenant, Battersea

Others felt that their attachment to London was weakened because they perceived their area as too inconvenient or – a recurring theme – too run-down:

... I find places like Camden a bit depressing but, I think if you live in, the type of people who live in Camden must like it cos I know people who rave about it. I mean, every time I drive through Camden it's a litter strewn, sort of litter strewn dump, but I think that's the effect of the market and the fact that there's so much going on there of a certain type. There's so many sort of, you know, pubs and clubs and bars and all the rest of it, going on there. Er, but you know, you look at areas like Docklands which, you know, you think what's happened in Docklands, an incredible transformation, the reason we didn't live there is, there's no sort of, amenities at all. And if you live in places like Surrey Quays you've got ... there's no restaurants, there's no shops there's nothing, it's all, it's just houses basically.

David, male cohabitee, thirties, self-employed, white Jewish, homeowner, Battersea

... and Moving On Again

In several areas we found a strong desire to move on again. This was overwhelmingly the case with respondents in Heston, who told us that they intended to move out because they saw it as going downhill and thought they should realise the equity on their houses. It seemed to be equally affecting different ethnic and cultural groups. The people who remain in Heston are even perceived to have failed in some way. And this equally affects people from different ethnic groups and different lengths of residence in the area, as Betty told us in her interview, reported in Chapter 5:

...round here, no one seems to have any self respect... Well, they all moved away cos Hounslow, everyone laughs about it, you know if you're still in Hounslow they think you're either mad or as bad as the ones who live here, all my friends moved away years ago, years and years ago.

Betty, married mother, fifties, employed, white, homeowner, Heston

Most did not go far, she explains: just across the M25 motorway into Surrey. But some were moving out a long way:

We've got friends now though who are going further, you know, friends who like us stayed, they're going further, they've gone to the New Forest, so people now, older, like our age group, will move away, don't move in that little bit, they go the whole hog, or they seem to be.

Betty, married mother, fifties, employed, white, homeowner, Heston

They were able to move becasue they could realise the equity in their houses, Betty explained in discussing the prospective move of her daughter and her partner:

Maybe because their houses allow them to, the equity in their houses has allowed them to, don't think it's for any other reason … when he's finished doing The Knowledge and he's a taxi driver they'll move out, and they'll move to Ashford or Staines or somewhere, cos that's what everyone does round here. If you get out, you get out that way, but the house prices are ridiculous .

Betty, married mother, fifties, employed, white, homeowner, Heston

The main reason for moving out, it appears, is the influx of asylum seekers in recent years:

Everyone wants to move from here now… Yeah, yeah, the Asian people like us, you know, I live here 25 years and sometimes we are thinking, my son said we should move from here, it's not safe area now.

Sandhya, married mother, forties, part-time employed, Indian, homeowner, Heston

Interestingly, the same reasons were cited by a Sikh respondent on the other side of London, who had moved from Newham to Gants Hill, and whom we quoted in Chapter 7:

I was getting er a lot of er refugees in that area at the time especially er from Africa and er all the people in all the houses that were being sold, there was people who were actually buying them they weren't buying them to live in, they were buying them to rent 'em out. So that was a deciding factor, as you understand so they were lowering the tone of the area and all that.

Ranjit, married father, fifties, employed, Sikh, homeowner, Gants Hill

A Sikh respondent, whose parents were originally from India and had moved from East London, living first in Southall and then in Heston where they have been for about 8 years, and who herself had attended school in Hounslow, told us that her parents were moving out of London, mainly to get away from the noise and pollution. She has no particular ambitions about moving out of London herself, since it is all she knows, although she jokes that if she did:

… Somewhere like England but hotter, would be nice.

Sewa, single woman, twenties, employed, Sikh, homeowners
(living at home), Heston

Another couple, Sikh of Malaysian origin, were contemplating a return to their homeland, but were constrained because they found education for their children so much better in London:

… because my husband's got a Malaysian passport we're hoping that when we retire we'll retire in Malaysia cos it's, it is very nice there weather wise, the weather's nice all year round, they don't have seasons like they do here and food is very, very cheap, in fact it's cheaper to eat out sometimes than actually cook food, and the social life's very good there. The only drawbacks, we were actually planning to move and live there a few years ago but the drawbacks was the education ... in England the education facilities are very good, especially if you want to specialise in a field, the facilities are there for you. So we're hoping maybe once they're educated then we will both retire and live in Malaysia.

Faizah, married mother, thirties, employed, Malaysian parents, homeowner, Heston

Bermondsey was another area where people expressed considerable enthusiasm for moving out. Many, they suggested, had already made the move:

I mean, if you go to places like Eltham and Mottingham and Sidcup, you'll find the amount of Bermondsey people that live in them ... them three areas alone, would amaze you... Yeah, because they now call it, like, a mini, like a mini Bermondsey, because they all move out ... they're bigger places, obviously, because they've had children, and so, you know, they just move, and they all seem to move the same way.

Cheryl, married mother, thirties, employed, white, council tenant, Bermondsey

Sometimes they spoke of a generalised sense of oppressiveness:

I still, and I must be honest, I still feel claustrophobic, I feel too closed in... So I find that hard to cope with and I still do.

Gary and Dawn, married parents, forties, employed, white, housing association tenants, Bermondsey

But the great majority, as in Heston, think the area is going downhill: they quote crime and education, but underlying this is almost certainly a racial motivation:

... a lot of them have moved out, bought their own places. A lot of them have gone into new towns. You know what they started out and that a lot of them has bought their flats. Like Peter he's bought his flat but he's on his own. But the majority has moved out, bettered theirselves. But as I say the old Bermondsey people we are just dying off fast our generation ... we was all in the same street, we was all brought up together so we all knew one other but today you don't know no one. As I say our children when they grew up and got married they all had to buy outside. I mean when we was married we had to be on the list for 2 years before you was even thought of. But we took it as granted because we was all the same but now when you see strangers coming in I mean they are finding the properties for them. I mean I don't know.

Rosemary, married mother, sixties, retired, white, council tenant, Bermondsey

... as much as we do like it, it is going downhill, and so ... you know, we just take the opportunity now that we can... Well, we keep applying for the Right to Buy, so once we get that, well, hopefully we can go.

Cheryl, married mother, thirties, employed, white, council tenant, Bermondsey

She: This is another thing the Council are trying to do, they're trying to sell off all the housing stock and actually bring in people like that and really try and move all us away.

He: ... I don't mind moving somewhere nice, they can send me tomorrow, it'll be cheaper than this round here.

She: ... If you'd asked him 5 years ago he would have said no wouldn't you?

He: ... they could take me out of here in a box, but not any more. I've seen too much happen round here.

Gary and Dawn, married parents, forties, employed, white, housing association tenants, Bermondsey

Specifically, they were worried about the drug culture that they saw taking hold:

We're more worried about the children really and the crime and everything and what they can get into, this is the problem.

Gary and Dawn, married parents, forties, employed, white, housing association tenants, Bermondsey

We heard the same views in Battersea. But here, coming from professionals, the motivation was less specific and the geographical range was wider. Sometimes it was just a generalised need for more space:

I did actually got through a period of quite severe depression a few years ago and I think a lot of it was to do with coping with two very boisterous boys in such a tight ... space, which actually ... can be really daunting, especially when they're throwing each other around and they're quite lively cos they're always fighting and I really felt that I was going mad ... it's quite small, it's got a small dining room, sitting room there, next door, the size of this, then it's got a kitchen and then it's got, upstairs it's sort of a small bathroom, one double bedroom and one small other bedroom. So it's only, yes, it's very small. Postage stamp of a garden. It's not enough for two boisterous boys. Boisterous boys need a lot of space, and there isn't space here, and it's very upsetting to see them constricted as well, cos you know they get really hyper when they're ... they have so much energy they need to be on the go all day ... and when they're bored they get very destructive.

Carol, divorced mother, fifties, unemployed, white, private tenant, Battersea

Perhaps more surprisingly, we found the same sentiments in Greenhithe, a newly-developing area. Here, many people seemed to display a weak attachment to their locality, perhaps because of all the recent growth: they were clearly juggling with the idea of moving:

I think I'd rather realise some of the equity and move into something smaller. But probably wouldn't stay actually in Greenhithe. We're not sure where we would want to go.

Emma, married mother, fifties, employed, white, homeowner, Greenhithe

Some confessed they would like to move even further out, but were constrained by lack of money:

If I had lots of money, you know, I'd probably move right to the heart of Kent I suppose. Country type of house. But I'm not in that league.

Karen, married mother, thirties, part-time employed, white, homeowner, Greenhithe

Others felt that the economic tradeoff made it worthwhile. This respondent was actively contemplating a move to a more rural area in mid-Kent:

It is a nice area to live. And you get quite a lot more for your money than what you do down this area to be honest. So, yeah, that's it.

Jill, married woman, fifties, self-employed, white, homeowner, Greenhithe

It's a place to live. It's quite nice but if I had to leave I'd leave … as long as I can get to work within a reasonable amount of time, where I live isn't that important to me… But if I saw something I really liked and it was affordable in another area, I would leave here.

James, divorced man, twenties, employed, white, homeowner, Greenhithe

That last reply was typical. Lack of money to buy something more desirable was one constraint; but lack of time was even more critical. Everywhere, respondents described the conflict they felt between the desire for space and rural (or suburban) calm, and the length and cost and strain of the daily commute:

… you're tied to the area where you work, it's the travelling. Move out in the country where most people would like, move to the seaside, something like that, you've still got to travel into London. That's the problem.

Rob, married father, forties, employed, white, homeowner, Eltham

Within driving distance basically.

Zoe, married woman, twenties, employed, white, homeowner, Eltham

One frequently mentioned travel cost as the reason why she would not move out: if she lived in the country, she would have to spend so much on petrol. Her parents also have free train passes which they would lose if they lived in a different borough. Another thought she might move when her children grew up:

… to me it's ideal until the kids maybe have grown right up and left home, then I would maybe think of moving out a bit into Essex. But at the moment it's like, it's fine.

Rachel, married mother, thirties, part-time employed, white Jewish,
homeowner, Gants Hill

The Unrooted Society

One place where we found an almost American-style mobility and lack of attachment was Reading, boom town of the Thames Valley. Here, many reported that they were struggling to keep their heads above water financially:

… we're both working, I mean, together we pull in a pretty decent amount of money … but we're still struggling … to, you know, meet the mortgage, which is just crazy because it just shouldn't be like that. But that's the way it is, and if there was just one of us who had an income and the other one didn't, there's no way, I mean, there's no, you know, we'd have to rent.

Rochelle, female cohabitee, twenties, employed, white Australian, homeowner,
Newtown, Reading

And some gave up the struggle, returning to their old homes:

… at one time there were an awful lot of Scottish voices around in Reading and people, I would hear people saying 'Oh yes, we came down to work in the whatever the Silicon Valley places are, but we're going back we can't, can't afford to buy anything here, we can't afford the rents'. Seems awful doesn't it when there's unemployment somewhere that something can't be done to encourage people to…

Margery, widowed stepmother, sixties, retired, white Australian, homeowner, Earley,
Reading

While others were seriously contemplating a move:

I know for a fact that if I went up north I'd be able to buy something really quite nice. And that's the reason really that I'd, you know, think about moving away.

Helen, single woman, twenties, employed, white, private tenant, Newtown,
Reading

Here, a recurrent theme was rapid mobility and lack of community. This was true even in Newtown, an older inner area, originally developed as a company town for the biscuit works:

I lived here for 3 years and there's a couple moved in next door at the same time as we did, and we didn't really get to know them at all. But, I mean, it's like they weren't, I wouldn't say they were unfriendly, but they just they weren't social at all. This side, there was some guys lived there; like this house is rented out next door. The last people were there only 6 months. I do know some people to talk to up the street. Not as many as I thought. You know, I didn't, I thought it would probably be a bit more, people would be more sort of easier to talk to really...

Paul, married man, thirties, employed, white, homeowner, Newtown, Reading

This respondent explained that it was his work in telecoms that kept him here:

I'm a telecoms engineer. That's probably why I'm still here, for the work. It's the place to be, really...The labour market in telecoms, and specifically mobile telecoms at the moment, is unreal. If I got the sack tomorrow, I probably wouldn't be worried at all. I've got a, if I went contracting, I'd probably be into a job within 2 to 3 weeks.

Paul, married man, thirties, employed, white, homeowner, Newtown, Reading

In Newtown, it was remarkable to find how many people here had come to study at the University and had stayed, simply because it was convenient. One, originally from Brixton, had graduated with an English degree the previous year. She had chosen Reading because someone recommended it to her. She came to know the Newtown district as a student and liked it, so she continues to live there in rented accommodation:

I lived here before, I lived in here this side of Reading in my second year, sharing a house and when I was, I had to move out of student accommodation... It was just sort of get the free ads and look and see what was available really and it was quite nice cos I knew this area before and I liked it.

Dionne, female cohabitee, twenties, employed, British-born Afro-Caribbean,
private tenant, Newtown, Reading

Another took a degree in history and then a Postgraduate Certificate in Education at York. She currently teaches in Bracknell, where she travels to from Reading:

My boyfriend was down here as well, which is the other reason that I came back down and a lot of my friends and things are in this area, but as a teacher I could have got a job, sort of, virtually anywhere in the country, although there are more available down here, it is still easier to get a job down here than it is in some places up north...

I'm actually leaving my teaching job at the end of this year and I've already been offered four jobs, because people just, people are desperate, people can't get, can't get them and that's without looking.

Helen, single woman, twenties, employed, white, private tenant,
Newtown, Reading

But lack of attachment was even more true in Lower Earley, a 1970s estate, where the sense was of constant change, of incessant mobility, of growth that had been too fast, and of a community that had become too big to maintain a good quality of life:

… it's grown, grown, no-one seems to be able to stop it, there is something in the newspaper about stopping building tonight, they were going to extend more houses, I think that's being stopped, so the voice has been heard at last, it was, I think why we moved to Lower Earley was because there was houses available and we wanted to move quickly … we had a dog we could walk miles around here, but now there isn't anywhere.

Brenda, married mother, fifties, employed, white, homeowner, Earley, Reading

Here, she told us, people were always upping sticks and moving on; there was no longer any sense of permanence or of community:

They are mostly, a big turnover in this estate of people, I think they are mostly white here; age, we have bungalows so in this little bit it's I think quite varied from probably early twenties to I don't know what age, we might have people about eighty, I think just, but they have been here quite since the probably since the bungalows were first built, so it's a mixture I think…

Brenda, married mother, fifties, employed, white, homeowner, Earley, Reading

She said she might move back to the North of England:

I might want to move back. I just find life in this area so fast, everybody wants to make money and time, there's no time is there, the pace is too fast, I'm finding it very hard at the moment.

Brenda, married mother, fifties, employed, white, homeowner, Earley, Reading

Yearning for the Country

In many of our interviews, not merely among the older people contemplating a move on retirement but also among much younger people, we found a disillusionment with life in the big city and a determination to move. Very often, these interviewees were quite geographically specific: they wanted to leave London, most often for the country, sometimes for the coast:

If given a choice, I would like to buy my own place and move out, not round here… Outside of London… I think I've had enough of like kind of I've been there, I've done it, I've seen it and I wanna buy a new place and find a woman and start a family or something like that, and I don't want my children to be here, no … yeah, somewhere outside.

Amir, single, forties, employed, African, council tenant, Battersea

If you were somewhere like, living on the South Coast, Portsmouth, Southampton they're still, you know, they're still thriving towns but you've got much more, sort of, in the way of outdoor facilities … as a child I really enjoyed being in the country so, I, I, it's something that I wouldn't want any children of mine to miss out, being able to run around, outside really, sort of, fresh air and…

David, male cohabitee, thirties, self-employed, white Jewish, homeowner, Battersea

David explained that he did not use Central London and did not like it:

… in 5 years I'll definitely be out of London, yeah… I think London's very functional and I don't, I don't make much use of the centre of town at all. You know, so, I just don't like the crush of people and going up there very much so.

David, male cohabitee, thirties, self-employed, white Jewish, homeowner, Battersea

Very similar sentiments were expressed by other Battersea residents. Perhaps, we felt, the same restlessness that had brought them here would also take them out again:

Buy me a house in the country. I'd live, I'd love to live in the country… I think I've had enough of London. It's just bustle and bustle of every day life, it's just rush rush rush rush, you know what I'm saying, it's just go to work, get up, come home, go to bed, get up, go to work, go to bed, get up, come home, you know?… I don't care where in the country as long as it's not London. I would like to move in the country.

Sandra, single mother, forties, employed, Afro-Caribbean, council tenant, Battersea

Interestingly, though, this basic desire – for more space, more peace, more rural calm – emerged equally strongly in our interviews with people in suburban areas like Greenhithe and Earley:

Wilmington is not far from here … it's the country. It's countryside. And like Sutton-at-Hone, all those places. It's sort of probably like this was when we first moved here. Do you know what I mean? It's more green and less buildings. So, I mean, you know, if I had a choice I'd have a massive five bedroomed detached house in Wilmington.

Sharon, married mother, thirties, part-time employed, white,
homeowner, Greenhithe

Well, obviously it's financial, but we would like to move out to New Barn–Longfield

Way. We wouldn't move too far away. We'd move within the vicinity because obviously we've got ties here. But it would be nice to sort of ... a bit snobby really. We'd like a bit more land, you know, to be a bit more secluded and a bit more detached. Also family reasons. I've got a brother who I'd like to sort of bring up and have a granny annexe for him as well. But we would move ... we would look at Longfield, Fawkham, New Barn – that way.

Emma, married mother, forties, employed, white, homeowner, Greenhithe

I'd probably, probably Wokingham or we go out a lot on weekends and we drive round all the little places and sort of more the, it is, there is quite, you're in a town and then suddenly you're in the country, I'd probably, like Saturday we went from here to Windsor on all the back roads, there's lots of little areas I'd probably, but can't afford to.

Brenda, married mother, fifties, employed, white, homeowner, Earley, Reading

In Reading, as in Battersea, we found many respondents who expressed no particular attachment to – or affection for – the area; they were characteristically rootless, and many expressed a wish to move farther away from London, generally to a town which they clearly saw as having more architectural or cultural character:

Yeah I'd go like a bloody shot... I'd go further out actually, I'd go to Bath. I'd go, I'd move away from London.

Dionne, female cohabitee, twenties, employed, British-born Afro-Caribbean, private tenant, Newtown, Reading

Others, though less critical of Reading, think that they are likely to move, probably further afield. They were very averse to London life. Noticeably, many named university or cathedral towns like Canterbury, Oxford or York:

Canterbury is a prime place really, but it would probably be down South still, somewhere, yeah... Unless it's in Scotland, because he's Scottish, so...

Rochelle, female cohabitee, twenties, employed, white Australian, homeowner, Newtown, Reading

I would dearly like to live in Oxford actually, again, and yes, I did actually consider several jobs there. So yes that was probably the place I considered most, so yeah, I would be very happy to live in Oxford. London I wouldn't because I didn't like it at all, I think it's completely different from anywhere else in the country, and the people are strange and I don't feel safe there... I don't like the feel of the place, it's so dirty and crowded and...

Kate, single woman, thirties, employed, white, private tenant, Newtown, Reading

… because York's a really nice place, people go, they get a job and they stay, they would rather, they would, you know, they call it the graveyard of ambition in York, because people would rather stay in a nice place than actually move on to promotion, where down here people move more regularly and there's always jobs available.

Helen, single woman, twenties, employed, white, private tenant, Newtown, Reading

The Sense of Belonging

These young people, clearly, are attached to Reading not as a place, but as a network of social relationships. They don't particularly value its qualities and they aspire to live somewhere else, in a place they think has greater aesthetic or social distinction. They define themselves more strongly in what they do not like: London has a very negative image, and they see themselves as belonging almost to a different country, small-town (or medium-town) southern England. And that could be a strong force in mitigating London's magnetic pull for young professionals like themselves.

Back in London, many of the people we interviewed would love to have a sense of freedom, a sense of choice. They are trapped in council property that they often dislike and say they are occupying only because they had no option: they had to have a roof over their heads. Others still value their home and their neighbourhood but feel that it has gone down socially, because the 'wrong kind of people' have come in; they complain of owner-occupiers who have let their homes to irresponsible tenants, and many are planning an exit strategy if they feel financially capable of it. And others feel the same could happen to them because they have no control over letting processes; the Council just does things to them, over their heads, without consultation and without warning.

The owner-occupiers were quite different, of course, because they had made a conscious choice: for many, to move outwards, often in the same geographical sector, from the place where they had been born and grown up. (Surprisingly, many mentioned family ties, especially to ageing parents.) Theirs was often a constrained choice, of course: many described how they had to balance their basic desire, for more space in and around the home, and for rural peace and quiet, not only against the need to be close to family and friends, but also against the time and the cost of the daily commute. And this balance had put many into new estates on the urban fringe, beyond the London border, where they complained about the pace of change, the loss of the tranquillity they had sought, but also the lack of basic facilities.

Schools were a matter of obsessive concern for those with children. Many had moved, or were contemplating moves, in order to be closer to what they saw as good schools – and even more so, to avoid bad ones. This was a key factor in the movement from some inner boroughs to the outer London suburbs.

It mattered a lot to people that they felt comfortable in their neighbourhood and fitted in with congenial neighbours. Most did, but a minority clearly felt they did not, and this seemed to affect their view of the world more generally, making them apprehensive and negative about almost everything in their lives. And in some neighbourhoods, this sense was much more general: a feeling that the area was not what it was, that it was going downhill, that the sense of community had been eroded, and that it was essential to get out while they could. These areas were a minority of those we visited, but in them the general sense of disillusionment and despair was quite palpable.

Commuters

© Bill Knight

Chapter Eleven

Getting There

Everywhere we went in London, people were obsessed by transport: how to get where you wanted to go, how long it would take, how big a risk there was that something would stop you getting there at all, whether there was a better way through (or round) the traffic jams and the apparently endless failures of train or bus services. But, given that basic obsession, there were some fairly big differences in the way people filtered and interpreted the basic problem, depending on age, gender, occupation, income, lifestyle and – above all – geography.

For inner-city residents, many of them young and most of them working, transport was a recurrent theme – both for old-time residents in council blocks, and for the newcomers. This was very evident in Bermondsey, where the new Jubilee Line extension had just brought a dramatic improvement in access to central London, and in the opposite direction across the river into East London. Consider these typical reactions from three different Bermondsey residents:

Like one thing'll improve, like they put the railway in, yeah? We've never had a railway station, right? Like, we had Rotherhithe, but like, the mother of my kids used to come from Stockwell, near Brixton, and to actually get to Stockwell from here, right, it was like Mission Impossible. It was … you needed a Sherpa! It was like going up a mountain! You had to get a bus to the Elephant, right, and another bus from the Elephant, or a train from the Elephant, yeah, and, like, for Christ's sake, I mean, in a motor, I could be there, like, in … if the roads are clear, 5 or 10 minutes. Yet they put this train station in down here, which is truly wonderful, I mean, like, you know, it's 30 years too late, but who cares! As long as people can get to the Dome, that's what I always say! That's what it is, isn't it, it's the route to the Dome, yeah!

Del and Kenny, single and divorced (father) brothers, thirties, unemployed/
employed, white, council tenant, Bermondsey

It is really, yeah, cos you've got the Tube now so that's a godsend really the Tube, because it gets you there very quick. You haven't got all the traffic, you've got plenty of bus services and you're only a little way from the Quays and right on top of the Blue, there's shops down the Blue there. So there's a pub across the road so we're right on top of everything really here.

Gary and Dawn, married parents, forties, employed, white,
housing association tenants, Bermondsey

Liz explained graphically how the new Jubilee Line had made life easier for her:

Whereas before I used to, I used to have to walk to Rotherhithe and get a train to Mile End and then a train to Stratford, which is a shopping centre, I just walk over, takes you straight through into Stratford. Also, I can get it to my sisters, save me having to walk to Rotherhithe but I have to change twice, but that's no problem. And also people go to the West End... Yeah, so and you can go, so no there's no...

Liz, divorced mother, thirties, unemployed, white, council tenant, Bermondsey

This Bermondsey resident works in Wimbledon in south-west London, and reports that the new line has shrunk his commute time:

It seems like it's quite a long way away from where you live. How did that come about?

It might seem long at first, but because of the Jubilee Line and trains opened, I can get to Wimbledon in just about half an hour, be at work in half an hour, so I don't have to get up until about 8 O'clock in the morning, which is good.

Mark, single man, thirties, employed, white, private tenant, Bermondsey

But another Bermondsey resident feels that there could be a downside: in the past inaccessibility has kept the area in a sense protected from change, but now property values are likely to rise, exposing people much more to market forces:

But there has always been, until the Jubilee line ... a transport problem, maybe it's just one of the rather nice things about it [*laughs*] there were only two buses and no trains or Tubes, so maybe that kept it backward a bit, and then the Tube stations boosted...

How do you feel about the Tube stations being built, what impact did that have...?

Well, not that much on our personal lives but I'm sure it's had an impact on property values and stuff. And certainly on the sales of these flats by the developers ... saying there's a Tube station within 5 minutes walk, that would [*laughs*] make a difference...

Francesca, married mother, forties, self-employed, white, homeowner, Bermondsey

Farther out east, in Upton Park, one respondent explains that it is all a matter of having sufficient alternatives, should any piece of the system fail – an ever-present worry for Londoners at the time we were interviewing, and subsequently:

Yeah we can get the bus, we get the bus from outside there at the end of the Faraday Road there, the 25 bus and it goes to Central London, or I can get the, well I suppose I'd go on the Central line that's it really … I mean there's other ways of getting there, you can go to Docklands and change at Bank if you're ever stuck or, there's this new Jubilee line link.

Padma, single woman, twenties, employed, Asian, private tenant, Upton Park

It is very different out towards the outer edge of the London region. Here, people see that their location, close to the M25 and its interchange with major radial highways, gives them potential access to a huge range of opportunities within about an hour's radius – but, of course, that access depends on having a car. Here are two representative answers from Greenhithe in Kent Thamesside:

I don't … I mean I can't really say there's any negatives that we've come across. I mean, cos we've got local towns, as I said, we're quite local to most things really. We've got Greenhithe one way, Gravesend, Bexleyheath's only down the A2. It doesn't take too long to get anywhere. We've got Thurrock. We've got Bluewater.

Emma, married mother, forties, employed, white, homeowner, Greenhithe

I suppose it's a convenient place to live. You know it's straight on to the A2. As I say you can be straight up into London or straight down towards the coast. Or straight on to the M25 so you can get pretty much wherever you want to. It's a very very convenient place round here.

James, divorced man, twenties, employed, white, homeowner, Greenhithe

But this accessibility is uneven: it does not apply so much to journeys into London, where congestion and lack of parking become major factors and most people are compelled to use public transport. Rather, it is relevant for orbital journeys around London, and to reverse journeys away from the capital:

It's very central and I do a lot of work in Kent and really the motorway's just up road 5 minutes from a motorway and I don't have to travel really any further into town. That's the other choice I suppose if you're going from, say, Lewisham and then you're further in town and then you tend to hit more traffic. But here, no, I can go on the motorway. I could be through the tunnel in 10–15 minutes if I choose the time right. I can be across the ferry, or get on the M25 in 10 minutes. And my work is the South-East, so I that's quite important.

Mick, married man, fifties, employed, white, homeowner, Eltham

For this Greenhithe resident, the area's excellent accessibility is actually a factor inhibiting a move farther from London to the coast:

Yes. I did think about moving. I did think about moving down to the South Coast and then I thought, don't be stupid, you're no longer at the centre of a radiant, you have removed yourself 60 miles away, which gives you another 120 miles on top of every journey you do.

Oona, divorced mother, fifties, employed, white, private tenant, Greenhithe

The same sentiment is expressed on the other side of London by a resident of Heston, which – she says – combines excellent accessibility by motorway to all parts of the compass around and outside London, with direct access via Tube to central London:

One thing I would give this area, without any doubt, it's a very very centralised area, which is very good, you've got the main roads just up the road, you've got the M25 ... you've got all the motorways, you've got the M4, the M3, M25, you've got the Tube station, which you can walk to in Heston West, you've got London, you know, on the Tube which is 10 mile away, so you're in, you've got the coast 50, 60 mile away, you're in a very very centralised and convenient area.

Sewa, single woman, twenties, employed, Sikh, homeowners
(living at home), Heston

And she stresses that here in addition, unlike Greenhithe, the Underground offers a level of access to the centre that could not be equalled beyond its limits:

I think jobs tend to tie people in a lot. Because the further out you go, if you've got a job in London it's very hard to get in, well, it can be anyway, can just be a pain. Whereas here you can get the Tube. We've got, you know, three Tube stations very close to us, within walking distance.

Sewa, single woman, twenties, employed, Sikh, homeowners
(living at home), Heston

In between these two extremes, in the outer parts of East London, people feel that a recent spate of highway construction has brought a totally new level of car-based accessibility, especially for journeys out to areas beyond the London boundary:

And it's not that far up that new A13, it's not far at all. The roads are making life so much easier now, everything's so much shorter isn't it? Journeys, I mean, to say this new road from Redbridge roundabout down to Stratford is like unbelievable and now you've got the new one up from, on the A13 right the way through to Lakeside and the Greenhithe Tunnel, it's you know, it's, it just makes everything so shorter and the new … and the 406 I suppose that gets a bit blocked and you can sit in traffic, but you know, up to Beckton, everything's so much shorter, it's such a … I think it's quite a good area to be in.

Jenny, married mother, forties, white, homeowner, Gants Hill

But perceptions can differ from one resident to another, as we found in Battersea. This resident thinks the area had excellent access by public transport:

Oh it's all right. You've got Battersea Park station up there, that's not far. You've got all the buses going to Chelsea way and Kensington, that way and you've got buses, all buses going down to Clapham Junction, you've got a bus going to the Arndale Centre in Wandsworth. So it's a very, it's very, very good around here for that.

Lloyd, single father, thirties, unemployed, white, council tenant, Battersea

Yet this resident takes the diametrically opposite view:

Oh, that's right, buses, you can't get here, that's the main problem, transport to this area is appalling, it is like an island, because A you haven't got a Tube, B you have to walk to Clapham Common and the tube is packed, and transport in morning is not good. So you have to either get on a bus, or…

James, gay cohabitee, thirties, self-employed, white,
housing association tenant, Battersea

The Daily Commuter Grind

In the south-east part of the capital, in Eltham and Greenhithe, we interviewed at a time when the local commuter line was experiencing particularly acute problems due to the collapse of a tunnel. So it was no wonder that we were overwhelmed by a constant chorus of complaint:

Anything you would care to name I think. Equipment failure happens an awful lot. Train failure happens a lot. Of course, this year, we've had the Strood Tunnel collapsing several times, which obviously nobody could have foreseen, but my God, it's irritating though… Very wearing, because you just do not know. You can get to Charing Cross and there's nothing up on the boards. Nothing. The station is packed and nobody's telling you anything. No excuse. No excuse for not keeping people informed.

Emily, married mother, fifties, white, employed, homeowner, Greenhithe

She stresses the uncertainty and consequent anxiety of the experience, repeated day after day:

On a good day, when the wind's in the right direction, I can do it door to door in an hour and twenty minutes. But it can be anything. The worst journey I've ever had, is leaving work at 5 O'clock, which was a good night, and walking in here at ten to ten in the evening. And that was a night when there was a fire between London Bridge and Cannon Street and they just stopped all the trains. They had to. But, when you're stuck on the train, you can't … it was before I had a mobile phone, you know, they didn't know where I was. But it's one of those things… It is wearing. I can tell you, you're fit for nothing at the end of the week, which is why I don't bother too much about the social side and why peace means a lot to me. Relaxation for me is pottering about in the garden, but obviously to people with different age groups, it would be exactly the opposite.

Emily, married mother, fifties, white, employed, homeowner, Greenhithe

She again underlines how wearing the experience is, and how it leaves her with little energy for anything else:

… I wouldn't consciously spend a lot of time up in town, say, meeting people after work for a drink because of the journey home and the fact that the trains … they've really gone down hill. And you just never know when they're going to cancel or when something's going to happen. And you'll get weeks where it seems every morning, every evening, there's a delay and that is very wearing. And quite honestly, sometimes, I just come in and have something to eat and go to bed and then go and do it all again the next morning.

Emily, married mother, fifties, white, employed, homeowner, Greenhithe

One respondent is acutely aware of the social nuances that attach themselves to the three parallel commuter lines that run through south-east London into this part of Kent:

Much worse, yeah. Eight trains an hour through Woolwich now. It's the level of service, yeah. Again there's the social aspect of commuting. I mean, again there's different social mix that get on at Woolwich on the Woolwich [line] than there is on the Eltham line than there is on the Sidcup line, so you're aware of that, but there's a lot more people who work on building sites and whatever who get on at Woolwich and there's less than that at Bexleyheath and there's less than that if you go on the Sidcup line.

Jeff, divorced father (living with partner), forties, employed, white,
homeowner, Eltham

In Battersea, because of the area's location between Clapham Junction and the London termini, people notice that the trains are always overcrowded with short- distance transfer passengers:

Clapham Junction connects Waterloo and Victoria a lot of the overcrowding is caused by people just trying to get from Waterloo to Clapham Junction to change, and they jump on trains going, you know, right out so, an easy solution would be to run a shuttle service continuously back and forth. And it would reduce overcrowding on all the platforms and for all the Clapham people... London will, I know it goes through cycles, but I do think the transport will probably ... the, the reason why it goes into its next downward cycle, transport, probably house prices going down.

David, male cohabitee, thirties, self-employed, white Jewish, homeowner, Battersea

This resident, interviewed before the event, looks forward to the impact of the Mayor's congestion charge:

Well, I mean, it's 15 minutes to Waterloo, and there are trains, but even sometimes that, just doing that short journey, can break down. So, well, everybody knows, the transport system is vastly overcrowded, and there's a long way to go, in terms of making ... moving round the capital easily. And, obviously, the first steps are going to be the congestion charges.

Scott, single man, forties, unemployed, white, council tenant, Battersea

Some respondents speak of their physical revulsion in entering the Tube at the peak hour:

... this idea of er, of Ken Livingstone's to charge for cars, I don't know what the details are, on the one hand I very much agree with an environmentally friendly policy, but you have to have an alternative and I'm, you know, I went, I had to go in on the Tube yesterday morning, at rush hour, and I feel really sorry for people who have to do it every day. It is such an unpleasant experience and, er, I don't think, I don't think politicians have ever been, you know, they've forgotten what it's like, they don't go on Tubes. You know, you've seen pictures of, of ... on the news of trains and you think that's not crowded that positively empty, you've only got a few people standing on there. And you go in and you're packed with your face in somebody else's hair and it's just absolutely disgusting. For a civilised country it's appalling.

David, male cohabitee, thirties, self-employed, white Jewish, homeowner, Battersea

And things are little better, it is suggested, on the national rail commuter services where, at the time we interviewed, there were serious problems:

Yes, yeah, I mean, some of the intercity services are fine. Er, and if you've got the luxury of going First Class it's quite nice. But commuting, the commuter routes into London and things like Network South East is ancient, you know, carriages which are 40 years old. You try and fit three people in a, on a 6-foot seat, it's just, just not funny.

David, male cohabitee, thirties, self-employed, white Jewish, homeowner, Battersea

Despite these evident discomforts, especially on the older rolling stock on the commuter lines south of the river, one respondent talks of how for him commuting has become a habit, despite the existential boredom of a day-by-day routine totally governed by the train timetable:

Because nowadays … get to work and you sit down in a railway carriage sometimes and look around and think, I might be the oldest person on this carriage. So, how do I find it? I'm increasingly intolerant of it yeah, which is why I moved … to London Bridge now, that's knocked another 15 minutes off before I get the train. It's the time keeping. It's the fact that you have to turn up for the overground train … you have to be there at a certain time and you're pushed out the other end and [at] a certain time, just like a sausage machine and the same back. You turn up and you're pushed out the other end at the same time. It's the same thing day in and day out. And unlike the Tube, you're … seeing the same faces half the time. You've got to get different trains to see different set of faces… It's a real pain. Underground could be better because there's different faces and you know different trains, but so it's an important part of my life the commuting.

Jeff, divorced father (living with partner), forties, employed, white,
homeowner, Eltham

There might come a point, he seems to be suggesting, when he would have had enough. So we ask him whether he has ever thought about moving out of London. He replies:

No I haven't. I wouldn't do it now. I'll do it when I retire … I think so, somewhere quieter yeah. Then you can vegetate more. But I wouldn't do it now, because I'm not prepared to do the commuting. But I'd never find a job locally as well paid or … it would be difficult to find a job as interesting and as well paid outside … there's lots of conversations about commuting whether it's a Tube or you know the overground. I'm getting increasingly intolerant of it. I think that's of age as well. You talk to other people…

Jeff, divorced father (living with partner), forties, employed, white,
homeowner, Eltham

But others are contemplating a move in order to travel on a more reliable commuter line.

If the rail link was better and more reliable, then yes we will probably stay around here, but it isn't. There's much, much better rail services, you know, the other line, that goes through Longfield… Although it is more expensive, but my God, it's more reliable than here.

Emily, married mother, fifties, white, employed, homeowner, Greenhithe

Those who use buses, too, complain mainly about their unreliability. And this seems to be true both inside London, which operates a controlled system of franchised buses, and outside it in places like Greenhithe and Reading, where there is a completely deregulated free-for-all competitive system of services. Here are two representative London responses, from opposite sides of the capital:

... I use the public transport, Oh that's a bad point, I mean, [*laughs*] sometimes I wait for bus for a long time. I get two buses at the bus stop, 111 and 828, but they don't keep the timetable so, you know, I know it's normal in London but Oh, sometimes I waste my time waiting just for bus. So...

Seung-yun, single woman, twenties, student, Korean, private tenant, Heston

He: Well, they can improve on it in terms of timing, especially on Romford Road, the timing is absolutely, I, you know, for example, if you go to the shopping centre people can stay for ages because there's only two buses that runs on Romford Road... And at times, by the time they leave the city centre they are completely full, and even the next stop which is just by Co-operative, they keep on driving, they don't stop.

Nadira and Coffie, married parents, forties, both employed, African, homeowners,
Upton Park

This seems equally true of Earley on the east side of Reading, except that this respondent thinks that the service is at least better than in the deep countryside:

However, it could be a lot worse in the country as well I know, and there is a train service also so really we're well off, except that we complain about Reading buses because I expect you've heard people say that they're 28 drivers short... So you stand at the bus stop and I go frequently to the hospital and I always leave a half an hour before I have to in case that bus doesn't come and I'm going to be late otherwise. That's not their fault, I don't blame them, it's like being a policeman I don't know how they can recruit people to do such a horrible job because the stress and strain of the traffic and the snappish people, passengers like me saying 'Where have you been'?

Margery, widowed stepmother, sixties, retired, white Australian, homeowner, Earley,
Reading

Car commuting could be just as stressful, as told to us by a Greenhithe respondent who now works near home:

Yeah, I've worked up London. I detest it, absolutely detest it ... What I do now I don't see any traffic, it takes me 20 minutes to and 20 minutes ... it's nothing, I mean friends of mine 3 hours in a day they're travelling to and from work, you know if they are driving up to London from here, it could be an hour and a half, an hour and a half driving home, to me that's 3 hours I'm at home.

Richard, married man, thirties, employed, white, homeowner, Greenhithe

The husband of another respondent has had an even worse experience. She tells us that he has been commuting daily right across London from Greenhithe to Uxbridge on the capital's far western edge, a total journey of about 35 miles each way:

Absolute nightmare … it takes 2 hours for my husband to go out to work, 2 hours to come back and it's a long way. So, we can't really do anything in the evening, because by the time he gets home, it's like gone 8 O'clock…

Karen, married mother, thirties, part-time employed, white, homeowner, Greenhithe

The most striking point about these different experiences is that the time spent on the daily journey seems to have very little relationship to distance travelled, as people could discover for themselves if they changed jobs. Here is a story from Heston in west London:

Well he, he used to drive 2 miles to Bush Corner in Isleworth and now he drives, I'm not sure it's 14 or 16 miles to Stoke Poges and it takes him the same time. [*Laughs*] That's 2 miles into London against, no it's 14 miles out against 2 miles in.

Betty, married mother, fifties, employed, white, homeowner, Heston

As we move out from inner to outer London and then beyond the M25 into the Outer Metropolitan Area, the most noticeable fact is that very rapidly people become completely car-dependent. Out here, the daily car commute is just a fact of life to which people become accustomed, almost on auto-pilot:

… I think on average it takes me about 55 minutes to get in and perhaps a little bit less to get back. I mean it can take, it can be worse than that, but it's not generally more than an hour… It's the sort of thing you get used to really. I'd prefer not to have to do it really but well you just get used to it I suppose.

Vincent, single man, thirties, employed, white, homeowner, Newtown, Reading

This respondent from Lower Earley, on the edge of Reading, describes the daily nightmare of leaving her home for work:

It can be horrendous, traffic in this area is, just getting out of Lower Earley, go to work early on a morning … if anything has happened on the M4 so you get tailbacks on the 329, so, it's no use going through Wokingham because it's busy there, if you leave it too late … you've got everybody taking their children to school, which is not good, so this morning it was a 20 minute run, tomorrow morning it could be an hour, coming home was bad, just getting out of Bracknell, from where I'm actually based just getting out onto the 329, it was queuing for about 20 minutes, so it varies.

Brenda, married mother, fifties, employed, white, homeowner, Earley, Reading

People like Brenda may or may not have public transport alternatives. But these seldom work effectively in practice. She believes that when everyone comes back from holiday, she will have to leave for work at six in the morning to find a parking space at work in nearby Bracknell:

Yes, I could go from Earley and they have now got free, we have a mini-bus that, say I wanted to go into Bracknell on a lunch time we have a free mini-bus, but they have extended that, they used to pick up from Bracknell Station, I think it was 8 O'clock and half eight, but now they are doing it from about half six in the morning to about half nine, then on an evening I think they start at 4 O'clock until I think half seven, so they are trying all these things, but at the moment I go by car, it's just so convenient, if I want to go out at lunch time, you know, if I want to go into Wokingham or Bracknell, it's easier to go in by car … than waiting for a free bus even, but I think I might consider getting the train if I don't find someone [to share the car], but then again it's going to cost me I've got a car standing there costing money and you've got to pay train fares which are not cheap … no, so you can't win can you?

Brenda, married mother, fifties, employed, white, homeowner, Earley, Reading

A similar answer comes from the other side of London, in Greenhithe down in Thamesside Kent:

Do you use public transport yourself?

No, not a lot, I must admit. You need to have your own transport to live here basically, it would be difficult to commute, OK if you are commuting to London by train but you know other areas would be very difficult on buses, if you're working anywhere else.

Richard, married man, thirties, employed, white, homeowner, Greenhithe

One explanation could be the cost of bus travel, about which people in Greenhithe seemed to complain a lot. Here are representative comments:

She: I mean I think public transport around here is quite expensive, especially for, you know, sort of people that haven't got cars. You know, I mean that would be quite a big expense to go there, but there again, they've got to make a profit as well haven't they?… I think they'd get far more people using it if it wasn't as expensive. Because it costs £2 to go single from here to Gravesend… My daughter came up the other Sunday because her husband had the car and she came up with the two children and it cost her £2 for herself and £1 each for the children – one 3, one 6. So it was £4 for her to come up.

Dorothy and Bill, married father/mother, fifties, employed, white, homeowners,
Greenhithe

Well, we very rarely use the buses. But when I do have to use them, I find those quite expensive cos obviously I'm not used to paying out… Everything goes up. But I do find that if I've got to take the two on the bus, it's just as cheap to get a taxi.

Emma, married mother, forties, employed, white, homeowner, Greenhithe

And in terms of this contrast, outer London proves to be a confusing cross between Inner London and the Outer Metropolitan Area. Ranjit lives in Gants Hill but does shift work in Dagenham, which is not on a radial route but involves a cross-journey through suburban East London:

Are you driving into work at the moment?

Well I have to, because if I don't, I have to take two buses from here to get to er Dagenham which by car it only takes me 15 minutes. By bus, change two buses because I work on shifts, different shifts, I'd probably have difficulty getting a bus after say, if I leave home about, for a start if I want to start work at half six, I have to leave here at 5 O'clock by bus. I don't think there are that many buses running at 5 O'clock. So then I have to take two buses and er then it cost me more than running a car, but more than the fare, its the time, the amount of time it's going to take me to travel by bus. Yeah. If I was working in the City, I'd take a Tube it's no problem because I've got a station round the corner, no problem. It's er, it's just the buses. You know it all depends where you live.

Ranjit, married father, fifties, employed, Sikh, homeowner, Gants Hill

And this Gants Hill resident clearly finds the bus an inferior alternative, but they have only one car and her husband takes it to work:

Buses are not too bad, sometimes you'd be waiting a long time for a bus, usually they are late but occasionally they'll be on time but must admit I do take the transport I usually have to wait long and comes two, two or three comes at once.

You tend to go in the car mostly then?

My husband takes the car to work, we only have one car in the weekend when we're shopping and things I go in the car but weekdays I rely on public transport.

Shirin, married mother, thirties, Bangladeshi, homeowner, Gants Hill

It was not always like this. Another respondent in Greenhithe, who grew up here, recalls her parents' lives:

My parents were very happy here. They didn't have any need of a car or anything. They went everywhere on the bus and, you know, and so we know that you can get to both places. There isn't a difficulty. Even if you didn't have a car.

Dorothy and Bill, married father/mother, fifties, employed, white, homeowners,
Greenhithe

The explanation of this paradox comes from Margery, a woman with mobility problems living in Earley: once, even in outer suburban areas like these, the pattern of land uses and services were perfectly adapted to an era before mass car-ownership. But now they have gone:

It's funny you should ask that! There's a little parade of shops which, when the estate was built, catered to every need. It was before the days when people had cars, it was before there were supermarkets everywhere. The result now of that is that we've lost our butcher, our greengrocer, our baker, it's a couple of, a take-away, an, an Indian restaurant, a Chinese restaurant and a sort of a, what do you call it, a convenience store I suppose, so I wouldn't shop here. Now when my husband was alive we went to Tesco by car. It's very difficult for me to get there, as of this week particularly it means two bus journeys and there used to be from the town three buses an hour which this week was changed to two buses an hour which didn't come today so I, it took me three hours of waiting before I even did any shopping, to get to Tesco and to come away again. The bus service has just been extended so that it goes to Asda … at least I'm going to be able to get there and get back and carry stuff which is my big problem. My stepdaughter takes me about once a fortnight and I try to get the heavy things then but things like, well, you know, you're supposed to eat fresh fruit and vegetables they weigh awfully heavily to carry and to get yourself on the bus with.

Margery, widowed stepmother, sixties, retired, white Australian, homeowner,
Earley, Reading

But among a few younger and more recent inhabitants, this pattern of car dependence extends even as far as inner London:

… it comes back to the, the traffic and lifestyle, I hate public transport with a passion.

Timothy, single man, thirties, employed, white, private tenant, Bermondsey

He clearly would derive big benefits from using the new Jubilee Line, but he will not do so – even though he complains bitterly about traffic:

Purely because I just love the freedom of being able to do what I want to do when I want to do it. The trains here are generally very good and when you want to go out drinking they are excellent… But the car is great for anywhere you want to go, go off, as long as you leave plenty of time, don't, don't get hassled by traffic and you've got a good piece of music to … listen to. No problems, no.

Really, really? So would … the benefits of … the car sort of outweigh all the traffic jams and everything like that?

Oh yes. Sadly so, for me, I'm very much a motorist. And, although the price of petrol is astronomical they would really have to hack the price up, make it basically bankrupt type price.

Really, really?… Why do you dislike public transport so much when … you've got this actually quite good line, the Jubilee line, what sort of puts you off using that?

It's the inflexibility of it. If all of a sudden I decide I don't actually want to go down that appropriate line, I actually want to make a quick detour and stop off at Halfords, you can't do that and sod's law will say that when you arrive there you've just missed a train. I know this is probably my fault as well, because I'm so bad at using it, I've never mastered it… So every time I go on it I generally think … the problems I find tend to compound because of my ignorance.

> *Timothy, single man, thirties, employed, white, private tenant, Bermondsey*

The View from the Road: Parking and Roadworks

Those who drive seem to be obsessed with two things: parking problems and roadworks:

Well, again, me personally, more parking facilities. Especially round the Eltham area. You can't park. You know, this is what you want … you know, you're interested in. You could … to go shopping in Eltham High Street, sometimes you've got to park half a mile away. Otherwise you're on yellow lines or restricted areas. So, you know, more parking areas within the Eltham High Street area.

> *Rob, married father, forties, employed, white, homeowner, Eltham*

Nahar in Upton Park relies on his van for his job as a salesperson, and is incensed almost to incoherent rage by the behaviour of the local traffic wardens:

This is I mean very, very trouble and you see within 2 minute they will come and they will not think about the man from where he will pay £30, where he will pay £40 I mean the service of traffic warden is better than police. The police come within 20 minute, half an hour and traffic warden come within 2 minute… Yeah, ticket and also they are very, very cruel people I say because they don't think about how man will pay. I mean if somebody park in the … block the traffic or somebody block the road or hassle for somebody else must have a ticket, but I mean just to park on the side and they put yellow line and I mean they should be little bit think about that I mean.

> *Nahar, married father, sixties, employed, Bangladeshi, private tenant, Upton Park*

For others, even in the same area, roadworks were the obsession:

They love doing roadworks, absolutely love it with a passion, but they're not very good at finishing them. They love starting them and then leave them for a long time, and they love their diversions… I'm sure they sit there planning their wild and wacky diversions, just to see if the public can cope with them for no apparent reason. The traffic is absolutely awful but you tend to, as it doesn't seem to change year in, year out there's always a problem, it really makes no difference. Therefore you just … if it all of a sudden got worse then there would be uproar. It's par for the course really.

Timothy, single man, thirties, employed, white, private tenant, Bermondsey

Mel and his wife, in Gants Hill, had witnessed a sequence of events that seemed to be producing a surreal landscape in front of their eyes:

He: Often you do see roadworks with nobody there for days.

She: … There was an electricity failure and they had to dig up the road to find out the fault, and that was open for weeks before it was – I said they left it open for the next power failure, which did happen – we've had three different power failures.

He: All they do to the roads is they put on another layer of tar, which means that the road vis-à-vis the pavement gets higher and higher.

She: Higher and higher.

He: So every time this happens it means that the houses are now becoming below the level of the road.

Mel, married father, seventies, retired, white Jewish, homeowner, Gants Hill

The View from the Picture Window: The Impact of Traffic

Parking is not just a problem for the drivers. It is also very much a bone of contention for local residents, especially in inner-city areas where people find their streets invaded by alien commuter cars:

… er, I don't know not, not really specific to this area. I mean, some things like the leisure centre just being round the corner means that parking's sometimes a problem for us, because this road gets choc-a-block with people parking their cars here. They're already in a parking consultation exercise and may bring in permits here, I don't know if that will help or not.

David, male cohabitee, thirties, self-employed, white Jewish, homeowner, Battersea

An identical view comes from the partner of Angie, another Battersea estate resident:

Partner: Get rid of all the cars. One good idea. Do you know about 90 per cent of the cars that are parked up around here do not belong to people in this area... Yeah I mean if you come down here on any evening time you've never seen the amount of cars that there is parked up there now, right, and it's getting to be worse and worse around the estate.

Angie, single mother, twenties, unemployed, white, council tenant, Battersea

Mayhem could result if one borough introduces controls but the other does not, causing a flood of overspilled parking across the boundary line:

Umm, some of them, no, very few is residents, most of them are people that don't live around this area, because Lambeth has pushed all their transport to our side, because Lambeth has made theirs [resident] zones only... So now everybody comes into the estate, 2 years ago the Council didn't wanna know our estate because we had no problem, no traffic problem, no nothing, now they're talking about putting permits cos it's gone crazy. See, this is what our roads used to be like.

Shirley, single mother, sixties, unemployed, white, council tenant, Battersea

So parking controls and restrictions, when eventually they did come, are seen as a positive step, as here in Bermondsey:

But they've put that in, so that's good, right? That's a positive. Then they've put all these parking restrictions in, to go with that station, so said people, yuppies and that, won't be parking their Porsches everywhere in our flats, right? But that's a lame excuse, because they're penalising all us, like I have to park my firm's van over in Spa Road, and yet I live here, because I ain't got a parking permit, I won't pay for one. It's ridiculous. So, like, what they give with one hand, I feel they take with the other. I mean, at the end of the day, you can't please all the people all the time. Well, they've succeeded in never pleasing us!

Del and Kenny, single and divorced (father) brothers, thirties, unemployed/
employed, white, council tenant, Bermondsey

But even this does not always bring relief because, it is alleged, the controls are not enforced:

They have made it parking zones now.

Partner: Yeah but it doesn't mean anything because the parking people don't come down here, they don't walk onto the estate yeah, and if they do they just fly by, maybe they'll park at schools and they'll frighten a few of the drivers that are parked up outside the school collecting their kids. But other than that everywhere along here is parked up with cars that don't belong in the area and as soon as half past five, 6 O'clock comes all they come across from the Tubes and the buses and they jump in their cars and drive off.

Angie, single mother, twenties, unemployed, white, council tenant, Battersea

A similar reaction comes from this resident in Upton Park:

And this road, too, parking is a problem… No parking at all. Sometimes they block my road and I can't even … walk on my driveway here… But they know – the people that are not enforcing it, they just say check – I think I spoke to one environmental officer last year, I said: 'This spot check – why did they introduce spot check?'.

Essien, married father, fifties, self-employed, African, homeowner, Upton Park

Traffic noise bothers people a lot, particularly in places where it has recently got worse. This seems especially to be the case in Greenhithe because of all the new development, including construction traffic. Here residents complain of multiple nuisances – speed and danger as well as noise, for one:

Well, from my own personal point of view, the same thing is happening here as happened at New Eltham. And I really notice it. Because I literally am housebound at the moment, the traffic at the moment isn't quite so bad, but in the mornings, people are using … they're obviously using this road as a cut through … as a rat run. And that is what will make me move on… I've got a car myself so I can't really criticise it, but the constant noise just drives you mad. It's so unnecessary. The speed that the cars go down this road… I think they're cutting through to get to the new road … this road is straight, people come in at one end and just put their foot down. It's unbelievable the speed that they go. And there's been a couple of near misses with parked cars where people have had to slow down. There's something coming the other way and they almost haven't made it.

Emily, married mother, fifties, white, employed, homeowner, Greenhithe

She: There is little parking facilities at all along the road. And of course with people with their cars there, there's been a lot of damage to cars, you know. There's not parking restrictions, there's no yellow lines or anything like that, but it restricts the road and you get a lot of heavy lorries and things like that come past.

Dorothy and Bill, married father/mother, fifties, employed, white, homeowners, Greenhithe

And congestion induced by shopping traffic, for another – especially in Greenhithe, because of the adjacent Bluewater centre:

Bluewater for a start, you know. We're trapped in this little corner really. There's always road blocks from Bluewater. And then at the main road down the bottom, they're building a roundabout. I mean the road blocks have been going on for a year … we've been trapped here.

Deidree, married mother, fifties, employed, white, council tenant, Greenhithe

It's only the traffic. We're just concerned about the traffic, cos at the moment, certain times for Bluewater, we can't get off the roundabout, the first roundabout. Because they're all coming from the Tunnel and they block the roundabout. So even if you want to go right round the roundabout and down Crossways Boulevard, you just don't stand a chance. I mean you can sit there for about 10 minutes.

Emma, married mother, forties, employed, white, homeowner, Greenhithe

But for some, evidently, the ever-present noise is the hardest of all to bear:

She: The noise of the traffic can be horrific and we've got double glazing, but you can still hear it. And if you open the windows, you can hear the traffic, you know, quite a lot… I don't think road traffic noise you would ever really get used to you know. Although you know it's there, it's in the … it's always in the background, you know. The televisions are always up loud because, you know, they would be a lot lower if you didn't have, you know, so much traffic. We thought of moving into the back, because it's quieter, but this is really the lounge. They built them round the wrong way, but there wasn't the traffic in those days…

Dorothy and Bill, married father/mother, fifties, employed, white,
homeowners, Greenhithe

The same is reported from Eltham, a much more stable area, where background noise from the A2 is always audible but where local noise is the more pervasive problem for one respondent:

Well it's noisier than I thought it would be because it's on the main road, other than that, yeah, it's fine. You can also hear the A2 which is alright, but if you live anywhere in Eltham you can hear the mush from the road, so you can easily forget that. You can deal with the mush… I can filter out road mush if it's in the background, so you can forget that… I mean you get aircraft noise. Doesn't bother me. You get the A2 noise. It doesn't [bother] me. No, because you expect that. That's what you expect by living in a big town, in London somewhere don't you? So that's not, you know, unusual. That's part of the course. That's fine.

Jeff, divorced father (living with partner), forties, employed, white,
homeowner, Eltham

We ask Jeff one of our basic questions:

… in terms of like improving your situation, however you want to define it, what would make it better?

Close the road off. This is a serious comment…Yeah, that is it. Do something about the road noise. Of course you could turn round and tell me to move, but anyway…

Jeff, divorced father (living with partner), forties, employed, white,
homeowner, Eltham

He realises that he always has the option to move farther out into the country, where it would be quieter. But that would mean a trade-off he is clearly reluctant to make:

It's a major thing yeah, it is. It's not just the noise, it's the pollution, but mostly the noise. I should be living in the country shouldn't I? Anyway, I'm not prepared to live in the country because I'm not prepared to commute that distance. So I'm not prepared to move further out and spend half my money or time on a train.

Jeff, divorced father (living with partner), forties, employed, white, homeowner, Eltham

A very similar sentiment is expressed by Linda in Heston, on the other side of London:

I suppose the only negative thing I, is the amount of traffic … growing up in the country, or always living in the country is that … there's loads of cars, but you're not so aware of, like here, it just seems like, with the planes and the cars, you're just surrounded by pollution.

Linda, female cohabitee, mother, late twenties/early thirties, employed, white, private tenant, Heston

And another Heston resident claims that growing traffic noise and pollution are already causing many people to leave for quieter places beyond the M25, where they hope to recapture the world they have lost:

Yeah, well, everybody, all my friends now, and the last one moved out this area in April, have got out of Heston … coming home from work tonight, I can do it in 15 minutes normally, it took me about, nearly three quarters of an hour, cos I was late, and once you hit all that traffic and all that, and queuing, you want to get out of that, if you know what I mean, and it's all round this area you know, it's definitely part of the Great Metropole …

Donald, married father, fifties, employed, white, homeowner, Heston

Others are equally concerned about pollution from traffic. Here is a representative quotation from a Bermondsey resident:

… you don't notice how dirty it is until you go away somewhere and so they are going to have to do something about the traffic, the number of cars the pollution and stuff. Cause here it is really in the centre of London. The pollution coming from the cars across the bridge and stuff it's really heavy.

Henrietta, single woman, twenties, employed, white, private tenant, Bermondsey

And another, from a resident in Battersea who sees it as a hazard throughout central and inner London:

I'm quite in favour of keeping unessential traffic out of the centre, I think purely from the health point of view, for all the people that live in this capital. We're just slowly poisoning ourselves, I think. I mean, I was asthmatic. Fortunately, I haven't ever felt the effects of living here, you know, as yet. But who knows, one day it could turn into a Los Angeles if we don't do something… I think it would be a totally different environment in the capital if there became traffic-free zones, like Trafalgar Square, and like Piccadilly, places like that. That would make a vast difference to people. And it would be hugely popular, I think.

Shirley, single mother, sixties, unemployed, white, council tenant, Battersea

Others, in residential neighbourhoods, are concerned about the danger from traffic, especially for children:

He: It's just a traffic kind of thing. But we have to live with that. You can do nothing about that. We have complained about the speed limits and they are now bringing things together, saying what they want to do is slow the traffic down. I mean it's a 30 mile an hour speed limit out here… And it's 30 mile an hour from the bottom of that hill right to Gravesend. But they travel along here at 60/70 mile an hour …

Dorothy and Bill, married father/mother, fifties, employed, white,
homeowners, Greenhithe

But – just as with parking controls – when traffic calming is introduced, it does not always seem to work, as Layla in Heston tells us:

Well, those humps were just put in this year, there weren't any, any humps there, we er, did a petition and we got the humps done, thinking it would slow down the drivers, but over this summer, I mean, this is the first summer it's been in, drivers go over them like maniacs, they just shoot, fly over them. I mean, God, your suspensions. But it's really bad this road, there is no safety. It's very dangerous to the kids. I don't allow my kids to play out anyway, but, whenever I'm outside washing the car, on that side, it's so dangerous, you should see the speed they're going through.

Layla, married mother, forties, part-time employed, Egyptian parents,
homeowner, Heston

Betty, a lifetime resident in the same neighbourhood, compares life here now to her own idyllic experience as a young mother:

Well, you can see, I mean even when I was, my children were small, used to have a skipping rope out the front, well, you can't do that now can you, because it's like a great divide, you know.

Betty, married mother, fifties, employed, white, homeowner, Heston

And traffic calming measures are useless because they do not get enforced, says this resident of one such zone in inner Reading:

Generally .. there are people that do behave, you know, really stupidly round here when they're driving. Generally, I don't think there's a problem, but it's so dangerous with the way, with all the cars parked, and there's a lot of young children. It would be so easy for them going too fast to... You know, it's a 20 mile an hour limit down there, but I've never seen anyone enforcing it. I agree, it should be a 20 mile limit, but if nobody enforces it, nobody takes any notice, it's not going to make any difference.

Paul, married man, thirties, employed, white, homeowner, Newtown, Reading

Traffic dangers might even cause some people to move for the safety of their children, as one Greenhithe resident tells us:

There was a chap living there with a young child. His wife had a young child. And that was why they moved out because of the traffic. Because they had a young child, they felt it was a potentially dangerous situation ... well, this is only my opinion.

Emily, married mother, fifties, white, employed, homeowner, Greenhithe

Some blame traffic for structural damage to their homes. We heard this in Greenhithe, which is full of construction traffic, but also in inner-city Battersea:

... it will take a lot of the traffic from this side, which is damaging and cracking our houses. So we've got a lot of cracks in the houses, we've had a lot of repairs done which we've never had done for 27 years, but in the last 18 months they've had to do so much work on the roads and the houses I think it's shocked them.

Shirley, single mother, sixties, unemployed, white, council tenant, Battersea

Transport: A Capital Obsession

Londoners are notoriously obsessed by transport; almost any conversation, in pub or dinner party or casual exchange, naturally turns to it. That, obviously, is because it is so complex, because Londoners rely so completely on it in the course of their work and their lives, and because too often it fails to work well – or work at all. And so it proved in our interviews.

But interestingly, as many people seemed to speak positively as spoke negatively about their transport experiences. They were proud to tell us that they had invested a lot of thought in their choice of home location, so as to give them good access to the things they needed, whether job or shopping or schools for their children. In some places they quoted new opportunities – new roads in Newham and Greenhithe, a new underground line in Bermondsey – as having transformed their quality of life for the good. But others, equally, spoke of nightmarish daily commuter journeys which they felt, with good reason, were getting worse.

It must be said that these responses may have been conditioned by the fact that when we interviewed, in mid-2000, the national railways were experiencing serious problems occasioned by the escalating management deficiencies of the Railtrack company. Yet the discontent equally seemed to affect users of all forms of public transport, especially buses, and also those who drove – many of whom told us quite vehemently that they either could not or would not use public transport. Theirs was the familiar litany of lengthening delays, road works, and parking problems both on the street and in dedicated parking places.

Interestingly, location did not seem to have much to do with their complaints: those beyond the London boundary seemed to have quite as many problems as those within the M25. And they were evidently more car-dependent than their London counterparts, who – especially in inner London – had at least the hypothetical option of switching to public transport, even if some resolutely refused to entertain it.

Perhaps such travails are the everyday stuff of life in a great global city anywhere, whether London or Paris, New York or Tokyo. Evidently, big cities are more congested than smaller ones – and, just because they are so big, average journeys are longer than in small or medium-sized towns. But they seemed to have a special quality for many of those we met. It was impossible to avoid the conclusion reached around so many bars or dinner tables: that, as a world city, London and Londoners were being let down by their transport system. The fact that so many people successfully schemed to avoid the worst consequences is, in a way, further testimony to that inadequacy. Here, as in the struggles of so many people to maintain a bare minimum of existence, is another sign that as a city London could do much better for many of its citizens.

Rush hour

© Bill Knight

School run

Chapter Twelve

Friends and Neighbours

In this chapter we look at some of the most basic social relationships: the ways in which people relate to other people within their local area. It proves difficult to generalise, because we found a great deal of variation. In some neighbourhoods residents spoke of knowing many dozens of people. In others they barely knew anyone beyond their front door. Many factors influence this huge range of experience – among them, rate of turnover, level of cultural homogeneity, layout and design. Yet on the whole, among neighbours almost everywhere, there is a very general and widespread system of reciprocity: people watch each other's houses and perform small errands for them if they fall ill. This then is a very general system of informal social capital. But it seems to be governed by informal rules, and it has some kind of informal limits.

Most people, almost everywhere, seem to have approachable neighbours. This is very evident in Greenhithe, a former village in the course of transformation into a new outer suburb:

… this is really a close community…Yeah. If you've got troubles, you can always knock on someone's door.

> *Deidree, married mother, fifties, employed, white, council tenant, Greenhithe*

I say perhaps the immediate neighbours, one each side. As I say things like you know when they go on holiday, perhaps going to switch a light on every now and again and putting rubbish out for them.

> *James, divorced man, twenties, employed, white, homeowner, Greenhithe*

But it is equally evident in Battersea, a gentrified inner-city working-class neighbourhood:

If I needed something, I wouldn't feel frightened to go and ask, there is a couple of neighbours that I would go and kind of say help or … or if I felt frightened or something.

Lisa, widow, thirties, employed, housing association tenant, Battersea

People, we found, perform a wide variety of conventional services: they turn lights on when neighbours are away, take in their post, open a neighbour's door for a repair or maintenance person, and – perhaps most crucially – notice if something is amiss, as evidenced by these quotations from different places in the wide London region:

… if post comes, or if you're getting anything delivered or stuff like that, and you're at work, then you know you can rely on a neighbour to … I mean, she doesn't work upstairs at all. Them kind of things, yeah, but no major things.

Simon, male cohabitee, thirties, employed, white, council tenant, Bermondsey

… just last week I'd taken a parcel for her, so maybe that's a sign of trust in itself. So I just signed it for her, and then just gave it to her.

Mark, single man, thirties, employed, white, private tenant, Bermondsey

… there's times when she's having delivering she call me to say 'Can you come to help me carry this thing upstairs?' She's alone there, no male person to help her. I do go give her a hand, anybody, yes, if you are in difficulty, call anybody to come and help you, they will.

Barnabas, married father, thirties, employed, African, council tenant, Bermondsey

I could probably trust Debbie, Wendy, Veronica, any of them, to hand over my keys, and say to them, 'Can you let so and so in?'

Serena, divorced mother, twenties, unemployed, white, council tenant, Bermondsey

Joan: And … people used to take notice of their neighbours. If they saw someone's milk wasn't taken in, they'd be concerned or, and I find that kind of community atmosphere is still going on here.

Val, fifties, unemployed, white, Battersea, and her daughter, Joan,
a homeless single mother

… if Ken goes away on holiday or something, I'll have a little look to make sure that papers are gone and all that. Those sort of things. But they're just neighbourly things aren't they.

Mick, married man, fifties, employed, white, homeowner, Eltham

I've got the key to a neighbour's house over the road just in case the alarm goes off. Or if there's any problems … we look for papers and things on the doorsteps. If people are away, I make sure that if I do see anything, it's not there. Or if there's anything sticking out the letterbox, we push it in. And obviously if the alarm goes off or whatever, we'll go and have a look…

Emma, married mother, forties, employed, white, homeowner, Greenhithe

Most respondents were inclined to put a limit to this: it was 'neighbourly', nothing more. However, in some cases it seemed to go rather further:

I wouldn't class that as being friends. If I knew that they were away, I wouldn't go by and see papers sticking out the door and all those sort of silly things. I would do that, but I would class that as neighbourly. I would class that as enough.

Mick, married man, fifties, employed, white, homeowner, Eltham

We always watch their house and everything when they're away. And I go and do their watering and what have you. They all have our keys

Joe, married man, sixties, employed, white, homeowner, Eltham

… when we went to Pakistan on holidays, we hand over the key of the door to them and she look after the house, every day she comes in…

Saqib, widower, sixties, retired, Pakistani, council tenant, Heston

Many neighbours would act as a kind of informal social service for ill or elderly people. We noticed this particularly in Greenhithe:

Like the old man when he was sickly and ill over there. You would all pop over there, you know. I would bake pies and I would go over and take him a pie. He would grow tomatoes and he would give me a punnet of tomatoes. And he would say, put it under your shirt, he would say, I don't want her in the corner…

Oona, divorced mother, fifties, employed, white, private tenant, Greenhithe

… had a heart attack a few weeks ago and I went round and said I cut your grass for you and I did that until he was back on his feet.

Harry, married man, sixties, retired, white, homeowner, Greenhithe

… he's just had a hip operation and I mean, you went up to the hospital to see him didn't you?… I took him to the hospital in the car. I mean if they want something, they want to go to … or something like that…

Dorothy and Bill, married father/mother, fifties, employed, white, homeowners, Greenhithe

But there were interesting formal limits to this process: the informal system of mutual aid was real, but it did not signify what people called real friendship:

I would know without any hesitation if I was in trouble then Stuart the young fellow from next door would help me out. I know this, but I wouldn't call him my friend in any sense.

Harry, married man, sixties, retired, white, homeowner, Greenhithe

For some, such casual contacts were vital, representing virtually the sum total of their world, as one Greenhithe resident told our interviewer:

Mark and Gaynor, who are a lovely couple, she would pop in and see me. But she's got two young children and I don't really feel, Oh my God ... I mean, you're my highlight of the day. You're my human company, you know, now, I'm going to meet Jo. And, you know, when you rang last night, I bet you thought, when I said yes 11 O'clock tomorrow, my God...

Emily, married mother, fifties, employed, white, homeowner, Greenhithe

This close mutual contact and mutual aid has geographical limits, as is only to be expected; it seems to extend at most about half a dozen houses each way from one's front door.

Community spirit, you know, neighbourly spirit. And you feel safer... No, I must admit there's direct neighbours, but along, say within six houses either way, we really don't know them.

Rob, married father, forties, employed, white, homeowner, Eltham

Local frictions do occur, but generally they do not affect neighbourly relations:

We have had a little bit of friction sometimes, only because they've, they've had a lot of festivals where, one where Sam, he's only a young baby, 10 months now, but he was very young and the music would go on all night til the early hours. So ... but you could have that anywhere. But no, we chat and I say, 'Hello'. And next door we're very friendly with and they come round and what have you.

Linda, female cohabitee, mother, twenties/thirties, employed, white, private tenant,
Heston

Neighbourhood watch, although it has existed for a long time, does not seem to be particularly effective. Instead, informal relationships take over:

I was in hospital for 3 months last year and people sort of made sure there wasn't stuff left on the doorstep and came in and opened the windows for a day so that it looked as if it was lived in, that sort of thing.

Margery, widowed stepmother, sixties, retired, white Australian, homeowner, Earley,
Reading

I mean, as I say, you know, we had like the lady down the road rung me last night and she's, you know she's had her hall decorated and she wanted some curtain rails putting back up so, I went down and did that for her. Her next door neighbour takes her shopping you know and, and I think people just sort of basically look out for each other. I mean like we're on holiday, if we make sure that we let Steve know we're gonna be on holiday he'll keep an eye open. He'll probably have a key in case, and same for us, you know, and he'll, he'll borrow the lawn mower it's sort of little things like that! You know it sounds small things, you know, but it's sort of and like he'll come round for a barbecue and stuff like that; it's just a nice place to live. It's just a nice atmosphere.

Tony, married father, forties, employed, white, homeowner, Earley, Reading

… needed anything, you know, you know that they'd help you out, and again two doors away you know she'd help you out at any time if you needed it.

Sheila, married mother, forties, white, homeowners, Gants Hill

Because any time our alarm goes off they make sure that they ring up all the numbers we've given. They're really good. And they don't give up.

Ajit, married mother, thirties, employed, Sikh, homeowner, Gants Hill

He: …silly things like Oh, we feed their cat, we used to feed their dog when it was all … we're cat people, we feed each other's cats, but er that's worked well, quite well, cos…

She: And that side when they're away, I have to water the garden.

He: Oh, we water each other's flowers in the garden.

She: Plants, there's that's not much to do.

Leslie and Miriam, married father/mother, sixties, retired, white Jewish,
homeowners, Gants Hill

There thus seems to be a kind of ideal relationship with neighbours; it is found across all areas, although perhaps it is less evident on council estates. It seems to be typified by knowing your immediate neighbours to say hello to and exchange a few words with, perhaps helping one another out in small but important ways, but with none of the obligations which might come from friendship or any closer kind of socialising. For many, the unspoken distance maintained between neighbours is important to a good quality of life:

We swap plants with the lady next door, and we have another couple next door whom we occasionally say hello, that it.

James, gay cohabitee, thirties, self-employed, white, housing association tenant,
Battersea

There are also age gaps that affect the depth of the relationship:

Very friendly with them. If that makes sense, but not as friends. I mean I wouldn't go out for a meal with them or things like that. But again that's purely because of circumstance I guess. People that side are retirement age and the people the other side have now got young children so, again it's circumstance I guess.

James, divorced man, twenties, employed, white, homeowner, Greenhithe

But some people claim to know an astonishingly large number of others on 'Hello' terms:

...how many people would you reckon you'd know to say hello to, sort of as many people as fifty?

Oh no I would say about 80 per cent. [estate of about 3500]

Ronnie, male cohabitee (father), fifties, employed, Afro-Caribbean, homeowner, Battersea

Because everybody knows everybody on the estate, you see.

Megan, single mother, late teens, unemployed, white, lives with the family of the father of her child (council tenant), Battersea

Well I'd know everyone in that block to say hello to, and everyone in this block to say hello to... No I can honestly say it's a nice, it's a nice area to live, I wouldn't live nowhere else, I wouldn't go back over the East End... I suppose it's the same with anywhere, you know, you know, people go, 'Oh they're all cliquey', but they're not, it's just who you are. And like I say, I suppose I'm different because I talk to people.

Liz, divorced mother, thirties, unemployed, white, council tenant, Bermondsey

This landing is, yeah! [*Laughs*] Yeah, this landing is very sociable!

Cheryl, married mother, thirties, employed, white, council tenant, Bermondsey

And while all of these people live on council estates, the same kind of camaraderie also seems to develop in newly-built residential areas – perhaps through the children:

Oh this street's brilliant. I mean this street is. I mean it's not, it's not quite as good as it used to be I mean about 3 or 4 years ago we knew all the neighbours like the neighbours next door were here when we moved in ... we've been here best part of 10 years. And it's great. It's one of those streets that if you need something you can always go and knock on somebody's door, you know, cos it's very close knit.

Tony, married father, forties, employed, white, homeowner, Earley, Reading

But Val, who had many years' experience of living on council estates, felt that they lacked the kind of community spirit which you found living in a conventional street:

Joan: It's a lovely street to be in and you've got the common up one end and the market [*talking together*] you couldn't get a better place to live.

Right, and do you know many of the people?

Val: I know them all.

Joan: All of them… I find that kind of community atmosphere is still going on here. It goes when you, especially on estates, you find although people know each other, there's a…

Val: A fear.

Joan: A fear of, of allowing people to get too close, because you never know, you never know what's going on really. People come and go …

> Val, fifties, unemployed, white, Battersea, and her daughter Joan,
> a single homeless mother

People Coming and Going

But in some transient areas, it seems that there is little sense of mutual recognition or mutual solidarity. A Battersea respondent compares its friendly spirit with Ladbroke Grove, where she used to live:

So it's different here from in Ladbroke Grove?

I think so anyway. I think so. Ladbroke Grove is just rush rush rush rush rush rush, d'you know what I'm saying? Everyone is in a hurry to get somewhere.

> Sandra, single mother, forties, employed, Afro-Caribbean, council tenant,
> Battersea

This, it seems, is especially typical of tower blocks on estates, which are unpopular so people are always coming and leaving:

And I'd lived in a tower block for like … well, I'm 28. I'd lived there all my life and I've never known so many people as I have since I lived here… In tower blocks, people come and go – quick turn over…

> Zoe, married woman, twenties, employed, white, homeowner, Eltham

But it could also be true of a mixed area where traditional public housing, much of it now sold under right-to-buy legislation, was combined with new housing rented by companies for short-stay executives:

… it's a somewhat floating community, lot of company flats. They get together to protest, as we did, about a problem, which is fair enough, but I would say there wasn't a socialising kind of factor, and you don't, I don't think they're in and out of each other's flats all that much.

> *Francesca, married mother, forties, self-employed, white, homeowner, Bermondsey*

Perhaps, too, relationships are quite selective and may not extend far from one's front door:

... we know the nice, nice neighbours anyway, we know each other.

Sandhya, married mother, forties, part-time employed, Indian, homeowner, Heston

So, this chap come in. I thought, he looks familiar. And I said ... can't think of his name now. I said 'Do you live in Eltham?' He said 'Yeah, Shawbrooke Road'. I said 'What house'. He said '32'. Four doors from me, I didn't know him.

Joe, married man, sixties, employed, white, homeowner, Eltham

And, it seems, there are some transient areas where there is virtually no sense of community at all. This was perhaps most evident from our interviews in Newham. Here is a typical response from an established couple:

So do you feel as though there's any sense of community around here or not?

She: I don't think so.

He: I don't think so.

She: I don't know, I don't know how you find out other people, I think everybody just do their own thing and try to be, you know, good neighbours, or good people, not neighbours good, you know, people, and that's it really, try to be good citizen, but neighbourliness, I don't think so er certainly I haven't had much to do with my, you know, neighbours ... the next door neighbour, the, the property is rented so and the tenants change very frequently.

Nadira and Coffie, married parents, forties, both employed, African, homeowners,
Upton Park

And we heard the same story in Hounslow:

... they're renting out that house and the guy who actually owns it, he never comes in, well, hardly ever, and so they're renting it out so it's like every month we have like new people, and so, you get, you get to know them and they're all right, they're pretty friendly at times.

Rajiv, male, teenager, at school, Asian, tenure not stated, Heston

This Reading interviewee did know the people who lived in the house, but no one outside it. There is no communal area as such, but there is a shared staircase:

... when I moved in I thought you know you'd meet people a lot more than you actually do but unless you actually make an effort to get to know people. Cos everyone is sort of in and out all the time, you don't meet, you don't bump into people very often really. Probably less so than you would do if you actually lived next door.

So would you know the neighbours say either side in the street?

No not at all no. I don't know anybody outside the house, you know, at all.
    Vincent, single man, thirties, employed, white, homeowner, Newtown, Reading

This, we felt, is a situation typical of residential areas with a high rate of 'churn' or turnover, such as some new estates:

So, I mean, in terms of neighbours, would you know the people either side?

… sort of either side and probably just to say hello across the road because as I say you can, if someone lives 2 years with a two bedroomed houses, usually after 2 years they move on… Probably one they move to another area, probably moving to larger like a bigger house, or we seem to have a lot of the young couples who are not married and then suddenly they split up and that's it then, yeah that's probably why.
    Brenda, married mother, fifties, employed, white, homeowner, Earley

The same problem was related in inner east Reading, an area with a high proportion of university students and of young professionals who were out of the house all day:

Not really, only, there's only really one person in this block that I know a bit, no, typical in a modern block of flats where people don't really talk to each other and I happen to work with someone who lives further up the road, but that's just by chance, I don't really know her. I only know her by sight, but probably wouldn't even say hello, and I've been here 4 years, yeah.
    Kate, single woman, thirties, employed, white, private tenant, Newtown, Reading

… my next door neighbours are ex-work colleagues so that's like, so I know them and another friend who's like a neighbour a few doors down but no on this street I don't know anybody really.
    Dionne, female cohabitee, twenties, employed, British-born Afro-Caribbean,
    private tenant, Newtown, Reading

This is most evident in outermost areas beyond the London boundary, with young people working long hours, such as Reading and Greenhithe. Here, people were much more explicit about it – as in these responses from Greenhithe:

… it's a sort of a dormitory thing. Because I do come home a lot later… I'm trudging up the road … half past seven is average. If I'm in at say half six, that's a good day. An some days it can be later than that and as I said earlier, I haven't got the energy.

And you just tend ... and especially in the winter, you don't see a soul... I don't think it's a good thing. I think communities ... no, if Dennis was here, he'd get on his hobby horse. He blames our generation for the way things are now, you know, we work all the hours under the sun to keep our jobs and it's wrong. We should actually tell our employers to get stuffed because it's more important for more people to be employed for say slightly less hours and to have a life and...

Emily, married mother, fifties, employed, white, homeowner, Greenhithe

... even the neighbours, you don't really get to know the neighbours because they're out at work. Rarely around. When they are around, you know, they're doing, their doing their own thing. Obviously because that's the weekends. They only have the weekends.

Emma, married mother, forties, employed, white, homeowner, Greenhithe

But we found it also in older-established areas of outer London like Gants Hill – in fact wherever long work hours and long commuting journeys were typical. Witness Sally, a divorced Gants Hill mother:

It was coming home at night and, I suppose, because the phone... Thank God there are things called phones. Cause then I could speak to my mum, my brother and everybody else and it was... Cause I'm the youngest and my brother, both my brothers had left home. But they all lived in that area... I didn't know anybody here. Because I worked, I used to leave home at 8 O'clock and not get home till 7 O'clock. I didn't know anybody. I really didn't know anybody.

Sally, divorced mother, forties, employed, white Jewish, homeowner, Gants Hill

And the same kind of response comes from Battersea, an inner-city area, where it seems to be a matter of deliberate choice of lifestyle:

... my lifestyle isn't really a community one, I don't tend, this is very much a place, or used to be very much a place where I would just, you know, leave in the morning and come home to at night. Whereas if you can get hold of the chap downstairs you probably get a very different response from him. And he's been here a very long time, he knows a lot of people in the area, er, and he's sort of, a pillar of the community, effectively.

David, male cohabitee, thirties, self-employed, white Jewish, homeowner, Battersea

The Importance of Children

By contrast, where there are children, people are more likely to be at home all day. And children, always in and out of each others' houses, seem to provide a form of social bonding:

But they'll come to me for their bumps and scratches and…

… *you're the first aider…?*

Yeah, first aider on the street. But, you know, it ain't a bad street really, it could be a lot worse.

And do you know people outside the street a lot or not really?

Oh yeah, yeah. I mean, you know, when your kids start school and they get to know people, you get to know them.

And do you help people outside the street in the same way?

Oh yeah, yeah. I mean … if anything goes wrong with the computer, he comes up here. If he wants a babysitter, he rings up. If he wants to know about his fish, he rings up, you know, comes up.

So you all help..

Yeah, there is. Not like in London at all. It's not there… There's people moving in and out the area all the time. There's a constant ongoing thing. You don't get so close to people I don't think.

> *Deidree, married mother, fifties, employed, white, council tenant, Greenhithe*

… myself are the sort of people that, we make ourselves known to people… I know quite a few of my neighbours. But my eldest knows more that I do actually. You know, he comes home with all the news, 'Mum, four houses up the road someone's just had a baby', he's told me, told me all about them and I have never met them…

> *Layla, married mother, forties, part-time employed, Egyptian parents,*
> *homeowner, Heston*

School gate networks, waiting to collect the children, prove especially important:

… by the time 3 O'clock comes the mothers are actually sitting up, lined up outside … they're all talking about what's going on for the rest of the day. Oh the people done this and Oh got this party going on and Oh yeah we'll organise that.

> *Angie, single mother, twenties, unemployed, white, council tenant, Battersea*

Sally in Gants Hill describes how children transform your entire social network:

It wasn't until I actually stopped work and I was pregnant that I actually started meeting people. I had my own friends that we used to see in the evening, but I didn't know my neighbours, or anybody. I still don't know anybody who lives down here.

> *Sally, divorced mother, forties, employed, white Jewish, homeowner, Gants Hill*

Local social networks also seem to be more important to those who have young children. Through the school they build up contacts which become an important part of life. For mothers who represent the interests of their children, it is the local schools and leisure facilities which might be particularly important:

How did I know? Well, it's when you go … you don't really start talking to people until your kids go to playgroups. And it's once you get into the playgroup routine and they make friends and you start talking to other mums and that and then you start talking about schools, when it comes to school age. And it's just people say, Oh that's a good school, you know, yeah, they've got a good reputation. The children do well there. It's a nice school. The teachers are nice. And it's sort of word of mouth. Because obviously not being from the area, I wouldn't have known anyway. So not being a Greenhithe lass or a Dartford lass…

Emma, married mother, forties, employed, white, homeowner, Greenhithe

Yeah, and people are really friendly… They are really, really friendly round here. I mean I know a lot more people. I suppose it's 'cos I'm going over to school as well. I find people a lot friendlier round here…

Sharon, married mother, thirties, part-time employed, white, homeowner,
Greenhithe

But, as children grew older and changed school, the amount of contact can wax and wane:

A lot of it's to do with children, so since they've moved school we've not … it's difficult.

Jeff, divorced father (living with partner), forties, employed, white,
homeowner, Eltham

And lack of children can mean absence of community:

First of all there are very few kids because it's not a terribly good area for kids this. Its a long way to go to a park or something, and erm … very difficult for cars, which people rely on with kids so much. What else? Maybe the way the flats are structured, with their entry phones and their caretakers, like little fortresses and maybe people moved here, many of the people, for isolation. Because they are flats and they are a little cut off from the rest of London, this is a little backwater, this north Bermondsey, with Jamaica Road making this like a little island almost. I don't know, people erm … suspicious of each other [*laughs*] for some reason.

Francesca, married mother, forties, self-employed, white, homeowner, Bermondsey

But even the presence of children does not automatically generate inclusive networks; private education and social cleavages may inhibit them:

No, they'd have nannies. I mean, a few of them have already got nannies for the babies, and they're the sort of people who, you know, take them off in their jeep up to the Northcote Lodge so they wouldn't be interested in sharing the school run, they would either, they probably have a nanny to do it, or if they didn't want to work they'd do it themselves, and they'd look down on you ... state school. [*Laughs*]

> *Carol, divorced mother, fifties, unemployed, white, private tenant, Battersea*

Fear of New Arrivals: the Sense of Uncertainty

In some areas the newcomers may be of similar cultural background to the current residents. Yet people who have lived in an area for a long time still feel uncomfortable when there are many newcomers whom they simply don't know. This is equally true for an inner-city area like Battersea and a new suburb attached to an old village, like Greenhithe:

I don't know as many people now because, well, people are, are, are changing, people move. In these, these streets now they seem to change a lot and there are young couples who are going out to work so you don't actually see them, even in the 8 years I have, there has been a lot of changes... Not at all, no, but I would still know people to say hello and, you know ... the property is rented so and the tenants change very frequently.

> *Mary, widow, fifties, unemployed, white, homeowner, Battersea*

Well if I went down into the pier, the heart of the village, the old pub, there has got to be somebody in there that knows me.

> *Oona, divorced mother, fifties, employed, white, private tenant, Greenhithe*

In such an area it seemed that comfortable local social relationships could be rudely upset by new arrivals of different age groups, cultures or income, who are seen as not conforming to local social mores. This is a widespread fear in many different kinds of community, especially in older-settled, stable residential areas:

She: ... you've still got one or two older people living in here, but the Council have let them out ... there's one or two of them where they've had single mums with either a baby or two children and it's like a stop gap until they move them on and things like that...

He: Their gardens don't get tidied up.

She: Yeah, they don't take an awful lot of pride in what they've got, you know.

*Dorothy and Bill, married father/mother, fifties, employed, white, homeowners,
Greenhithe*

… It's not conducive to put old people and young families together because it just
causes a lot of hassle … you put a group of young children with very elderly people
you are gonna get problems.

Anonymous respondent in Bermondsey Focus Group

But Hounslow, an old-established Indian community now affected by
new migration streams from overseas, seems to tell a different story. Here,
people have close reciprocal relations with family but not with neighbours.
This is very unusual, as also is the high degree of resident turnover found
there. Thus some respondents described their neighbourhood as stable and
very good to live in, while others described the reverse:

… we know 'em all, even the ones in front of us as well.

And is it a fairly stable type neighbourhood in terms of people going in and out?

Yeah, I mean, you do have a chat every now and then, it's not like there's any trouble
between us, it's friendly neighbours, you can chat to them, ask them if you need any
help with anything, they ask you.

Milad, single man, twenties, employed, Lebanese, homeowner, Heston

… ever since I've been here we've had the same neighbours apart from two, the ones
next door and those in the corner over there, other than that we've known the rest
for about 15 years now.

So you seem to have a fairly positive view, I mean, just sort of general description.

Yeah, there's nothing to … nothing negative at all really about the area.

*Milad, single man, twenties, employed, Lebanese, homeowners (living at home),
Heston*

… this side of the road white, that side of the road Asian, but I don't do any more
than that with anyone, so I don't think it's cos they're Asian, just think it's cos people
don't any more.

Betty, married mother, fifties, employed, white, homeowner, Heston

I know how to deal with people … new tenants came in front of my house … and
er … they became the friend. I said hello and I talked to them and if you talk to each
other then they come closer and easy to understand these kind of people.

Saqib, widower, sixties, retired, Pakistani, council tenant, Heston

Problems seem to occur where there is a dominant group with a fairly
clear sense of its own identity, affected by new arrivals who are perceived not
to fit in. As a result, an older generation may move out of the area as a new

one comes in. This is particularly evident in communities which were seen as homogenous and neighbourly a generation or more ago, but are so no longer. Theresa told us about the Bermondsey in which she grew up:

…the borough is not the Borough of Bermondsey how it was when I was growing up in it. And neighbours, I don't think people today are like they used to be. Like when I was a kid growing up I can remember my nan used to live in the block across the road to us and she always had a key on a string on her letter box up until the day she died so that if we ever went to her house you just put your hand through the letter box and you pulled the string out and you let yourself into her house and many times they key was just left in the door and no one bothered.

Theresa, married mother, forties, part-time employed, white,
housing association tenant, Bermondsey

She told us that people don't know each other now to the same extent that they used to then. And she attributed this to people coming in from outside:

I think a lot of it is to do with being from different boroughs you know. I think … people are just different you can tell they are different… Bermondsey used to be a really tight community and everybody knew everybody and I don't think it's like that … most people's dads was either dockers or the brewery across the road.

Theresa, married mother, forties, part-time employed, white,
housing association tenant, Bermondsey

Others, too, emphasised how Bermondsey had changed:

… we was all brought up together so we all knew one other but today you don't know no one. As I say our children when they grew up and got married they all had to buy outside … now when you see strangers coming in I mean they are finding the properties for them. I mean I don't know.

Rosemary, married mother, sixties, retired, white, council tenant, Bermondsey

Almost invariably, in these recollections the question of race would appear:

Here it's just one race you don't really find a lot of black people on this estate so it's a lot harder for them to accept other people coming into their space which they have been here for a long time, well that's what I find.

Anonymous respondent in Bermondsey Focus Group meeting

… people are nice, the people that are Bermondsey people, they're nice … it's like their parents and grandparents. I mean, it's people that's sort of born and brought up in Bermondsey, I've always known, cos everyone knows everyone, because it's quite… I think it's got worse, yeah. I mean, a lot of people moved out now, and unfortunately, you get … I mean, I know you've gotta live somewhere, but you've got these, all these immigrants, and they don't care.

Pete (son): … they should be done with by now shouldn't they mum?

Shouldn't be allowed in the country, love. We should be looking out for [our] own country.

> *Cheryl, married mother, thirties, employed, white, council tenant, Bermondsey*

This resentment could take various forms. In Battersea and Newham it is directed against new arrivals who are said to be engaging in systematic Benefit fraud on a huge scale. Ironically this is seen as quite different from fiddling the Social, as practiced by the white English host community:

It's little for the normal everyday person that's lived here and grew up here, but the foreigners are doing it on a very big high scale… We had one lived on this estate and … we never involved the police cos we didn't know how big it was, but when he went into hospital, seriously ill, we found so many Social Security books we were shocked. Different addresses, all in the one name… And this was an African bloke. The Indians and the Africans are doing it on such a big scale… I think how dare they take the mickey out of our country.

Yeah. Yeah. But are there also people like English people who are also doing that?

Oh yes. Oh yeah. But not as bad, but they are doing it. But I wouldn't say that they got ten, twenty, thirty Social Security books, they would have one or two.

> *Shirley, single mother, sixties, unemployed, white, council tenant, Battersea*

Like I said, I live on £73 and I find it very hard, and then that Rhodesian woman was getting £770 a month, in the paper, plus she was begging at £20 an hour, her husband was working on building sites and they had a mansion given to them rent free. Now why, you got pensioners living on £55 a week… That was in the *Daily Mirror* 3 days ago, or 2 days ago. It was on the telly as well, and now she's done a bunk… We've got, let's see, Chinese, India, we've got two Chinese, Indian … Portuguese, we've got Moroccans, we've got quite a few Africans moved in here, but we're lucky, the ones in the houses are lovely.

> *Shirley, single mother, sixties, unemployed, white, council tenant, Battersea*

But it goes further than this, to a kind of defensive mentality in which all strangers are viewed with intense suspicion:

… you get a lot of older residents and they have been there for a long long time and they take it as though it's like their block and they don't really want other people into it…

> *Anonymous respondent in Bermondsey Focus Group meeting*

Yet some of the most harmonious communities are the culturally heterogeneous ones, where there are no dominant ethnic groups. Battersea is a prime example, and some of the interview remarks from Chapter 2 bear repeating:

It's mixed, yeah. It's mixed. You've got a lot … you've got certain people who's unemployed, you've got people who's working, you've got people from Guyana and there's Jamaicans and there's … there's a Spanish family from Spain, and you've got … some Italians, so it's a different mixture of people. Different ethnic minorities. It's kind of cool though.

Daniel, single father, twenties, employed, British-born Afro-Caribbean, council tenant, Battersea

Everybody's very friendly around here, I must say… If anything happens to anyone everyone's interested to know why, who, and … you know, and what happened.

Sandra, single mother, forties, employed, Afro-Caribbean, council tenant, Battersea

Is that just in this block or do you mean in the area in general?

The area in general, cos you're walking up the road and somebody'll just say, 'Hello, good morning, good afternoon'. People don't usually do that, you know, people just walk straight past you if you drop down in the road, nobody bothers they jump over you to go over to what they're doing, but here people are different.

Sandra, single mother, forties, employed, Afro-Caribbean, council tenant, Battersea

In Reading, likewise, we heard similar stories:

Yeah well I mean, if we're talking that sort of thing different sort of races and stuff, I mean the guy next door is I think he's West Indian, the family about three doors up from us West Indians, you know the nicest family you ever wanna meet and, you know, it's just all mixes really and we all get on… Yeah, yeah I mean Steve next door is about the same age as me, lives on his own and then you've got the sort of older person lives a bit further down. I mean it's all sort of all, ages and, you know, if anyone's sort of got problems really I mean like last night I went down to an old lady down the road who wanted some work doing on her house, just went round and did that. Got loads of friends in the street, it's a really friendly street.

Tony, married father, forties, employed, white, homeowner, Earley, Reading

Yet it is difficult to identify exactly what accounts for a good community life in a place like Battersea. In Heston and Gants Hill, similarly quite ethnically mixed areas, relations appeared to be relatively cold:

I know there are some streets where, you know, everyone knows everyone, but no, we don't really know people that well. And we've lived here, as I say, for 8 years…

Sewa, single woman, twenties, employed, Sikh, homeowners (living at home), Heston

… it's not a friendly environment here at all you know, I don't think … it's not a friendly area as such I would say. Not like it was years ago when I lived in North London or even Walthamstow.

Jenny, married mother, forties, white, homeowner, Gants Hill

I don't know really much, we say 'hi/hello', that's it, but I don't know much about them, because I think I don't give them much time, or they don't give me time…

Selina, married mother, forties, employed, Asian, homeowner, Gants Hill

So in some racially mixed areas there often seemed to be very good relations between neighbours, with few tensions, while in others the different communities tended to have distinctly cooler relationships. The key could be the age of the inhabitants and the length of time they have spent in the neighbourhood. A place like Battersea seems to attract certain kinds of people, more outgoing and sociable – and indeed younger and less fixed in their lifestyles – while places like Heston and Gants Hill have older-established communities that feel more threatened by any new incursion into the neighbourhood:

… it's quite diverse, you've got one side our neighbours we've got Irish, English, we've got South African, Pakistanis, it's just diverse, there's no set race in this area.

Milad, single man, twenties, employed, Lebanese, homeowners (living at home),
Heston

And this little part of Newham is quite mixed is it?

It's mixed yeah between white and black and Asian, yeah… I think it's cos a lot of people rent as well so it doesn't, people just come in from all over the place… I know about like three houses on that side and three houses on that side so that's as far as we go when we invite people to parties… No well we only had two and the last time we had what, one of these blokes next door here he actually called the environmental health cos he got pissed off with it.

Padma, single woman, twenties, employed, Asian, private tenant, Upton Park

…both two houses that side are young couples and next-door's a young chap with a lodger, and next to him there's a young Ukrainian woman, and yeah, and all are really friendly, really friendly, and yeah, I mean, it's quite nice to live in this area.

Rochelle, female cohabitee, twenties, employed, white Australian, homeowner,
Newtown, Reading

Neighbours from Hell?

'Neighbours from hell' can really blight the quality of a person's life. But we found few cases, surprisingly few in fact, reported to us. They could take various forms and were found in different types of neighbourhood.

One involved an older woman whose peace had been invaded by the arrival of new residents with new and incompatible lifestyles. This seemed more likely to happen on council housing estates, as in this case, where letting policies had changed to bring in younger people to an area previously reserved for old people:

Nine O'clock you said that party was going to be over. I must have looked a right state I 'ad no teeth in my 'ead I had my nightgown on running up and down the stairs telling them to be quiet... Anyway they went through a stage slamming and banging the doors. Coming in and everything they dropped you could hear ... thinks she can do just as she pleases and she mustn't be told. I said it to her in a nice way. And if I say anything I'm racist. And when that kiddie runs across it's as if she's got hob nailed boots on... They must be out at the moment. I wish she was in so you could hear it. But I'm not allowed to say anything and it's wrong... Nothing about when he was nearly murdering her upstairs and she was screaming and shouting and hollering. But that's what you got to live with.

Rosemary, married mother, sixties, retired, white, council tenant, Bermondsey

So really this area, if I had money I wouldn't purchase a house here ... it's really, it needs a lot of improvement because the people put themselves in a category of low if you like, because it's not tidy, it's not clean, and the children just wild ... some areas when you're, even when you're driving along, you could see plants, flowers, you know, and houses are different, and the streets are clean – you don't see it here, you just see rubbish, just people don't care, they just chuck junk in front of the ... you know, it makes the place low, it really...

Dafina, single mother, forties, part-time employed/student, African, housing association tenant, Upton Park

Some of the most difficult cases concerned neighbours with mental problems:

I think that the only thing that we had a lot of problem, probably about 3 years ago and 4 years ago, it's still at the moment, was this so-called care in the community. So because St George's is a one bedroom flat, a lot of them you know in St George's, you know and sometimes, you know you've got needles down there. You've got needles on the landing if the lift is not working and you go down the stairs. You know, so that can be quite stressful, you know so, you know... So the main problem is, which you get on all the estates through London, Birmingham, Manchester is the drugs. It is a major problem.

Ronnie, male cohabitee (father), fifties, employed, Afro-Caribbean, homeowner, Battersea

She: ... except for this one who lives on the other side of Usha, who's a, he's a schizophrenic, he's a lunatic.

He: The police have been round there loads of time, he used to bang on their wall and play loud music in the middle of the night … he's already, to our knowledge has chased three previous tenants out well not, owners out of that house.

She: He lives with his mother, and when you're in the garden sometimes you hear him shouting and screaming at his mother.

He: F'ing and blinding away, yes.

She: … at his own mother, but apparently the police, unless the mother herself em…

He: … wants to, take some sort of action.

She: … wants him taken him away, there's nothing they can do, and they've lived there a long time, you know.

He: Which is a pity, cos they're such nice neigh…

She: But other than that, then the neighbourhood's…

He: Yeah – it's a nice neighbourhood.

She: It is nice, we…

He: He's the only fly in the ointment, there's always one. Sorry, I mustn't talk across… Oh no, he's weird.

She: Oh he, he is schizophrenic, there's no, you know.

He: Yeah, yeah. It's unfortunate, one might almost feel sorry for him, but er except he makes everybody else's life a misery.

> *Leslie and Miriam, married father/mother, sixties, retired, white Jewish,*
> *homeowners, Gants Hill*

Very different was this case, where a very large extended family had moved into a small suburban house:

Yeah, I think maybe it's because it's a very large extended family when I came here it wasn't so extended and now it's so extended and it's very noisy … people live the way they want to live, fine, but there must be consideration for the change of culture, you know … the houses are very close to each other, it's a very small home, smaller than mine and so many people in it and … I can't get the peace, doesn't matter which room you go, there is a spare one upstairs, but the noise comes out and it's just impossible to work.

> *Sharmaine, married mother, fifties, employed, Afro-Caribbean, homeowner,*
> *Gants Hill*

In this case, the next-door house probably houses eight or nine people, living in a three-bedroomed house. She is trying to move. But here is another case from suburban Greenhithe, incited by the neighbour's children, with the same response:

Her children are absolutely awful to my grandchildren. And I have dared to say something to one of the girls, or her girl, and she didn't say anything to me. The girl screamed and shouted at me and she actually now doesn't talk to me, the woman … and I can't live in an atmosphere, you know. I just can't stand it. And Bernie wants to move any rate, so I've really given in.

> Jill, married woman, fifties, self-employed, white, homeowner, Greenhithe

The Importance of Design

Geography and layout, it seemed, could have a significant effect on perceived sociability and neighbourliness. In general people preferred traditional streets to the high-rise blocks of postwar housing estates. But even comparing estates, design meant a great deal: small blocks were seen as more friendly than large ones, and long decks were seen as particularly negative for neighbourly feeling. Generally people preferred a small estate to a huge anonymous development, as one fortunate Bermondsey resident reported:

I think it's because it's so small, and all the blocks face each other, and they've got, like, a communal area, obviously, in the middle … if they want to cut down on crime, and things like that, if they really wanted that to work, then they should bring back small estates like this, where everyone can see what's going on the estate, everyone knows everyone else, and they all protect each other. So … apparently, the council won't do things like that.

> Serena, divorced mother, twenties, unemployed, white, council tenant, Bermondsey

The same response came from a satisfied resident in Battersea:

Joan: Definitely. I keep coming back here because the atmosphere's nice, the community spirit's nice. They have thought … I mean there are estates, but they, they've been well thought out and well planned, they're smaller usually, generally not so high, they're not so high-rise, they're two or three floors high and they … on those sort of estates they do try and get a decent mix of people, it's not all one class of people or all one economic structure of people, they're, they're very mixed, you get a nice mixture. On such a large estate like Doddington because it's so big it becomes very impersonal so you'll find that you've got one block and there's a community spirit within that block, but they might not even know the people that live in the next block, whereas if you've got a smaller estate the community spirit is spread out a bit more and it's easier and the layout of the estate as well, it's very important.

It makes huge differences?

Joan: Oh yes I mean if you've got a nice small estate, well you've got trees and I do find with a lot of the smaller estates, they make the walkways or the pavements and the streets look like streets which has a profound impact on people. When they walk out of their, their flat and they're in what seems to be a road or a street, there's a different atmosphere to walking out into like a, a precinct that has a very cold, non-community-type atmosphere. No matter how much you try and get involved in, in creating a community, the actual buildings and the layout of the estate can, can make all the difference, all the difference. If you've got dark alleyways, places where people can be dragged and raped into, although they don't seem to care nowadays, they do it in the middle of the street in broad daylight but it doesn't make you feel like you want to be on that estate because it's, you feel wary.

Val, fifties, unemployed, white, Battersea and her daughter Joan,
a single homeless mother

But even so, some inner London residents spoke of the lack of space, especially for children's play, and the effect that density had on quality of life:

So it's a good place to bring up, the only thing I think, there are no parks, no, you know, space for people, children to go and play, and er ... and to ... if you talk in terms of where we live, you know, some people make hell of a noise, that affects the children. So that will make them to be all the time fearful, when they hear the bang, you know.

Barnabas, married father, thirties, employed, African, council tenant, Bermondsey

What would you rather have? Kids on street corners, or kids kicking a football? I know what I'd rather have. I mean, kids play down here, it drives you nuts sometimes, but they've got to play. They've gotta play somewhere. People get old and forget that they were kids, you know what I mean? I remember running round the streets, knock down ginger, driving the old people mad! But you've gotta give them somewhere to play. There's nowhere here to play. And I would say nine out of ten boys play football, or some sort of sport where you'll need a caged in area – rounders, cricket.

Cheryl, married mother, thirties, employed, white, council tenant, Bermondsey

And this could be compounded by catastrophic design failures, like deck access:

Yeah. Well you used to have got lots of bridges like that, linking all the blocks. It was just like, there's a place in Stockwell, I think it's built by the same contractor, there's an estate in Stockwell, called Stockwell Park Estate and that was notorious. Cos, and the whole area was linked, it was like, you know you had to go outside to get to another building, you didn't have to go downstairs. There used to be bridges linking everybody together like, which was dangerous for the boys then, you know. So if they break into one flat, they can easily get away, you know and this was the main problem, you know.

Ronnie, male cohabitee (father), fifities, employed, Afro-Caribbean, homeowner,
Battersea

Like the tower block you are less likely to get a community feeling... I've lived in a tower block before, because the chances of bumping into the same person in the lift of a different floor is very remote. You can have lived there for years and there might be one person twice in 2 years. And there is no common meeting ground.

Anonymous respondent in Bermondsey Focus Group meeting

... on the courtyard there is more everyone knows each other cause you see each other you see people come in and you say hello. But in the long stretched out blocks you have less of that because again you are less likely to see people. It's about seeing people isn't it when you are leaving the estate or coming back on to the block.

Anonymous respondent in Bermondsey Focus Group meeting

It's better. We've ... still got a little element but it's nothing like that. About ... yeah, the small estates are friendlier anyway, cos you get to know the people... In there people won't even talk to someone that lives opposite, you know, cos they just don't know what they're up to.

Barry, married man, forties, employed, white, council tenant, Battersea

This, one respondent emphasised, was not an invariable rule: it depended on people:

You can have a tower block in it ... with a hundred people in it and they are as good as gold and you can have one in ... and they are murder.

Anonymous respondent in Bermondsey Focus Group meeting

Social Networks and Social Capital

Looking at the ties which bring people together in their neighbourhoods, the final question is to what extent they constitute social networks and to what extent, in turn, these produce local systems of social capital. Some found that local social networks were most important for their quality of life, while others depended on a wider network of friends with whom they could stay in contact:

I've got quite a few. I've got quite a few. Cos I go down to the Seven Islands twice a week Tuesday and Thursday swimming and erm and course we all meet up there and its more like a little community. In fact when I was at school I was taught to swim 'n that.

Rosemary, married mother, sixties, retired, white, council tenant, Bermondsey

For, the dinner lady job I, I was talking to a friend and she works inside … there's always jobs there so I goes, 'OK'. And she goes to me, I goes to her, 'I'll get me application form'.

Tiffany, divorced mother, thirties, part-time employed, Jamaican-born
Afro-Caribbean, council tenant, Battersea

It was one of the teachers. I was reading a poem in the class and one of the teachers said to me 'You can do that for us if you want'. And I said 'Oh all right then'. She said 'You can be a primary helper unless you've got any experience and then you can be something else'. I said 'Well I've only worked in a nursery before, so I haven't really worked in a school'. So she said 'Oh you can just help the children with reading and things'.

Angie, single mother, twenties, unemployed, white, council tenant, Battersea

If people had grown up in an area, as many council tenants had, and if they had a strong sense of attachment to it, local friends and family and neighbours seemed more important to quality of life. These networks were not just a point of social contact but served a much wider range of functions as well:

… yeah so Druid Street charities and we got a week's holiday with them. But I only find out about that from going swimming and chatting to the different people. Other than that I wouldn't have known it existed. And when my mum was alive I could maybe have got a holiday through but I didn't know it existed.

Rosemary, married mother, sixties, retired, white, council tenant, Bermondsey

For people who spend a lot of time in the area or have some form of long-term attachment to it, a sense of community is important. Older people seemed to complain more about loss of community: because the population has changed, they don't know as many people as they knew when they were younger. So stage in life cycle affects people's experience of community.

Another Bermondsey resident described the loss of an old place-bounded community:

Well it's like a little village really, that's all I can … you know, everybody comes from Bermondsey, born here, their mums and dads come from here, their grandfathers come from here, so they're all like close-knit and you could leave your door open, well I mean you can't do that now because of the way society's changed anyway. So it's really closed in the community, where everyone was more friendly and they're not quite so friendly as they used to be.

Gary and Carol, married parents, forties, employed, white, housing association
tenants, Bermondsey

For such older residents there was a real loss:

I don't think they'll ever have what we had – a sense of belonging. Cause we did belong. You know. As I said we never 'ad much but we was happy enough in our little way.

> *Rosemary, married mother, sixties, retired, white, council tenant, Bermondsey*

But, where people – especially long-time residents – talk about a strong community, newcomers can end up feeling excluded or even the object of hostility:

And if you're not from Bermondsey, if you're from Orpington or Welling, or whatever…?

I don't know. It just because everyone's so … they just know each other. It's not hard to get to know people, it's just … it's awkward for people who don't come from … do you know what I mean? It's not like they push them out on purpose. I think they feel more pushed out because everyone does know everyone else, more than actually being pushed out. Do you understand that?

> *Serena, divorced mother, twenties, unemployed, white, council tenant, Bermondsey*

In other words, one person's community is another person's clique:

It's cliquey. It's what I would describe as clique, right? At the end of the day, you've got your little cliques, and these people, like, they all think the same. It's like the mutual admiration society, like, they're all great, funny enough, by … just purely by coincidence, and they all keep telling each other so … round here, well, I wouldn't know where to begin, because there is very few people that, like, I'm likely to, like, leave my money on the table in front of … you don't put your wealth on offer, and you don't let on too much. You know, you play, what is the saying? You play your cards close to your chest.

> *Del and Kenny, single and divorced (father) brothers, thirties, unemployed/*
> *employed, white, council tenants, Bermondsey*

No not really cos at one time it was like a closed shop down there. If you walked in there and you felt that you was the stranger … it was like cliquey but I think it's altered now. See we don't drink and it's more like the social down there.

> *Rosemary, married mother, sixties, retired, white, council tenant, Bermondsey*

The Sense of Neighbourhood

So, in much – even most – of London, neighbourliness was alive and well. In fact, the lack of it was so rare as to be noteworthy. People had a very acute and fine-tuned sense of their mutual social obligations, and these went beyond mere reciprocity – taking in each others' parcels – to a wider sense of social obligation to neighbours who had fallen on temporary misfortune and needed help. And it might extend to a system of informal social control over deviant behaviour – a point to which we return in our next chapter.

But this system had its limitations. It did not go beyond certain limits: being good neighbours did not mean becoming good friends. And, in a few areas, it seemed to break down. These were the transit zones where people came and went all the time, hardly getting to know each other at all. Particularly, this was true of areas of young workers who were away from home for long hours, returning home late after dark. Neighbourhoods with children were never like this, because the children, always in and out of each others' houses or being met at the school gates, provided a natural social bond.

People tended to fit into their neighbourhoods and feel comfortably in them, rather like wearing comfortable old clothes. They could become disturbed by new arrivals, even if they seemed to be like themselves, very much more so if that were not the case. The unhappiest were those facing a sudden incursion of people they saw as very different from themselves in age or race or – the significant point – lifestyle. This tended to happen in social housing where tenants had no influence on letting policies. But the strangest and hardest-to-explain finding was that in some areas, like Battersea, people of entirely different backgrounds seemed to live amicably together, while in others, like Heston or Gants Hill, they did not. The most likely explanation seems to be the perceived threat posed to the old community by the newcomers. If they did not evidently disturb existing ways of life, they would easily be accepted. But if they did, whether because they were suspected of crime or simply because they were noisy neighbours, they would be greeted with suspicion and resentment, and the older-established residents might actively contemplate moving. Design could make a difference here: everywhere, 'estates' were seen as performing badly in comparison with conventional 'streets'.

Finally, in the best integrated neighbourhoods, it was really possible to see the existence of that much debated asset, social capital. And it was perhaps no coincidence that this was most evident in less affluent working-class areas, even in the much-derided 'estates': here, long-established traditions of mutual solidarity and mutual aid survived, albeit in diluted form. This could have its negative face, where newcomers told us they found a neighbourhood to be cliquey, dominated by long-established – almost tribal – social norms, and excluding those who failed to follow them. But, for those within the club, there can be no doubt that it represented something of huge value in their lives.

Itinerant market

© Bill Knight

Newham incident

© Bill Knight

Chapter Thirteen

Fearing Crime, Avoiding Crime

Crime, clearly, is an important element in deciding where to live – or, more potently, where not to live. But overall, crime in London does not turn out to be the issue that most Londoners might imagine. People do not seem over-worried about it, and that is directly related to the fact that – as just seen in Chapter 12 – they know plenty of people in their local area and feel that there is a good sense of community there.

But this is not true everywhere: we found a sharp polarity. In a few areas – Upton Park, Eltham, Bermondsey, Heston – there is a feeling that crime is widespread and getting worse:

… crime is too much crime.
Nahar, married father, sixties, employed, Bangladeshi, private tenant, Upton Park

The crime and the fear and the scariness of London is getting worse... I'll tell you why I don't feel safe, I like London, but I don't like going to night clubs there are so many drugs and drug dealers and even people you think are really normal are taking drugs and it really really gets to me. I don't like it at all, I don't like it at all... I don't feel brilliantly safe in London. I don't feel safe sitting in a bus with my headphones on unless there are loads of people sitting on a bus.
Henrietta, single woman, twenties, employed, white, private tenant, Bermondsey

This could be associated with a feeling that strong social ties, once powerful in linking people together into a community, have been loosened:

People looked after their own in Bermondsey and stuck together which was nice because everyone knew one another and I never ever felt it was rough or a frightening place to be when I was growing up here. But that's starting to change now. You know sometimes I frightened for … you know my dad's 78 now and you know he doesn't care, he'll go out and I often think you know… I do worry about my mum and dad.

Theresa, married mother, forties, part-time employed, white, housing association tenant, Bermondsey

Among these respondents and in these areas, there is a widespread fear that crime is rising out of control. Some were positively unhappy with their neighbourhood, and felt a real sense of fear – like these residents in Greenhithe, where their fears may have been triggered by the murder of a local girl:

… people didn't worry about this a few years ago but now they do. This is not withstanding the fact that I don't think crime has risen here at all but there's always that nervousness particularly since Claire.

Harry, married man, sixties, retired, white, homeowner, Greenhithe

Yeah it worries me, I've got a big bolt on the back gate, I've got locks on all the windows, I never go out and leave them open if I'm going out because even though they are small windows I still think that someone that can get through the window. That's why I leave the trees like they are at the back… I mean when we lived in Swanscombe I didn't even have a key to my back door and any one could walk in, you didn't it not then but now you have to. I never used to worry when my husband was here because he was a big man and I knew he could handle his self, but my back door isn't very secure, it's old and my son in law is getting me a better one, a more solid one…

Ann, widowed mother, seventies, retired, white, homeowner, Greenhithe

We found one respondent in Eltham, a retired white homeowner, who was in a state of almost paranoid fear caused by gangs of young people congregating outside his house. He returned to the problem again and again:

… the effect is that you have to be on your guard all the time … before we move to that front door, I mean we've got a wide view here across everything. If you can't see [them], they've got these peaked caps on all the time, you know. If you see them wandering about you won't go out. In other words you don't want anyone to know that you're going out … er we don't go on long holidays … it's got to the stage now where … well I'm thinking we have a paper delivered, I'm thinking I'll cancel that paper … once you cancel the paper people know you are away… And it's that sort of thing you got to be on your guard all the time… I mean on my bottom fence now I've got carpet gripper. I don't know if I'm breaking the law or not … but I made sure. If any one grabs the fence they've had it now.

Joe, married man, sixties, employed, white, homeowner, Eltham

But in places as wide apart as Greenwich, Heston, Upton Park and

Peckham, there was a more general sense of menace and fear, which residents described quite graphically:

About what's happening, we have to lock our doors every time we go out. It is a bit freaky though really.

What, is crime quite high round here?

I think, I think it is because there's a lot of cars get burnt out on the side roads there. I used to park my car there, now I have to park it over there.

Because cars are getting burnt out on the side roads?

Yeah. I think crime is quite high in this area of Forest Gate.

Kamal, married father, fifties, unemployed, Indian, private tenant, Upton Park

Others reported a sense of unease, but felt that there was nothing much they could do about it, because they were too closely tied to their area to contemplate leaving. Here is Joe from Eltham again:

We would like to move away ... groups of youths ... it's the smaller side of things, burglaries, petty crime, touching your car you know em ... but we've always have, you know, break even ... but two bedroomed places are few and far between I mean no way would I live in a maisonette ... for the time being we are going to grin and bear it ... the wife wouldn't want to move away from the grandchildren ... and I don't think there is anywhere in the country where you could do it ... go away on holiday or go out for the day and feel at ease, you know your place wouldn't be broken into.

Joe, married man, sixties, employed, white, homeowner, Eltham

Del and Kenny, young men who might be expected to show strong links into Bermondsey's matriarchal society, were very cynical about 'community' relationships and were aware that their faces didn't fit. This went along with a hand to mouth existence and a lack of access to the material goods which they noticed that others all around them had. Not exactly afraid, they were very conscious of all the 'thuggery' and thought that there were very high levels of crime. Others, even in suburban Greenhithe, feel that crime seems really close to their front doors – in the case of this resident, for a special reason:

... if I do see anything, I do call the police. And I suppose in 8 years, I've called them about four or five times. In once, when a girl got stabbed, she came in because I brought her in. I mean she was stabbed fifteen ... thirteen times. And we brought her in and, you know, sorted her out until the police got here.

That must've been...

Yeah, it was frightening because I mean we'd been … sort of a couple of years previous, a young girl got murdered on the corner. There's a plaque to her on the corner now. That was up past the station. But they think it was the same person that did it, but he's never confessed to the murder… So, I mean we've had major crimes. Such as, I mean not every road in a village has got a murder you know, that sort of … and then Christmas time I had to call the police out again because the chappie that was looking after the … well pulling down the factories, he and his girlfriend were having a real big row outside and he nearly run the chap down. It was 2 O'clock in the morning … that house on the corner, not the people that are there now. It's been robbed since they've been there. They've only been there 18 months. But that's been done about three times.

Jill, married woman, fifties, self-employed, white, homeowner, Greenhithe

A Gants Hill mother felt safe within the immediate neighbourhood but not when she ventured any further from home – and would not even allow her children out:

I think it's not fair. Yes, if older one come late, I get worried, and little children they can't play outside, I think, and they don't mix with neighbours, because I don't let them … allow go out.

So they don't know the children up the road or anything…?

No, they don't know at all.

Because they're not playing out?

But before my children … other one was young, she used to do bike riding and other children used to come out and they used to have little chat, and now this little one I'm stopping completely.

Selina, married mother, forties, employed, Asian, homeowner, Gants Hill

People who did worry about crime sometimes seemed to be unhappy in the area for quite other reasons, as with this Battersea mother who felt out of place in her gentrifying neighbourhood:

The over-riding fear of crime, it's, it's always there and if I walk along the street, it's an ever present thing … I think it's horrible… I don't think it's imaginary. What I would actually like is … one of those metal doors which go in front of your street door and then you can open the door without them breaking in. That's what I would really like.

Carol, divorced mother, fifties, unemployed, white, private tenant, Battersea

Some people seem to have had so much experience of crime that they have almost got used to it as part of their everyday lives:

Burglary well we've been done three times since we got married and before I left home we'd been done another three times but being that we were in a shop I think they used to watch our places and we were burgled a week after we were married.

Pam, married mother, forties, employed, white, homeowner, Gants Hill

Many others have built defensive measures into their lives. Consider these two typical responses from Greenhithe:

Is crime and safety an issue for you around here?

This area has got a very good record, a very good record, er, I'd say all the new houses that have been built around here, and most of them are newish so they've all got good security measures built in to them you know when they are built, er, every house has got burglar alarms and what have you, so crime isn't a problem, I'm not saying it doesn't exist but it isn't a problem that I notice, there again everyone takes preventative measures, so…

Richard, married man, thirties, employed, white, homeowner, Greenhithe

But, yeah, so I mean you're aware that you've got to lock your gates up at the back and you've got to lock your windows and you've got to have an alarm, you know. Other than… As I say, I'm not physically frightened.

Jill, married woman, fifties, self-employed, white, homeowner, Greenhithe

The problem might be that when everyone does this, it creates a fortress mentality and erodes all sense of neighbourhood, as Donald in Heston suggested:

… and so yeah, people shut themselves, without any doubt, people shut themselves in and lock themselves up a lot more now, there isn't the air of being 'I'm safe' around any more, it's a sort of thoughts 'I'm gonna be safe' so they lock themselves in, this sort of problem, and it's happening more and more. I never thought it would happen to me but it does, it does happen to you, the only other area, the only other thing I see people doing more and more and more, is buying dogs and things like that, more and more people I see, even, you know, even my Asian friends and all that, a lot of them are buying animals, or dogs, obviously, and it's to, obviously to help to make them be aware of things that are happening around their houses and things like that, there's definitely a great change in the environment, without any doubt.

Donald, married father, fifties, employed, white, homeowner, Heston

It reduces people's sense of freedom, their sense of what they could and could not do. Especially this was true for parents of small children:

It's about … I suppose for her to walk, it would take her about half-an-hour, em, but there's been a … a couple of incidents that … to get from one side of the road to another you have to go under a subway and that's the only way of doing it, and there's been a man who has been attacking some of the children, so … em … I prefer to drive her to school.

Sheila, married mother, forties, white, homeowners, Gants Hill

The same is true of public anti-crime measures like closed circuit TV, which cumulatively leave some residents feeling less comfortable about their neighbourhood:

It was, when we lived there it was OK and I knew everybody but now you hear all kinds of stories about the estate and everything. So I don't, it's a lot rougher now, a lot rougher so, and they're got all cameras up, you know, CCTV cameras everywhere and they didn't used to be there but they're everywhere now, so.

Does that make you feel more … how does that make you feel like having those cameras?

If I was there I would be a bit scared, you know, cos they move.

Do they?

Yeah. I walked past one of the cameras up high and I was watching it and things, and that's kinda scary if it's watching you but it's for your own safety yeah, but I don't know it's a spooky feeling. If somebody else is watching you walking down somewhere, although you're not up to anything it feels like they're watching you.

Susie, single mother, thirties, unemployed, white, council tenant, Battersea

People also question the effectiveness of such measures, wondering about the extent to which they simply shift the crime elsewhere:

We've now got cameras as well, which have proved to be … well, in street crime, one of the biggest deterrents. It basically means the crime goes somewhere else, outside of the cameras.

Scott, single man, forties, unemployed, white, council tenant, Battersea

Crime and Urban Churn

Rising crime in neighbourhoods is often attributed to urban churn, particularly noticeable in some parts of London, bringing in new arrivals to old-settled stable areas and destabilising them: asylum-seekers in Heston, decanted council tenants from Peckham in Bermondsey, beggars in Battersea.

… everyone round here gets burgled … they get away with it really, they get away with it, they burgle and burgle and you know, the proof you have to get, you know, to take them to court, next minute they're out again, and it's going on and on.

Donald, married father, fifties, employed, white, homeowner, Heston

… you know I think it's scary there, I, when I see bullet proof glass and everyone's got a video camera on them and things like that, I don't wanna be anywhere like that, I don't want to know about all that, scares me a lot, so, and I, you know, I'm a … strong person, but I sit … I see a lot, I observe and because I observe a lot I realise they're not doing it for nothing, you know.

Betty, married mother, fifties, employed, white, homeowner, Heston

… there's an awful lot of people knock on your doors, I'd say once a week there's somebody knocking on your door… Asking for charity or something… Nothing to do with, nothing to do with charity, oh, you know it's a scam, you know, say, 'Oh, I'm collecting for this', such and such a thing, a school or…

Amy, married mother, thirties, employed, white, homeowner, Battersea

Similarly, the arrival of new residents on housing estates, arising from a change in local letting policies, could trigger a local crime wave:

When … an older person moved out or something like that, they was putting young people in there and they was breaking into people's flat, into, you know so I think they stopped it or slow it down… Because a lot of these people, they're not from Wandsworth. They came from Scotland, Liverpool, Manchester, end up in London, end up in prison and then the social services and the welfare find accommodation in the area under the special need policy, you know, but off the wall you know, the local lads that was getting blamed. Cos I had a quiet word with them, you know, so they just leave, they went about their business you know.

Ronnie, male cohabitee (father), fifties, employed, Afro-Caribbean,
homeowner, Battersea

This victim of crime, an Indian mother from Heston, reflected sadly on her family's own value systems and the effect of crime on their children; it gave all the wrong messages, she thought:

… my house is broken two times, in Hounslow … But, but it's not good impression for the children. We understand it's not good future if you're stealing the things but children, they think it's easy…

Sandhya, married mother, forties, part-time employed, Indian, homeowner, Heston

She runs a launderette, and reported many instances of people stealing from her. She thought they were asylum seekers, but could not identify their origin, except that they wore long dresses and covered their heads. It had happened more than once, she said, and appeared to be different people each time:

You know it's happened three or four times the same refugee people come to me and they ask me, 'Give me that bottle of foam', or soap or a box of soap or a bottle of liquid or something, then they gave me £50 note, it's happened three or four times, when I give the change … she hide the £20 note … It's happened three times before, the same thing, £50 note and hide £20.

Sandhya, married mother, forties, part-time employed, Indian, homeowner, Heston

There were many ways in which crime affects people's quality of life. Most of all, it eroded their trust in their neighbours and their neighbourhood. Tracy in Eltham, living on a 'rough' estate, describes how she came here after she was harassed by one stalker in the place she used to live:

I never used to really do the curtains. Just the blind. Pull it up in the morning. And he had his face against the window. And when I'm taking the kids to school and that … in the end he kept sort of like, trying to get cigarettes off me. As I was crossing the road, he'd cross in front of me. And … I don't know, he was just … really, I think he thought I was scared of him and he was just trying to pester me really, you know? And then I said to my mate, I want to move. She said she knew somebody. I didn't really want to move here. Personally. But it was off of there.

Tracy, separated mother, forties, unemployed, white, council tenant, Eltham

But it was out of the frying pan into the fire, because here she never felt safe from the constant fear of being robbed.

Comparing Places

Often, people compare their area favourably to another they know, perhaps somewhere they once lived, or think they know. Very often, this other area is an inner-city one. South London respondents, in particular, seem to have a negative image of certain neighbourhoods:

I mean, I don't… It's not like Lewisham rough… I'm not frightened to go out.

Sharon, married mother, thirties, part-time employed, white, homeowner,
Greenhithe

… to be absolutely honest with you, we've had a stabbing, we've had a murder since we've been down here, but I mean, that's obviously frightening. But, you know, I mean, it's quiet compared to a lot of other places where you live … we had the car bashed in 3 weeks ago. Someone come on the drive and done it… Yeah. There was a big fight outside … that could happen anywhere, you know, it's you know… But for a village, it's sometimes … you think, God I'm living in a village and it shouldn't be happening, but it has and, you know, you just live with it really don't you? So…

Jill, married woman, fifties, self-employed, white, homeowner, Greenhithe

These suburban respondents directly compared their exposure to crime with the inner-city places where they had previously lived:

But it's safe. I don't see any ... I don't feel it here at all, er, places like Kennington, I used to live near the Oval, at Kennington I used to feel it.

Why was that...?

I think there was a lot of drugs and a lot of er, it was a very rough area there was a lot of drugs and, and my car had got broken into quite a few times, right outside my house, virtually every other week my car was brake, was broken into. But er, I don't feel that here. I feel it's all safe and everything. It's so safe I...

Layla, married mother, forties, part-time employed, Egyptian parents, homeowner, Heston

I'd still be wary but I don't think I'd feel quite as instantly tensed up as I would in East Ham or in Dagenham.

Ajit, married mother, thirties, employed, Sikh, homeowner, Gants Hill

But it was not always a matter of inner and outer London, central versus suburban. In Battersea, Lisa felt safe living on a street in comparison with a nearby estate:

I feel safe, I feel quite safe here ...I have lived in an estate and everything so being on a street I do feel a lot safer...

Lisa, widow, thirties, employed, white, housing association tenant, Battersea

But equally, some particular local area – almost never the respondent's own home patch – is invariably seen as 'bad'. Here is Joe in Eltham:

There's an estate... I don't know, it might be on your list, the Ferrier... They come wandering over, but... But, do you know, I was talking to the chaps at work. And they say no matter where you live, I mean you talk about Bexleyheath... It's pretty general, you know, and erm at the moment I don't feel that the law is doing enough about it.

Joe, married man, sixties, employed, white, homeowner, Eltham

And here is a Heston resident, likewise talking about a local estate with a reputation:

I mean it's known to be rough, I mean by the police and that, there's always trouble going on around there ... like kids bashing in cars and like bashing in windows and like stuff like that. Cos there's always police cars going, driving down there like, with their sirens blaring and stuff.

Rajiv, male teenager, at school, Asian, tenure not stated, Heston

And so too in Reading:

…there's two or three places. I wouldn't really like to live in … too much or Whitley. I used to go to school in Whitley. Or sort of, you know, sort of [Dee?] Road area of Tilehurst. Sort of, West Reading generally. I have lived in West Reading, but sort of off the Oxford Road area. I'm not that keen on it.

> *Paul, married man, thirties, employed, white, homeowner, Newtown, Reading*

I wouldn't want to live in Whitley Wood.

> *Brenda, married mother, fifties, employed, white, homeowner, Earley, Reading*

Almost any kind of place could get this reputation, even in a newly-developing area like Greenhithe:

If you just go through the alley and across the road over there called The Crescent … you would not think you were in the same area… It was like being back in London. And it was like a real shock for me. You know when they're got all like half motorbikes taken to pieces on the front lawn and, do you know what I mean?

> *Sharon, married mother, thirties, part-time employed, white, homeowner*
> *Greenhithe*

Local shopping centres and bus stations are perceived as unsafe, especially at night, but in Stratford even during the day, because they attract unemployed and unattached people:

I used to walk through there to shop at Hounslow West, I wouldn't walk through there now, I wouldn't walk through there at all.

> *Betty, married mother, fifties, employed, white, homeowner, Heston*

First female: I wouldn't say it's safe … there's a lot of mad people around in Stratford but you know around here you do feel a bit safe.

Second female: I don't think I'd like to live the other end of Stratford I think it's a bit unsafe.

First female: Which way?

Second female: You know a bit nearer to the shopping centre it's, I think all the weird people seem to congregate around the shopping centre it's a bit rowdy round there.

First female: But then I think they come from far and wide though, don't they just come from wherever I mean … we've got Westbourne House across the road, do you know what that is? It's basically, you know for prisoners that haven't got anywhere to go after they've offended like no-one wants anything to do with them, they go into like this rehab house over there and it's like across the road from here, do you know what I mean it's like, so you know all the nutters live in there anyway … that's really no different from most areas anyway.

Padma, single woman, twenties, employed, Asian, private tenant, Upton Park

Padma felt that the only answer was to shut the Stratford shopping centre at night, even though it was the only direct route from the train and bus station to the high street:

I think they should close the shopping centre in the night time actually would be a … make a big difference. Yes normally when you go into a shopping centre it's really lovely and bright and clean and, because that one's open all the time and it's basically a short cut through it's just really filthy because some people sleep there.

Padma, single woman, twenties, employed, Asian, private tenant, Upton Park

But perceptions about crime are to a large extent subjective, reflecting the extent to which one knows any particular area. Sometimes, residents who may have had a standard of comparison actually thought that things are improving:

… the publicity on the Aylesbury estate is not as bad as people think it is… Jobless, too much crack people round here… They think there are too many drug related crimes around here, and there isn't any way … that's about it.

OK, so has this area got better or worse over time?

It's gotten better, it's all right… It was a bit bad… There was a bit of crime there before… Burglary, robbing, theft, car theft.

Eze, single man, twenties, student, African, lives with family (council tenants), Peckham

… on the Aylesbury, I found you had a lot of people that would, like, steal cars, and mug you, and … things like that, you know, a lot of fights would go on. But it's quite hard. And living here, you've got more or less the same thing going on here as well. So I think, I don't really think it matters where you live, because bringing up children, I think, is going to be hard anyway.

Janice, single mother, thirties, unemployed, British-born, half-white, half-Afro-Caribbean, council tenant, Bermondsey

One very laconic Peckham resident thought that things used to be bad but had improved:

OK, what's the crime rate like around here?

Low.

So, there is not a lot of criminal activity around here? So how about the old estate?

Back in the olden days there used to be.

In this area or the old estate?

The old estate.

Like what?

Burglaries.

What else?

Robbery, muggings.

Was it frequent?

Yeah.

> *Kosey, single man, twenties, student, African, lives with family (council tenants),*
> *Peckham*

Children Running Wild

Almost everywhere, children are seen as a problem, sometimes because of harmless horseplay, but often because it degenerates into something worse – and people widely think their behaviour is deteriorating compared with some fondly-remembered past period. Joe in Eltham sees the whole area going downhill because of the activities of a gang of local youths:

… well, we think it's going down … you know, you are getting groups of youths … whatever you'd like to call them. And they're sort of roaming about and creating a nuisance more than anything, but erm, yeah, you never used to get this. You know, er, well not to my knowledge, did we? We never used did we … we found out afterwards, that a car had been stolen, some yobbos in it, doing wheelies, spinning on the grass, tearing round. The police turned up. They all ran and erm … they're doing that sort of things, that was a couple of weeks ago.

> *Joe, married man, sixties, employed, white, homeowner, Eltham*

He and his wife clearly felt no longer tranquil or safe in their own area. But they were doubtful that moving would be an answer, because they sensed that the problem was almost universal:

… if we could find somewhere where we could go away and go out in safety and we didn't have all this hooliganism of an evening or anytime really, you could walk out, take the dog for a walk in the evening at ease, they're no gangs wandering round, that is where I would like to live. But if there is such a place, it's probably on another planet.

> *Joe, married man, sixties, employed, white, homeowner, Eltham*

Older inhabitants in other areas reported the same sense of unease, which they had never felt in the past:

… there are gangs of youths apparently, been vandalising the buses, and apparently in the evenings the buses won't come down from Hainault – they've diverted down the road as there was so much vandalism on the buses … they've had to divert the buses in the evening.

That's not something that used to happen at all, is it?

Oh good heavens … well, I was telling you that you could leave the baby in the pram outside.

Mel, married father, seventies, retired, white Jewish, homeowner, Gants Hill

But this Greenhithe resident thinks that the children are a problem elsewhere, not here:

Oh no, I wouldn't like to live in Swanscombe and I wouldn't like to live in Dartford. There looks quite a lot of trouble in Dartford there's a lot of shop windows smashed and whatever and in Swanscombe I've heard it's not too good either, from people I know in Swanscombe … a lot of children they are quite destructive, they're not a lot of how can I put it, they seem to cause the disruption, some of the children but you can't blame them, it's their parents…

Ann, widowed mother, seventies, retired, white, homeowner, Greenhithe

The problem age group for these Bermondsey respondents is the 13 to 15 year olds in the area, who are the main agents of trouble. But they are few and far between:

… It's mainly setting fire to the public bins, wheelie bins at the end of the road seem to be a common game, and throwing balls across the road when you're driving down… It's stayed about the same. It hasn't changed really.

Timothy, single man, thirties, employed, white, private tenant, Bermondsey

… we did have trouble a little while ago with the kids on the motorbikes, but they wasn't from this area. Some of em were, I mean, I'm not being, you know, up and down on the night and all. And anyway they had meetings, and they've gone, the only trouble is I've heard they've gone to another estate … down Jamaica Road somewhere. So really it's only, we've got 'em off our estate, and some poor other estate's got it all, so … you know, I mean, I don't know what you do about that, it just seems you move 'em from one, they go to another and another.

Liz, divorced mother, thirties, unemployed, white, council tenant, Bermondsey

The same reaction came from Dave in Battersea:

… there are, there are some things I think, which I see in the area, which annoy me slightly … packs of kids running, running wild, and, you know, playing football in the middle of the street, when it's packed with cars and stuff like that, when they've got a perfectly good park over there. Dropping litter and with no regard for it and, you know, when I was a child there was no way I would ever, you know, throw litter around and you know, over your shoulder goes a Coke can and you just, there's no… Er, this street, a lot of people make an effort to, you know, for the street to look nice and to have a good feeling to it, and you get a gang of kids going through and in 10 minutes it looks like a bomb's gone off.

David, male cohabitee, thirties, self-employed, white Jewish, homeowner, Battersea

Often, this seems to be general hell-raising, perhaps resulting from boredom as much as anything. But there are also strong suggestions that older children are engaged in more systematic crime, in particularly drug-dealing. Joe in Eltham again:

Round the corner comes a car and then they're in the phone box. So you've got to assume… Drug related, you know. Erm, er you know, we see all this and er…

His wife: It frightens me. It's not very nice round here… I'd never go out on a night on my own in the dark, never. I'll take the dog for a walk if it's light.

Joe, married man, sixties, employed, white, homeowner, Eltham

He goes on to describe an actual incident involving a neighbour:

When he come back, there was a group, Oh we didn't even know it was happening, apparently they told us about it afterwards, about eight or nine standing in the road. He was trying to park his car, you know, and they just wouldn't move. That sort of thing. Just petty. He got a lot of abuse, bad language and he's little girls ran in crying because they were upset with it all. And his wife was there. She picked up the phone. She said 'right I'm getting the police'. 'Alright' he said. 'We'll come back and do your car'. And they did do his car… Because they're only 15 to 16, you can't go out and thump them. They'll have you up in court, so you can't win. You've got to stand there and listen to them. The language they call out. It's not very nice.

Joe, married man, sixties, employed, white, homeowner, Eltham

Likewise for Mark in Bermondsey:

… on Saturday night just past, there's always a lot of kids walking about there, I actually saw a group of about five or six kids there, and it was almost a military-like operation, they just walked along … one guy has a look-out here, another one at the corner there, and they went … maybe it was six of them, I think it was another four in the car park there, belonging to those flats, trying to steal a moped … they came in with their sirens and … when the police turned up, obviously they know this area, and they just split, and there's a hundred different places to run round here, so I don't know if they actually caught any of them.

Mark, single man, thirties, employed, white, private tenant, Bermondsey

And for Barry in Battersea:

I come through there, was it last week? And there must have been ten or twelve young lads, 17, 16 beating the hell out of each other in the street… It's like a running battle. It's the first time I've seen it on the street… But I know a few of the boys that float through and they're all up to no good.

What, you mean sort of dealing and…?

Yeah.

That sort of thing?

Yeah. Bit of bent gear and stuff, you know, that just…

Barry, married man, forties, employed, white, council tenant, Battersea

Generally, much of the crime is seen as drug-related:

Oh yeah, it's getting quite bad… I think a lot of it is now, is to do with drugs unfortunately… There are burglaries, yes there's a lot of burglaries and…

Gary and Dawn, married parents, forties, employed, white,
housing association tenants, Bermondsey

For these Bermondsey residents, the problem is that addicts steal to feed their habit:

I think that's probably happened with all inner cities. In the last few years there's so many now drugs that people are dependent on, you know … now things have changed. They've got … to get money for drugs. They'll break into a car, you know, and nick a £400 radio … to sell it for £20, you know, just to get something to shove up their nose.

Gary and Dawn, married parents, forties, employed, white,
housing association tenants, Bermondsey

But underlying the addiction, they feel, is a deeper story of unemployment and lack of alternative ways to occupy their time:

Yeah, 99 per cent of the trouble in this area is drugs. I mean there's not enough, there's not enough work, I mean that's all to do with technology I think. There's no clubs for them, there's no youth clubs for the kids to go to.

Gary and Dawn, married parents, forties, employed, white,
housing association tenants, Bermondsey

Drugs can affect a neighbourhood badly, and even if the police attack the problem, all they may succeed in doing is to move it:

There are security cameras… The cameras are good but it forces it into other areas.

Scott, single man, forties, unemployed, white, council tenant, Battersea

Policing – Official and Unofficial

Some residents mourn the departure of the old-style local policeman who was known to all, especially the children:

I think we should have a Bobby on the beat. I really do. Because when I was little, we had a Bobby on the beat and he was, I can't remember his name now, but he was always walking around and, you know, you were just too scared to do anything in case he caught you. But I suppose kids haven't got respect for policemen these days have they? I think I'd love it to have police round Greenhithe… Just to put them off or perhaps, you know … if there was more police around, I'd feel safer.

Sharon, married mother, thirties, part-time employed, white, homeowner,
Greenhithe

P.C. Cole. I even remember what he looks like as well, yeah. Harry Cole his name was. And he used to go to every single school. He knew every child down Walworth Road, and he knows who your mum and dad was. And I think that they're the sort of policemen that they should bring back. Because if you saw him coming down the street and you were doing something wrong, you knew you were going to get in trouble. And your mum and dad used to threaten you with him, and … he would come round to your house as well, if you'd been naughty.

Serena, divorced mother, twenties, unemployed, council tenant, Bermondsey

The one we had in Walworth Road, he knew all the kids. He used to even go into, like, the school, my kids were all there, and always talk to the children and everything. He was really nice.

Janice, single mother, thirties, unemployed, British-born half-white, half-
Afro-Caribbean, council tenant, Bermondsey

But in some areas, people feel that there is an effective neighbourhood watch – whether or not it officially exists:

… there are people that are about. There's a few pensioners here and a policeman and fire officers. People do work odd shifts. So there are people around here in this particular road. Whereas a lot of new type estates perhaps out this way you'd get almost commuter land where people just completely disappear during the day. But it's not like that here.

James, divorced man, twenties, employed, white, homeowner, Greenhithe

It's died down and the good thing about this estate is that everyone knows each other so there's a sense of unity and that's important. Everybody knows each other… We do have neighbourhood watch, yeah. But I think that the people on the estate prefer to do things by themselves. Because the police has, on a number of occasions they have let us down.

Daniel, single father, twenties, employed, British-born Afro-Caribbean, council tenant, Battersea

In a few places, there is a strictly informal and old-fashioned system of crime control, independent of the police and more reminiscent of a peasant village of old than of a twenty-first-century metropolis. We found this especially in these two stories from Battersea residents:

… we had another one that moved here and we had him out in 5 minutes because we knew him. And when we done the flat up we were doing it up because we got told a homeless person was moving in and they'd been living on the street for a while and we thought, fair enough, we'll help them, and when he moved in I went 'I'm not having you here'. And he said, 'You don't know me'. I said 'Yes, I do'… So I took my daughter who's is big now and she was quite little at the time… 'You're Michael so and so, you're my headmaster and my mum took me out of your school'… I said 'her mother's never realised what you done but I did'. So … 'Where am I gonna go and live?' I said, 'I don't care'. I said, 'But you can move here but I'll be watching every bit of your move', I says, 'so you better ask 'em to find you somewhere else to live very quick and you can take all the furniture and carpets with you', I said, 'but we don't want you on our estate'.

Shirley, single mother, sixties, unemployed, white, council tenant, Battersea

In this case, the response is slightly more formal but, it seems, equally effective:

We've never had a lot of crime on this estate cos we always knew the families that were crime, but … they've all grown up and then their children started it and we started neighbourhood watch, and through neighbourhood watch we watched the crime go down to 1 or 2 per cent… We have got two families but the police are looking into them. We've warned them, we've put them letters in their doors, we've put it in the newsletters and if they ignore them, 6 months, bang, right, now you've got the police involved… But now you do it quietly, you've got a police phone number where nobody has to know you've phoned up.

Shirley, single mother, sixties, unemployed, white, council tenant, Battersea

Shirley also blamed criminals who came from across the borough boundary from Lambeth:

We've got a Lambeth estate that brings a lot of crime into this area and we, we've gradually shown them we're pushing it back to them, we don't want it over here and we're letting them know 'You get caught, we nick you'. And we just tell 'em straight, 'If we catch you again we give your name to the police, we know who you are, we know where you live'. We don't know where half of them live but you bluff them and it's stopping them selling drugs on our estate ... it's always been known around here, Lambeth is the worst place for selling drugs. It's the ease, you can go to any park, we all know where to go to get drugs if we want them. It's easy as that, but we won't have them on our estate.

Shirley, single mother, sixties, unemployed, white, council tenant, Battersea

Areas are seen as having bad individuals or families or groups; people invariably knew who they are:

Not a few hundred yards from here, there's a chap. He's always in trouble. He's always being picked up by the police. He's always being arrested and he's still walking about. So it all comes down to the law of the land. In other words, all these people, all these law breakers, they're not frightened of being caught today. That's what it comes down to. And that's the law of the land. That's got nothing to do with the police.

Interviewee's wife: I think the police are so disheartened, I think.

They're saying now that if this trouble maker, and they're getting complaints about him, at the local council office, they will evict them. What about a house-owner. You can't evict a house-owner can you? Or can you? I don't know. I wouldn't have thought so. They own it, you know?

Joe, married man, sixties, employed, white, homeowner, Eltham

This correspondent and his wife clearly felt nothing could be done. And some spoke of an unwillingness to get involved; people, they claimed, simply wanted to look the other way and keep out of trouble. Ronnie in Battersea tells of anti-social tenants who play loud music:

They open the window or sometimes they've got a door like this ... open the door like that right, and they put the speaker there and then they will play it until the guy come and tell them to turn it down. But they know that he's going to take a little while to get here anyway and they, you know they don't ... you can't say nothing to them, so it's best to leave them alone like, do you know what I mean?

Ronnie, male cohabitee (father), fifties, employed, Afro-Caribbean, homeowner,
Battersea

People are reluctant to intervene even when they see crime being committed, Battersea respondents told us:

... if they come into your corridor and you're on the top floor, they can rob you. Do you know what I mean? They can just break the door in, no one's gonna even come out and have a look, in fear that they might see something they don't wanna and then they're a victim, so they just don't.

Barry, married man, forties, employed, white, council tenant, Battersea

Del and Kenny in Bermondsey condemned political correctness, which they said made people unwilling to intervene:

I'll tell you what happens when people stick together, right? I'll tell you what happens. Their idea of sticking together round here is, at the end of the day, if somebody was having a battle, right, next door, if you was fighting for your life in your house, and you was trying to make as much noise to create attention, like, 'Get me some help', and you was screaming 'Help' at the top of your voice, right, and this is a proven thing, they teach women this on, like, unarmed combat, right? Don't ever shout 'Help'. People turn the volume up, they don't wanna help. They go the other way... They always tell women, 'Don't ever scream "Help"', cos you won't get it. And that's terrible.

Del and Kenny, single and divorced (father) brothers, thirties, unemployed/
employed, white, council tenants, Bermondsey

All these different elements seem to have left people feeling that there was little that can be done to combat crime. Either the police appear to be powerless to take action:

He: And there's been a couple of break-ins like in the streets. A couple of old ladies got burgled. We heard that the police basically come round and checked it out, but at the end of the day, you know...

She: Nothing was done.

He (too faint to hear): ...you can't really do nothing about it.

Zoe, married woman, twenties, employed, white, homeowner, Eltham

Or, when they did manage to arrest someone, the lawyers were all to often able to negate what they had done.

One family does not have a neighbourhood watch on the street, nor do they have a burglar alarm – although all the other neighbours do. Their approach has been to not have too much to steal; for example she simply did not replace her jewellery after it was stolen:

It was scary at one point because we did have, like a burglary a week, so that we ended up with no possessions. I mean ... you become immune to it, like tellies and things, you just sort of gave up on them... But that I have to say is better now. They

don't break in so much.
Francesca, married mother, forties, self-employed, white, homeowner, Bermondsey

Ronnie in Battersea has the same approach:

…when I first moved here I used to work from six till about two. I used to do all the morning reports, like damaged lamp posts that night and things like that, you know and I had a beautiful stereo that I bought from Belgium and they had stole that. So I says bollocks, I have never bought once since, you know. I mean that one is a… I used to love my music.

Ronnie, male cohabitee (father), fifties, employed, Afro-Caribbean, homeowner,
Battersea

And a Peckham respondent is fatalistic, feeling that crime is everywhere:

Would you like to move anywhere else?

Maybe Fulham or Chelsea if I had the money, but realistically I don't mind living in the area, because wherever you go there will always be trouble. There is always umm … but an apple in the barrel as they say, wherever you decide to live.

Rafi, married father, thirties, employed, British-born Afro-Caribbean, council tenant,
Peckham

Crime and Urban Design

Some features do seem to help crime prevention, especially but not exclusively on estates – through 'streets' are almost always seen as better than estates:

Because the houses are back to back and stuff, it's like if somebody is going to break in, they're going to have to make a concerted effort to sort of like, you know.

Dionne, female cohabitee, twenties, employed, British-born Afro-Caribbean,
private tenant, Newtown, Reading

I dunno it's a funny feeling but it's, I feel safer around here cos I'm in a street now rather than on an estate, it is a nicer feeling like that … if you see what I mean, without making myself sound big headed or anything, I've bettered myself by coming off a council estate. Although they call this the Latchmere estate it's not a real estate, it's not a proper council estate, so in that way I've bettered myself and I really and truly don't want to go back on an estate… Nicola, my daughter, she's 13, and she's at that age where I don't want her to mix with certain people, so, and I know that on an estate that is what's going to happen.

Susie, single mother, thirties, unemployed, white, council tenant, Battersea

Residents are quite specific that small units are safer than massive tower blocks. Here is a representative view from Bermondsey:

I think it's because it's so small, and all the blocks face each other, and they've got, like, a communal area, obviously, in the middle. And it's got such a different age range … they don't have a community any more, like the Aylesbury Estate. I can't see them having a community … the tall blocks, because you don't know who lives two floors down from you. Whereas probably everyone in that block could tell you who lives on the ground floor and … and who lives opposite them as well… if they want to cut down on crime, and things like that, if they really wanted that to work, then they should bring back small estates like this, where everyone can see what's going on on the estate, everyone knows everyone else, and they all protect each other. So … apparently, the Council won't do things like that.

Serena, divorced mother, twenties, unemployed, white, council tenant, Bermondsey

But someone suggests an alternative explanation: that, because tower blocks are unpopular, they acquire a bad tenant mix:

Tower blocks, they seem to generate, I don't know, they seem like, I dunno, there must be a kind of system. You'll be lucky if you find one or two people in the whole tower block who actually get a job … cos most of them, irresponsible, a lot of them. So, him doing nothing, the mother's doing nothing … There's quite a lot of drugs going on around the tower blocks.

Amir, single father, forties, employed, African, council tenant, Battersea

Yet design does matter. Design faults, like internal corridors or easy escape routes, are seen as particularly conducive to crime. Here are three eye-witness views, two from the Five Estates in North Peckham, the other from the Doddington estate in Battersea.

Concrete jungle innit … like a maze, brick and bricks and more bricks. If you are running from the police you can get away, like I used to steal mopeds and take it on the estate, me and my mates, and when the police come they can't find you.

Kosey, single man, twenties, student, African, lives with family (council tenants),
Peckham

… fighting, robbery … it's quietened down from what it used to be but it's still there, cos now you've got doors, entry doors on every floor. So you know, they were getting mugged in the corridors before they were getting to their flats… Oh, they did from the outside but the inside is still … yeah, it's like a prison camp.

Barry, married man, forties, employed, white, council tenant, Battersea

I would say it had got slightly worse… In respects to not having enough, or a large enough police presence around here, and because the estate being as big as it was, it was like there was so many escape routes for people who committed crimes to escape. It like, a bit like a maze although they are redoing the whole of the estate and redeveloping the area, but it seems to have got slightly worse.

Rafi, married father, thirties, employed, British-born Afro-Caribbean, council tenant,
Peckham

We found it particularly interesting to compare the Doddington and Rollo estates in Battersea and the Five Estates regeneration programme in Peckham. Both had similar designs, with similar problems, but they have taken radically different approaches in dealing with them. While the Five Estates had been all but totally demolished and replaced by small maisonettes of traditional design, the Doddington has been significantly modified to design out some of the problems:

Not the blocks they just knocked down the walkways, about eleven … of walkways, so there was no way for anybody, basically this was a really bad crime scene round here cos you could basically get to this estate and you disappeared. It's not easy to catch somebody round here. But then they started saying 'Right block this area off, put bollards up'. And now it's like the estate seems to have quietened down a heck of a lot compared to how it used to be like. Much the same as Peckham. The design of the estate was a haven for people who wanted to get up to trouble … it basically just went from one very noisy bad estate to one very quiet and no one's ever heard anything on this estate any more. I mean the trouble's moved from here, it's gone all the way to Winstanley area.

Rosemary, married mother, sixties, retired, white, council tenant, Bermondsey

Safe Places

Yet – save for some women and some older people – most people seemed relatively unaffected by neighbourhood crime and unconcerned about it. True, most could report some experience as a victim of crime, ranging from theft from the shed to fairly violent personal assault and robbery. Many reported that they had taken precautions to protect themselves and their property – and frequently that of their neighbours – as part of their daily routines, interestingly even where neighbourly relations were strained. But only in a very small minority of cases did fear of crime seem to permeate all aspects of everyday existence, with major effects on quality of life. More typical was this reaction from Greenwich:

No. I mean, apparently in the area there's meant to have been quite a few break ins. But no. I'm one of these people, I've got to be honest, I sort of live in the past. If I go to bed and forget to lock the front door, then it doesn't bother me, which is wrong really … but as regards safety, it wouldn't bother me to walk down the road at night, but if I did, hubby wouldn't be quite happy about it. No way would he be happy about me going down the road at night … appreciate that at all.

Margaret, married mother, fifties, part-time employed, white, homeowner, Eltham

Of course, respondents like these might have been affected directly by crime themselves. But surprisingly perhaps, such people seem not to worry about their experience. Generally, fear of crime seems to have little relation to the reality of crime. People who know their neighbourhoods, who feel they belong there, seem to have no fear. Contrariwise, when someone does not identify with people in the area, that person tends to be more concerned with crime. Where people feel that they live in a strong community, even if they had experienced crime, that experience never grows into a fear. And, when a person moves out of an area and has lived elsewhere for a time, they perceive crime in their old area to have gone up, although the continuing residents seem blissfully unaware of the fact. So fear of crime is much more a reflection of a person's relationship to the community than a gauge of actual crime levels.

Some areas seem to be perceived as generally crime-free: Dartford, for instance, despite the recent murder:

I wouldn't be overly struck on my wife walking about late at night on her own, but I'd say if she had to I'd think this would a good enough area as any, I would think, to do that.

Richard, married man, thirties, employed, white, homeowner, Greenhithe

I don't think the crime is more or any less than it was, of course the crime has changed. No, not really, we did get the odd dreadful murder of someone, but of course that's exceptional. There are car crimes now that when I was your age people didn't have cars so that's something that's grown up since.

Harry, married man, sixties, retired, white, homeowner, Greenhithe

Likewise in Greenwich – which is interesting, because other residents gave a very different picture, suggesting that here, one local neighbourhood area might be very different from another:

No problems at all. We like it here. The neighbours are wonderful and I've never seen any trouble. I accept that there has been trouble, but nothing, nothing that I've ever seen.

Mick, married man, fifties, employed, white, homeowner, Eltham

If you've been on holiday or something like that, always get a pint of milk when you get home. Loaf of bread, you know, things like that… Community spirit, you know, neighbourly spirit. And you feel safer.

Rob, married father, forties, employed, white, homeowner, Eltham

And also in Heston and in Upton Park, again contradicting other evidence:

They own, own their own houses round here I mean, you know, most of them are Asian, as you know, but you met lots of Asians here. And I think they've been living here for a long, long time, so, at the moment they are settled down and they've got extended family and that kind of thing, so. I feel much safer than other places.

Seung-yun, single woman, twenties, student, Korean, private tenant, Heston

It's peaceful, we don't have, you know, burglary, well touch wood, burglary, no racial harassment. So far since we've moved into the area.

Nadira and Coffie, married parents, forties, both employed, African, homeowners,
Upton Park

But perhaps most significant because they totally contradict the picture given by other residents, are these views from Bermondsey respondents.

Bermondsey's quite good, you know, compared to other areas I've said.

Barnabas, married father, thirties, employed, African, council tenant, Bermondsey

I do know, sort of, everyone to say hello to, so I would feel safe, yeah, walking round here, I wouldn't have no qualms about…

Any time of the night?

Yeah, I wouldn't have really no, that is because I know everyone and…

Liz, divorced mother, thirties, unemployed, white, council tenant, Bermondsey

Reading, in particular, was perceived as generally safe:

I haven't found it an issue except probably I don't go out very often sort of late at night, you have young kids hanging around but that's always been.

Brenda, married mother, fifties, employed, white, homeowner, Earley, Reading

I've been here a year now and these guys have been here a year and a half and we've never had any trouble at all. I've never had any trouble with my car, we've never had any trouble with the house, so …I mean, I walk, I mean, I walk, sort of, from my boyfriend's and stuff, round at night on my own and I don't, I don't feel unsafe, so .. not really.

Helen, single woman, twenties, employed, white, private tenant, Newtown,
Reading

… you get, sort of, people going through late at night, drunk on a Saturday, and sometimes coming up here, and there is some level of crime although not huge, in my perception.

Kate, single woman, thirties, employed, white, private tenant, Newtown, Reading

No, I'm not aware of it at all. I wouldn't know if there'd been burglaries or anything around here.

So you feel safe then, do you?

Yeah totally, yeah, yeah.

> *Rochelle, female cohabitee, twenties, employed, white Australian, homeowner,*
> *Newtown, Reading*

A Gants Hill respondent does not know of anybody who has been burgled or experienced car crime:

Do you feel safe in the local area?

Yes... Yeah, I think so. I mean I can't really say that I walk out at night by myself, because I've got the car... So, if I go anywhere I take the car, em, but I think it's ... I think it is quite a safe area compared to some.

> *Sheila, married mother, forties, white, homeowner, Gants Hill*

Likewise with this respondent:

I haven't had to er, er deal with any problems so far. I mean its co-operation I haven't been burgled so I've never been burgled anywhere. I've been lucky so far.

> *Ranjit, married father, fifties, employed, Sikh, homeowner, Gants Hill*

When discussing why she has chosen to live here and what could be done to improve the area, this respondent focuses quite strongly on issues of crime and security:

I don't know, but I have found this is peaceful... I feel safer than other areas, I don't know why, maybe I live in this area, I feel more confidence about the area.

> *Selina, married mother, forties, employed, Asian, homeowner, Gants Hill*

Interviewees from inner-city council estates in Battersea and Bermondsey suggest that a great deal depends on informal social controls: in particular, the degree to which teenagers are socially integrated:

Well, we look out, like for our neighbours, immediate round our block, or people we know, if we see something going on untoward we would step in... Anything, we would back each other up. That's the good side. You know, within your own sort of block, you do help each other out that way.

> *Barry, married man, forties, employed, white, council tenant, Battersea*

So people here feel total confidence; they feel they 'belong':

I'm a South London person, so I'd rather stay here where I know. It goes back to feeling safe, you know. I know my little bit of South London, so I feel safe here.

Cheryl, married mother, thirties, employed, white, council tenant, Bermondsey

In Greenhithe, likewise, there is the same story of close social supervision:

Oh, yeah, yeah. Always in and out each other's houses. There's always someone to keep an eye. So it's not really a dangerous place… Someone to keep an eye on the kids, you know. I mean, I attacked a bloke in the park once. Our park down there … I was going down to with kids, someone says, there's a bloke with a little girl. She was screaming her head off. She was screaming and kicking and thumping… I said, that little girl, it doesn't look like she wants to go with him… I said to the little girl, does this man…? She said, it's my dad… He said, I wish there was more people about like you, even though…

Deidree, married mother, fifties, employed, white, council tenant, Greenhithe

Lisa in Battersea describes how she feels safe in the area and thinks that there is a kind of community. She is also happy to let her son play out:

In the summer, to be honest most people along here have their doors open in summer because we all have children… I don't mind him playing out because of lots of other children and I know everyone has got their door open … I feel as though it is as safe as you can be and there are lots of adults about.

Lisa, widow, thirties, employed, housing association tenant, Battersea

One of the factors which determines whether an area feels safe is if there are other people around during the day:

We've been burgled, it was quite a while ago, but lucky enough, I'm fortunate enough that my wife stays at home, and I think that's helped quite a bit.

Donald, married father, fifties, employed, white, homeowner, Heston

And when those who around are vigilant this can help even more:

They didn't go into the house, but they knew we weren't there because we was on holiday and they heard it through the walls sort of thing. Someone was in our rooms. They knew we was on holiday so they know there must be an intruder like, so, phoned the police straight away … they didn't have the time because, you know, hearing straight away, they didn't have the time to…

Rob, married father, forties, employed, white, homeowner, Eltham

Sanjula in Upton Park feels that the presence of older people in the daytime is a positive factor, but that they may make themselves more open to crime themselves:

And it used to, you used to feel much safer round here...?

Yeah, definitely. And I think at the moment, because there are quite a lot of elderly people on this road, you know, I seem to think that...

Do you think that's why it's been targeted?

Possibly, possibly ... the elderly people seem to be at home most of the time, so, you know, it's almost as if they're our neighbourhood watch.

So they're watching over what's going on?

Yeah, yeah, but on the other hand, I feel that, you know, they may be easy targets later on.

Sanjula, married mother, thirties, employed, Indian, owner occupier
(lives with in-laws), Upton Park

But likewise, the absence of bystanders could be a problem – and this could be exacerbated both by social mores and by defects in design:

Yeah, the neighbour, here and here yeah, unfortunately with the modern sort of ways of building and development, one of the things you'll find is people obviously when the winter comes they shut themselves in more, you know, they shut their doors, this is a British disease, a Southerner's disease I call it, cos if you go up North you don't get that sort of problem, they all mix more and they go out to social clubs, but round this area you'll find when night time comes everyone shuts up, and like that's unfortunately with the new modern sort of building specs, people have got double glazing and triple glazing, so you don't hear nothing outside, so any sort of problem point of views, you could be outside there shouting and a lot of it you wouldn't hear.

Donald, married father, fifties, employed, white, homeowner, Heston

The Unbonding of Society

To emphasise finally, as at the start: for most people in most areas in our study, crime does not appear a serious worry. But for a substantial minority of respondents, it is a major concern, even an obsession. Though they were able to tell us of specific incidents that they had suffered or their neighbours had suffered, they seemed far more concerned by a general sense of menace, by a sense of the disintegration of the social bonds that had earlier united different individuals in a neighbourhood. These people repeatedly spoke of their ever-present sense of danger, of being unable to feel safe in going out of their front doors, certainly after dark, in the worst cases at any time. Much of this fear stems from gangs of youths who they say were roaming their neighbourhoods, looking for trouble and menacing law-abiding citizens.

Some of this is just teenage bad behaviour, but there is a sense that in some cases it is shading over into straight gang criminality, especially to do with drugs. These people see the police as virtually powerless to intervene: the system is stacked against them.

Sometimes this is attributed to new arrivals in an area, especially into council housing; such people are seen as wrecking long-established norms and relationships. Even those who feel safe tend to compare their areas with others, often those from where they have moved, which – especially in south-east London – they perceive as distinctly unsafe. And, more locally, everywhere there seems inevitably to be an area universally regarded as 'bad' by reputation, whether or not the respondent has direct experience of it. Invariably these are areas of council housing, and 'estates' are seen as crime-ridden compared to 'streets', simply because of their physical characteristics.

There is a widespread desire for a return to the old-style local 'Bobby' whom some can remember from their own childhoods. But evidently, his effectiveness depended on shared social norms that would be inconceivable in the London of 2007. Even so, in some traditional working-class neighbourhoods there seems to be an extraordinary degree of informal social control: if people, especially young people, are seen as out of control 'the lads would have a word with him', with the clear implication that drastic penalties could follow. Such areas seem naturally to produce social gatekeepers: people, quite often mature women, with great personal presence and moral courage, who can control even the most difficult local teenagers with a subtle yet firm hand. But these, we sensed, were few and far between. Elsewhere, it helps to have people around during the day: a rare enough occurrence in many areas, where both adults in a household would be out at work, unless there are older retired people to hold the fort. Thus, even though many areas report feelings of solidarity and neighbourliness and everyday small kindnesses, in many areas there seems to be an underlying sense that in important ways the social cement that bonds society has become significantly loosened, even dissolved: a loosening that may bode ill for the future.

Gants Hill subway

© Bill Knight

Two flags above Newham   © Bill Knight

Chapter Fourteen

Melting the Pot

Many Londoners celebrate the fact that theirs is one of the most racially and culturally diverse cities on earth. Over four decades their city, once almost homogeneously white and European, has become a bewildering rich mosaic of colours, creeds and cultures. But, when it comes down to the neighbourhoods where Londoners live their lives, it gets a lot more complicated.

A few – mercifully, very few – places in London are prone to violently racist behaviour. We will describe them later. But, very often, much is subtle and half-hidden. And in so many cases, it proves very difficult, involving subjective judgement, to establish what exactly is happening. Again and again, we heard of incidents that caused uncertainty and embarrassment and resentment. But it proved hard to say what exactly was at issue. Very often, it seemed a question of linguistic or cultural misunderstanding.

The 'bad areas' are in some ways the simplest case. Worst of all are traditionally white working-class areas in east and south-east London, which for decades were isolated from the wider community by reason of the jobs people did and the tight-knit nature of the society that formed in the streets around factories or docks:

Not really – other things are basically all right. When we first come back to this country we were in East Ham where there was a bit of racism, so we had to move to Camden Road.

What sort of racism did you experience?

When me and my brother went to the park there was like these boys throwing stuff … cricket, when we were playing cricket…

What, they were, they were throwing stones and stuff?

And when we informed the police, police said: 'We can't actually do anything unless you are hurt, so they didn't do anything like that, we can't do anything, unless you're physically hurt'.

Kamal, married father, fifties, unemployed, Asian, private tenant, Upton Park

But we heard the same story from Heston in west London, a traditionally working-class area with a large old-established Indian population. Here, it seems, the problem arose from a small part of the host population:

… the only crime we suffer from, we get lots of bullying … one summer it was just living in a hell, and that was neighbours from hell … and even when they stare sometimes, they even call you … 'Oh don't bother … just you have every right, don't bother about the Pakis … don't bother about these bastards'. … it's quite difficult, it's very hurting as well. Sometimes you feel inside it hurts you that you do so much, you help your neighbours and then the neighbours … they just come and start saying these sorts of thing.

Jalil, married father, sixties, retired, Asian, homeowner, Heston

Not merely those of Asian descent, but also the Irish, could suffer the same treatment, again – it would seem – from a small section of the population:

That was Surrey Lane estate which is near Battersea Bridge. That flat were lovely, it was just the people who were terrible … first of all we were Irish and I know … I'm afraid it was a problem. The other thing was we went to work and a lot of the people didn't go to work, and our children went to a different school and, and you just got, you know, niggles and … you got a great deal of aggravation because also we were kind of in an end flat and the children used to play, you know, in the, on that corner and I mean if you said, if the police, the police would come, you know, and the aggravation would start and they would say, you know, the children would say, 'Well, we had nowhere to play!' but aggravating people wasn't, you know… I mean you would get anything thrown in your garden. You would also, we had our, our front door broke, the, the glass in the front door broke Christmas afternoon because they threw something at it… So I suppose they didn't actually mix that much with the children that were there, you know, or if they did the few times, well, the few times they went out, you know, you'd have a mother coming to the door and saying [*whinging voice*] 'Your son's hit my son', and you'd know very well that your son hadn't the courage to hit theirs, they weren't streetwise, so you know…

Mary, widow, fifties, unemployed, white, homeowner, Battersea

But, more often and much more subtly, people describe small incidents which they see as racial slights, but which – just possibly – they may have misinterpreted. It is very difficult to judge them at a distance. Take this example:

She's actually a classroom assistant at Namjot's school and she was the assistant in Namjot's sort of first year, so it was all nice, and they're really lovely… Mary used to come to the door, and they always remembered the kids' birthdays. Amazing… But there was a time when she'd just be at the door and just give us a card and a present at the door and not ever come in… We used to wonder why doesn't she want to come in. Is it because, you know…

Ajit, married mother, thirties, employed, Sikh, homeowner, Gants Hill

And this sensitivity evidently extended to other aspects of their relationship:

It's funny, the kids come over here a lot to play with Namjot and they come out over the garden and we're fine about that, but they hardly ever have Namjot over. I don't know whether that's racism. I can't say whether they just don't…

Ajit, married mother, thirties, employed, Sikh, homeowner, Gants Hill

Out of such small incidents, seeds of distrust are planted and take root. It was very similar with this encounter in Battersea – a misunderstanding, it seems, but one that rankled:

I went to the Turkish baths last Thursday, in Lewisham. I'm not being funny, but this lady … I drove my car into the car park and got a parking space, you have to put money in the meter and you get the little … ticket, you know the little ticket you stick on the car, so this lady, this elderly woman, had a daughter about my age but the other one was a bit older than me, white lady, and she said, 'Would you like this ticket?' but I didn't take any notice because I thought she was talking to her daughter so I kept on going and I went to the meter to put my money in, and she said, 'Scuse me'. So I turned around, and she said, 'Would you like this ticket? I've still got an hour on there' … I said, 'Yeah'. I said, 'Are you sure?', she said 'Yes'. She said, 'We're going anyway'. I said, 'Would you like something for it?' she said, 'No, no, no, cos we're going, we don't need it'. So she gave me the ticket, next minute she turns round and she said, 'Would you like my blood as well?'

Sandra, single mother, forties, employed, Afro-Caribbean, council tenant, Battersea

Was this extreme over-sensitivity? Divorced from the immediate context in which it took place, it is almost impossible to say. More straightforward, perhaps, is this encounter from Bermondsey, where a white working-class couple seemed convinced that 'coloureds' in their neighbourhood were bent on poisoning or drugging their child:

… but there is a lot of like coloureds round here and well, you couldn't really let him go out of your sight too much, you know… I said, 'What are you doing going in there, going in people's houses?', so he said, 'Mum, I wanted a drink'. I said, 'I live down there', and this man, apparently, had give him some Ribena … he wanted a drink, this man give him a drink. I said, 'Well, what's he give you?', 'Only Ribena', I said, 'Well, how do you know what he put in that Ribena?'

Shaun and Katie, married parents, thirties, self-employed, white, council tenants,
Bermondsey

Older people, we were told, are the most intolerant of differences, and so the most openly racist. Here are two almost identical views, one from Heston, the other from Bermondsey:

... well, not everyone, but especially the older ladies, English older ladies, they're completely racist ...

Sandhya, married mother, forties, part-time employed, Indian, homeowner, Heston

I don't know, but what I've come to realise that the older white people, the older people, they're the racist ones ... the young ones will try to get on with you, because we're all the same, we're just different colour. But it's the old ones that are insulting. You know...

Sandra, single mother, forties, employed, Afro-Caribbean, council tenant, Battersea

And, it seemed, this stereotype was confirmed by this middle-aged Battersea woman who told us that she felt she was no longer living in her own country. One senses her real confusion about the changes that had occurred in the stable, homogeneous London she had known as a child:

Val: There's only one doctor here that I go to, I've been going to him for years but they're all Indian now, there aren't any English and I object to going to the Post Office and finding all Indian and Indian music, I don't feel as if I'm in England. All our basic needs and dentists are all served by foreigners... If you go to a, a doctor and the person speaks in a dialect, an English dialect that you can't understand then it, it really defeats the whole object and that happens with, throughout the, the health, with the Post Offices, people are beginning to feel alienated and not, and that they're not in their own country, they can't explain [how to] get they want or they can't understand what's going on and if they complain or say anything, then they're classed as racist or difficult people.

Val, fifties, unemployed, white, Battersea, and her daughter Joan,
a homeless single mother

Notice, though, that she stresses the sheer difficulty of communication in a multilingual society: 'They can't explain [how to] get what they want'. But another and very potent source of misunderstanding is a clash of lifestyles, perhaps especially – since the newcomers tend to be younger – as between different age groups:

... they've just a completely different, different outlook on life ... he'll turn up on a Saturday or a Sunday night at 11, 12 O'clock and she's got the children with her, you know what I mean, our children would be fast asleep at, and they're taking the children and they're visiting people at midnight, you know. And they've got to go to school in the morning and ... whatever you say, you know, 'Oh you're being racist' and that, it's not, it's a fact because you live with them and you see that there's so many differences, and there's deep-seated differences... I'm not saying that what they do is wrong but it's not what I'd want to do. It's wrong from my point of view...I mean what we do is probably wrong from their point of view, you know, as far as they're concerned...

> *Gary and Dawn, married parents, forties, employed, white,*
> *housing association tenants, Bermondsey*

Perhaps as a result of such encounters, some ethnic groups simply would not consider moving out of their traditional areas, which they felt gave them a kind of natural protection, allowing them to feel comfortable. Here are two representative views:

I wouldn't want my child to grow up in a typical white neighbourhood ... for cultural reasons, I don't want them to get lost.

> *Kevin, male cohabitee, thirties, employed, African, council tenant, Peckham*

We tend not to go that far afield because we like to see other black people when were going around. You don't want to be in an area where you don't see a black face ... so I think we tend to move Catford, Lewisham. People in Brixton go to Streatham, Thornton Heath Croydon, not far out...

> *Wynette, British-born Afro-Caribbean, Southwark Borough Council official*

Areas of Tension:
Bermondsey, Dagenham, Newham, Hounslow

But certain areas of London seemed to be in a particularly problematic class of their own – above all, as already told, old white working-class dockland areas like Bermondsey:

... you've gotta bear in mind, right, this is the Dockland area, it was one of the last areas to get integrated, right? And that ain't nothing to do with the people who live here, right? And they're as anti anything new, as they would be the yuppies, or anything else, right? Give them a bit of time, people get their heads round it. But it's ridiculous, because we're all in the same boat.

> *Del and Kenny, single and divorced (father) brothers, thirties, unemployed/*
> *employed, white, council tenant, Bermondsey*

This, another long-time resident explained, was a product of history. Bermondsey and places like it were long-established working-class areas where people had a tradition of being housed, first by charitable landlords and later by the local council:

... it wasn't a place where people new to London came, because you couldn't get a place to live and people were on the council list for donkey's years … but nowadays there is much more because we are Southwark and we cover a larger area there are more newer people. I notice in the church we have newer people from Africa so it's brought in a different perspective.

Maria, married mother, sixties, part-time employed, white, homeowner, Bermondsey

Most relevant here, perhaps, are the views of a Bermondsey housing officer with widespread experience of the local estates:

Bermondsey is very close knit because of the old docks and you find people who have been here for years and then they have their children and their children. You find people living in the same block and people round the corner marrying each other that sort of thing. So they resent anybody coming in and if you are black it is worse cause if you are white and you live across in Peckham and you come in you are still an outsider as far as they are concerned… I don't know whether they have accepted it or they are forced to. I think perhaps they are forced to, but I know certainly they tolerate it more.

Bermondsey Housing Officer

The culture here is graphically described by a white Scotsman, who explained that he too felt like an alien:

… sometimes, it's almost intimidating to go in the pub there … everybody knows each other… A very close community … not racist, but…

Mark, single man, thirties, employed, white, private tenant, Bermondsey

As a result, a pattern of informal yet deep segregation had evolved in Southwark, in which the Old Kent Road formed a critical boundary line:

… they haven't got a lot of people from Peckham. Generally very few, because people wouldn't choose this area. Not really. People on Peckham on the whole don't really want to go to Rotherhithe. And people round here don't want to go to Peckham. They don't want to cross the Old Kent Road.

Bermondsey Housing Officer

Faced with ethnic and cultural change, the logical response of people here was to move out of London altogether. Thus, in a sense, working-class London has steadily exported itself to Essex: *+to Kong !!*

What's happened to all the white families is there is a lot of people moving out of the area because they don't like the blacks. They will move out … the Essex thing is still happening…

Shaun and Katie, married parents, thirties, self-employed, white, council tenants, Bermondsey

Here, as might be expected, the two sides told totally different stories, real enough to them: blacks reported abuse and harassment, whites reported problems with noise and mayhem:

When you were living in Aylesbury, Walworth Road, did you experience racism there?

No. They say that all areas have got it, but I've never experienced it when I lived there. It's only since I've come here that I've noticed it … the only coloured children around here are mine. So sometimes, when they have arguments, they always bring it up.

Janice, single mother, thirties, unemployed, British-born Afro-Caribbean, council tenant, Bermondsey

But it steadily came to appear more complex. They had suffered violence from young people, but some of them were actually black:

I've only ever experienced it in Bermondsey, like down this part.

And do you think it's mainly just older people who are racist, or is it the younger people?

I find the younger ones as well… My mum would like to move, because she's on a big estate, and because she's old and got a bad leg and everything… She said it's too noisy for her and everything else that, I mean, she's been attacked, she's walked down there and she's been attacked down there, even. The younger kids have come along and flung stones at her, and … you know, it's just … my mum's frightened to walk certain parts now, so she comes… I showed her a different route, where she ain't gonna really buck up with anybody.

Has she lived there for long, in the Blue?

My mum's lived there 3 years… My mum's been … when she lived on the Aylesbury, she was mugged twice, and that was by two black boys… And then in this area, she gets attacked by the … they're not even big boys, they're little.

Janice, single mother, thirties, unemployed, British-born half-white, half-Afro-Caribbean, council tenant, Bermondsey

Partly at least, this Bermondsey respondent suggests, the problems are not racial but cultural – a matter of different lifestyles, in particular a different way of occupying space:

… nobody speaks to Africans I don't know why it's awful… But the family on the balcony, she sometimes in the summer time, you don't hear them on the winter time but sometimes in the summer time she'll have 18 children on her balcony and that's so intense you just want to run away. I means it's just so so intense in these little concrete flats that kind of reverberate with sound. They don't go into the playground at all, they are just on the balcony.

Shaun and Katie, married parents, thirties, self-employed, white, council tenants,
Bermondsey

A black housing officer confirmed that this was a generally expressed view:

But I think people…people out in the street they don't like black people but you work in the office so while you are in the office you're okay or if you go to visit you're okay. If they are talking on the phone or if they are talking to you … they will still say things about black people … if you are on the waiting list, if I was black I'd get it, that sort of thing or that black person next door is making noise or what have you and that sort of thing or I don't want any black people living here I don't want that sort coming….

Bermondsey Housing Officer

But the tensions could equally well work in the opposite direction, as he confirmed:

… this man had this really big dog on the walkway. And I asked him 'do you mind moving your dog?' … 'don't you fucking tell me what to do you fucking black so and so … you fuck off back to Africa'… I've never been to Africa … 'fuck off back to Africa take your f-ing disease with you…'. He was really angry. And I was a little bit… Ann who was with me said don't you speak to like that, and you can fuck off an' all.

Bermondsey Housing Officer

And they could well flare into open violence, where the police intervene only with difficulty:

I have just had a case on the squares and they will constantly break windows, they will … what they did, they tried to put, how can I say it without being really rude, shit they will try to put things like that through the letter box, they will put chocolate and all sorts on people's cars … there was a group of youngsters and in the end they sort tried to beat him up and he tried to fight back and there was some sort of stabbing. He was arrested… But I spoke to a police officer last week and he give his version of it, because sometimes you really don't know because … he said the … our tenant was arrested because he feels that even though he was a victim he was also responsible for hitting another chap so they argue.

Wynette, British-born Afro-Caribbean, Southwark Borough Council official

Some of the worst incidents have come from traditionally white estates like the Blue Anchor Lane estate off Southwark Park Road, like this one seen by a resident:

I think it's more like towards the Blue, my neighbour witnessed a really horrible assault last week and she said that there had been a few recently because her brother-in-law lives over there. She saw a black guy being beaten up by thirty white men on Jamaica Road and all the cars had stopped and there was lots of tooting, and there was one police car and the guys just ran off through the park...

Shaun and Katie, married parents, thirties, self-employed, white, council tenants,
Bermondsey

In East London we got a very strong sense of the barriers against Asian migration into traditionally white areas, including actual violence and not just the threat of violence. Dagenham, we heard more than once, is an area with a notorious reputation for racism:

We don't want to move there, mainly because we think it's a lot of the old white East End people who are racist move out there.

Ajit, married mother, thirties, employed, Sikh, homeowner, Gants Hill

Ajit graphically described the kind of incident that drove Indians out of Dagenham:

I had some relatives who'd once lived in Dagenham and had been driven out. They moved to East Ham. Because they'd had so much racism they'd just moved out. Our friends that I was talking to you about, the teachers, when Jasmine was 18 months or less than that, under 2, they had a petrol bomb through their window. They had their house set alight. They've had the troublemakers coming round and having fights on the lawn with Brian … broken his nose. I mean they've had so much. They've had their tyres slashed, their car regularly trashed. And they're still there! They've had a video camera...

Ajit, married mother, thirties, employed, Sikh, homeowner, Gants Hill

But there was an additional and rather strange factor, she said: a social one, because they were professionals:

She: Because she's Asian. Plus there's an added factor there, which is a weird one, because they're teachers. He teaches in Dagenham, and people in that area don't seem to like authority …

Is Dagenham sort of white, old East End?

She: Yeah, white, old East End.

He: Dagenham has a history of being white, working class, and it had a great history of racism. It's changing over a period of time, but the abuse that we had was from the kids. Kids will do it anywhere. But they get it from somewhere.

Ajit, married mother, thirties, employed, Sikh, homeowner, Gants Hill

Eltham, of course, acquired the same kind of reputation as a result of the Stephen Lawrence murder. But one respondent indignantly refuted the idea that it was justified:

How about the media attention? What impact do you think it's had on the area?

They're treating everybody in the area as though it's racist. It just isn't… And it's easy to write, you know, clever people write clever things in newspapers. And it's a story. And they move on to something else. It's not a fact, it's very much fiction isn't it?

Mick, married man, fifties, employed, white, homeowner, Eltham

The New Arrivals

But in Hounslow there is a different kind of culture clash: there, we found that people want to move out in reaction to the asylum seekers who have been moving in. There appears to be no clear ethnic pattern in the people who want to move out: it seems to affect both whites and those from the Indian subcontinent alike. This had been an old-established and stable multi-ethnic community, we were repeatedly told. But now it seemed to be in a state of turmoil:

Everyone wants to move from here now… Yeah, yeah, the Asian people like us, you know, I live here 25 years and sometimes we are thinking, my son said we should move from here, it's not safe area now… Yeah, we are thinking to leave, we go on the side, you know, where there are not many refugee people there.

Sandhya, married mother, forties, part-time employed, Indian, homeowner, Heston

Southall, she suggested, had gone completely downhill – and Heston could easily go the same way:

Yeah, yeah. So I go there [Southall], you know, now sometime, it's completely different, you know, it's full up of the refugee people or the Somali people, and it's, it's messy there, it looks dirty… Hounslow is looks a bit better than Southall. Maybe later on this one is the same place, but Southall is a really dirty place now.

Sandhya, married mother, forties, part-time employed, Indian, homeowner, Heston

In this tale, the villains of the piece seem to vary. Sometimes they are asylum-seekers housed in hostels:

something should be done about this is the travelling … there's so many laws they're breaking … the kids don't go to school so they're getting up illiterate, and they're with kids with the caravans all day long and things like that, so that's not gonna help them when they get older.

Donald, married father, fifties, employed, white, homeowner, Heston

Sometimes they are Irish travellers:

... OK they might be OK but a lot of them are causing trouble, you find the kids all over the place, and you know, they're dumping things everywhere, and junk in their gardens and things ...

Donald, married father, fifties, employed, white, homeowner, Heston

One Indian shop worker reports many experiences of people, who she thinks are asylum seekers, stealing from her. She can't identify where they come from:

I don't feel safe, if I am alone here I just try to lock the door... Because they are nicking so many things ... nick the money or something, they are after the money.

Sandhya, married mother, forties, part-time employed, Indian, homeowner, Heston

Sandhya identifies herself as British and distinguishes herself from the asylum seekers, whom she sees as a bunch of common criminals:

So ... our living standard, our thinking, everything is like English now because it's a long time we live, but that people is completely different.

Sandhya, married mother, forties, part-time employed, Indian, homeowner, Heston

Invasion and Succession: Gants Hill

A more complex set of conflicts appears to be occurring in Gants Hill, where a traditionally Jewish area is becoming progressively more Asian. Here, it appears that the new arrivals are mainly second- or third-generation migrants from the East End, who – as one respondent pointed out to us – are actually following in the footsteps of the original Jewish migrants who came here 70 years earlier:

I don't know ... well, a lot more Asians have come into the area, but they're doing the same as what Jewish people did, they've come from the East End and they've come out, so they've done exactly the same.

Rachel, married mother, thirties, part-time employed, white Jewish, homeowner,
Gants Hill

And – rather as in Hounslow – older-established Asian residents are also concerned as to where this process might lead. Rachel again:

... that time there wasn't a Jewish secondary school, so half my class in *** were Jewish, because Gant's Hill predominantly, half were Jewish. It's taken over now because Asians are in the area so it's like, now it's like half the class are Asians, so it's just taken over.

Rachel, married mother, thirties, part-time employed, white Jewish, homeowner, Gants Hill.

And here from her Bangladeshi counterpart:

It's quiet, it is nice area but you're getting a lot of Asian people, Tamil people mainly moving into this area … for Asian people it is better I don't know not for white people… I wouldn't like it to be like a ghetto or you know, it's alright, so far it's alright but, I don't like East London that's just a ghetto … well their children also are striving to do well, you know there's a lot of competition and things the parents also have high expectations would like them to do well whereas in East London it's not really like that and um, I don't have very much time to mix with the people so I don't fight with them.

Shirin, married mother, thirties, Bangladeshi, homeowner, Gants Hill

Traditionally, many of the older Jewish population were taxi drivers working in central London:

… when I went to school there was always Jewish people in my class but there's more and more and I mean they say the Jews move out and the Asians move in, that's definitely how.

Right so you think they've moved further towards Clayhall and…

Definitely from Redbridge roundabout they're coming up from there cos the houses are slightly cheaper, they're the slightly smaller so they're getting in there and then they'll creep up here.

… and you think that's what's happened with the Jewish population it's moved up from Gants Hill roundabout up to Longwood and…

Yeah and then they're going to Chigwell you know they go to Chigwell and er, yeah definitely.

Pam, married mother, forties, employed, white, homeowner, Gants Hill

In other cases, though, it appears that the newcomers are actually from abroad and are jumping the queue for social housing:

I think that it's … they're not so much worried, but it's the fact that there's people waiting for houses and they come straight in and they get the houses that people who live in this borough are waiting for, and I think that's the thing that gets them.

Sheila, married mother, forties, white, homeowners, Gants Hill

In next-door Newham, where the pressures on affordable social housing are almost certainly greater, there are concerns that new arrivals, flocking into areas of existing ethnic concentration, might lead to the formation of ethnic ghettos. Here is the view of Roland, himself a member of an earlier wave of immigration into London:

I think it's cos a lot of people rent as well so it doesn't, people just come in from all over the place so it's… People like living near others of a similar ethnic identity to themselves, leading to concentrations of people from particular groups… Well, it's all right, you know, because em well, most of the neighbours them are Indians, you know, my next door neighbour, she's English, and my next door neighbour is em Indian, so you know, everybody kind a keep themself to themselves.

Roland, married father, sixties, retired, Afro-Caribbean, homeowner, Upton Park

Clearly, for Roland, it is important that people from different backgrounds live quietly together, respecting each other's space. But he has seen a huge change:

… now 90 per cent of this people live on this street are Muslim… Because they're near to the church. One bloke offered to buy my house.

Roland, married father, sixties, retired, Afro-Caribbean, homeowner, Upton Park

And, as in Heston, so in East London, older-established Asian residents are now concerned about a recent incursion of asylum-seekers:

We've always had migrants into Newham. But refugees and asylum seekers. And Redbridge, but Newham probably has more than Redbridge. The whole of the East End I think has had more than their fair share in terms of proportion.

And they've been mostly coming from what, Eastern Europe?

Yeah. For a time it was Somalia wasn't it. So there's quite a few Somalians… The Somalis seem to be more around the west side.

Ajit, married mother, thirties, employed, Sikh, homeowner, Gants Hill

The New Melting Pot: Battersea

Battersea, we found in our interviews, used to have a lot of racial tension – but most of it seems to have dissipated, making it culturally and racially a very heterogeneous area. Here is Angie, a white woman with a black partner; their children appear to be mixed race and white:

I think people have just slightly got smartened up. What's the use of arguing over people who come in here and live with you all their lives yeah?… I mean I've got, my cousins are all black and I've got one, two, I can say I've got about three black friends. Most of the rest of them are white... Well most of my family were black people, all my brothers and sisters except one, two.

Angie, single mother, twenties, unemployed, white, council tenant, Battersea

We did however get some anecdotal evidence of white flight from Battersea, probably of working-class people quite a few years earlier:

Yeah. And ... they were very friendly with my sister ... very nice. They moved to Kent and two black people bought the place and came in... Yeah, they told me, yeah. They encouraged me to get out.

Because of the black people?

Yeah... They said there was too many black people and they wanted to move out ... 'my daughter she's the only one there' and all that ... they all say that the kids are rough and that.

Amir, single father, forties, employed, African, council tenant, Battersea

Reading too seems well integrated, perhaps because of the huge influence of the university:

I mean, I really like it. I mean, I like the fact that it's, sort of, multi-cultural and stuff, I like the fact that you step out of your door and there's just so many, sort of, different people, I like, sort of, the community, sort of, the local shops, I've actually got quite a lot of friends that live in this area and, sort of, towards town as well. I like the fact that it's in walking distance to town.

Helen, single woman, twenties, employed, white, private tenant, Newtown, Reading

Possibly, this respondent suggests, the actual degree of mixing was less than might appear on the surface – but there was a mood of live and let live, which she finds agreeable:

Well ... I mean, I haven't noticed anyone really, sort of, mixing, everyone seems to sort of go about their own business, but it's just nice having that.

Rochelle, female cohabitee, twenties, employed, white Australian, homeowner, Newtown, Reading

Race in the School

London parents generally express a strong view that they want their children to be educated in multicultural schools with a good mix, but they worry a great deal about schools becoming overwhelmingly ethnic. Here is a view from Heston which we reported in Chapter 5 – clearly a response to recent developments:

… my youngest is 22 now, she, I took her out of that school and moved her to another school which I wouldn't have thought I would ever consider sending her to, and I don't want you to think it's, I'm a racist if I say it, but it was because in the morning, instead of going in and saying 'Good morning' to the teacher, they had to say '***' or whatever it was … so please don't think it's because I'm a racist cos I don't, I'm not that way, but it, culturally it's changed completely in the space of two or three years. It went from being an English, a school in England where a lot of Asian children went to, to a school in England that was like an Asian school, if you know what I mean.

Betty, married mother, fifties, employed, white, homeowner, Heston

These remarks show that parents react very negatively to the prospect that their children might go to a school with a very high proportion of ethnic minority pupils. But interestingly, many of these positively affirm that they want their children to enjoy a true multicultural education:

I sat outside there about 2 months ago and I counted the children, 53 children I counted coming through there, and 5 of them was white.

Gary and Dawn, married parents, forties, employed, white,
housing association tenants, Bermondsey

That was a view from white parents in Bermondsey. But similar is the reaction of this African mother who says that, reluctantly, she would have to send her children to a private school:

I like that fact that it's a multicultural … I mean the Catholic schools you know, there's only one or two black faces there.

Adeola, divorced mother, thirties, employed, Nigerian, housing association tenant, Heston

And the same sentiment comes from this British-born Afro-Caribbean respondent in East Reading:

I'm not sure I'd like to send my children there either because I'd want it to be more ethnically diverse than it is now… Yeah I would want that, at least 50:50 but not sort of 95:5 as it is now and I'd probably go private as well, I have to say so… 95 per cent Asian and 5 per cent white.

Dionne, Female cohabitee, twenties, employed, British-born Afro-Caribbean,
private tenant, Newtown, Reading

A specific worry concerns the different attitudes of Muslim parents to the upbringing of teenage girls, as Betty from Heston was reported as saying in Chapter 5:

… because of the way the Asians are, which is fine for them, they, they don't let their daughters, they stop letting their daughters do things like that, so you are then, your, your white girl is then in a minority because she's got no one to go to pictures on a Saturday afternoon with, so what's happening now is people are trying to find schools where there's other girls of the same ilk, so that when they get to about 12 or whatever, they're not going to be isolated.

Betty, married mother, fifties, employed, white, homeowner, Heston

There is, perhaps, a mixture of racial and class attitudes here, as seen in this comment from a Bangladeshi mother in Gants Hill:

… plus also it's a ghetto you get too many Bangladeshi children going there it's like a ghetto you don't… Here there are a lot of Asian children, lot of Tamil and Indian and Gujaratis you know varieties but they're more from professional classes so they have an incentive to do well, whereas some of those children their parents are not educated and they're not from professional classes they don't really want to work as well, you don't get that incentive from home for them to do well because they've got different ideology as well.

Shirin, married mother, thirties, Bangladeshi, homeowner, Gants Hill

But, as this long-time Heston resident explained in Chapter 5, part of the problem is cultural-linguistic:

… when we went to school there wasn't a language problem, you know, obviously with the schools today the kids going into school today, you've got a 50:50 split, you've got half the Asians I think are really westernised, maybe more than 50, very westernised, no problem with English or whatever it is, going to school, but … certain kids are being held back because the others have got to learn the basic English before they can pick up the general education and I think that is a problem … not only the 4 or 5 age level, I think it's more also the 6 and 7 age level, and it's not all the, sorry, it's not only Asian, to be quite honest, it's Eastern European … what they don't obviously understand is before the kid can understand what is being taught, he's got to know the language, so that will hold back others and I think that's been coming up more and more now really.

Donald, married father, fifties, employed, white, homeowner, Heston

There seems to be a general fear of the consequences of having your own child in a class with too many children for whom English is a second language:

I mean they're putting more and more people in classes, special needs are put in the same classes and I could go on forever, being married to a teacher you know it's, but it's just sad and they expect them to come out with all these qualifications but at the end of the day, Richard says he turns round and tells the kids what to do and then, and they have to turn round and say in Urdu or something because they can't speak English... I mean as Richard says it's all right when you're playing a game of football but when it's in an English class or a Maths, there's not really much hope!

Pam, married mother, forties, employed, white, homeowner, Gants Hill

But it proved difficult to disentangle such purely educational worries from attitudes that appeared frankly racist. This same respondent in Gants Hill, again:

And did you, which other schools did you go to?

...I actually know a teacher that teaches there she said don't let Simon go there [*laughter*] and ... [it] had so many Indians in, the Asian, and I mean let's be honest we are white, I want him with the majority of people like ourselves.

Pam, married mother, forties, employed, white, homeowner, Gants Hill

Such attitudes seemed rare, at any rate in being expressed so starkly. But they did not seem to be at all shared by the younger generation who had direct experience of latter-day London schools. Consider these two comments from Heston:

There was Asian and white mainly. Mainly Asian.

And was that, did that create any sort of, issues in terms of people getting on with each other within the school?

No, not at all, cos er the group of friends was like so diverse, we've got Moroccan, Ethiopian, er, Indian, Pakistani, Lebanese, English, just you know, nothing, no-one grouped themselves in terms of race or things like that.

Yeah, and where would er, where do people tend to come from, do they all come from this local area?

Yeah, they're mainly local area.

Milad, single man, twenties, employed, Lebanese, homeowners (living at home), Heston

I think there's a mixture, total mixture. I mean I, I can't see racism going on at all, but I mean it does exist obviously, otherwise people wouldn't be talking about it, but I mean in our school there's a total mixture of people and people just hang around in any type of like groups, no matter what colour really.

Rajiv, man, teenager, at school, Asian, tenure not stated, Heston

However, it appears very difficult to achieve a truly multicultural school. As this respondent from Peckham Youth Club explains, cultural mores enter into choice too – as does the fact that in London, many of the better-performing schools select their children:

… it's a combination of factors, you will find that in the black and Asian communities you will have more Muslims so you will have more who are opting for a single sex education. Also more that are fundamental Christians, again single sex education… I also suspect that … most black parents in the area would prefer to send their child to a school where they would be in a majority rather than in the minority or at least in a very significant minority and I think that is acceptable but I also know that there are other schools that stay largely white. What can I say? I don't know, it seems to be more the selective schools that stay more white than mixed, and you can draw your own conclusions from that. I don't have any evidence for people's criteria that they operate a racist admissions criteria, however if you look at the ethnic composition of some schools and then look at the ethnic composition of other schools there is a huge, huge disparity and you find it in the primary schools as well, because although there has been an increase in black and Asian young people they are not 75 per cent to 90 per cent of the community so you draw your own conclusions, but you find other girls' schools that are 75 to 80 per cent white – again the community is not 75 to 80 per cent white … so I think it's a combination of factors really.

Respondent, Peckham Youth Club

The observations of the following respondent illustrate how some of the processes of segregation take place:

Well, at the moment *** are coming off with very good results, but *** has caused a problem as well in my view … they … because since it opened it seems like all the Jewish children have come out … aren't going to the local state school and all going to ***, so therefore there's very few Jewish children left at the local state schools. So then my child … I mean they'll be in a minority religious wise if they went to the state schools … they're all going to *** … and I don't want that, I mean *** isn't a particularly religious school … it's a school for Jewish children, I feel…

Rachel, married mother, thirties, part-time employed, white Jewish, homeowner,
Gants Hill

In Gants Hill we found a strong sense among the Jewish population that schools are going downhill because of an influx of Asian children. At the same time, in Hounslow there is a feeling among the Asian population that minority children are being ignored and allowed to under-perform:

… [*sighs*] I don't know how to describe it but it is, it is really disgraceful that the teachers are not … taking the full potentials of the people from the, er … from sub-continent. Because it is admitted fact that people from sub-continent … they are very intelligent people, given … opportunities or given proper education and proper incentive and ex', er, little bit encouragement … but they are not being encouraged, and this education is going down and down, down drains … predominantly white school, they have better standard, which are predominantly Asian schools the teachers just give in and they just don't do anything. They just say 'Oh well, we don't want [*mumbles*] ... they are from, they just ...' as if they think that they have come from a ... 'Oh they don't, they are alright as it is'.

Jalil, married father, sixties, retired, Asian, homeowner, Heston

But other minority parents feel that, comparing London schools now with their own experiences a generation before, there have been very significant improvements in the ways in which schools approached multicultural issues:

... it was quite a good experience, when I went there it was quite predominately white, but it is good to see having been back there in the last 2 or 3 years off and on, that they are more aware of issues such as ... how should I say it ... ethnicity. Like they have black awareness day and certain aspects ... which was totally unheard of when I was at school...

Rafi, married father, thirties, employed, British-born Afro-Caribbean, council tenant, Peckham

Political Correctness and Reverse Racism

We got a strong sense from our interviews that now, a process of reverse racism is occurring: a belief that political correctness and positive discrimination had gone too far:

It's totally wrong, mobs of kids having a go at kids because they're black, right? But it's totally wrong mobs of kids having a go at kids because they're white. It's wrong, full stop... But I resent the fact that, like, round here, things, everything happens, and it's a racist motive, right? Now, if I was black, right, and something happened to me, and I could get something out of it, I'd call it racist. I don't blame people, you know what I mean? But I resent the fact that, like, at the end of the day, that somewhere, somehow, someone has got it into their head, that we're all walking around here in fucking SS uniforms. You know what I mean? Because I truly resent that. I really really do. But it's, you know, I mean, everybody's in the same boat. It ain't a question of the colour of your skin, it's everybody's in the same boat.

Del and Kenny, single and divorced (father) brothers, thirties, unemployed/ employed, white, council tenants, Bermondsey

Most interestingly, this view is also strongly voiced by older-established minority respondents:

... first of all, right, police should be a police... The black people will not communicate or assist the black police. They ain't going to want nothing to do with them and

that's a fact… The black police will be more corrupt than the white corrupt ones
what we've got now and I'm a black man saying that.

> *Ronnie, male cohabitee (father), fifties, employed, Afro-Caribbean, homeowner,*
> *Battersea*

This respondent tells us about her sister-in-law, who is black, and who gets
very angry with positive discrimination:

Joan: What you find is a lot of people, specially people who have been brought
up in this country, get very irritated. My sister-in-law gets so angry with positive
discrimination.

She's a black woman?

Joan: Yeah, and she says: 'If I go, if I go to get something and I know they're only
giving it to me because I'm black, not because I deserve the job or cos I can do the
job, that makes me more angry because it's more discriminatory than if they don't
give me the job because I can't do it. I want that job because I can do the job and I'm
right for the job and they think I'm, I'm going to be a benefit to them'. Not, Oh you
can have the job because you're black. It's so patronising.

> *Val, fifties, unemployed, white, Battersea, and her daughter Joan,*
> *a homeless single mother*

Longer-standing white working-class residents, especially in traditional
areas of council housing like south-east London and Newham, are doubly
frustrated: on the one hand they see council property gradually disappearing
through right-to-buy, on the other they resent council property going to
'outsiders':

… the Council are not building any new property, they're getting rid of all their
property … So you've got a brand new place like this, you know, and there's sort of
hundreds and hundreds and hundreds of new houses being built and there's people,
can't speak a word of English, and these people are still stuck up in the tower block
or some really old block of flats round on Manchester Road or something. And you
can't, it's resentful, it makes them resentful, you can't blame them. You can't say 'Oh
yeah we're giving them because they deserve…'. They don't deserve it, they've only
just arrived in the country. They don't deserve it.

> *Gary and Dawn, married parents, forties, employed, white,*
> *housing association tenants, Bermondsey*

Gary and Dawn specifically accuse the housing authorities of racism in
reverse:

…it's wrong for me to be at the top of the list because I'm white because that's, that's racist, but it's all right for them to be in front of me because they're either black, lesbian, gay or Hindu or whatever. I mean that's something it's absolutely stupid. I mean like ... they're saying that...

Gary and Dawn, married parents, forties, employed, white,
housing association tenants, Bermondsey

Here, one problem at the time of our interviews was a policy of the Southwark borough council, which involved systematic emptying-out of council estates prior to modernisation coupled with mass movements of tenants from one part of the borough to another, and which seems to be deeply resented:

... in the last years it's changed because the Council they've done it as a purpose, they've decided that they'll make like 50 per cent of the Borough, well not of the Borough, 50 per cent of any new properties will be an ethnic thing, like which can be Irish, so, African, whatever, you know. So a lot of the people that lived here, they're getting the hump because they see places like this being built, we was lucky, you know, and they...

Gary and Dawn, married parents, forties, employed, white,
housing association tenants, Bermondsey

Significantly, these views were shared by a member of the black community who appeared equally apprehensive about the new arrivals:

... when I complain about these people moving from Peckham you cannot call me a racist because I am black and I'm complaining about black people moving from Peckham... I would love to move out.

Anonymous Respondent in Bermondsey Focus Group

It is also associated with a view that the authorities generally adopt a double standard for the new arrivals:

I think they should stop, you know, stop 'em coming in. I mean, it's, you most probably have seen 'em, you know they beg with their babies, but if I was on the street begging with my babies, I know my babies would be took off of me.

Liz, divorced mother, thirties, unemployed, white, council tenant, Bermondsey

A similar view comes from Battersea, from a respondent who accuses Lambeth council of the same reverse racism:

It's positive discrimination, which causes unrest between races. Now if you're homeless, if, if you've just come over from another country, you've come from a war torn area where you were in poverty, you were scared to let your children play outside in case they get blown up by a mine or something and you come to a country like England and they say: 'Here's an interpreter, this is what you can claim, here's temporary accommodation and then we'll have you into a flat within 6 months. Who in their right mind is going to turn round and say: 'Oh no I'd better not take it because it sounds like it's racist'. No one's going to say no… So it's not the people themselves that are being offered these things that are wrong, it's the government and the system that allows one group of people to take preferential treatment purely because of their race. They are the racists, that's not positive discrimination, that's racism, so when you have a bunch of people on a housing list, regardless of what colour, or creed or religion they are and they see people coming into the country and 4 weeks and getting not just what they deserve but more, and help, they're going to get upset by it, anybody would.

Val, fifties, unemployed, white, Battersea, and her daughter Joan,
a homeless single mother

The problem seems to be especially stark in East London, which has housed exceptionally large numbers of asylum-seekers:

I don't think they liked the idea of having them there, I think if you go to Ilford and go to Ilford station and see them all begging… Ilford shopping centre itself, em, and you see them with their mobile 'phones and their Reebok trainers and their, you know, and you think 'well, hold on a minute', you know, 'you've got all this stuff', you know, 'why should we give you money'.

Sheila, married mother, forties, white, homeowners, Gants Hill

We found a widespread belief that there is a new race relations industry, devoted to imposing political correctness not so much for the benefit of the client as to serve the interests of the bureaucrats themselves. Here are two representative views from white working-class residents in Bermondsey:

… if they turned round and said to me 'Would you like a £45,000 a year job and tell us, keep finding problems, you know, about racism, political correctness?' I could go and find out some bloody ridiculous ones but if it keeps me in work, you know, it's in my interests to stir up trouble.

Gary and Dawn, married parents, forties, employed, white,
housing association tenants, Bermondsey

I think … the Council, at the end of the day, once again, they can never actually get to the meat of the facts, because of all this political correctness shit. I mean, to fill out a form now, like I'm well appreciative people are from different cultures and countries, but you've gotta talk through 8 pages from, like, Bangladeshi to, like, Russian, before you can tell them, and then their first question is, 'Was you born in this country?' like, and all that. And it's like, you shouldn't even be giving me this form, mate, there should be a separate form to say … well, what do I need to do all that shit for, and why do you? You know what I mean?

> *Del and Kenny, single and divorced (father) brothers, thirties, unemployed/*
> *employed, white, council tenants, Bermondsey*

Racism in Reverse: Black against White, Black against Black

Several respondents told us about behaviour that they regarded as black racism. Del in Bermondsey had an incident up a back alley in Peckham:

I pulled into these flats, I went to the bottom, I turned round. And it's took me 5 or 10 minutes, because I'm worried about scraping up someone's car with this van. I've turned round, I'm coming back out of there, right, and there's a BMW, right, sounds like I'm making this up right, there's a BMW full of these coloured fellas, right? This geezer is looking at me like he wanted to kill me, and I'll be honest with you, I thought to myself, 'Well, if anyone around here is likely not to be going home, you're definitely a candidate, mate'. And he felt obliged to call me a few names and everything. All right, they was 5-handed in the motor, right. Now, bear in mind I'm coming down this side of the motor, they all leaned over like that, you know, and these people looked older than me. And I'm like, 'Ain't you got nothing fucking better to do? You're driving a top of the range BMW for fuck's sake, you ain't skint', you know what I mean? They've all got their gold on and everything. And I thought, 'I'm in the Bronx, ain't I? I've just walked into Harlem'. And they give it a bit of verbal, and I drove out of there, and I thought to myself, 'Well, that's racism, surely'. Do you know what I mean?

Yes, yes, well, racism comes both ways.

Yeah, but, like, not officially, not officially it doesn't.

> *Del and Kenny, single and divorced (father) brothers, thirties, unemployed/*
> *employed, white, council tenants, Bermondsey*

And this white woman in Brixton complained of a sense of being viewed with racist hostility:

I just don't feel as happy going into Brixton, and I travel there in my car most of the time I wouldn't be happy walking around the streets or anything… In Brixton, I feel that white people are a minority and not part of there so … it is difficult, really difficult…There's no way that I am racist, I love working in a multicultural school, but it feels quite hostile I feel, being here is totally totally different.

> *Lisa, widow, thirties, employed, housing association tenant, Battersea*

This view is shared by some in the black community:

... they say a white person can be racist against a black person because they in the minority, yeah, but a black person cannot be racist against a white person, just how stupid...

Tiffany, divorced mother, thirties, part-time employed, Jamaican-born
Afro-Caribbean, council tenant, Battersea

In South London we found more than one example of mixed marriages. And here complications could arise, as with this Bermondsey white mother and her black daughter, who is talking:

My mum's been ... when she lived on the Aylesbury, she was mugged twice, and that was by two black boys. She got mugged twice, two different occasions. And then in this area, she gets attacked by the ... they're not even big boys, they're little.

Children?

Yes. And she gets attacked by them. But it makes it quite hard really, especially, like, when they see my mum with me, and they look at her and think, 'Oh, she's ...' you know what I mean. It makes it quite hard sometimes.

Actually, I forgot to ask, because I don't know, is your mum black?

No, my mum's white! (*Laughs*)

Your mum's white! Yeah, yeah. So ... yeah, that can ... because people don't ...
I mean, this is what I've heard, it's like ... they get really upset when people mix
together ...

Yeah.

Janice, single mother, thirties, unemployed, British-born half-white, half-
Afro-Caribbean, council tenant, Bermondsey

The strangest evidence we found was that of inter-racial prejudice: black against black, brown against brown. Africans look down on Afro-Caribbeans; Afro-Caribbeans report prejudice as between one island and another; Africans express distrust of Indians; people from the Indian subcontinent report racial prejudice based on skin pigmentation; even Bangladeshis seek to differentiate themselves from other Bangladeshis. Here is Jamaican prejudice against Africans:

No, maybe back in the past, Jamaicans used to hate Africans.

The eighties?

They used to say 'African boo-boos' ... you lot are boo-boos.

And you Africans should go back to your country, but they're stupid because they should go back to their country.

Why do you say that?

Because we are all visitors really ... this is another man's country.

> *Kosey, single man, twenties, student, African, lives with family (council tenants),*
> *Peckham*

And here its reciprocal:

... we always at war, the West Indian and African, cos they saying that we haven't got any culture... And then this man said, this man said to me that ... this man literally got in my face, 'You ain't go no, you ain't got no language, you ain't got no culture, you ain't got nothing, you West Indians ain't got nothing ... my fore-parents sold your fore-parents into slavery'. And he, yeah, he said it was all about...

> *Tiffany, divorced mother, thirties, part-time employed, Jamaican-born Afro-*
> *Caribbean, council tenant, Battersea*

And here antipathy between the Caribbean islands:

I mean the Barbadians, Granadians, St. Lucian, Dominican, and a lot of them don't get along with Jamaicans because they think, they think that we think that we know too much, there's too much of us around - anyway, we're into everything.

> *Tiffany, divorced mother, thirties, part-time employed, Jamaican-born Afro-*
> *Caribbean, council tenant, Battersea*

We were told of similar conflicts between young men from the Indian subcontinent in Gants Hill:

There's a lot of rivalry between Sikhs, Muslims, Muslims and Hindus. You know, there've been gang fights and all sorts. These horrible young men.

> *Ajit, married mother, thirties, employed, Sikh, homeowner, Gants Hill*

This Nigerian mother expresses doubts about living in Hounslow, a community with a strong Indian presence:

Lots of Indians, I don't like it very much ... the ones that are nice are very nice, and the ones that aren't are terrible... I never expected things to get this way, and, Oh, I don't know, maybe I think I'm too good for this place... I'd rather be in Chiswick, I like Chiswick, I don't like it here, never did, never will do, don't know, there's lots of things.

> *Adeola, divorced mother, thirties, employed, Nigerian, housing association tenant,*
> *Heston*

And several respondents from the Indian subcontinent suggested to us that there are racial distinctions, subtle and less subtle, among their communities:

Asian community is very bad because Asian, Asian community don't like Asian each other, that is a problem.

    Sandhya, married mother, forties, part-time employed, Indian, homeowner, Heston

It's not just white children then that are being difficult?

No, it's other Asian kids who are fairer skinned. I mean culturally, in our culture, you know, white skin is preferred.

        Ajit, married mother, thirties, employed, Sikh, homeowner, Gants Hill

Some Asian Londoners, it was suggested, identify themselves as English in order to distinguish themselves from others in their community, while others condemned them as unrealistic:

… you find that sometimes in the Asian community there are some people that are even against their own people sometimes and they think that they will be respected more by being nicer to an English guy or, you know, which is so ignorant because they'll never be, I mean you can be westernised but you'll never be English, you'll always be what you are, you know.

    Faizah, married mother, thirties, employed, Malaysian parents, homeowner, Heston

And such reactions caused some people to find themselves in a kind of cultural void, as Ajit recorded in Chapter 7:

We're in a weird situation where … I mean we don't know what white people round here think of us, but we know that our family think we've become white… So we can't win really. We're not white enough for the white people. We're not Asian enough for the Asian people.

        Ajit, married mother, thirties, employed, Sikh, homeowner, Gants Hill

Most interesting of all, perhaps, was this reaction of a middle-class Bangladeshi mother in Gants Hill to her own compatriots back in the Brick Lane area of Whitechapel:

I wouldn't like it to be like a ghetto or you know, it's alright, so far it's alright, but I don't like East London that's just a ghetto. And they actually misrepresent Bangladesh they call themselves Bangladeshi but they don't represent the whole of Bangladesh… It's a different dialect and they're the ones who don't like to progress in life um, because of their parents you know mainly they were originally from the villages and living in extended families.

        Shirin, married mother, thirties, Bangladeshi, homeowner, Gants Hill

Small wonder, then, that people from ethnic communities report real confusion and conflict in their everyday lives:

My neighbour for instance Corrina, she used to say to me that you would get people just coming and allowing their children to go and mess on the landing, I don't want to name anyone, but once you pulled them over about it they were not too happy. It could be a case of that type of thing is acceptable to them, and they don't care but here is a different story … so umm … in general I would just say that as for that question I haven't seen any real segregation.

Rafi, married father, thirties, employed, British-born Afro-Caribbean, council tenant,
Peckham

These confusions extend widely, above all in attitudes to new immigrants:

I had to sit through a conversation with Vandit's aunt, which was, these people are coming over here, taking our jobs and so on. I was thinking, hang on a minute, didn't people say the same thing about you 20 years ago. Have you forgotten all that?

Ajit, married mother, thirties, employed, Sikh, homeowner, Gants Hill

The same middle-class Sikh respondent, again:

We were at my sister's place once when she had a friend round who used to be a Communist, she says, and worked in the homeless unit in Newham and experienced so much of the refugees coming in for a council house that she's just gone full circle and doesn't believe a word of it anymore. And she's just tarred everybody with the same brush… You just can't say … every case is different and has to be judged on its merits. We were in the minority and there was about ten of them screaming us down, so we just said, okay, and we shut up.

Ajit, married mother, thirties, employed, Sikh, homeowner, Gants Hill

The same self-doubts about identity come from a professional woman, originally from St Lucia, who complains that she is not understood by fellow Afro-Caribbeans:

I think there is a general stereotype within culture, when I say within culture, not necessarily people from St Lucia because I hardly see any, or black people, there are a kind of stereotype as to how you should behave or how should you speak and so on, but I came from an island, I behave just the way, in a sense that I have integrated here with the sentiments that I carry from there here.

So within … from other members of the black people you have experienced prejudice because you've married a white man, because…

Because I'm educated, because…

Because you've got a certain standard of living?

Yeah.

> *Sharmaine, married mother, fifties, employed, Afro-Caribbean, homeowner,*
> *Gants Hill*

Tiffany, a young black woman in Battersea, complains that both blacks and whites tend to segregate themselves and to identify either with one community or the other:

> … my friend, Wendy here, she's white, yeah, and, but if we go out anywhere, I go to the pub together, friends or whatever, you see the white people will stay together and the black people will stay together… But then, like most of the white people I know that lives around here, they're married to either, they're black, they go out with black, yeah, actually majority of the white people I know around here is with black men … there's not a black or a white, when a black person or white person actually gets together, yeah, there is not, there's not, one of them always lose their, like, as I say, lose their identity. One of them either becomes white, or the other one becomes black, they don't mix the two together, which is quite silly, because that's the whole purpose of going out with each other, ain't it, cos one is white and one is black or whatever, but they don't, they cross over, which means one of them always go the other way, one go the other way, totally.
>
> *Tiffany, divorced mother, thirties, part-time employed, Jamaican-born*
> *Afro-Caribbean, council tenant, Battersea*

The same kind of voluntary segregation seems to occur at weekends when, as Tiffany told us in Chapter 2, the whites all seem to disappear from Battersea:

> … there's things going on in the park tomorrow and you'll see all the black people going over there…

Really, and not the white people? What the white people do?

I don't know, they go out, they go away, they go camping, go somewhere… Yeah, I think they feel threatened by so much black people together. Which is quite silly.

> *Tiffany, divorced mother, thirties, part-time employed, Jamaican-born*
> *Afro-Caribbean, council tenant, Battersea*

And she suggests that in the black community there is a reverse prejudice among the black community, against black women who go out with white men:

> Now I'll tell you a secret … they say a white girl will give them what they want, give them anything they ask for … whereas a West Indian woman would moan and groan

... say, 'You stay out late, where have you been?' and whatever, make a big fuss about it... Yeah ... a white man will tell you that he's afraid to ask the black woman out because she will say no ... but you don't get many black women that goes that way, with a white guy... And it's harder cos a lot of black guys will accept, accept black guys going out with white girls but they don't accept their sisters going out with a white guy.

Tiffany, divorced mother, thirties, part-time employed, Jamaican-born Afro-Caribbean, council tenant, Battersea

But conversely, in African society, it appears that there is a prejudice against black men who date white women:

Lots of African people don't like their, especially their sons, dating white women. They would like them to marry an African ... that's how it is. Unfortunately, that is how it is.

But they accept you?

Yeah, because he loves me, that's all, you know! So that's all that matters. But, if the truth be known, I think she would prefer it if I was of ... you know.

Megan, single mother, mid teens, unemployed, white, lives with the family of the father of her child (council tenant), Battersea

There is a special challenge for the Asian, above all Bangladeshi, communities of East London, where an older conservative generation has difficulty in coming to terms with the mores of the host community which their own children are adopting:

... there really is a problem ... so many of them, even the Asian girls, running away from home, committing suicide... In this area, yeah, there's a lot of them. In Newham Hospital, my daughter's got a part-time job there, she was telling me that lots of them are Asian girls, they just want to kill themselves ... yeah... Because part of change of environment is like the things that you never used to do in your country ... you come to this country and you are allowed to do them, and it just tips your head, you feel like I can be an adult before the age ... I can do what I want. I think change of environment has got a lot of impact into children's lives, especially for black people... I don't think it is a good idea if you're living in a country like this one where the children are given freedom of choice ... you come and sort of give them some little restriction, it's just not ... it doesn't work.

Dafina, single mother, forties, part-time employed/student, African, housing association tenant, Upton Park

This especially affects Asian families with a Muslim background, where the clash of generations and of mores could be exceptionally severe. But, we were told by a white woman in Battersea with mixed-race children, there were almost equally severe strains between Afro-Caribbean generations:

Joan: ... what a lot of Asian families are finding it so hard because their family is being eroded because, London especially, and England it separates, you move away, you don't have that, that community atmosphere where your mum lived across the road and your grandma lived down there and you know your family was all around you. Now the Asians came from that kind of community and brought it with them but after the second or third generation, that started to be eroded so they're finding the same problems that the Jamaicans and black people found when they first came over and their children and grandchildren started behaving differently. Cos you find, you find that Jamaican families, of mum's age, they're Victorian, very English attitude and they, they cannot understand the attitude, they can't understand the attitude of grandchildren any more than the white families can understand or the Asian. It's a problem with age, it's a problem with culture, it's a problem with the way, the way the world's going at the moment and I think it happens in every city, every built-up city.

Val, fifties, unemployed, white, Battersea, and her daughter Joan,
a homeless single mother

Race and Class

Race discrimination is less evident then than we thought at first – but still evident, even virulently, in some places. Our strong sense is that it is a matter of culture. In the melting-pots like Battersea where young people come together on a basis of equality and shared lifestyles, race is no longer a factor. In Bermondsey, as in Battersea long ago, where a white working class finds itself economically and socially and culturally beleaguered, it is a very different matter. Many poorer white people appear to be affected by a form of discrimination which is directed against them on the basis of the way they dress, their 'class', or the way they speak. It is an unarticulated, veiled form of discrimination but none the less insidious. And it can affect white and black working-class people alike. That single white mother in Battersea told us:

Joan: I find the most discrimination you get nowadays is class, class discrimination. It matters not whether you're black or white, it depends on what car you drive, where you live, whether you've got the right trainers on, that dictates how people treat you... Everybody, schools, Council, neighbours, anyone really, they will, they will judge you according to what they see and if you don't display your poverty, people don't really understand that you, you're still in the same sort of situation as the person who looks poor, you just don't show it, so you're penalised for it. How dare you be happy and poor at the same time, we can't have that.

Val, fifties, unemployed, white, Battersea, and her daughter Joan,
a homeless single mother

And this is confirmed by the experience of Barry, a middle-aged white man, in trying to get a sales job:

Have you ever experienced any form of discrimination in getting work or anything like that?

Yeah. Long hair and an earring.

Really?

I went for a job as a car salesman and the owner had long hair and I walked in in my suit and he swore at me and said 'Your hair's too f'king long, get out'. [*Laughs*] … no, just … wouldn't entertain me. And … his loss.

> Barry, married man, forties, employed, white, council tenant, Battersea

And recall the middle-aged African woman on the other side of London, in Newham, who suffered a huge loss of status when she had left her native Nigeria and had had to fight her way up through education to a professional position in a London. Asked in Chapter 4 how she saw herself in terms of class, she gave this surprising reply:

As low really, as very low-class.

Why?

Because of the way I am.

In what way, what about the way you are?

Well language for a start … even sometimes some black people classify each other, some people, you know, language, and if you can't speak fluent or if you can't do … you know, the lifestyle like this, you know, for that social class, and then you … maybe sometimes I push myself to the lower class, because you find that that's where you feel safe … you know, that's where I belong, that's where this is comfortable.

> Dafina, single mother, forties, part-time employed/student, African, housing association tenant, Upton Park

Race, Class and Culture in Contemporary London

Racial differences, then, play a huge role in London. In one of the most multi-ethnic, multi-cultural places on earth, this is hardly surprising. But what does prove really surprising is the complexity. There are prejudices all over: of one non-white group against another, of Afro-Caribbeans against Africans, of Caribbeans from one island or island group against another. There appears to be anti-white feeling on the part of some black people, especially against those who 'marry out'. And there is certainly evidence of the old-fashioned racism, of whites against non-white races.

But viewed more closely, even this becomes complex. A lot of it concerns children and schools, and it proves to be less racial than cultural: parents are worried that the traditional European (or British) culture is being overlain and even overwhelmed by other cultures, and they are concerned to maintain not all-white schools but culturally-balanced schools. They positively want their children to go to schools that are ethnically and (still more) culturally mixed, but they worry that this quality can be quickly eroded if the school fills up with children from one culture or religion. Paradoxically, though their attitude may seem superficially racist, in fact it is the opposite.

Of course, old-fashioned white racism survives. But interestingly, it does so most evidently in certain working-class enclaves in east and south-east London. (It may exist in similar enclaves in other parts of London, where we did not interview.) These areas have suffered more than most from the huge economic changes that have swept London since the late 1960s. They were the places with concentrated blue-collar employment in docks or factories, which simply disappeared in the great economic transformation of the 1970s and 1980s, leaving huge communities faced with long-term structural unemployment and – even more problematically in its long-term implications – psychological difficulties among the children in adjusting to the demands of the new post-industrial advanced-service economy. Many of them also happened to be quite isolated communities, sometimes geographically, certainly psychologically, with a strong sense of internal solidarity born of long years of hardship and working-class struggle for better pay and conditions: they were and are more like factory towns than integral parts of a great metropolis. So it becomes more understandable that they should react to any change, whether the arrival of new racial groups or the onward march of the gentrifiers, with resentment and hostility.

Many, even most parts of London were never like that; they were part of a constant process of dynamic change, as new arrivals modified the ethnic or religious or cultural mix. Gants Hill, where today Bengalis follow in the footsteps of Jews in their progress from the Whitechapel ghetto to the leafy suburbs, is the archetype of such a London place. And in turn new groups arrive to take their place in melting-pots and transit centres old and new. London has accommodated such changes before, not always without trouble to be sure, but in the long run successfully. The evidence is that it will continue to do so.

Multicultural groceries

© Bill Knight

School's out   © Bill Knight

Part Four

London Futures

In this final section, we first asked Londoners about their future and the future of their city. In particular, we wanted to discover whether they feel they have any influence over the course of events. We asked about political involvement and political apathy. We find that most people are not involved, nor do they want to get involved; at most, they are prepared to vote. They give various reasons, most commonly lack of time. Yet many are involved in local activities, often around their children. And a few have taken action to change their local world.

Finally, we bring together the book's main conclusions, asking first what all these London lives seem to have in common, and then how they may differ significantly from one area of London to another.

Click for yes

Chapter Fifteen

Changing the World

Londoners, we found, grumble a lot about things they dislike in their local area. But they prove strangely reluctant to do very much to put them to rights. They tend to do so only when they are confronted with some threat: something that, to a greater or lesser degree, affects their current quality of life and that they want to see removed, or – conversely – some threat of change in their local environment which they don't like and want to stop happening. Then, they may act – and it seems that people on council estates tend to do so, through tenants' and residents' associations, more than other people. But other than that, we did not find enough evidence to show whether some kinds of Londoners were more prone to action than others, whether because of where they lived or because of income levels, or for some other cause. If they do act, unhappily, it seems that often they end up disillusioned.

The Non-Participants

Very many respondents, like Rob in Eltham, simply said that they were not involved at all. But Rob said this was because he had never been asked:

Thinking about involvement in like organisations, are you a member of any kind of groups or organisations at all?

No.

Is there things like residents' associations around here, neighbourhood watch?

Yeah, there is. I'm not involved with it at all.

Why not?

No. Not because I'm not interested, but I've never been asked to become involved.

Do you think if you were asked, it would be something that you would do?

Yeah I think it is. And you've got to know it exists.

> *Rob, married father, forties, employed, white, homeowner, Eltham*

Others, like Sewa in Heston, did not even offer excuses:

Are you actually, sort of, involved in any, sort of, community type things as well, or anything like that ... churches or sports or anything like that?

(*Laughing*) No. No. No. Sorry.

It's okay. You don't have be!

(*Laughing*) I do nothing for my community. I'm sorry.

> *Sewa, single woman, twenties, employed, Sikh, homeowners*
> *(living at home), Heston*

And similarly with Jill in Greenhithe:

Doesn't interest me really. I suppose because we just, I mean, we go to work, we come home, we go out for a meal. I don't seem to need it, which is not a good thing because I think you always need something outside work and family, but no. I'm not.

So even things like, is there like residents' associations and neighbourhood watch?

No. There isn't a neighbourhood watch around here. There must be ... there is a residents' association. And no I don't belong to it.

> *Jill, married woman, fifties, self-employed, white, homeowner, Greenhithe*

Asked about his local neighbourhood watch scheme, Amir in Battersea replied:

We don't believe in all that, yeah. We don't believe in all that ... this neighbourhood watch it's like run by, they, they don't get you involved you know, they do not explain to you, this is what's going on, they just want your signature and that's it, you know what I mean. And if you happen to be in a discussion with them, you are nothing, you know, you don't matter that much. They listen to each other and all that ... you know very well what they think of you and then it's, well, I'll ... get there and be disappointed so I might as well not get there first, you know.

> *Amir, single father, forties, employed, African, council tenant, Battersea.*

This young Reading resident clearly found local affairs boring:

...I mean we've even got a sign on a door saying no free papers. So, but things like you get clogged up, there's so much bloody freebie crap and it is crap a lot of it, though I don't buy the local newspaper because it's just full of things like, you know, I don't know it's really sort of like, you know, a shopping trolley stolen and things like that, it's like oh.

Dionne, female cohabitee, twenties, employed, British-born Afro-Caribbean, private tenant, Newtown, Reading

But another living not far away, somewhat older and certainly more involved, saw that his sole involvement in the political process was his vote:

… well … do I have a voice? Well, I guess I can vote for someone else, but would they be any better than the people we've got? I think if you make the effort, you can get to know the people that are in the Council. If you make the effort. I suppose I could go to council meetings if I wanted to, but I don't have the time, really. I see my influence in either voting for them or not voting for them. That's something I always do. You know, I always do vote.

Paul, married man, thirties, employed, white, homeowner, Newtown, Reading

That was a fairly common reaction. But some went further: they said they voted, but they were cynical about its usefulness:

Always take part in elections. Always vote.

Do you think you have influence over what happens?

Not really, no. Anybody that says that they do is conning.

Ranjit, married father, fifties, employed, Sikh, homeowner, Gants Hill

The same reaction came in less vehement fashion from a voter in Greenhithe, who thought that her local MPs could do little or nothing to influence a development process that was well-nigh inevitable:

I think you try don't you? You've got the local MPs. We've got about two or three independent MPs, sort of independent that you can try and follow, who are all for Greenhithe … keeping Greenhithe as a village, but they do have a say to a certain extent, but I think it's already taken care of.

Karen, married mother, thirties, part-time employed, white, homeowner, Greenhithe

Many people said in various ways that they simply didn't have the time to bother getting more actively involved – even in neighbourhood activities centred on a housing estate or school. They quoted long, sometimes very long, hours at work:

… the housing association came round and surveyed and they actually said you know

'Your husband's was put forward to say he'd be a really good person run it', but it ... you know we didn't have the time to actually, it would of been nice but he's got like a 24 hour job and so you know you ...

> *Theresa, married mother, forties, part-time employed, white,*
> *housing association tenant, Bermondsey*

Unfortunately not. Again because we both work. I mean I, I, normally I work from nine 'til half past five but recently I've been finishing, I never finish work before 6.30 and usually I'm home 7.30, you know, I finish 7.30, 8 O'clock sometimes, so it's just so time consuming, you know, it would be nice if I could afford to work part time and do other things, you know, maybe join some clubs or help, I'd love to be able to help, find out if there's anyone in the area that needs their shopping done and things like that, you know, because I'm sure there's some old people that find it difficult, in the winters, to shop, and we've got cars and, you know, that would be great if we could do something like that for someone. The children are members of scouts, in fact this weekend they have a family camping thing, so that's the first time we're gonna attend one of these, go camping. [*Laughs*]

> *Faizah, married mother, thirties, employed, Malaysian parents, homeowner, Heston*

I don't really have the time for them, I really don't have the time. Like, with two kids and a husband, and working ... it's ... hard. It is quite difficult. I mean, I mean, you know, like, over the school, if they ask for stuff to be sent in, and all stuff like that, I'll always contribute, but it's the time factor, you know, when they say, 'We want 3 hours of your time', it's ... how difficult for me and you try to ... it's crazy! It's only because they've been told off tonight, they're upstairs, so we've got a few minutes!

> *Dawn, married mother, thirties, employed, white, council tenant, Bermondsey*

This could be further complicated by irregular patterns of work, such as shift work, which made it impossible to attend evening meetings on a regular basis:

I work shifts like you know, I work one week 2.30 to 10.30 and nights 10.30 to 6.30 in the morning or if you start half six to half two although I might have time, have time on my hands, it's at different times like you know, it's not like working er, er the same shift or same pattern and you would have a certain amount of time er at set times which I don't... I like to er do some voluntary work which I don't have time for it, although I have time for it, but it's just not at the right times, preferably if I had er time in the evenings I would like to help out a couple of hours a day like you know, driving taking the elderly people out or whatever.

> *Ranjit, married father, fifties, employed, Sikh, homeowner, Gants Hill*

One Battersea respondent had actually tried to do it, but conflicting pressures of work had forced him to give it up:

So I was there and then I used to be the chair of the leaseholders, so you get a chance to go to the council meeting at night and also I was on the committee for the estate, you know but then it was getting too much. As you can see I started bringing work home and rubbish, you know and it started piling on me. Some nights I'm working to 11 O'clock, you know so I says no, no I don't, you know. So I had to give up a lot of it, you know.

Ronnie, male cohabitee (father), fifties, employed, Afro-Caribbean, homeowner,
Battersea

Betty in Heston cited another kind of time pressure: from domestic duties. For her, home and children came first:

No, no. Because I think I would either be, I'd have to be 100 per cent, I know it'd take over my life, and my family's the most important thing in my life and I wouldn't want anything to change that.

Betty, married mother, fifties, employed, white, homeowner, Heston

Yet others had serious health problems:

… I got ill myself and I, I, I certainly couldn't join anything or belong to anything. Although I look healthy but it's terminal and I take, have chemotherapy quite frequently and that makes you very tired, I expect you know and I couldn't take on any sort of charity or anything like that. That was the sort of thing I'd looked forward to doing if I had a retirement flat, you know, during, most, most of them have activities that you can join in, you know, theatre groups and that sort of thing which I would have liked but, I can't do that now.

Margery, widowed stepmother, sixties, retired, white Australian, homeowner,
Earley, Reading

And sheer inability, or unwillingness, to contribute time might prove fatal to an activity, such as a local voluntary organisation, that depended critically on such input:

Are there any residents' associations in this area, that kind of thing?

… There was one next door but I think … I started finding it time consuming so if there is still one, then it's run by probably people that have got a lot more time than perhaps the rest of us don't get involved.

James, divorced man, twenties, employed, white, homeowner, Greenhithe

Reasons for Detachment: No Problem, No Hope

When we probed more deeply into the kinds of local issues that might involve people, we found a strange paradox. For many, there was no need to get involved because they felt there was nothing to arouse their passionate concern. Scott in Battersea seems to have been one of the apathetic majority, because he did not feel sufficiently dissatisfied with anything in his neighbourhood:

Oh, there's always the opportunity to write to a councillor, or get on to the tenants' association. If I really felt where I am living was deteriorating, you know, really badly, say if I kept coming across people doing, or dealing drugs on the stairs, if I kept walking into people doing that, then I would feel, perhaps, I was in a … you know, a harmful situation to my person. So I would make something of that. But, as yet, it hasn't got to that stage.

Scott, single man, forties, unemployed, white, council tenant, Battersea

Likewise, one Greenhithe respondent, asked whether she would be interested in any form of local involvement, realistically replied:

I don't know … they normally start for a reason don't they, you know, and it depends what the reason is… If I feel strongly about an issue, then yeah I'd be at the start of it, but I don't think there is a big issue in this area is there at the moment?

Zoe, married woman, twenties, employed, white, homeowner, Eltham

The same was reported in inner east Reading:

There's a local network, that's down, that's the sort of situated around the canal, cos they had a big thing about sort of getting the bridge over to Tescos fixed and they had a whole thing about a big building thing being built next to the gas works, on the other side of the river. And that, and they had a, they were quite strong about that actually but again they were sort of done down by local apathy, I have to say it was like a few residents. But they had a newsletter and they did lobby the Council…

Dionne, female cohabitee, twenties, employed, British-born Afro-Caribbean,
private tenant, Newtown, Reading

Yet some others were very angry indeed about what they saw as the failings of their local council, but had become disillusioned about the possibility of changing it. Betty in Heston, again:

I complain about a lot all the time, but I try not to any more because it does, they don't do anything, doesn't change, it just upsets you and you get, you know, over involved in things. When on the corner here, somebody's built like a shack on the back of their house, and it's so ugly, and there's no way they could have got planning permission for it, or they just, round the corner they've just taken out the kerb stones and they just drive across, they've taken out the kerb stones and put a bit of old tarmac down themselves, to make like a drive across, well, we paid 600 quid for ours. They're allowed to do it and get away with it, you know, and it's just, so you moan, you say to them 'Well, how did they get planning permission for that?' and the only plans I can get for my house, I've got to have it 3 foot back and this, that and they come and look in the hole and, and they've got permission, no. You know, it's all wrong, all wrong.

Betty, married mother, fifties, employed, white, homeowner, Heston

She also found her local council services, from Hounslow, very poor:

You phone the civic centre, you're put on hold for 15 minutes, and you get through to someone who's actually not their department, and then they take a message and say they'll get someone to call you back within 3 working days, and a fortnight later, someone who doesn't know what you phoned about in the first place leaves a message on your answerphone while you're out, and then you call back and they say 'Oh sorry, what was that about?' And then you tell them, and they say 'Oh it's not my department, I'll pass it on'. You never ever get to speak to anyone who cares or can do anything.

Betty, married mother, fifties, employed, white, homeowner, Heston

She felt that it was useless to try to act, because of local apathy: people simply could not be bothered to vote in local elections:

… you get to a point where you don't care any more, cos people have got no respect, and friends, not a friend of ours, my daughter's friend at school, her father fought in the last local election, as an independent, and everything he said was absolutely right, yes, and I went round delivering leaflets, knocking on doors, doing everything what was properly and my husband for one hour on election night stood round the school at Hounslow Heath, wearing his, this man's rosette, and ticking off names you know, on a bit of paper, and he said that he didn't see more than a dozen people he knows go in there to vote and he wasn't just there the hour, it was like an hour before talking, an hour afterwards, so he was there about three hours, and he didn't see more than about twelve people he knows, knew, go into vote, so he said 'It can't ever be any different cos people don't bother any more', if you don't vote, you're not gonna change nothing are you. You don't change, the only way of changing what's there is by voting differently and bringing in someone else … albeit, but it doesn't, it doesn't change, people don't bother any more, we've gone past it in Hounslow.

Betty, married mother, fifties, employed, white, homeowner, Heston

But we found occasional people who were passionately concerned about a single local issue that affected their lives or those of their children. Deidree in Greenhithe felt strongly about Kent's selective system of education, which retains grammar schools:

I wish we had fair education. You're supposed to be able to choose for your kids, you know. You can't. Not unless you can afford it. It's keep the poor in their place. Don't let them rise above their selves, you know. Keep them down, keep them down, keep them down. It's my favourite subject at the moment actually.

So what did you think of the school there then?

I think that school down there's crap actually … if you're clever, you're fine. But if you're not, if you're not that bright, they don't want to know. They're not going to rise above nothing. They're not going to come out of the woodwork … if you're bright … but if you're much slower than the others, no. I mean, when I went to school, we was sort of roughly the same, you know. And it wasn't until recently, say the past 5 years or so, I've been trying to get into this business, otherwise how many people … not so much of our generation, but of my kids' generation, my elder ones, have left school unable to read or write, you know… Couldn't see it says M40 to Oxford. Then we asked around. There's so many people who can't read and write. It should be the basic right of everyone in this country… I love reading, so you know…

Deidree, married mother, fifties, employed, white, council tenant, Greenhithe

Consultation and Cynicism

People, especially those who lived in areas of rapid change like Greenhithe, told us that their local council often consulted them. Some tended to be cynical about the process and the outcome; others were more positive:

No. No. I've got too many… Can't commit myself to any more. But I don't think really, as a resident, I don't think you have a lot of say in what goes on. I think it's all done up at the council at that level. They might do polls or questionnaires, you know, through the door. I've just got one back about the hospital from the Liberal party, the Liberal Democrats. But then what are they going to do with that information?

Will you fill that in? Is that something you feel is worth filling in?

I will fill it in, yeah. I've had a quick read of the paper … the questions and that. So yeah, I will fill that in. But I don't really feel … I don't think … no. I don't think you have a lot of say. I think it's all decided for you. I mean I wouldn't know if I could go along to a council meeting or not. Nobody actually tells you whether you're invited or, you know.

… you mentioned the land next door … have you taken action…?

Well, we used to have inside information because the gentleman who lived next door was a councillor, so he used to let us know what was going on. But since then, we just rely on the residents' association newsletters and things. I mean I suppose I could ring the Council up and sort of ask, but then at the back of my mind also, if I keep pestering and asking, what will they do with it, you know? Am I going to push something that I don't really want to be there.

Emma, married mother, forties, employed, white, homeowner, Greenhithe

Rob in Eltham was more optimistic about the force of public opinion:

Think about like how you can influence them, whoever they are, how much influence do you think that you have?

Zero.

Really? OK. So, you've got no sense of having any kind of power or influence over what goes on?

… none. No, tell a lie. We've had questionnaires from the Council asking similar questions what you're asking. I suppose, you know, the fact that they've bothered to send questionnaires, they're interested in the tenants in the area, what their point of view is. To get some sort of idea what needs to be done.

Is that something that you bothered to fill in?

Yeah, it was. Again it's similar questions what you've been asking, you know. You know, is there a drug problem in the area, is there vandalism, you know, etc. Just tick boxes asking your point of view. I suppose they, you know, see what everyone says and then come to some decision what they're going to do about it, you know.

So you felt it was worth kind of filling that in?

Oh yeah.

So do you think it will have any impact?

Yeah, I think it could do. Because if, you know, enough people the questionnaires in, they've got some idea what generally worries people and what they feel … people in the area. It seems commonsense that they'll come to some decisions that work for the majority of the people.

Rob, married father, forties, employed, white, homeowner, Eltham

Some felt they were too new to their area, like Rochelle in Reading:

…I want to get more involved in the Council … and what's going on, but we haven't lived here that long, it's only been since November, so we're just sort of getting to grips with this … and I wasn't actually entitled to vote this time round because of moving house and I wasn't on the Electoral Register, so I missed out on that as well, which I was annoyed about. So, yeah, I mean, we'd both like to … but because we haven't lived here that long, it's something that's still got to happen.

Rochelle, female cohabitee, twenties, employed, white Australian, homeowner, Newtown, Reading

Another young Reading resident felt that her local Labour Party newsletter connected her to her local neighbourhood:

It's, it does, you know, a very minor level, but it says things like, you know, actually we're going to be installing bollards in this road next week, or we're going to deal with this parking problem, or there's a … next week or, just, it makes you feel more, you know, it makes me feel more plumbed in to what's going around me. In a way that I think it's sometimes hard as a single person living in a flat that doesn't come from the area to be, plumbed in, yeah, yeah.

Kate, single woman, thirties, employed, white, private tenant, Newtown, Reading

Very often, people seemed to have only a vague idea of who exactly was consulting them at any given time – whether it was the Council, a political party, or maybe some interest group:

I mean at the moment there's a … there's two particular things I know of, there's a racecourse that they want to build at Fairlop and over the top of the night club *Faces* they wanted to build … em, self-contained flats, basically for the illegal immigrants, and there was an uproar about that, and also about the racecourse … a lot of people signed petitions, went to the Council and that, I didn't have anything to do with that, but…

Did they come round and…?

We had letters … it must have been through the Council, I presume, because the letters are on County paper, or … you know, it was on headed paper…

What, saying 'come in to – come to a public meeting about…'?

Yes.

Aha … and who was organising the petitions? You don't know…?

I presume it's residents.

Right … did they come round to you?

Em, no, I believe that the sweet shop along the road had a … that you could sign.

You could go in and sign?

Em, but with the racecourse, they actually sent out questionnaires to all of the families around that sort of area, and they were asked whether they thought it was a good idea or a bad idea, and what they felt it should be made into if it wasn't a racecourse, and I believe that they've now decided that it's not going to become a racecourse now.

Sheila, married mother, forties, white, homeowners, Gants Hill

Emily in Greenhithe explained that she found a message from:

... Dartford Council inviting you to go along and say what you want done with Greenhithe. That I think is a very good thing. One of them's already gone. The dates are coming up very soon.

And was this stimulated through the residents association or was this...?

I don't know. It was one of the things ... when we came back from our holiday, it was one of the things that was on the floor with all ... no, it wasn't on the floor, it was on the worktop because mum had been in and gathered up the post. So when it actually came ... but at least they're inviting you to go along and partake and put your oar in.

Emily, married mother, fifties, employed, white, homeowner, Greenhithe

But we found widespread cynicism: meetings could take place, people could be consulted, but at the end of the day they were not heard:

But the people, I mean some time if they got a meeting on the estate and things people, their views is not taken on board, you know.

Do you think that's worse than it was or it's just always been like that?

It's, has always been like that, has always been like that... At local level you might get something started on that, but then after a while before ... it just fade away.

Ronnie, male cohabitee (father), fifties, employed, Afro-Caribbean, homeowner, Battersea

The same sentiment came from Donald in Heston:

... they're not, people are not listening to us any more, to the actual work force, whatever you want to call it, or the people of the Borough, we're not listened to, and unfortunately that's gonna cause problems later on in life, without any doubt.

Donald, married father, fifties, employed, white, homeowner, Heston

Getting Involved

At the most basic level, very often people get extensively involved very locally with voluntary activities like Guides or Brownies, running playgroups and the like. Here is Ronnie in Battersea:

And that catered for people with mental problems, it's called, it used to be called a family centre. So I was the chair there, I've been there for about 17 years, 12, 17 years, I've been the secretary there, treasurer and the chair and also I work, I used to work in there. So I used to drive for them sometimes, you go trips to the seaside, whatever.

Ronnie, male cohabitee (father), fifties, employed, Afro-Caribbean, homeowner, Battersea

This is particularly true, for obvious reasons, of mothers. Here Sally in Gants Hill:

And then when I got divorced, things changed yet again … it was basically finding some single friends, because all my other friends were married, and that was very hard. But at the same, roughly at the same time, my son started football… Um, well yeah. I've got quite involved in the football. I'm now secretary of the club. Um, and I got quite involved and, yes. I mean it was literally going to watch the kids play football, standing chatting and that's how it sort of happened…

Sally, divorced mother, forties, employed, white Jewish, homeowner, Gants Hill

…I've got two big girls, the ones who live ten doors away. The elder one [her stepdaughter] went to all the local things, nursery, toddler group, nursery school, local primary school Maiden Earley school and is now at college doing PE. She's very heavily engaged in Brownies and Guides and all that sort of thing. Her mother ran the nursery school group, playgroup so you can't walk 10 yards along the road with them without people hailing them and knowing them, you know, from grandparents to little tiny children.

Margery, widowed stepmother, sixties, retired, white Australian, homeowner, Earley,
Reading

Emma in Greenhithe tells the same story.:

Joanne was a Brownie. They were short of a leader and they're were going to close the pack down. So I said, Oh I don't mind coming along, but I do have a younger one. That's alright, bring her along. And that was it. They then … I didn't go in as a helper. They then said, Oh you're the Brown Owl. So, they were obviously looking for somebody to take it over and being me, I couldn't say no. And it just went from there really.

Emma, married mother, forties, employed, white, homeowner, Greenhithe

But it is a big step to move beyond that kind of casual voluntary activity, to forming an organisation that would promote change. In Gants Hill, people are trying to form a local association to improve the quality of their area. It was not clear how effective it is going to be:

What things do you think you could do to improve the area?

Oh God … we set up … a little association for the road in fact, because I think that they ought to have some ramps or something like that, to stop this cars from going so … speeding up and all that. I've seen the change even since I came, there are young children around and if you're pulling out you know, it's very difficult there and dangerous. So we've said something like that to improve that side of things and people dropping litter and things like that and the noise, but I think it's a difficult task but the association has been set and is ... the little bit down Perry Farm we meet there every 3 months and the Council has come to sit on that.

And is it like a neighbourhood association?

A neighbourhood thing, you know talking about you know, keeping ... and we're talking about buying some trees 'cause I say 'How can you have houses no trees...'. I know I've got a tree in front, I've got a nice oak tree in front of the house, I'm lucky, but it would be nice to have trees ... it's so dry. So we're thinking about that and trying to do this sort of improvement.

Sharmaine, married mother, fifties, employed, Afro-Caribbean, homeowner,
Gants Hill

When they did challenge the Council it was mainly owners who came on board:

Well, I have to say that it was mainly the kind of owners, you know, like we own this building and some of the flats are owned by people who tend ... like there's one couple who've been there right from the start, they're two blokes, and he's actually a market ... a gardener, so he was very interested in the environment, he was, they were exceptional, I think, in taking a kind of personal interest in the environment. Mostly it's quite difficult to arouse people's ... cos they're going to work and they come back and they go into their flats and they look at the river ... a big ship, they look at the river and er...

Francesca, married mother, forties, self-employed, white, homeowner, Bermondsey

Margery in Earley suggests that local activism depends on a minority of socially minded people:

Well there is a Maiden Earley residents' association which I must admit I don't go to any of their meetings but they have a little magazine that comes round every quarter and people are really community minded, you know. They do things like getting traffic calming and speed cameras and traffic lights and crossings and things like that and parking improved at the shopping precinct and, Maiden Earley lake they, they work on, it's quite an attraction in the area, they look after that, they have a, a park ranger sort of man there looking after the wildlife and so forth, yes. They are well, very well socially minded I think.

Margery, widowed stepmother, sixties, retired, white Australian, homeowner, Earley,
Reading

Harry in Greenhithe describes a successful local action to stop a proposed development:

Certainly ... people felt quite passionately about it, I did, I did, so much so that the local MP was there, so too was the television people and the radio, newspapers, the local mayor, this is how strong we felt about this, but it worked…I don't know, I could not tell you how it started off. There's a chap that lives next door to the Pier Hotel that it would affect and I think he started it off or started the ball rolling and that was the result, there were, people were putting it in his window 'Say No to Bendigo Wharf development' I wouldn't have been that strong and I certainly wouldn't hit a policeman over the head with a banner but I would give my voice.

Harry, married man, sixties, retired, white, homeowner, Greenhithe

Dorothy in Greenhithe describes herself as an inveterate letter writer:

I do write letters. I'm a great, you know, sort of peeved of Gravesend or peeved of Greenhithe … we don't sit back and just say, Oh it's somebody else's problem, you know… You've actually got to … there comes a time when you've got to say, right, enough's enough. You've got to ring the Council. They're not going to do anything without somebody complaining are they, you know?… I think it becomes, you know, you can put up with things for so long and so long and then you say, right, enough's enough and you've got to stand and do something. And I think a lot of people are like that. You know, you put up with things for so long and that's when people get really angry. They should actually, as soon as soon as something happens, they should be on the case immediately and then it wouldn't get to that stage, you know.

Dorothy and Bill, married father/mother, fifties, employed, white, homeowners,
Greenhithe

She tells us that her previous career has given her contacts, which are essential for effective action:

I don't just sit back. I have … I've been actually … you sort of hide your light under a bushel sometimes because you just don't realise some of the things that you have been involved in. I mean, through my work, I have been involved a lot of things. I used to be the secretary for the community relations and things like that in Gravesend when we lived there, so, you know, I do know quite a lot of people. And obviously my job, I mean, being there, I mean, I've been in the Education offices and the Education Service in Gravesend over 40 years and you just really know everybody.

Do you think that's important being able to knock on…?

Yeah. Call in favours and things, yeah.

Dorothy and Bill, married father/mother, fifties, employed, white, homeowners,
Greenhithe

But some are resentful of their council estate neighbours who they feel were too inclined to interfere:

… now, like, now a few little Hitlers have got their hands on running Fawlty Towers and its twin over there, like, basically, I've ... that's why I didn't say nothing in the lifts yesterday, because I've... I'll be honest with you, a couple of people have pulled me, coming into this block, and I've been rude to them, because I think to myself, like, I mean, I've had people who probably don't even go to work or whatever, but they've got on, they're on this committee or whatever, and now they want to make all our lives better. But mine's all right as it is... They now want to sit on little committees and decide who's eligible to live in them blocks. So you've got to go up before a tribunal of people who know nothing, but have got opinions. I wouldn't do it. I personally wouldn't do it.

What, if you want to live in this block, you've got to go up ...?

The Council will refer you, and the committee will sit in judgement, high judgement over you, and they wanna decide, they interview you, and they decide whether ... you're a bit of them, whether your face fits. It's not a question of whether you need a roof over your head, or nothing like that, it's making it into like another little clique, I'm afraid. And I'm not the cliquey type ... given half a chance, I'll be honest with you ... I don't think me or him would fit the bill if they was making decisions... Turn me out, and a few others in here, and just have, like, the whole block of clones of their selves.

> *Del and Kenny, single and divorced (father) brothers, thirties, unemployed/ employed, white, council tenant, Bermondsey*

Yet Serena, not far away, feels that her Tenants' Committee did a good job:

At the moment, I'm the secretary of the tenants' association ... There's quite a few people go to the meetings, we have one meeting a month, over at the Housing Office, so we take up our grievances with the Housing Officers. And we just discuss, basically, what we're going to do... It's just things like broken windows and things like that, that haven't been fixed in the time that they should have been. And if the teenagers have been making too much noise on the estate, then somebody has a word with them. But, basically, no, it's a very, very good estate. I think we've had one burglary in 3 years, because everyone knows everyone on here, and they know who shouldn't be on here at certain times, so...

> *Serena, divorced mother, twenties, unemployed, white, council tenant, Bermondsey*

She tells of the long years of struggle and negotiation they experienced in creating a secure play space for children:

This used to just be green, and the kids, in the summer, when the dogs used to come on the grass and do their business or whatever, couldn't go on to the grass. The year before, the Jubilee Line dug it all up. The year before that, I think it was Cable and Wireless put their cables in, so they didn't really have anywhere to play for 3 years. And in the end, we finally got the funding... You're allowed a certain amount for community development and … well, if it's going to a good cause, then you usually get grants from different places… The Council tell you … what happened was, the kids were playing football on the grass, and, basically, what was happening was, the balls were hitting the windows. So, rather than that happen, I think everyone thought they'd rather have the kids inside… I know it sounds wicked, but put them inside a cage, and then they can go and smash the ball about wherever they like.

Serena, divorced mother, twenties, unemployed, white,council tenant, Bermondsey

This Bermondsey respondent feels that it had been easier in the past:

Well, we post, we used to use flyers and posters when there was some particular issue, I would go round with flyers and knock on doors and say 'Do you know about this?' and if they said no you'd give them a little quick low-down… So that was sort of face to face contact. What else did we do?… I think we just publicised meetings and people would turn up and the … centre and in those days you could put notices in shops, I don't think you can do that, we could do that now… Well … the Post Office doesn't have a notice board and you used to be able to stick things in the butcher's shop, I don't know, people don't like you doing that any more. [*Laughs*]

Francesca, married mother, forties, self-employed, white, homeowner, Bermondsey

But Deidree in Greenhithe is sceptical about the efficacy of her local residents' association:

There's a very strong residents' association now. But they can only do so much… They can suggest the Council do this or suggest they do that, or say, look this can't be allowed to go on. But it doesn't mean to say they're going to take a blind bit of notice of you.

Deidree, married mother, fifties, employed, white, council tenant, Greenhithe

But she finally admits that residents could become effective if they get organised:

It's all 20 mile an hour now through Swanscombe. They've managed to bring that into force. But that is by lobbying County that is not through lobbying Dartford, you know … that is down to the residents' association.

Deidree, married mother, fifties, employed, white, council tenant, Greenhithe

The same sense of disillusionment comes from Ronnie in Battersea:

I was the chair of leaseholders and I remember some policy at one time that I was unhappy about and it was supposed to be a consultative paper, that means nothing's supposed to happen then and then later on in the meeting when I object to certain things, she says to me that it's already been before the main Council officials. The

Council they have their main meeting, I think on a Thursday night or something, so it was like literally already approved. So it was only before us for amendment and it wasn't going to be amend, so I was horrified … so I just came off it, you know… You don't get nowhere, you know.

Ronnie, male cohabitee (father), fifties, employed, Afro-Caribbean, homeowner,
Battersea

Sandra in Battersea started her local tenants' association:

It was just … my friend came here once, he's a college lecturer and he came here once and he said, he said, 'You live here?' I said, 'Yes'. He said, 'Why don't you ask for a transfer?' I said, 'Why?' So he said, 'The block looks so and so and the block is this …' and when he came there was writing all over, graffiti all over the walls and I felt really really ashamed so I just, I said 'Right, that's it'. So I sat there and I drafted out a letter, piece of paper and I said right, we're going to get this done. And I started from the top floor, I worked all the way downstairs and I started rolling the ball and then this other lady took it over, cos like I said, I go to work and I don't always have the time in the day and that's it. So we want this and we want that and now we're fighting for a concierge, I don't know. It doesn't really matter whether we have that or whether we have the camera, we just need something.

Sandra, single mother, forties, employed, Afro-Caribbean, council tenant, Battersea

In Chapter 2 she described to us the efforts she made:

… cos the lifts kept breaking down every so often and they'd come and fix it, and they'd come and fix it and then you come upstairs and you sit here with me for about half an hour, we have a chat and a cup of coffee and when you're ready to go downstairs the lift's not working… And I thought 'What the … going on?' and I used to be phoning up, phoning up, phoning up, and there's people in, there's old people in the block and there's people in the block with kids and babies, and some of them lives on this floor, some of them live on the top floor, you know, higher level, and I thought, no, that's not right, man, so I thought they have to get, and I used to go every single day I used to go to the Council, every single day… Soon as I walk in they said, 'Oh, here comes trouble'. … I said, 'I don't care what you call me, mate'. I said, 'If you do your job right I wouldn't be coming here so often'. So I said, 'You can call me whatever you like, I don't give a shite'.

Sandra, single mother, forties, employed, Afro-Caribbean, council tenant, Battersea

You could change things, she told us, but you have to keep resolutely going on, and never take no for an answer:

I said, once you are determined to do something and you say right, and you don't sit on it, you will get it done… I don't stop asking for it until it's done, until I get it done. Cos when you want something done and you keep bugging and bugging and bugging, they're gonna get fed up with you, in the end they say 'Oh, fed up with this woman, we'd better get her work done'. You know, but if you ask for it for this week then you leave it for another 6 months they don't bother with you, if you just keep asking and asking and asking they say 'Gosh, we might as well get rid of her cos we're fed up with her phoning up every day'. So they get it done, so I don't stop asking for whatever I want until I get it done … not in this block, but some people have said to me 'Gosh, I've been living in this flat and I haven't had any hot water for 6 months and I've got a baby'. I said, 'You haven't what?' I said, 'You do not want hot water, darling'. Do you know what I'm saying?

Sandra, single mother, forties, employed, Afro-Caribbean, council tenant, Battersea

The Silent Majority and the Unsilent Minority

Sandra, evidently, is in the minority: one of those born political leaders who, faced with an evident problem, simply have to get up and do something about it. The great majority, we found, are not like that at all. If there is one cliché about Londoners that seems to be true, it is that they are politically apathetic. They combine rather perfunctory apologies – most commonly (and here they seem to have some justification) lack of time – with a kind of world-weary cynicism about the state of their neighbourhood or of their borough and the impossibility of ever doing anything about it. They tend to view any effort at consultation – either on the part of their council or by some other involved body like a political party – as a piece of tokenism or, worse, of political manipulation. (And sometimes, they do not even seem to understand who exactly was consulting them.) They seem to feel that local services are bad and getting worse and that there is nothing they can do about it: the sense is that local politics is a kind of racket in the hands of a small clique, and – even more disturbingly – that anyone who becomes involved would be doing so for the wrong motives, because they are hell-bent on power for its own sake.

Strangely, the only widespread active involvement we found was at a very local, very a-political level: in local sports teams and in boy scouts and girl guides and the like, invariably by mothers as a service to their children. This seems be both an extension of motherhood and, in some cases, a way of getting involved in a very local community by people who, for one reason or other, feel a need for greater integration, for instance a lone parent who might be a stranger to the area. Beyond this, people could find themselves coming together over a single local issue, like a traffic hazard that threatened their children. And it seems that such issues more often arise for council tenants, because they depend more on collective services to give them the basic necessities of life like heating or hot water. Here, such associations might acquire a permanent and institutional character, spawning a social side that can bring members together in shared experiences. But it must be said that the reverse could be true: such associations may develop in such areas because they have always had a stronger sense of local solidarity, and that might be associated with negative characteristics – such as a distrust and fear of strangers, as noted in earlier chapters. Local action is by its nature like that: by definition, it is carried through by a small geographically-bounded face-to-face group, and that can entail a drawing of boundaries, a building of mental walls against a hostile external world.

Perhaps such local solidarities are a fleeting and fading part of the contemporary London scene; perhaps Londoners are all destined to become parts of a vast cosmopolitan society without any obvious bounds, a sort of nonplace urban realm as forecast by the Californian urban guru, Melvin Webber, in the 1960s (Webber, 1963, 1964). But it may be premature to pronounce the death of locality for a while – at least, to judge by our conversations with Londoners.

Riverlink: Millennium Bridge

© Bill Knight

Chapter Sixteen

Bringing it Together

No one could claim that the people we interviewed were that ultimate holy grail of the social scientist, a statistically significant sample. True, we found them in a way that was far from random: we carefully chose our areas to be representative of trends we thought significant in millennial London, and within them we sought by precise methods to produce a representative sample. But a total of some 132 interviews, dotted in and around London, could never be truly representative of a total population of some ten million. And very probably there was a semi-conscious bias in our choice of areas: we were seeking places that represented significant trends, and so we tended to ignore the many other places where perhaps less was happening: the more stable, and therefore perhaps more boring, parts of London. That basic health warning needs to be underlined before we start to sum up.

First, then: the most important conclusions about the stories told in *London Lives*, the book's second half. And second: a look back at key conclusions from *London Voices*, telling us something about how those lives can differ from place to place.

London Lives

Making Ends Meet

Perhaps because we did go to the interesting places which attracted more than their share of newcomers – either to that particular area, or to London overall – we found significant numbers of people who were struggling to make ends meet. They told us that they were coping, but only just; they felt that they were constantly at risk of going under. Aspiring younger couples told us how they needed two incomes in order to survive. Sometimes this was to achieve a standard of living that left money over for small luxuries like consumer goods or holidays; often, it was to bring up children – especially where, as in a significant number of cases, these parents were paying for a private education. And those who lacked such a supplementary income – such as lone mothers with small children – found life an endless struggle. Worst of all were those who found themselves assailed by a combination of poor health and resultant unemployment: for them, existence could become positively a nightmarish struggle to survive.

The interviews very often illustrate the fact that comes starkly out from the statistics, analysed in the study to which this book forms an accompaniment (Buck *et al.*, 2002) and other sources (Hamnett, 2003; Mayor of London, 2004): that increasingly, London is a city polarised between the very comfortable rich and the desperately insecure poor. One resident of Newham put it graphically as he struggled to find words:

I mean example I want to buy house, I mean they'll ask me, give me £10,000 as a deposit for mortgage or something but I have no, how can I get house.

And what do you think will change to help things get better?

Because the richest people they are going to richer rich and poor people they are going to poor, it is very hard I think.

Nahar, married father, sixties, employed, Bangladeshi, private tenant, Upton Park

That response shows how basic insecurity is massively complicated, for many interviewees, by the problem of access to housing. For those on low incomes, some kind of affordable housing is essential. That means social housing from the borough or from a housing association. But such housing is supplied according to rules that are often complex and difficult to understand, involving a process that can drag on for years, in which people may come to feel that the system has completely forgotten about them. Those people languish in some of London's worst accommodation: privately-rented housing with shared or substandard facilities. And even those who finally succeed – such as lone mothers, who receive top priority and therefore can bypass other applicants – may find themselves in unsuitable substandard accommodation, or at least accommodation they dislike and which may drag them into psychological depression.

Some battle the system and win; many others eke out a marginal existence. Here, life can be a constant battle to survive. Finding a place to live for you and your family can mean endless hassle; but, even for those who succeed, the system often offers little choice, and at worst it may leave people living a marginal life with difficult or impossible neighbours. More affluent Londoners, some of whom may also experience minor troubles with their neighbours but have the freedom finally to move, may never fully understand the hellish conditions that obtain on some of London's worst estates.

Finding a Place

Thus, many of our interviewees desperately crave the sense of freedom, the sense of free choice, that most Londoners take for granted as a basic human right. These are the people trapped in social housing they dislike; they live where they do only because they have no option. Other social housing tenants are so far secure, but feel a great uncertainty that they could be impacted because they have no control over their council's or housing association's policies, which may introduce difficult neighbours without consultation and without warning. There may be a racial element here; but the real reason often appears to be a clash of lifestyles, particularly associated with age, which may, for instance, bring an incursion of younger noisy partygoers into a formerly-peaceful estate of older people.

Others, more favourably placed, are owner-occupiers who have that basic freedom to move, but who feel that their neighbourhood has declined because 'the wrong kind of people' have come in. Again, there often seems to be a racial element to these complaints, but it is far from simple: an older Afro-Caribbean in Newham complains about the arrival of Muslims from the Indian subcontinent, Indians in Heston complain about new white asylum-seekers. They tell of rising crime levels, they object to owner-occupiers who have disappeared and let their homes to irresponsible tenants, and above all they talk of falling standards in the local schools. Many are themselves planning to leave; they quote many cases of neighbours who have already gone, they describe their own exit plans in detail, and some are in the course of moving.

Many owner-occupiers seem to have made, or to be making, a deliberate choice: to move outwards, often along the railway lines within the same geographical sector in London, from the inner London locale in which they had been born and educated. But many told us that they could not move very far – because of family ties, especially to ageing parents who themselves found it hard to move, especially if they were tenants in social housing. Many described how they really aspired to have more space in and around the home, plus rural surroundings, but how they had been forced to compromise – not only because of the need to be close to family and friends, but also because of the constraint of the daily journey to work, which for many was still in central or at least inner London. For some, that compromise meant buying an interwar house in an outer London borough; for others, it resulted in life in a new estate just outside London, in Kent or Berkshire. Here, especially, people complained endlessly about the pace of physical change: the endless construction, including heavy construction traffic, the steady erosion of a sense of tranquillity, the stress and strain of the long commute to work whether by car or train, but also the need to travel for shopping or other basic local services.

For those with children, schools were a major concern – perhaps *the* concern. Every parent seemed to talk endlessly about it, and all seemed almost alarmingly well-informed about the merits and demerits of the choices on offer. Some had moved, others were contemplating a move, to the catchment areas of what they regarded as the best schools – but even more so in order to avoid what they saw as bad ones. They might do so locally, but in addition schools appeared to be a key factor for those who moved from inner London boroughs to the outer London suburbs or beyond. Again, there could appear to be a racial element here, but it was complex: an Indian mother in Newham could describe how they were moving out because the local schools were overwhelmed by new arrivals with learning problems.

It clearly mattered hugely to almost everyone that they felt comfortable and settled in their local neighbourhood, with a general sense of physical security, and with neighbours whom they felt to be congenial and to whom they could turn in an emergency. In this sense, you might say that almost all Londoners shared middle-class values. And certainly, this is the impression you would get from tramping or driving down the endless streets of impeccably-maintained terraced or semi-detached housing where we did most of our interviews: semi-detached London is still the London that most Londoners know, even though the people who live behind the lace curtains or the double-glazed picture windows may be very different, ethically and culturally, from the people who first lived here 70 years ago. Most did have such a sense of living a good life in a good neighbourhood.

But a minority clearly felt they did not, and sometimes this seemed to cloud their entire view of their world, giving them a general sense of insecurity and anxiety. This seemed equally true of an inner London neighbourhood like Upton Park and a middle London neighbourhood like Eltham; it invariably appeared to reflect the presence of a relatively few anti-social young people. In some such neighbourhoods, especially in parts of middle and outer London, there was a more general feeling that the area was going downhill, that the former sense of community had been eroded, that everyone was leaving and that it was essential to join the stampede as soon as possible. This was a far from general response: these areas were exceptional, but in them there was a sense that newcomers were bringing with them an erosion of the entire social fabric. This was one of the few really negative findings of our study, but we felt that it was a significant one.

Getting There

One stereotype proved true: Londoners are obsessed by transport, for the good reasons that they rely on it to get to work and live their lives, and that often it fails to work either as well as they would want, or even at all. But people were positive as well as negative about their experience of transport. Many had invested considerable intelligence in choosing where to live, in order to get access to their jobs or their children's schools. Some – especially in east and south-east London – quoted new roads or train services as major new advantages.

But many spoke of appalling experiences, especially on their daily commuter journeys, and claimed that they had got worse – perhaps because, when we were interviewing, there were special problems with rail services. Yet the problems seemed to extend to all forms of public transport, especially buses, as well as to private car drivers. Particularly notable were those who told us of their refusal to use public transport, even where it was locally available. They told us again and again about their problems with congestion, road works and parking. Here, those living in the new suburbs outside the M25 seemed to suffer as much as Londoners – and they confessed that they had far fewer and poorer choice of public transport than did the latter.

Transport and traffic are bound to be a concern in any big city. But it was impossible to avoid the conventional, often-quoted conclusion: that London and its region were suffering from a seriously inadequate transport system. Here again, there is a clear indication that London could serve its citizens better – with the difference that here, almost everyone seemed to suffer.

Friends and Neighbours

In partial compensation, our interviewers found that most Londoners seemed to find a good sense of neighbourliness – so much so, that it was noteworthy to find its absence. Londoners had a very highly developed sense of their social obligations, and in may cases these went far beyond a mere formal reciprocity – such as taking in each others' parcels, which was almost universal – to embrace a wider sense of obligation to neighbours who might fall on temporary misfortune. And this might extend to a system of informal social control over deviant behaviour – a point to which we return below.

But this system had its quite strict formal constraints. For instance, it did not go beyond certain limits: being good neighbours did not mean becoming good friends. And, in a few areas, it seemed very largely to break down. These were the transit zones where people were always coming and going, barely getting to know each other at all. Particularly, it seemed true for areas that housed large numbers of young workers, who left their homes early in the morning and returned late in the evening. These might typically be in inner-city neighbourhoods, especially the gentrified or gentrifying ones, but they could also include new suburbs. However the latter tended to be different in one key respect: they often had large numbers of children, and that meant that the children, always in and out of each others' houses, provided a natural social bond for the parents.

People, we concluded, tended after a time to fit into their neighbourhoods and feel comfortable in them. So they could become quite disturbed by the arrival of new and different groups of people, even if these people seemed to be like themselves – and of course very much more so if they were not like themselves. The unhappiest of all were those facing a sudden incursion of people they saw as very different from themselves in age or race or – the really significant point – lifestyle. This tended especially to happen to tenants in social housing, who had very little influence on who came into their neighbourhoods.

But we found strange variations, which were hard to understand: some localities seemed to act as amicable melting pots where people of very different origins and backgrounds got on with each other, while other areas seemed not to achieve such a happy outcome. It seemed that the happy places contained mobile and inclusive types of people who positively liked change and variety, while the people in the other places were suspicious and inward-looking and defensive of traditional ways of life. Age could have something to do with this; so could social homogeneity maintained over a long time; so perhaps could income levels. But perhaps the key variable was the perceived difference between the existing residents and the newcomers. If they 'fitted in' they would be accepted, even if different in important respects. But if they failed to conform to some local social norm, or because they were suspected of crime or they were noisy neighbours, the shutters would come down and the existing residents would talk of moving out. Urban design and architecture could play a role here: everyone seemed to feel that 'estates' of flats were less good places to live than conventional 'streets'.

There seemed to be an upside as well as a downside to this, though. Some of the most defensive areas were also remarkably well integrated in a social sense, simply because people had lived together here for generations; this seemed truest of all in working-class council estates, where extraordinarily strong traditions of social solidarity survived, even though we were told again and again that they were under threat. It could have the effect of freezing out newcomers, but for those inside it, this world did have some of the sense of living in a huge extended family.

Fearing Crime, Avoiding Crime

One of the most surprising things we found in our neighbourhoods was that – contrary to what everyone seems to think – most people in most areas of London do not appear much concerned about crime or personal security. But, equally strangely, for a substantial minority it seems to be a major worry, in some cases overshadowing their lives. These people told us of unpleasant events immediately outside their front doors or a neighbour's door, often caused by a tiny minority of delinquent youth. They and others seemed to share a general fear that the social cement that had structured their lives was eroding away, leading to a sense of anarchy, a sense of danger always present. They see the authorities, particularly the police, as powerless and ineffectual.

In some areas they blame new groups arriving in the area, such as asylum seekers or travellers. In others they see a general decline in standards. Many told us they felt safe in their neighbourhoods – comparing them with others, especially those from which they had moved, which they see as crime-ridden. Indeed, this seems to have been a significant reason for the out-migration of many, particularly out of inner south-east London. And many people talked about some local area they saw as a 'bad' area, a place to which they would not willingly go and whose residents they regarded with distrust – almost invariably an 'estate'.

Many, especially in more traditional working-class neighbourhoods, express nostalgia for the old-style local 'Bobby' or community policeman – though this is invariably mixed up with a desire to put the social clock back, returning to an era when authority figures commanded respect. Yet one of our most surprising discoveries was that in such areas, there continue to be systems of informal social control and social policing: if someone showed delinquency 'the lads would have a word with him', with a clear note of menace. In these areas we found some few extraordinary cases of mature women, of strong personality and character, who played key roles in their neighbourhoods, sometimes controlling teenage behaviour, sometimes leading campaigns to improve their neighbourhoods. In outer areas, it helped that mothers and children were around during the day; their absence could be striking in other areas, where the streets could be almost deserted on weekday afternoons. Thus, though most people in all areas could report a strong sense of neighbourliness and social solidarity, we often sensed a feeling that this might be in danger of eroding away in the future.

Melting the Pot

It is almost a cliché by now that London has become one of the most multi-ethnic, multi-cultural places in the world. And, in many areas, it seems to have achieved this with remarkably little tension in comparison with other cities in other parts of the world and even in Britain. But we were surprised by the complexity of the relationships that people reported to us. There are, we were told, all kinds of prejudices: of one non-white group against another, of Afro-Caribbeans against Africans, of Caribbeans from one island or island group against another. There does appear to be anti-white feeling on the part of some black people, especially against those who 'marry out' to form mixed marriages. And we certainly found evidence of the old-fashioned archetypal prejudice, of whites against non-whites.

Some of this, no doubt, was simple and unvarnished racism. But in the contexts that were reported to us and which we observed, it was subtly and confusingly mixed with other elements. Much of it is about schools, and appears to be far less racial than cultural: parents repeatedly told us that they were worried that the traditional European (or British) culture was being overlain and even overwhelmed by other cultures. And their concern, they insisted to us, was to maintain schools that were truly multiracial and multicultural: many positively wanted that experience for their children, but were desperately worried because they saw their local school filling up almost exclusively with children from one culture or religion. Their attitude, far from being racist, appears precisely the opposite. And interestingly, we found it expressed not exclusively by whites, but by respondents from different races and cultures: some of those most concerned, who were moving or contemplating moving, were actually Indians faced with incursions of asylum-seekers' children.

We were in no doubt that simple, old-fashioned white racism survives. But we sensed it most strongly in traditional very homogeneous working-class estates in east and south-east London. The people here were among the most defensive of all the groups we interviewed. They have suffered from huge economic changes that have destroyed traditional male jobs in docks or factories, bringing structural unemployment and real difficulties for the children (especially boys) in responding to the needs of London's new advanced-service economy. Many such communities are geographically isolated, with a strong shared sense of solidarity: we found them far more like northern English factory towns than parts of a metropolis. So one can begin to understand, perhaps, why they should react so defensively to change of any kind.

Such areas remain unusual though not uncommon. Generally, the London story has been a quite different, even contrary, one: a story of almost constant change and instability, as new groups came in and older groups moved out. Gants Hill, where Bengalis follow Jews out of the Whitechapel ghetto to the suburbs, is typical of such a place. What has happened in London since the 1960s is simply that the extent and the speed of such changes has become so much greater, affecting so many more areas so rapidly.

Changing the World

We earlier described a distinct type of born community leader, typically a woman of great moral courage and presence, who could have a real impact on her neighbourhood. (Interestingly, London's Afro-Caribbean community seemed to produce a number of such women.) But most Londoners are not like that: they seem to confirm the cliché that London is politically apathetic. They make perfunctory apologies about lack of time (true, we felt, for many of them) with a metropolitan cynicism about the uselessness of the political process and the consequent impossibility of bringing about real change. Indeed, we were surprised by the intensity of that cynicism, which seemed to regard any attempt at consultation as a piece of manipulation or of spin. We got a strong sense that many people regarded local politics as a kind of racket monopolised by a small clique, and that the only kind of people who got into politics did so for bad reasons. Consequently, though they complain about local services, they see no real possibility of doing much about it.

That might suggest confirmation from this side of the Atlantic of the findings of Robert Putnam, the American political scientist, whose research suggested a massive decline in Americans' civic involvement (Putnam, 2000). But that would not be completely true, because we also found quite intense and active involvement at a local and completely a-political level: in sports teams, boy scouts and girl guides and similar organisations, on the part of mothers for the sake of their children. We found many examples of this kind of activity: it seemed part of the experience of bringing up young children – but also, for many, a way of becoming better integrated with a local neighbourhood and society, particularly for those who might feel new or marginal.

And of course people might organise over a local issue such as traffic – though, if the hazard were dealt with, then the organisation might wither. Council tenants, we noticed, seem to get involved more than owner-occupiers, simply because they need collective action to provide the services which owner-occupiers get for themselves. So there, organisations might become a more permanent feature of life, with associated social events. But finally, we could not say whether this sense of solidarity might not be the other face of the sense of defensive insularity, which we have noticed earlier.

Such, then, were the key features of London life as we found them in that millennial year. They carry no great surprises, unless it proves surprising that for the great majority of Londoners, most of the time, life is not overwhelmingly difficult or hazardous or stressful. There are potential sources of difficulty and stress, to be sure – and one of these, transport, seems to have been something of an obsession for many Londoners when we were interviewing them.

But if there is one more basic and more abiding problem, it is economic insecurity. For many, this is represented by the sense that they are struggling to keep their heads above water – particularly if they need two incomes to support a decent standard of living, and particularly if they also have children. For a significant minority, especially those who cannot aspire to own their own home, there is a real feeling of life on the margin, particularly if they are assailed by other problems like bad health.

London Voices

There is another question, which needs reference back to the voices we recorded in the first half of the book. What difference does locality make to all this? Do London lives vary so much from one area to another? Do those local voices sound so different in Battersea and in Bermondsey, in Greenhithe or in Gants Hill?

The answer to that question is slightly difficult, because in each area there were so many voices and because they did not always tell the same tale. That was particularly true of some of the areas which we judged to be in the throes of rapid change, rapid transition. The incomers often told different stories from the long-time residents – sometimes almost diametrically opposed stories. Many of them seemed to feel that they were living a good life, while the old timers felt they had been invaded by people whom they did not understand and whose customs and lifestyles they did not share. Partly this was a function of age: of many parts of contemporary London, one could say with Yeats that 'That is no country for old men' – or old women either. But it was partly, and perhaps more deeply, a question of social identity.

That said, it seemed also to be true that people had more of a sense of social wellbeing in some areas than in others: simply, more of them felt they were living a reasonably good life. That again seemed to be in part a function of rapid change – demographic, ethnic, economic, social, physical. People felt less secure, less at ease with their neighbours, in areas of rapid transition than in more settled and more stable areas. Even when they did, as in areas with a lot of new development, they disliked the physical disruption and the loss of qualities they had experienced either years ago or more recently, like rural peace and quiet.

This is perhaps a case of social research proving the obvious: why should people feel otherwise? But it does remain a fact that many parts of London are experiencing upheaval of one kind or another, and that if anything the pace of change has increased and may increase further – if only because London is again a growing city, struggling to house hundreds of thousands of extra people within its borders.

We sensed that this conclusion might be slightly biased by our choice of areas, which may have stressed precisely this element of rapid change. Perhaps, if we had been able to survey more areas and if we had been more rigorous in choosing a random sample of them, we would have found more

Londoners living calmer, even uneventful lives. But this seems doubtful. Even apparently stable areas are changing in multiple ways as people die or move out, others come in. People may yearn for a lost peace they believed they once had, even though time may have caused them to forget the actual quality of life 30 or 40 years before.

What seems undeniable is that for most people who conclude they no longer care for London life, there is an obvious option: to leave it. The migration figures from the 2001 Census show that, as for decades previously, Londoners were moving out to the more rural counties around, indeed for increasing distances deep towards the edge of South East England and beyond, into regions like the East of England and South West England, presumably in search of a more rural or small-town life. What was relatively new, since the early 1980s, was that their places were being filled by new arrivals from other parts of the world, evidently happy to live the London version of the urban life – either because they were younger, or because they came from cultures more at home with vibrant urban living, or perhaps both. This, plus the fact that some of them were producing large numbers of children, was the basic reason behind London's dramatic demographic reversal after four decades of decline.

Perhaps they too in their turn will tire of London and will follow the endless trek out of the Great Wen. Certainly we found that to be true of older waves of immigrants, as in Heston. But others will be found to take their place, given the demographic explosion in so many parts of the world and London's remarkable achievement in opening its doors so relatively freely to incomers without too many questions asked – especially after their first arrival. The great debate about ID cards, of course, could have a political impact here. But London has become one of the most culturally diverse cities on earth, and the rich fruits of that diversity have still to be picked as new generations of young Londoners come out of its schools. If some future generation of urban researchers follow in our footsteps, half a century hence, that is the outcome that we would most confidently predict.

References

Anon (2003) London's Comings and Goings. *The Economist*, 9 August, pp. 23–25.

Beresford, P. and Beresford, S. (1978) *A Say in the Future: Planning, Participation and Meeting Social Need: A New Approach: North Battersea: A Case Study.* London: Battersea Community Action.

Buck, N., Gordon, I., Hall, P., Harloe, M., Kleinman, M. (2002) *Working Capital: Life and Labour in Contemporary London.* London: Routledge.

Geddes, P. (1915) *Cities in Evolution.* London: Williams and Norgate.

Hall, P. (2003) *Growing the European Urban System* (ICS Working Paper WP3). London: Institute of Community Studies.

Hall, P. and Pain, K. (2006) *The Polycentric Metropolis: Learning from Mega-City Regions in Europe.* London: Earthscan.

Hamnett, C. (2003) *Unequal City: London in the Global Arena.* London: Routledge.

Kellett, J.R. (1969) *The Impact of Railways on Victorian Cities* (Studies in Social History). London: Routledge & Kegan Paul.

Mayor of London (2002) *The Draft London Plan: Draft Spatial Development Strategy for Greater London.* London: Greater London Authority.

Mayor of London (2004) *The London Plan: Spatial Development Strategy for Greater London.* London: Greater London Authority.

Park, R.E., Burgess, E.W. and McKenzie, R.D. (1925) *The City.* Chicago: University of Chicago Press.

Putnam, R.D. (2000) *Bowling Alone: The Collapse and Revival of American Community.* New York: Simon and Schuster.

Rasmussen, S.E. (1937) *London: The Unique City.* London: Jonathan Cape.

Webber, M.M. (1963) Order in Diversity: Community without Propinquity, in Wingo, L., Jr. (ed.) *Cities and Space: The Future Use of Urban Land* Baltimore: Johns Hopkins University Press, pp. 23–54.

Webber, M.M. (1964) The Urban Place and the Nonplace Urban Realm, Webber, M.M. *et al.*, *Explorations into Urban Structure.* Philadelphia: University of Pennsylvania Press, pp. 79–153.

List of Respondents

An Important Note on Anonymity

All interviewees understood that their transcripts might be used for short anonymised extracts as part of the published outcome of the ESRC study. To protect their anonymity, all personal names – both of the interviewees themselves, and of their family members – have been changed. In addition, some local details such as school names have been removed where these might possibly allow identities to be surmised.

Battersea

BTH 1   ('Tiffany') Divorced mother, thirties, part-time employed, Jamaican-born Afro-Caribbean, council tenant.

BTH 2   ('Sandra') Single mother, forties, employed, British-born Afro-Caribbean, council tenant.

BTH 3   ('Daniel') Single father, twenties, employed, British-born Afro-Caribbean, council tenant.

BTH 4   ('Carol') Divorced mother, fifties, unemployed, white, private tenant.

BTH 5   ('David') Male cohabitee, thirties, self-employed, white Jewish, homeowner.

BTH 6   ('Mary') Widow, fifties, unemployed, white, home-owner.

BTH 7   ('Amir') Single father, forties, employed, African, council tenant.

BTH 8   ('Amy') Married mother, thirties, employed, white, homeowner.

BTH 9   ('Megan') Single mother, mid teens, unemployed, white, lives with the family of the father of her child (council tenant).

BTH 10   ('Scott') Single man, forties, unemployed, white, council tenant.

BTH 11   ('Seema') Married man, thirties, employed, Bangladeshi, lives with brother (council tenant).

BTH 12   NOT USED Single man, twenties, self-employed, white, private tenant.

BTH 13   ('Val') Fifties, unemployed, white, and her daughter, Joan, a single homeless mother.

BTH 14   ('Ronnie') Male cohabitee (father), fifties, employed, Afro-Caribbean, homeowner.

BTH 15   ('Barry') Married man, forties, employed, white, council tenant.

BTH 16   ('Susie') Single mother, thirties, unemployed, white, council tenant.

BTH 17   ('Angie') Single mother, twenties, unemployed, white, council tenant.

BTH 18   ('Lisa') Widow, thirties, employed, white, housing association tenant.

BTH 19   NOT USED Information not available.

BTH 20   NOT USED Single mother, forties, unemployed, white, lives with father (council tenant).

BTH 21   ('James') Gay cohabitee, thirties, self-employed, white, housing association tenant.

BTH 22   ('Shirley') Single mother, sixties, unemployed, white, council tenant.

Employment areas: Nine Elms, Clapham Junction.

Bermondsey, Peckham

BRH 1   ('Serena') Divorced mother, twenties, unemployed, white, council tenant.

BRH 2   ('Cheryl') Married mother, thirties, employed, white, council tenant.

BRH 3   ('Simon') Male cohabitee, thirties, employed, white, council tenant.

BRH 4   ('Janice') Single mother, thirties, unemployed, British-born half-white, half-Afro-Caribbean, council tenant.

BRH 5   ('Del and Kenny') Single and divorced (father) brothers, thirties, unemployed/employed, white, council tenants.

BRH 6   ('Mark') Single man, thirties, employed, white, private tenant.

BRH 7   ('Francesca') Married mother, forties, self-employed, white, homeowner.

BRH 8   ('Juliette and James') Married couple, twenties, employed, African, living with council tenants.

BRH 9   ('Gary and Dawn') Married parents, forties, employed, white, housing association tenants.

BRH 10   ('Timothy') Single man, thirties, employed, white, private tenant.

BRH 11   ('Barnabas') Married father, thirties, employed, African, council tenant.

BRH 12   ('Liz') Divorced mother, thirties, unemployed, white, council tenant.

BRH 13   ('Henrietta') Single woman, twenties, employed, white, private tenant.

BRH 14   ('Theresa') Married mother, forties, part-time employed, white, housing association tenant.

BRH 15   NOT USED Divorced father, fifties, self-employed, white, living on friends floor.

BRH 16   ('Maria') Married mother, sixties, part-time employed, white, homeowner.

BRH 17   ('Rosemary') Married mother, sixties, retired, white, council tenant.

BRH 18   ('Patrick') Married father, forties, employed, white, homeowner.

BRH 19   ('Shaun and Katie') Married parents, thirties, self-employed, white, council tenants.

BRH 20   ('Patricia') Widow, sixties, retired, white, council tenant.

PK 1   ('Kosey') Single man, twenties, student, African, lives with family (council tenants).

PK 2   (Azizi') Single man, twenties, employed, African, private tenant.

PK 3   ('Eze') Single man, twenties, student, African, lives with family (council tenants).

PK 4   ('Kevin') Male cohabitee, thirties, employed, African, council tenant.

PK 5   ('Rafi') Married father, thirties, employed, British-born Afro-Caribbean, council tenant.

Employment area: Bankside/Borough

Eltham

GRH 1   ('Joe') Married man, sixties, employed, white, homeowner.

GRH 2   ('Mick') Married man, fifties, employed, white, homeowner.

GRH 3   ('Zoe') Married woman, twenties, employed, white, homeowner.

GRH 4   ('Alan') Divorced father, fifties, employed, white, homeowner.

GRH 6   ('Jeff') Divorced father (living with partner), forties, employed, white, homeowner.

GRH 7   ('Rob') Married father, forties, employed, white, homeowner.

GRH 8   ('Margaret') Married mother, fifties, part-time employed, white, homeowner.

GRH 9   ('Heather') Divorced mother, thirties, part-time employed, white, homeowner.

GRH 10   ('Tracy') Separated mother, forties, unemployed, white, council tenant.

GRH 12   NOT USED Widowed mother, eighties, retired, white, council tenant.

Employment area: Greenwich Riverside

Gants Hill

GHH 1 NOT USED Married mother, forties, employment?, white, homeowner.

GHH 2 NOT USED ('missing') Widowed female, late sixties/early seventies, white, homeowner.

GHH 3 ('Sheila') Married mother, forties, white, homeowner.

GHH 4 ('Pam') Married mother, forties, employed, white, homeowner.

GHH 5 ('Rachel') Married mother, thirties, part-time employed, white Jewish, homeowner.

GHH 6 ('Ajit') Married mother, thirties, employed, Sikh, homeowner.

GHH 7 ('Sharmaine') Married mother, fifties, employed, Afro-Caribbean, homeowner.

GHH 8 ('Sally') Divorced mother, forties, employed, white Jewish, home-owner.

GHH 9 ('Selina') Married mother, forties, employed, Asian, homeowner.

GHH 10 ('Mel') Married father, seventies, retired, white Jewish, home-owner.

GHH 11 ('Leslie and Miriam') Married father/mother, sixties, retired, white Jewish, home owners.

GHH 12 ('Shirin') Married mother, thirties, Bangladeshi, homeowner.

GHH 13 ('Jenny') Married mother, forties, white, homeowner.

GHH 14 ('Ranjit') Married father, fifties, employed, Sikh, homeowner.

Employment area: Central Ilford

Greenhithe

DFH 1 ('Sharon') Married mother, thirties, part-time employed, white, homeowner.

DFH 2 ('Deidree') Married mother, fifties, employed, white, council tenant.

DFH 3 ('Ann') Widowed mother, seventies, retired, white, homeowner.

DFH 4 ('Emma') Married mother, forties, employed, white, homeowner.

DFH 5 ('Richard') Married man, thirties, employed, white, homeowner.

DFH 6 ('Oona') Divorced mother, fifties, employed, white, private tenant.

DFH 9 ('Nancy') Separated mother, thirties/forties, employed, white, homeowner.

DFH 10 ('Harry') Married man, sixties, retired, white, homeowner.

DFH 11 ('Jill') Married woman, fifties, self-employed, white, homeowner.

DFH 12 ('Dorothy and Bill') Married father/mother, fifties, employed, white, homeowners.

DFH 13 ('Emily') Married mother, fifties, employed, white, homeowner.

DFH 14 ('James') Divorced man, twenties, employed, white, homeowner.

DFH 15   ('Karen') Married mother, thirties, part-time employed, white, homeowner.

Employment area: Crossways/Bluewater

Heston

HWH 1   ('Jalil') Married father, sixties, retired, Indian, homeowner.

HWH 2   ('Rajiv') Man, teenager, at school, Asian, tenure not stated.

HWH 3   ('Surjit') Single woman, twenties, student, Sikh, homeowners (living at home).

HWH 4   ('Sewa') Single woman, twenties, employed, Sikh, homeowners (living at home).

HWH 5   ('Betty') Married mother, fifties, employed, white, homeowner.

HWH 6   ('Saqib') Widower, sixties, retired, Pakistani, council tenant.

HWH 7   NOT USED Single man, thirties, self-employed, Sikh, home-owners (living at home)

HWH 8   ('Linda') Female cohabitee, mother, twenties/thirties, employed, white, private tenant.

HWH 9   ('Donald') Married father, fifties, employed, white, homeowner.

HWH 10   ('Layla') Married mother, forties?, part-time employed, Egyptian parents, homeowner.

HWH 11   ('Sandhya') Married mother, forties?, part-time employed, Indian, homeowner.

HWH 12   ('Faizah') Married mother, thirties?, employed, Malaysian parents, homeowner.

HWH 13   ('Scung-yun') Single woman, twenties, student, Korean, private tenant.

HWH 14   ('Milad') Single man, twenties, employed, Lebanese, homeowners (living at home).

HWH 15   ('Adeola') Divorced mother, thirties, employed, Nigerian, housing association tenant.

HWH16   NOT USED Single female, very early twenties, student, Asian British (Sikh), homeowner (parents).

Employment area: Great West Road

Reading Newtown⁺, Earley*

+RGH 1   ('Paul') Married man, thirties, employed, white, homeowner.

★RGH 2   ('Brenda') Married mother, fifties, employed, white, home-owner.

+RGH 3   ('Dionne') Female cohabitee, twenties, employed, British-born Afro-Caribbean, private tenant.

+RGH 4 ('Kate') Single woman, thirties, employed, white, private tenant.

+RGH 5 ('Rochelle') Female cohabitee, twenties, employed, white Australian, homeowner.

*RGH 6 ('Tony') Married father, forties, employed, white, homeowner.

+RGH 7 ('Vincent') Single man, thirties, employed, white, homeowner.

*RGH 8 ('Margery') Widowed stepmother, sixties, retired, white Australian, homeowner.

+RGH 9 ('Helen') Single woman, twenties, employed, white, private tenant.

+RGH 10 NOT USED Cohabiting mother, forties, self-employed, white, homeowner.

+RGH 11 NOT USED Single man, twenties, employed, white, private tenant.

*RGH 12 NOT USED Married mother, thirties, employed, white, home-owner.

*RGH 13 NOT USED Married father, thirties?, employed, white, home-owner.

*RGH 14 NOT USED Married father, sixties, part-time employed, white, home owner.

Employment areas: Reading CBD, Thames Valley business park, Winnersh Triangle

Upton Park

NHH 1 ('Christian') Single man, thirties, French African-Caribbean, unemployed, private tenant.

NHH 2 ('Nadira and Coffie') Married parents, forties, both employed, African, homeowners.

NHH 3 ('Linda') Married mother, forties, part-time employed, white, homeowner.

NHH 4 ('Padma') Single woman, twenties, employed, Asian, private tenant.

NHH 5 NOT USED Married man, late thirties/forties, employment ??, Kurdish, private tenant.

NHH 6 ('Roland') Married father, sixties, retired, Afro-Caribbean, homeowner.

NHH 7 ('Nahar') Married father, sixties, employed, Bangladeshi, private tenant.

NHH 8 ('Dafina') Single mother, forties, part-time employed/student, African, housing association tenant.

NHH 9 ('Sanjula') Married mother, thirties, employed, Indian, owner occupier (lives with in-laws).

NHH 10 NOT USED Separated mother, age?, employment?, Estonian, private tenant.

NHH 12 ('Ian') Married father, forties, employed, white, homeowner.

NHH 13 ('Kamal') Married father, fifties, unemployed, Indian, private tenant.

NHH 14 ('Essien') Married father, fifties, self-employed, African, homeowner.

Employment area: Stratford

Index